In This Land of Plenty

POLITICS AND CULTURE IN MODERN AMERICA

Series Editors
Margot Canaday, Glenda Gilmore, Matthew Lassiter,
Stephen Pitti, Thomas J. Sugrue

Volumes in the series narrate and analyze political and social change in the broadest dimensions from 1865 to the present, including ideas about the ways people have sought and wielded power in the public sphere and the language and institutions of politics at all levels—local, national, and transnational. The series is motivated by a desire to reverse the fragmentation of modern U.S. history and to encourage synthetic perspectives on social movements and the state, on gender, race, and labor, and on intellectual history and popular culture.

In This Land of Plenty

Mickey Leland and Africa in American Politics

Benjamin Talton

PENN

UNIVERSITY OF PENNSYLVANIA PRESS

PHILADELPHIA

Published by
University of Pennsylvania Press
Philadelphia, Pennsylvania 19104-4112
www.upenn.edu/pennpress

Printed in the United States of America on acid-free paper

10 9 8 7 6 5 4 3 2 1

Library of Congress Cataloging-in-Publication Data

ISBN 978-0-8122-5147-0

Contents

Introduction

The United States is universally recognized as a land of great wealth and resources. Yet, in this land of plenty, millions of individuals—a dispropor- tionate percentage of them black—lack the financial resources necessary to achieve a life free of poverty.

—Congressman Mickey Leland

Congressman George Thomas "Mickey" Leland departed Addis Ababa's Bole International Airport on August 7, 1989, on a Twin Otter plane with his thirteen-member delegation of Ethiopian and American relief workers and policy analysts. They were bound for Fugnido, a town near Ethiopia's border with Sudan. This was Leland's seventh official humanitarian mission to Africa in his nearly decade-long drive to make U.S. policies toward the continent more closely reflect his black internationalist vision of global cooperation, antiracism, and freedom from hunger. In many respects, the Horn of Africa and southern Africa were his test cases. Over the previous six years, he had led the cause in the U.S. House of Representatives for the approval of consis- tent U.S.-government-sponsored humanitarian assistance to Marxist-ruled Ethiopia and several other African countries enmeshed in a food crisis web. By any measure, Leland was Congress's champion for U.S. humanitarianism in Africa during the final decade of the Cold War, while he simultaneously helped craft a new policy toward South Africa for the United States centered on human rights and antiracism.

Leland and his group were traveling to Fugnido to visit Pinyudo, one of three massive refugee camps operated by the Ethiopian government that sheltered tens of thousands of people, mostly children, from southern Sudan. Following an eleven-day walk and a stroke of good fortune, these children would meet soldiers from the Sudan People's Liberation Army

(SPLA), who would escort them to one of the camps.[1] When Leland planned his visit, the plight of these young Sudanese had yet to become the fashionable celebrity and media-driven cause that would emerge in the 1990s. They would become known as the "Lost Boys of Sudan" and the dramatic tales of their trek to Ethiopia would capture the hearts of Americans and Europeans. During the 1980s, however, they were merely casualties of a civil war with regional implications. Few individuals and institutions outside of Ethiopian, southern Sudanese, European, and American relief organizations had shown more than a passing interest in escapees from southern Sudan. Leland hoped his mission to Pinyudo would attract U.S. media, government, and public attention to the refugees' condition and the critical but wanting assistance the Ethiopian government provided them.[2] He trusted the power of these children's stories and images to spark an international relief effort and expose the complex contradictions of Cold War geopolitics that linked Ethiopia, Sudan, Libya, Somalia, and the United States.

Leland and his colleagues in the Congressional Black Caucus engaged African issues during a period in which African Americans reached their point of greatest influence on U.S. foreign affairs. The 1980s was the first time in U.S. history that African Americans as a bloc directly shaped U.S. foreign policy and the social and political narratives that influenced public opinion. Leland was motivated in his activism inside the U.S. Capitol, on the streets of Washington, D.C., and in his hometown of Houston, Texas, by an understanding that interrelated forces lay behind hunger, deprivation, and injustice throughout the world. The social and political milieu of 1960s Houston, as well as the broader, international dimensions of Black Power and the Third World, informed Leland's approach to global affairs.[3] He frequently expressed his sense of obligation to serve a global constituency, particularly the hungry and displaced in Africa. He envisioned the United States putting geopolitics and its Cold War ideologies to the side to lead an international humanitarian relief effort and to ultimately end the problem of hunger in the world.

African Americans' efforts to shape U.S. foreign policies from inside Congress, and specifically as members of the Congressional Black Caucus during the late 1970s through the 1980s, show that Black Power and related iterations of black radicalism in the United States neither completely died out in the early 1970s under state attack nor disappeared as African American politicians won offices as members of the Democratic Party.[4] As Global

South solidarity fractured as a force against Western hegemony and neoliberalism, activists continued in its afterlife to deploy the strategies of the 1960s and early 1970s New Left, Black Power, and civil rights movements to advance discreet political causes, even from within the government. The U.S. Congress was ill-suited for radical activist members, but Leland and his colleagues did their best with the power and political resources they possessed to redefine the United States' relationship with Global South nations.[5]

This book presents Leland as emblematic of the afterlife of international radicalism in the United States. Leland's political career, particularly as it relates to African affairs, highlights the global dimensions of black politics during the 1980s and the myriad ways Black Power and civil rights ideologies, organizing strategies, and political aspirations of the 1960s and early 1970s informed the rapidly transforming domestic and international political environment of the period. Once in political office, first in the Texas state legislature and then in the U.S. Congress, Leland continually affirmed his solidarity with the declining number of leftist regimes in the Global South.[6] Yet the Reagan administration's emphasis on anticommunism as the centerpiece of its foreign policies toward Global South nations was an obstacle to the goal of Leland and other African American politicians, ambassadors, and activists to elevate Africa's significance during the 1980s in U.S. debates on human rights, sovereignty, aid, and development.[7] They applied their energy and political capital to ending U.S. government and corporate support for white-minority rule in Africa, which they successfully forged as a consensus issue. Leland hoped that the food crisis in the Horn of Africa and southern Africa's Frontline States—Angola, Namibia, Botswana, Zambia, Zimbabwe, and Tanzania—might attract public attention in ways similar to the ways apartheid in South Africa had. His premise for a U.S.-centered movement to end hunger in Africa appealed to most members of nongovernmental organizations and received his congressional colleagues' endorsement, but he did not rally public support for ending hunger as he and his colleagues had gathered support against white-minority rule in South Africa.[8]

Despite Africa's prominence in Leland's activism and political thinking, his career shows that the continent was an ephemeral point of heightened political interest for African Americans.[9] One of this period's great paradoxes was that the movement against apartheid in South Africa contributed to African Americans' unprecedented prominence in U.S. foreign affairs.

Breaking down white supremacy in southern Africa was the glue between African American and South African activists. The two groups were not joined closely around other political issues in comparable ways. In the early 1960s, the South African Communist Party labeled state-sanctioned white supremacy in South Africa "colonialism of a special type." However, the end of this "special type" in 1994 was labeled a victory for democracy and the ballot, but not a liberation. The language of national liberation was no longer relevant in South Africa. Democracy, rather than liberation, had taken hold in the country.[10] Democracy is a political process, while liberation is a state of being. The end of overt white supremacy in South Africa removed the onus of equality and justice from the U.S. government and placed it on the African National Congress (ANC)-controlled government, ushering in a postradical era of waning activism. Absent blatant white supremacy in Africa, African American leaders applied differing interpretations of issues and events on the continent and pursued what often became conflicting approaches, which weakened their voice in U.S. foreign policy.

Leland recognized these contradictions in African American leaders' relationship with Africa and strived to draw public attention to diverse issues on the continent, from civil wars in Angola and Mozambique to humanitarian crises in Sudan and Ethiopia. He played a key role in the anti-apartheid movement, but Ethiopia's famine in 1983–85 rather than apartheid in South Africa was Leland's signature issue in Congress. As the famine became international news, journalists and reporters, together with relief organization workers, crafted a narrative of helplessness and state failure in Ethiopia. This narrative redefined the scope and mission of international relief organizations and the international politics of food aid in the Global South throughout the decade.[11] Leland also sought to sideline Ethiopia's complex issues in favor of a streamlined human-interest narrative of events behind Ethiopia's crisis. In speeches, interviews, and congressional hearings, Leland also repeatedly insisted that the U.S. government had an obligation to address the needs of poor and hungry people in the United States that equaled its obligation to end hunger elsewhere in the world.[12] Leland believed that if the U.S. public was made fully aware of the food crises in Africa they would find the U.S. response unacceptable.

These issues—the legacies of Black Power and civil rights in African American politics, the domestic and international anti-apartheid movements, U.S. humanitarian relief for Marxist Ethiopia, and the effects of the end of the Cold War U.S. involvement in African affairs—are at the center of this book, but they were far from being the only features of Leland's politics. Beyond African American economic and political empowerment, pan-Africanism, and humanitarianism, Leland held strong positions on most domestic progressive political issues, including Native American land rights, geriatric health care, anti–nuclear proliferation, minority representation on U.S. television, and, perhaps most prominently, hunger and homelessness in American cities. He remained ahead of his time by calling for immigration reform and celebrating Latino cultures as part of the fabric of U.S. society. He addressed his colleagues in Spanish from the House floor while making a statement in support of retaining bilingual clauses in the Voting Rights Act of 1965. He wanted his colleagues to appreciate the challenges many Latino citizens faced.

When he embarked on his seventh congressional delegation in August 1989, Leland was a forty-four-year-old, deeply charismatic, fiercely compassionate black radical American. He was also an elected Democratic official, representing Houston's largely African American and Latino Eighteenth Congressional District. Above all, he was a self-proclaimed "citizen of humanity." The events surrounding his death would help ignite a turn of events in the Horn beyond anything he had ever imagined, beginning with the Leland party's flight from Bole that never arrived in Fugnido. In hindsight, Ethiopian authorities should not have allowed the plane to leave the airport. Dense, low-hanging clouds over Addis Ababa, Ethiopia's capital, disoriented veteran pilot Captain Assefa Giorgis as he attempted to fly the plane through an impossible storm. For the aid workers waiting to welcome the Leland party at Fugnido and the aviation officials back at Bole, it must have seemed that the plane simply vanished. Nothing mechanical at takeoff had signaled trouble. During the six days following the plane's departure, friends, families, and colleagues held out hope that the Leland party was just missing and had survived. They would later discover the reality: just fifty miles from Fugnido, one of the plane's wings had clipped a tree and caused it to crash into one of the colossal mountains that define Ethiopia's landscape. To locate the plane and possibly rescue the Leland party, the United States and Ethiopia launched a historic joint mission that grew into the largest, most expansive search for civilians in Ethiopian and U.S. history. This unprecedented venture accelerated reconciliation and ultimately marked the end of Cold War antagonism in U.S.-Ethiopian relations.

During the days leading up to and following his funeral, Leland held the U.S. media's attention to a degree he would never have dreamed of when alive. Fellow lawmakers and activists celebrated him as a model politician and humanitarian. Newspapers and television news programs aired stories of him helping the oppressed, poor, and homeless around the world. Today, nearly thirty years after his death, Leland's place in the history of U.S.-African affairs and U.S. politics is easier to discern than in the weeks and months after his death. His political ideologies and aspirations were forged during the radical struggle for civil rights and Black Power and ultimately absorbed humanitarianism and human rights.

There were several memorial services in Washington, Houston, and Addis Ababa. The United States Agency for International Development (USAID) held a service at the Lincoln Memorial for its staff members who had died in the crash. The *Ethiopian Herald* reported that Abune Zena Markos, archbishop of the Ethiopian Orthodox Tewahedo Church, presided over a service beneath the beautiful stained-glass windows of the historic Holy Trinity Cathedral, "in the presence of archbishops and solemnly attired clergy representatives of various churches and monasteries in and around Addis Ababa," for the sixteen Ethiopians and Americans who died in the plane crash.[13] In Houston, five thousand mourners gathered for a two-hour service in Texas Southern University's gymnasium. Jesse Jackson was among the invited speakers and described Leland's political path as one worth following, stating that doing so would lead to the right side of history: "If you're for Mickey Leland, you'll choose a national health plan over a stealth [bomber] plan. If you're for Mickey, you're for ending apartheid in South Africa and freeing Mandela. You'll wipe out these slum houses in the Fifth Ward right here in the shadow of downtown where all these millionaires live if you're for Mickey."[14] He praised Leland for his "unselfish service to humanity." Jackson went on to predict, "They will be naming streets after Mickey, schools and highways and federal buildings."[15]

The burial service for Leland took place in Houston at St. Anne's Catholic Church on Saturday, August 19, where "a long line of sweating mourners," as Jim Simmon of the *Houston Chronicle* described, "curved around the driveway of the church yard on Westheimer and Shepherd." Over 650 people squeezed into the historic Spanish-style church's sanctuary and many stood in the side aisles. The more than 550 mourners who could not find space in the church gathered in a tent across the street and listened to the service over loudspeakers. It is unlikely that St. Anne's church had ever held a similar service. Its blend of Baptist and Catholic was characteristic of Leland's style. The "political power brokers sat knee-to-knee with common folk from Leland's inner-city district," Simmon reported. "Saxophonist Kirk Whalum filled the church sanctuary with the bluesy strains of 'Somewhere over the Rainbow' and the Rev. Jesse Jackson brought the crowd to its feet with a thundering eulogy."[16]

Bishop Joseph A. Fiorenza's more traditionally Catholic homily followed Jackson's charismatic eulogy. Fiorenza emphasized Leland's charitable actions, describing him as one whose "work put him in contact with the famous and powerful, but he never lost a special love and genuine concern for children and the elderly, for the poor and the homeless . . . for the powerless people of the world." Jackson and Fiorenza eulogized Leland with the central theme that his death charged all who knew him with the responsibility to push his cause forward. "Mickey is not in that box, just as Jesus was not in that tomb," Jackson declared, gesturing to the simple pine casket that would soon hold his body. "And because Mickey is not in that box and because Jesus is not in that tomb, death has not freed us of the burden of Mickey's mission. The challenge that we have today . . . is for those of us who remain to protect the integrity of Mickey's mission." Jackson concluded with his trademark exhortation to "keep hope alive!"[17]

In the decade after Mickey Leland's death, with the end of abject white supremacy in southern Africa, African American political leaders ceased to engage in African affairs as an ethnic bloc in a robust and informed manner. From the late 1970s to the early 1990s, African Americans had exerted a postradical influence in U.S. policy toward Africa, and the Global South generally, that had never been seen before and that has yet to reemerge. During the first decade of the 2000s, there were individual African Americans who had a far greater influence on U.S. foreign policy than those of preceding generations, but they operated with fundamentally different sensibilities, goals, and strategies. Most important, they were policymakers, ambassadors, and lawmakers, and one was even a president for whom race was secondary to national identities and interests. President Barack Obama, Ambassador Susan Rice, Secretary of State Colin Powell, and other members of the George W. Bush and Obama administrations who were African American shared links to diverse black communities, but their links to the typical black political communities were marginal.[18] Where the lawmakers and ambassadors of the 1970s and 1980s had their roots in the civil rights movement, Black Power, and trade unions, those who attained positions of influence in the 2000s had their political roots in the Democratic Party or, as in the case of Powell, the military.

This book examines how African Americans successfully influenced U.S. foreign policy, as well as failed to do so, from inside and outside the government during the postradical environment of the 1980s. It explores the links among the electoral politics, community activism, and community organizing that propelled African Americans to reach their point of greatest influence on U.S. policies toward African and other Global South countries. Congressman Mickey Leland and his colleagues drew on the ideologies, practices, and aspirations of the broader movement of black radical politics of the 1960s and 1970s in the United States and inspiration from pan-Africanism, decolonization, and revolution in the Global South to advance African American interests and represent African interests from inside the government. Their radical work marks a moment of transition. Global radical leftist activism and revolutionary political imaginings receded as neoliberalism and political conservatism emerged as the dominant paradigm in domestic and international affairs. The radical activism of the former period ended European colonial rule in South Asia, Africa, and the Caribbean and fueled the U.S. movement for social and economic justice in the United States and a number of political revolutions in Central America, the Caribbean, and Africa, including those in Cuba, Nicaragua, Guatemala, Maurice Bishop's New Jewel Movement in Grenada, and Thomas Sankara's revolution in Burkina Faso. Leland represented a vision of a black post–Cold War foreign policy that looked beyond national borders to try to benefit all of humankind. But he was one of the examples of radical politics during an era when the political left was descendant globally. Examining Leland in this context inspires a fundamentally different way of thinking about the relationship between African American political voices and geopolitics, as well as the relationship between Africa and the United States more broadly during the closing decade of the Cold War.

Chapter 1

"The Low Rising Against the High and Mighty"

Radicalism and Protest in Addis Ababa and Houston

Shadows scream! Freedom hopes!
    And tar colored bosoms swell
    with burden!

Kinky-haired "boys" build arsenals
of straw to hide slingshots and
bottles of lawnmower fluid to prepare
for guerilla wars against
blue-eyed Tanks and Blond-haired
missiles and blanch-skinned
militaires and Caucasians?
and law? and order? and justice?

Genocide? Suicide? Or Life?
Shadows are gaining substance
Much too slow!

The Sleeping women,
    She'll never know!

—Mickey Leland, "Mickey's Message"

Mickey Leland's route from black radical activism during the 1960s to electoral politics in the 1970s began in Houston, Texas, with protests and community organizing to address racial discrimination, police brutality, lack of community control of public institutions, and systematic barriers to African American political representation. He was known in Houston as "a rather flamboyant radical," a term that described his personality and his personal style.[1] He cut a striking figure with his signature large reddish Afro, freckles and green eyes, and solid build. Until he entered the Texas state legislature, he most often wore jeans and a dashiki. He fit well with the times. Years later, he described himself as a "child of the sixties" and "a disciple of Stokely Carmichael, Rap Brown, and the other brothers and sisters who challenged inequities and injustices we saw in the system. So, I was a soldier in the army of the Civil Rights Movement."[2] He said he had been possessed by a feeling of being at war with the white establishment in America. He did not serve in Vietnam, he said, because he was already at war: "My enemies were right here at home."[3]

With the end of de jure segregation and state-enforced discrimination in the United States in the mid-1960s, African Americans redoubled their efforts to build sustainable community-based institutions that they imagined would enable them to achieve control over their communities and interact with the country's white power structure on their own terms. The Black Power demands for economic and political liberation and empowerment galvanized African American communities throughout the country and grew out of grassroots civil rights and community development work.[4] Radical internationalists among black activists called attention to the movement's global dimensions and added the fight against global white supremacy, European imperialism, and the expansion of global capitalism to the domestic struggle against racial oppression.[5]

Leland's political philosophy was fortified by a strong belief in the power of protest for social and political change and to dismantle the pillars of white supremacy. But this period marked the turning point for a significant number of black radicals, as they gained a new perspective on the efficacy of the ballot to secure stability within African American communities. Yet others insisted that electoral politics ran counter to true empowerment because effective legislating demanded compromise and, therefore, ideological betrayal. They could see no grounds for compromise with the capitalist, white supremacist political establishment. Proponents of Black Power through elected office, however, regarded it as a means to set the terms of their civic engagement, including asserting direct control over communal institutions, from schools to libraries and community centers to police departments. After Congress passed the Voting Rights Act of 1965, the ballot became an instrument to pursue their domestic and foreign policy interests.[6]

The logic of community control, rather than social integration, inspired the push toward electoral politics among black radicals.[7] In other words, political integration was a mechanism to gain control over their ethnically distinct communities and institutions. In 1965, Bayard Rustin, one of the principal strategists of the civil rights movement, published an essay prescribing electoral politics as the next logical, even natural, phase following protests and political action centered on voter registration drives. "What began as a protest movement," Rustin wrote in his customary sagacious prose, "is being challenged to translate itself into a political movement."[8] Aggressive registration drives in the South, represented most dramatically through the Freedom Rides that began in 1961 and continued through the middle of the decade, transformed African American voters into a vital constituency for the Democratic Party. Rustin argued that free, unencumbered access to public accommodations, the centerpiece of the classical stage of the civil rights movement, was meaningless if economic and political discrimination continued to keep African Americans poor and disenfranchised. "What is the value of winning access to public accommodations," he asked, "for those who lack money to use them?"[9] Rustin called for the movement to expand from its narrow focus on race relations to address economic issues. The solution to the interrelated problems of economic and racial injustice was political power. The turn toward political action was, he said, the most effective way to get rid of the racist and corrupt "local sheriff."

Amid the radicalism of the 1960s and 1970s, African American electoral victories throughout the country, in both municipal and congressional elections, aroused African Americans' optimism for what might be achieved through electoral politics. Nonwhite and nonmale voices rose to unprecedented prominence in U.S. government. In Brooklyn, New York, in 1968, Shirley Chisholm became the first African American woman elected to Congress. Barbara Jordan followed four years later as the first African American woman elected to represent a southern congressional district.[10] She had already made history in 1966 as the first African American elected to the Texas state senate since 1882, as well as the first African American

Figure 1. Mickey Leland yelling into a microphone at the University of Houston, no date. Courtesy of Special Collections, University of Houston Libraries.

woman state senator.[11] For young Houston activists, like Leland, Jordan represented the possibilities of mainstream politics to achieve the power and influence necessary for community empowerment. There was an ironic justice in the growing number of African American lawmakers in Congress, a body that through the systemic exclusion of African Americans had enabled whites to inflict violence and even death on African American citizens and to ensure they remained economically and politically marginalized.[12]

Mickey Leland was part of the community of student activists at Texas Southern University, one of the nation's largest historically black universities, that marched, held rallies, and staged sit-ins against racial segregation and threatened the city's sense of economic well-being and self-image as a bastion of racial tolerance. Houston city leaders believed Houston was an exceptional city. It experienced a postwar economic boom that continued into the 1960s. It attracted Fortune 500 companies and NASA built the massive Lyndon B. Johnson Space Center. Moreover, Houston did not have the same level of civil unrest linked to racial injustice as other southern cities and towns like Mobile, Jacksonville, and Atlanta. The city not only avoided protracted violent confrontations between demonstrators and police, it also distinguished itself among cities of its size for its lack of a vibrant counterculture like that found in New York and Berkeley, which made them hotbeds of protest. As Gene Locke, Leland's long-time friend, explained, "While it was fashionable for students at Columbia and other schools to take over buildings in the administration and hold those buildings until their demands were met, that never was a strategy that we felt we had the luxury to entertain."[13]

Student activists exploited city leaders' fear of upsetting their carefully crafted image and their economic interests to force them to dismantle formal, state-sanctioned racial segregation and disenfranchisement.[14] Rather than defend Jim Crow at the risk of a headline-grabbing confrontation with TSU students, civic and business leaders chose to protect the city's image as a cultural and business hub. They quietly but expeditiously removed the city's Jim Crow signs from major businesses and public spaces to eliminate the rationale for large protests downtown.[15] But, as police harassment and brutality remained a scourge in the African American community, activists continued to stage relatively mild protests against police brutality and other forms of racism.

African Americans in Houston did not entirely avoid violent confrontations with the city's police. The FBI and Houston police monitored and harassed activists, and in July 1970 a police sniper stationed on a rooftop across the street from the Black Panther Party's Houston headquarters shot and killed Carl Hampton, the local chapter's leader. When they murdered Hampton, Houston police pushed African American activists to the precipice of violent uprising. Church leaders and white city officials worked together to ease tensions and prevent rioting. But as was the case elsewhere in the country, young African Americans were determined to assert their citizenship and relationship with the U.S. power structure and culture on their own terms.

In 1968 Leland and his friends Sammy Ford, Deloyd Parker, and Charles Freeman formed the Black Community Action Team—the Black CATs—a group that aimed to channel and organize the simmering tensions within the black community through social programs and political and educational forums. They set out to educate community members on how to understand and articulate the structural barriers to social, economic, and political equality. The Black CATs received much of their financial support from Reverend Guy of Bellaire Presbyterian Church. He was concerned—as were many African American ministers in Houston—that the city would be the next to launch a rebellion, similar to Washington, D.C., Los Angeles, Newark, and Chicago. The Black CATs organized political and cultural awareness study groups and invited guest speakers such as Stokely Carmichael, the former leader of the Student Nonviolent Coordinating Committee who had popularized the slogan "Black Power!"[16] Leland looked up to Carmichael and other nationally renowned activists of the period as major guides for his and other Black CAT members' political development. "They were expressing the anger and anguish of black people at that time," Leland said years later. "They were the ones who would step up and be bold enough to challenge the white establishment. I was impressed with that."[17] The activists believed the country was in a prerevolutionary state—and they were positioned to bring about real transformative change in alliance with students, women, nationalists, and veterans.[18]

They considered their connections to movements and peoples in the Caribbean and African as self-evident. The Student Nonviolent Coordinating Committee (SNCC), for example, established ties with the FLN in Algeria and President Nyerere in Tanzania. Robert Williams, former leader of the Monroe, North Carolina, chapter of the NAACP, self-exiled in Cuba and China in the 1960s and championed civil rights from those locations.[19] Black internationalism existed within a broad global milieu of radical left politics geared to revolutionary change. SNCC organizers regarded their work as inextricably tied to larger international movements against white supremacy and for liberation and self-determination.[20] At SNCC's first conference at Shaw University in Raleigh, North Carolina, in April 1960 the founders declared their unequivocal solidarity with and support for African liberation. They encoded this position in their charter: "We identify ourselves with the African struggle as a concern for all mankind." To reinforce this claim, Antioch College undergraduate Alphonse Okuku from Kenya was a featured speaker at the conference. SNCC leaders invited Okuku to address the radical implications of the "African struggle" and to express words of solidarity with young activists at the forefront of the student sit-in movement engulfing the U.S. South.[21]

U.S. activists' calls for solidarity across international borders had racial dimensions, but their conceptions of international connections were not limited to race. Many argued that African Americans' economic, social, and political condition was akin to colonialism or what scholars and activists defined as "internal colonialism."[22] This concept has an extensive history within African American political discourse, extending back to the black conventions of the decades preceding the U.S. Civil War. Throughout U.S. history, activists described African Americans as comprising a "nation within a nation."[23] For nearly 180 years, activists, including Frederick Douglass, Cyril Briggs, and W. E. B. DuBois, had employed versions of the concept. Most scholars who debated the term prior to the Black Power era had little regard for its suitability and utility. Still, it emerged in the 1960s as "internal colonialism" or, as progressive activists and Marxist-oriented scholars presented it, the "Internal Colonialism Theory."[24] In 1962, Harold Cruse explained the rise of revolutionary nationalism among African Americans as having sprouted from their colonial roots. "The Negro is not really an integral part of America beyond the formal recognition that he lives within the borders of the United States," he wrote. "From the white's point of view, the Negro is not related to the 'we,' the Negro is the 'they.' This attitude assumes its most extreme expression in the Southern states and spreads out over the nation in varying modes of racial mores. The only factor which differentiates the Negro's status from that of pure *colonial status* is that his position is maintained in the 'home' country in close proximity to the dominant racial group."[25]

Similarly, in the 1964 publication *Youth in the Ghetto*, sponsored by Harlem Youth Opportunities Unlimited, a civic organization, the celebrated African American psychologist Kenneth Clark, whose research on the psychological harms of segregation to children contributed to the 1954 *Brown v. Board of Education* decision, described Harlem's social, economic, and political conditions as essentially colonial.[26] There were broad structural issues that excluded the majority of African Americans from success within the U.S. economic system. Urban spaces shared many characteristics with South African Bantustans, including a core of deprivation with suburban rings of racial privilege protected by government and upheld by banking policies.[27] With a prevailing sense of black spaces as colonial, many black radicals found the civil rights movement's goals of pro-capitalist integration into mainstream U.S. society unimaginative and unacceptable. Instead of integration, they wanted political, economic, and cultural control of their own communities.

Omowali Luthuli-Allen, a close friend of Leland's from Houston, described his and his fellow students' mind-sets as revolutionary rather than activist. They believed, he said, that their organizing methods were antithetical to the social status and future employment their university education had otherwise secured for them. "There was this idea," Luthuli-Allen explained, "that it was incumbent upon us to commit class suicide. We had to betray the class we were being prepared to join. We had to shed ourselves of personal opportunities."[28] They were freeing themselves from participating within the "managerial class" of African Americans and within the broader colonial framework of the United States. With the term "class suicide," Luthuli-Allen drew conscious ties to the Guinean and Cape Verdean anticolonial theorist and liberation leader Amilcar Cabral. Using Cabral as an example, Luthuli-Allen expressed the connections that he, Leland, and other activists in Houston felt to the socialist revolutionaries throughout the Global South.

The student activists in Addis Ababa during the 1960s and 1970s also subscribed to the theory of class suicide as a revolutionary imperative of their country's social, economic, and political elite. Many of the Ethiopian nationalists, like their counterparts in the United States, read Cabral's writings on revolutionary theory. Cabral helped them conceptualize and articulate their role, within what he categorized as the petty bourgeoisie, as bringing about radical, even revolutionary, social change. They had two choices, according to Cabral: either become more bourgeois and embrace its class mentality or commit class suicide and "be reborn as revolutionary workers, completely identified with the deepest aspirations of the people to which they belong."[29] These were no mere words for the activists, and Leland continually repeated this aphorism years later, even while in Congress.

In cities around the world, activists shared ideas through the writings of radical intellectuals who later were classified as foundational to postcolonial studies. Pan-Africanists and a few budding Marxists aspired to codify a major insight of civil rights campaigns and earlier liberation struggles, namely, that black people could develop alternatives to the oppressive social institutions that dominated their lives.[30] Couching the push for radical change in the United States and tying it to a broader aspiration for revolution had influential critics, even among those who fit within the camp of African American radical critics of U.S. society. Harold Cruse criticized black radical internationalists' easy identification with Third World revolutions, Cuba's in particular. Cruse was troubled by the movement's evident faith in the liberating power of violence for their own condition, without sufficient understanding of the cultural and material differences between African Americans and colonized and formerly colonized communities in the Global South.[31]

C. L. R. James, a Marxist Trinidadian writer and activist, studied similarities between various struggles against colonialism and other iterations of white supremacy. "What is taking place in Africa today and what the people in other parts of Western Civilization—the Africans—must know," James wrote, "is that the struggle they are carrying on is part of an immense change in the whole social structure that exists in the world at the present moment. It may be Black Power here, another thing there, independence here, freedom, democratic rights there. But it is part of this tremendous change that is taking place in the whole social structure that exists in the world at the present time." Africans are setting an example for the diaspora to emulate, he continued, "and we, Black people in America and the Caribbean, must look upon the African revolt as a symbol of what is likely to take place everywhere and to which we are very closely allied."[32]

The spectrum of Black Power included Marxist revolutionaries, back-to-Africa separatists, cultural nationalists, feminist consciousness raising, reparations campaigns, Afrocentric intellectuals, black capitalists, and radical integrationists seeking economic and cultural inclusion.[33] Black Power, from the 1950s through the early 1980s, went in different directions, yet self-determination lay at the core of each of its iterations. Leland's idealism as a student activist and his early years of electoral politics fell in the middle of the spectrum of Black Power. He endorsed racial coalition politics and some integration to achieve African American economic and political empowerment. He and others aspired to apply power and resources toward developing African American communities, specifically targeting the poor and working-class families. They took many of their political cues from Stokely Carmichael, who articulated the conceptual and practical problems of oppressed classes integrating into neoliberal capitalist societies. Carmichael argued that the African American community's emphasis on middle-class assimilation as the key strategy of integration would ultimately contribute to the inevitable erasure of the African American community's rich character and distinctive culture. Mainstream American society viewed integration, he stated, with "the assumption that there was nothing of value in the Negro community and that little of value could be created among Negroes, so the thing to do was to siphon off the 'acceptable' Negroes into the surrounding middle-class community."[34] Instead, radical activists pursued development programs to underscore the self-sustenance and value of African Americans and their culture.

Each iteration of black radicalism had at its core the goal of economic and political stability in black communities across America. Leland chose to focus on public health. He found community-based health-care programs favorable. He greatly admired Walter Lear's Medical Committee for Human Rights. Lear launched his program during the Freedom Summer in Mississippi with a group of health professionals to provide civil rights activists with health care to address the lack of adequate health-care facilities for African Americans in the segregated South.[35] In 1970, when Leland completed the master's program in clinical pharmacy at Texas Southern University, he wanted to build free health clinics in the Fifth Ward and provide breakfast to schoolchildren in a program similar to the community service run by the Black Panther Party.[36] Independent black institutions exemplified the contemporary politics of personal and collective conversion. They were instruments of a stratum of radicalized, largely middle-class activist-intellectuals. But their control and hold on community institutions, and the private and municipal resources to sustain and grow them, were tenuous at best.

The steady proliferation of African American elected officials and George McGovern's inspiring, though failed, campaign for president in 1972 attracted Leland to politics.[37] According to Omowali Luthuli-Allen, Leland followed the McGovern presidential campaign closely and found McGovern's foreign policy ideas refreshing. His aspirations for a "new morality" to replace Cold War ideology closely resemble Leland's arguments throughout the 1980s against Cold War foreign policies.[38] Barbara Jordan's success in the Texas state senate certainly broadened the scope of what was deemed possible. But electoral office was not revolutionary in and of itself. Moreover, to win a political campaign, one necessarily had to tap into the well of privileges for social and financial capital. Rather than forgo the benefits of university education and an associated professional-class lifestyle, Leland and a number of Houston activists and artists received financial support from Houston's most powerful philanthropists, John and Dominique de Menil.

The de Menils' financial and emotional support of Leland's graduate education and his early involvement in politics was vital to his trajectory toward national politics. The French couple had escaped German-occupied Paris in the 1940s, where their experiences with fascism gave them a visceral disdain for injustice and a firm belief in the moral and political value of the many nonviolent operations of the political left. The de Menils supported

Figure 2. Mickey Leland and Dominique de Menil at Menil Collection Opening, Houston, Texas, no date. Crossley and Progue. Used by permission. Courtesy of the Menil Archives, Rice University.

a variety of political, educational, and artistic individuals and projects in Houston. But they were also personally and directly involved in civil rights activities. From the mid-1950s through the 1960s, John de Menil provided funds to support student protestors at Texas Southern University, including the court fees for the TSU Five, who had been beaten, arrested, and falsely charged by the police in 1967.[39] The de Menils also financially supported African American political candidates, including Barbara Jordan when she ran for state senate in 1966 and Congress in 1972. John had also been a strong advocate within the business community of desegregating downtown Houston facilities.

During a visit to Texas Southern University, John de Menil asked the university president to identify students who were particularly promising. He singled out Mickey Leland, who was an undergraduate pharmacy major. The de Menils would embrace Leland's distinctive brand of activism and make his political career possible financially. Although they did not find it at all out of the ordinary to forge bonds with Leland, Deloyd Parker, and other activists, it was unusual for the time.

Again, Harold Cruse's writing is instructive for making sense of the tension between white liberals and black radicals during the 1960s. In the early years of the rise of Black Power, Cruse tied black radicals' skepticism toward white liberals to the hollow promises of U.S. democracy. "[Black nationalists] have less respect for liberals and left-wingers than for the conservatives of the Barry Goldwater type," Cruse wrote. "The latter, they believe, at least honestly express real white attitudes on economics, politics, and race relations."[40] Considering Cruse's insights, John and Dominique de Menil's enthusiastic acceptance of the legitimacy of black radicalism was as exceptional as Parker's and Leland's acceptance of John de Menil as a mentor.[41]

Leland and John de Menil's close relationship was widely known in Houston. Without the friendship and support he received from the couple it is doubtful that Leland would have considered entering mainstream politics and working closely with white politicians. John took Leland on as a protégé and encouraged him to explore the possibilities that electoral politics could hold. Though Leland was twenty-eight and black, and John was a sixty-eight-year-old wealthy white philanthropist, art collector, and oil man, from 1969 to 1972 the two were practically inseparable. In 1972, de Menil pressed twenty-eight-year-old Leland to run for the Texas state legislature to represent Houston's Eighty-Eighth District. As an activist in Houston's predominantly African American Fifth and Third Wards who frequently expressed his affinity for Marxism, Leland was an untraditional candidate for the Texas legislature. But de Menil encouraged Leland to apply his commitment to Houston's poor and marginalized to mainstream politics, and he spared no expense in supporting Leland's activism and budding political career. He introduced Leland to well-connected people in Houston, and Leland often joined the de Menils at their home when they entertained someone they believed could possibly help Leland in the future. "I went to breakfast, lunch, and dinner at their house," he recalled. "I spent hours talking with John about world politics and philosophy. He wanted me exposed to every aspect of their life that would give me a chance to do things for my community."[42]

John de Menil financed a trip to East Africa for Leland. De Menil had spent enough time among young activists in Houston to appreciate Africa's special place in Leland's brand of black radicalism, and he knew Leland dreamed of traveling there to witness Black Power firsthand. Tanzania's president, Julius Nyerere, intrigued Leland. Nyerere was a former school-teacher whose homegrown socialism and commitment to pan-Africanism and African liberation made him a hero to black radical internationalists in the United States. The de Menils demonstrated to Leland that white people could be good and that he could love them. A week before he departed for East Africa, he wrote John a two-page letter. "I want you to know that I sincerely cherish our relationship which has grown sacred to me," he wrote. "Not for the material things that you've done but for the faith and confidence you placed in me." The letter suggests a deep affection for John and that Leland regarded him as much as a father as anything else. "It is very dangerous for a Black man to endear fatherhood by a white man. I stand by my convictions, and our colorless relationship, and say that you have become the father I always wanted and never had."[43]

By traveling to Africa, particularly Tanzania, Leland followed a path to the continent that earlier activists had taken. In 1964, for example, John Lewis, James Forman, and singer, actor, and activist Harry Belafonte organized a tour of West African countries for SNCC that became an important step in the group's political development. Eleven members went on the trip. In addition to Forman and Lewis, the group included Julian Bond, Bill Hansen, Bob Moses, Dona Richards, Prathia Hall, Matthew Jones, Ruby Robinson, Fannie Lou Hamer, and Donald Harris.[44] When they returned to the United States after seventy-two days on the continent, Lewis and Harris were eager to establish a unit within SNCC to focus on international outreach and collecting information on issues and events in Africa. Within a year of the group's return, SNCC fieldworker Dona Richards produced an outline for developing an African Bureau with her "Africa Project." It had many of the ingredients that would be used in developing TransAfrica Forum, an African American foreign policy lobbying firm, in 1977. She hoped that the Africa Project would be devoted to gathering information to educate the public on African nations and U.S. policies toward them. The second part of the project would involve gathering data to help SNCC develop a campaign to pressure the U.S. government to impose economic sanctions on South Africa. Richards and SNCC staffer Gwen Robinson collected donated books to create an African Library that was to be housed in SNCC's Atlanta office. They also founded the African Bureau to manage SNCC's correspondence with and research on countries and organizations in Africa.[45]

Figure 3. Mickey Leland, Sam Gilliam, and John de Menil at Menil Collection Opening, 1972. Hickey-Robertson. Used by permission. Courtesy of the Menil Archives, Rice University.

Leland and de Menil flew together to Los Angeles, then to New York and Paris, before they parted ways for Leland to experience Africa alone, with de Menil financing the entire trip.[46] Leland traveled to Ethiopia, Kenya, and Tanzania, where his enthusiasm for Nyerere's Ujamaa socialism soared. When Leland arrived there in 1971, pan-Africanism and the Third World project continued to have many adherents, and Tanzania was among the few countries with a head of state who actively supported leftist rebel movements. He provided safe haven for rebel leaders from Zaire, Rhodesia, and South Africa. Nyerere helped fill the void in pan-Africanism left by Kwame Nkrumah's political fall in the 1966 coup. Tanzania attracted black internationalists who wanted to witness Nyerere's political project firsthand. Ghana had been the heart of diasporic and expatriate pan-Africanist aspirations for Africa. President Nkrumah welcomed African Americans and diasporic Africans from the Caribbean to visit and settle in the country and lend their talents and expertise to its development.[47] Ghana's tangible historical links to the Atlantic slave trade, the years Nkrumah spent in African American communities, and his pan-Africanist outlook when he returned endowed Ghana with greater historical significance among people of African descent in the West than Tanzania. However, subsequent Ghanaian leaders lacked Nkrumah's pan-Africanist outlook and connection to African American and Caribbean communities, and Ghana's pan-Africanist star declined.

A small group of African American and Caribbean expatriates moved to Tanzania from Ghana, and countless pan-Africanists poured continuously into Dar es Salaam, its capital, as political tourists, pilgrims, expatriates, and exiles in the 1960s and 1970s, including Malcolm X, Angela Davis, Amiri Baraka, and Eldridge Cleaver. The country even offered safe haven to a number of Black Panthers.[48] President Nyerere welcomed diasporic Africans' enthusiasm for Tanzania. SNCC's International Affairs Commission met with Nyerere in 1967 to discuss ways African Americans might assist in "progressive" African nations' development.[49]

After Nyerere, a Christian, pan-Africanist, and former school instructor, led the former British colony of Tanganyika to independence in 1960 he appeared to successfully navigate his country toward economic and political autonomy through nonalignment in the international realm and Ujamaa socialism at home. He was part of a generation of African leaders in the 1950s and 1960s, including Guinea's Ahmed Sekou Touré and Ghana's Kwame Nkrumah, that championed African socialism. Pan-Africanist ideas had been part of Tanganyika's political landscape since the interwar period, and like Nkrumah he applied them to his struggle for national liberation.[50] With Ujamaa socialism, Nyerere presented the nation itself as an extension of Tanzanian families.[51] His brand of pan-Africanism, socialism, and sincere support of those willing to take up arms for liberation appealed to black radicals.[52]

The fact that Tanzania ostensibly remained politically nonaligned in Cold War geopolitics was paramount among his political achievements. Other African heads of state proclaimed the nonaligned status, but few managed to substantiate it through their foreign policies to the same degree as Nyerere. What young radical would not be enamored with an African head of state who hosted pan-Africanist conferences and harbored leftist rebels from Zaire, Rhodesia, and South Africa? Leland joined the legion of Nyerere-philes, and his East Africa travels would only strengthen his belief that the African American struggle for community control and self-determination was tied to the broader struggle of defending African sovereignty.

John de Menil arranged for Leland's trip to last several weeks, but the weeks stretched into months as the long-standing emotional and political connection Leland had to the continent evolved into a tangible, fully formed political commitment. "My mother thought I was dead," he said years later. "My grandmother had just given up on me. But the fact is that I got totally absorbed in Africa."[53] He returned to Houston three months later, engulfed in the optimism of African nationalism he had acquired in Tanzania. Rather than overturning U.S. power, he envisioned transforming it into a positive force for change in black America and the Global South. Totally absorbed, Leland carried around *We Must Run While They Walk*, William Smith's flattering portrait of Nyerere and Tanzania.[54] As his friend Gene Locke recalled, Leland kept the book with him almost all of the time during his initial homecoming to Houston.[55]

Reflecting on his trip in 1989, Leland described Nyerere's profound impact on him. The trip and Nyerere's nation-building project and philosophy that he had learned through *We Must Run While They Walk*, Leland said, "provided the concrete that built my foundation."[56] The experience of black people in charge of their own affairs energized him. What he had seen in Tanzania enabled Leland to imagine the possibilities for a generation of college-educated, socially conscious, and committed activists determined to lift the disenfranchised and the disposed, "the boats stuck on the bottom" as his friend Luthuli-Allen described, from within the mainstream political system.[57]

Leftist revolutions were transforming political landscapes in Ethiopia, Angola, Mozambique, Guinea-Bissau, and South Africa during Leland's travels in East Africa. But Julius Nyerere's socialist project in Tanzania inspired him more than the revolutionary changes in other parts of the continent. In Ethiopia, Student protests in response to Emperor Haile Selassie's policies, his neglect of the country's growing famine problem, and the deteriorating state of their university were ubiquitous in Addis Ababa. Few issues carried more weight within pan-Africanist and black radical politics in the 1960s and 1970s than the integrity of Africa's internal national borders and the national sovereignty of each of its countries. The primacy of sovereignty in international affairs, however, was dissonant with the domestic push for political reforms, secessions, and civil wars several African countries faced. For black radical internationalists and pan-Africanists, Ethiopia's successful resistance against European imperialism made it the ultimate expression of black power. While there is no account of Leland's opinion of Ethiopian student activism and revolution at the time, he would have been attracted to the students' demands for free speech, peasant control of farmland, and political reforms. But the students' slogans that expressed their disdain for Emperor Selassie would have likely struck him as detrimental to the progress of pan-Africanism and African liberation. During the late 1960s and early 1970s, the political kingdom that Kwame Nkrumah counseled his generation of leaders to seek remained precious. Attacks on African sovereignty and the champions of African liberation and pan-Africanism were sacrilegious.

A broader view of East African political affairs would have brought the region's food crisis into sharp relief for Leland. In 1972, the year after his sojourn in East Africa, the signs of a famine appeared in Ethiopia's northern provinces and in Hararghe, in the east near the Somali border. Chronic lack of rain caused the drought, but policies caused the famine. The hunger and famine powerfully symbolized Emperor Selassie's corrupt and anachronistic government to student activists. "Land to the Tiller!" was one of their most popular slogans. Leland may not have expressed an interest in the Ethiopian student movement, but the protests and ensuing revolution are essential to the story of U.S.-Ethiopian relations at the end of the Cold War and set the stage for Leland's involvement in Ethiopian affairs, particularly the hunger and famine crisis, during the 1980s. In Addis Ababa students and leftist activists pushed toward revolution with hunger and famine as issues linking their otherwise disparate grievances. When famine returned in 1983, it thrust Leland into the political world these leftists helped create. Hunger and famine were portals to the myriad issues that defined the political left and their protests during the 1970s. The story of the student activists behind the Ethiopian revolution is essential to the broader narrative of the international response to Ethiopia's food crisis in the 1980s.

Ethiopia's young activists planted the seeds of revolution in the same period of radical activism that brought change to societies around the world. Students in Ethiopia were the country's sole revolutionary class, while in cities in France, the United States, and even South Africa there were opportunities for alliances and cross fertilization between a variety of groups that sought revolutionary change. But like the groups in New York, Paris, and Dakar, students in Addis Ababa had the time and the capacity for critical study, analysis, and organizing to confront economic and political elites' hold on power.[58] Their protests were initially intended to bring about social, political, and economic reforms, not necessarily revolution.

The students in Addis Ababa perceived the emperor in ways that Leland and black radicals, Rastas in the West, and pan-Africanists throughout Africa and the diaspora would not have recognized. Over the previous three decades, Emperor Selassie had allowed social and political discontent in Ethiopia to fester and government officials' blatant corruption and cronyism to go unchecked. He expanded access to Western-style education and Westernized the civil service and army to further centralize his power and promote a sense of pan-Ethiopian identity among the urban elite.[59] Vast unemployment and his failure to provide opportunities for the growing educated population inflamed political activism and left him in a political trap of his own making. The emperor's lack of forethought contributed enormously to his eventual political undoing. In this milieu, teachers, students, and state functionaries channeled their grievances through protest.[60] Their hardships and the country's economic and political decline, as they saw it, contrasted with general optimism elsewhere on the continent during these years of African independence.

The humanitarian crisis in Ethiopia in the mid-1980s that the public in the West responded to had its political roots in the closing years of the emperor's reign. The country was stuck in a morass, and the peasants' worsening situation perfectly captured its existential crisis. Student and leftist activists advanced this economic paradigm shift as their core cause. They were not primarily concerned with the famine in and of itself. The food crisis was an outrage, but, to a degree, it served as a rallying point, a catchall for their myriad grievances with Emperor Selassie, particularly the slow, and in many respects stalled, pace of Ethiopia's political and economic development. The monarchy fomented activists' grievances in its effort to stem the effects of the country's food shortage. To avoid an urban crisis, the emperor ensured that urban markets remained stocked with food, but this was done at the expense of the rural areas, where peasants grew the food. In doing so Selassie created a rural crisis.

The emperor might have avoided the worst effects of the food crisis if he had taken advantage of his ties to the United States and responded earlier and aggressively. Ethiopia was a key U.S. ally in the Horn of Africa in the 1970s, and Emperor Selassie was an important partner for U.S. interests in the Middle East. The Ethiopian coast provided a base for U.S. operations in the Red Sea and the Persian Gulf. Quite naturally, the emperor had earlier strengthened these ties to his advantage.[61] In 1953, the United States had signed agreements with Ethiopia for access to military bases within the country in return for economic and military aid. The United States maintained Kagnew Station, a communications facility at Asmara in the province of Eritrea on the Ethiopian coast. The station was named in honor of the Ethiopian legion that participated in the Korean War as part of the UN force. Between 1963 and 1974, the United States provided in excess of $230 million in aid to Ethiopia, more than it provided to any other country in Africa during that period.[62]

The emperor benefited from close ties to Washington, but he claimed a nonaligned position in global politics. Therefore, he accepted economic and military assistance from the Soviet Union. With foreign assistance, the emperor built the largest and strongest army in Africa. His formidable military withstood Somali irredentism and Eritrean separatists. Internally, however, the nation fell into disrepair, and a nearly successful coup would expose the emperor's vulnerability.

Student activists shifted gradually from demanding reforms to the education system, reforms to the political system, and the right to freedom of speech to an outright end to the monarchy. Similar to their leftist counterparts in the United States, South Africa, and cities throughout Europe, they consumed socialist and Marxist literature that foreigners, expatriate teachers, and students returning from schooling abroad brought into the country and made abundantly available in the capital during the late 1960s. A radical Marxist-Leninist transformation of the Ethiopian state and society became the cornerstone of the student movement.[63] Had the new regime successfully empowered the peasantry and freed them from landlessness and hunger, these measures alone would have marked a fundamental transformation of the Ethiopian state, whose economic and social systems had rested heavily on feudalism.

In February 1965, the student protests intensified with a mass demonstration in front of parliament where they shouted the famous slogan "Land to the Tiller!"[64] The year marked the genesis of revolutionary fervor within the Ethiopian student movement. However, student activism at Haile Selassie I University had germinated after Mengistu Neway and his younger brother Germame's failed coup attempt against Haile Selassie in December 1960 while the emperor was on a state visit to Brazil.[65] The near success of a commoners' coup removed the veneer of invisibility from the monarchy, and new possibilities for political change suddenly emerged. Tenant farmers made up 75 percent of the population in some provinces, and peasants accounted for more than 90 percent of the overall population. Student activists held rallies on campus rather than attending classes and distributed leaflets among people in Addis Ababa with revolutionary and class propaganda to overthrow the monarchy.[66]

One student who participated in the movement remembers the "Land to the Tiller!" demonstrations as a catalyst for greater student activism: "Students were dismissed because of it and they experienced hardships as a consequence. . . . Although there had been earlier some visible signs of left-wing tendencies in the form of discussion clubs, they had substantially proliferated thereafter."[67] To another activist, "the implementation of this crucial watchword will once and for all remain the specter of famine from Ethiopia. The antagonistic existence of abject poverty on one side and luxury on the other, grain exports by some and famine for the multitude and potentially rich country and an actually poor one will be made to vanish never to return again."[68] Other slogans followed over the next few years and the protests took on a life of their own. "Is Poverty a Crime?" and "Education for All!" characterized the themes of the students' demonstrations.

Hunger and famine were the emperor's Achilles' heel. At the start of 1973, reports of a worsening food shortage in the provinces of Tigray and Wello spread through Addis Ababa. Indeed, food refugees themselves soon migrated to the capital. Ethiopia experienced its third consecutive dry season with as many failed harvests. No rain had fallen throughout the previous year, and then torrential downpours washed away the meager crops that had managed to emerge from the depleted soils. The country was unprepared to confront a catastrophe of this magnitude. There were 40,000 to 80,000 deaths, far fewer than during the famine a decade later, but peasants who lived through both the 1973 and the 1984 famines described the former as the more severe.[69] Tadesse Mollaw, a farmer, said 1973 was the worst year of his life. "There was no help from the government and no help from outside," he explained. "People were dying up and down this road. [The year] 1984 was also very bad, but we got aid then from Mekanne Yesus [the nearby Protestant church]." His family survived on handouts that his two young children received.[70] As Tadesse pointed out, the absence of a sizable, organized humanitarian response in 1973 marked part of the difference between the two crises.

Activists tried to step in where the government and international relief organizations, with some exceptions, were absent. They carried out humanitarian relief initiatives that led to direct confrontations with the Ethiopian state. Haile Selassie I University's Famine Relief Committee consisted of students and university faculty who commissioned a study of conditions in famine areas. In April 1973, the committee's three-person fact-finding team issued a report on the government's response to the famine. It described the government as deplorably unwilling to provide relief and noted that it had, in fact, belittled the significance of the crisis. The report described the conditions of peasants in the north and their general state of well-being and, finally, issued a call to action. The report accused the emperor of placing a premium on protecting his hold on power at the expense of building a strong agricultural industry for his country. The Relief Committee followed up its report with a relief effort. Volunteers distributed $67,000 worth of grain ($385,500 in 2016 dollars) to people in Wello and Tigray that had been purchased with funds raised from their colleagues abroad.[71]

These ascendant revolutionaries were also bound by their distaste for Tigrayan and Amhara highlanders' social and political dominance of non-highlander communities in the east and the south. Antifamine activism tenuously and only momentarily provided a basis for activists to close ranks. Ultimately, their unity did not endure; indeed, many argued it was illusory from the start. Subtle ideological differences and competing political aspirations erupted in two main radical political factions that grew out of the student movement: the communist Ethiopian People's Revolutionary Party (EPRP) and the All-Ethiopia Socialist Movement, or MEISON. These were the most prominent pan-Ethiopian organizations in the country, but both had been established by students studying and living abroad. They became antagonistic competitors for intellectual and political power within revolutionary Ethiopia. MEISON's members initially sided with the Derg, but ultimately they, too, became the Derg's targets for extermination.[72]

Herein lie the origins of the conflict Leland chose not to address. It did not cause the food crisis, but the civil war that grew out of this factional dispute precipitated the famine. Leland would never successfully address the issues that lay at the heart of Ethiopia's food crisis without tackling the country's complex political conflict that erupted from the revolution. Leading up to these events, the Ethiopian military turned the students' protests into a revolution. The military capitalized on the student movement's limitations and fractiousness, and on January 12, 1974, joined the revolution. Soldiers of the Fourth Division in the southern frontier post of Nagele Borana, in the province of Sidamo, mutinied. Economics rather than politics defined their discontent. The mutineers sent radio messages throughout the country demanding a pay increase and better living conditions, but they issued no political demands. As their message echoed throughout the country, other military divisions took up the mutiny. The army's Second Division, stationed in Asmara, the Eritrean capital, changed the army's message from reform to revolution by calling for the end of the Selassie regime. To cool the rising political temperature, the emperor futilely offered two separate pay raises, but his move toward conciliation was too late.

The emperor then doubled the price of petrol and pushed the crisis to the tipping point. He explained the increase as a necessary response to increased oil prices caused by the 1973 Arab-Israeli War, but workers found his explanation untenable. In Addis Ababa, taxi drivers launched a citywide strike in February 1974 and demanded a 50 percent fare increase commensurate with the rise in the price of petrol. The nation's teachers also launched a general strike. Encouraged by these developments, student protests grew larger and more aggressive. Civilian riots forced the emperor to reduce the petrol price. In addition, his inattention to mass hunger agitated widespread economic and political grievances and stoked the flames of revolution.

For six months, protests grew in size and frequency, and conflicts between student associations became common. Historian Bahru Zewde, an activist in the years leading up to the revolution, described the protesters as populist and endowed with an acute class consciousness. The students' tenacity and the size of their protests overwhelmed the monarchy. "The general tenor of the popular movement," he wrote, "was one of the low rising against the high and mighty—soldiers and junior ranks against the high officers, the poor against the rich, employee against employer and labour against management. The coercive arm of the state, with its tradition of stifling such opposition, was unable or unwilling to exercise its customary function."[73] The monarchy could not withstand the pressure and essentially deferred to the mutineers, but Emperor Selassie remained the de jure head of government.

Army officers established the Coordinating Committee of the Armed Forces, Police and Territorial Army to investigate soldiers' grievances. With the emperor's tacit approval, the committee, or Derg, investigated the grievances of abuse, poor living conditions, and corruption of various military units. The Derg had risen to power during a radical revolution, but the 107 officers who composed its leadership were neither revolutionary nor populist, and it is doubtful that more than a few of them were familiar with Marxism-Leninism. Initially, their concerns were limited to issues within the military, and therefore their movement had little affinity with the popular uprising. Nonetheless, during the next few years Derg leaders either became politically radicalized or took up the lexicon and symbols of radical politics.[74]

The Derg appropriated the left's outrage in response to famine and the general food crisis as their own grievance. But as an extension of the military, the committee had the power to accomplish what the activists could not. With the military involved on the side of the activists and against the ruling elite, revolution was possible. The Derg accused the emperor of willful neglect and presented evidence that he had been briefed on the severity of the famine. Indeed, his subordinates had reached out to him for help. In one piece of evidence, a memo from Mamo Seyoum, the governor and special imperial envoy in famine-stricken Wello, to Emperor Selassie, the governor warned him that the drought was extreme and directly asked the emperor to provide food assistance to the peasants who were faring the worst in the crisis.[75] The monarchy was blind to its own excesses of power and the extent of its people's suffering. Derg officials publicly described the emperor as "an expensive and unnecessary luxury."[76] The army simply stepped forward to deliver the final push over the edge but then refused to yield the levels of power it had assumed.

On September 11, 1974, the Derg imposed a curfew on Addis Ababa. Derg officials gave the emperor direct orders to watch a documentary scheduled to air on television that evening. He complied with their orders and reportedly sat alone in his palace except for a single aide and watched British journalist Jonathan Dimbleby's documentary *Ethiopia: The Unknown Famine* in silence. It had first aired in Europe in the fall of 1973 and had shocked viewers. Dimbleby estimated that nonprofit organizations and NGOs raised $150 million as a result of his initial report. The film consisted of twenty-five minutes of images of relentless suffering, children's dead bodies, and a veiled appeal for assistance.[77] The following morning, September 12, Derg officials escorted the emperor from the palace and arrested him. The Derg had the emperor murdered the following year, and he was buried in an unmarked grave on the Menelik Palace compound.

For the most part, the general population welcomed the Derg's rise to power, as the committee appeared to embody all the positive aspects and promise of the revolution, and augured stability and order. For the next three years Mengistu Haile-Mariam ruled Ethiopia from behind the scenes, first with General Aman Andom and then with Brigadier General Tafari Benti as the official head of state. In the long history of the twentieth-century U.S.-Ethiopian partnership, the Mengistu Haile-Mariam regime was an interregnum. After his rise to power in 1974–76, his fall between 1989 and 1991 was an ironic end to and then recommencement of formal U.S.-Ethiopian ties. He belonged to neither the socially, economically, and politically dominant Amhara nor the Tigray; his father was reportedly Oromo and his mother Amhara. Mengistu had been an obscure figure prior to the revolution, outside of Harar, capital of the province of Hararghe. His father was a sergeant in the Ethiopian army, and Mengistu followed in his footsteps. In 1957, at age eighteen, he enrolled in the Military Training School at Holeta with the rank of second lieutenant. He was assigned to the Third Division in Harar and traveled twice to the United States, first in 1963 and then in 1969, for specialized military training.[78]

Mengistu's political ascension marked the advent of a radical transformation of Ethiopian society. As an Ethiopian leader, he was like no other in the country's history. Over the course of seven centuries, every Ethiopian leader had claimed to descend from the union of King Solomon and Queen Makeda of Saba (Sheba). Mengistu was physically different from the Ethiopian nobility. His complexion was relatively darker and his features were described as stereotypically "African." Mengistu did not possess Emperor Selassie's "Arab" look. To most Amharans and Tigrayans, Mengistu did not look Ethiopian at all. He was a *barya*, representative of the denigrated phenotype commonly associated with the peoples of the south.[79] As Dawit Giorgis, head of Ethiopia's Relief and Rehabilitation Commission, which the Derg established in 1974, recalled, "By putting him into power we were clearly demonstrating our rejection of past values and putting the message across that all are equal, irrespective of race, creed or religion."[80]

If the revolution catapulted Mengistu to power, once there he defied activists' expectations. He initially appeared poised to bring fundamental change to Ethiopia that would culminate in social, economic, and ethnic equality. Mengistu charted a distinct political path from that of Emperor Selassie. For one, he pursued full independence from the United States' sphere of influence. However, his aspirations soon converged on building and sustaining his unrivaled position of power. Toward that end, he built an aura of fear that demanded formality and submission. Derg officials grew intimidated and fearful of speaking freely about the evolving state of political affairs.[81] His authority centered on personal power rather than ideology or social reform, and he cloaked himself in Marxist-Leninism as a shield against leftist intellectuals and radicals. Few around him had faith in the authenticity of his Marxist-Leninism before he came to power. According to Dawit, "The people who injected Marxism-Leninism into him were civilian intellectuals, such as members of the All-Ethiopia Socialist Movement. . . . They had a marked influence on the undeveloped political mind of Mengistu."[82]

Ethiopia's Marxist revolution was among several political and social revolutions of the 1970s and early 1980s that marked the final stage of political radicalism in the Global South, including those in Nicaragua, Grenada, Angola, Mozambique, and Guinea-Bissau. But Mengistu undercut its potential by purging the movement of its political architects, the student activists and leftist intellectuals. The Derg declared scientific socialism as the state's official ideology in April 1976 and pursued promising reforms to Ethiopia's feudal system. Landlordism was abolished and replaced by smallholder production. Peasant households gained usufruct status over the land that they cultivated, but those rights could not be transferred to others by sale, lease, or mortgage. The state became the landlord.[83] Tens of millions of peasants gained greater control over farmland and were freed from their oppressive tax burdens. Peasants throughout the country felt this change in their everyday lives. A beet farmer who worked on a collective farm described his experience in postrevolutionary Ethiopia as akin to a rebirth. "Now I am feeling like a new child," he said. "I have milk to drink." He was barefoot and desperately poor but described a sense of freedom he was experiencing for the first time: "Before, I worked like a slave for the landlord, but I never had enough to eat. I was tired and ashamed to be a serf."[84]

The Derg's economic and social policies initially had variety of positive outcomes throughout much of the country, but by 1976 the regime had embarked on a political and economic course that had deleterious effects on Ethiopian citizens. Government officials aggravated food prices in rural areas by distributing agricultural produce disproportionately in favor of the restive urban population and the military. Urban residents experienced the aftershocks of the revolution through Derg policies that nationalized industries, large businesses, banks, and insurance companies. After the revolution caused social and political turbulence, the Derg's economic program strengthened Ethiopia's economy. Under Emperor Selassie, farmers and other peasants divided two-thirds of what they grew between their landlords and the Ethiopian Orthodox Church. Ninety percent of Ethiopians outside Addis Ababa were subsistence farmers, most of whom grew their crops on ox-plowed fields that would never belong to them.[85] The Derg destroyed the feudal system in the rural areas and confiscated church landholdings and the estates of the imperial oligarchy. But the government did not allow the new system to mature and thus it remained vulnerable to environmental and economic crises.

The galvanizing spirit of the Ethiopian student movement continued after the revolution through political dissidents and the northern rebel movements, dominated by the Tigray People's Liberation Front (TPLF) and the Eritrean People's Liberation Front (EPLF), both of which espoused Marxism and claimed to be revolutionary. Tigrayan dissidents launched the TPLF in 1976 and remained the movement most loyal to the Ethiopian student movement's Marxist-Leninist tenets, centered as they were on class and national rights.[86] The Ethiopian revolution was, therefore, a drawn-out conflict of competing revolutions.[87] Rebel groups kept Mengistu politically vulnerable but also contributed to precipitating famine. Remarkably, in contrast to other leftist regimes in Africa, famine, rather than the Cold War, internationalized Ethiopia's crises. Without peace between the government and the northern rebels, food security in Ethiopia was impossible.

Soviet leaders initially welcomed Mengistu's overtures to Moscow, Eastern Europe, and Havana. Before long, however, they began to doubt the thirty-seven-year-old Ethiopian leader's commitment to Marxist-Leninism and struggled to balance support for Ethiopia with their alliance with neighboring Somalia, whose tension with the Derg increased rapidly after the revolution. Soviet officials had grave concerns about Ethiopia's economic and political initiatives, but these concerns did not prevent them from approving weapons and military training for Ethiopians in 1977. Fidel Castro also assisted with Cuban military advisors.[88] The Soviet Union redoubled its commitment to Ethiopia following the Ogaden War. Leaders in the

International Department of the Communist Party hoped that Ethiopia would serve as a showcase for Soviet-inspired modernism in the "Third World."[89] If Leland questioned Mengistu's commitment to Ethiopia's development and the welfare of its people, he left no evidence of it in his records. Leland's reticence to acknowledge the contradictions between Mengistu's socialist claims and his actual policies might be understandable in light of the black internationalist milieu that shaped his political outlook. Yet his insistence on centering his humanitarian activism on an ambiguous, amorphous, natural cause to the Horn's food crisis, devoid of any serious engagement with its political dimension, exposed Leland to sharp critiques from his conservative colleagues of his initiatives to thwart Reagan's constructive engagement policy toward South Africa.

It is difficult to discern how much Leland knew of Ethiopian politics at the time of his visit in 1972. However, as an elected official during the early 1980s, fully abreast of the facts on the ground in the Horn, Leland's initial tactic was to treat the famine as a natural disaster. Rarely did he refer to the ongoing civil wars. He was more concerned with the moral principle of humanitarian relief than with the legal construct of human rights. His Select Committee on Hunger held hearings on Sudan's civil wars as they related to that country's food crisis, but no similar hearings were held for Ethiopia. Though Leland expressed neither fondness nor support for the Ethiopian government, he rarely, if ever, factored the TPLF and the EPLF into the equation of food aid in Ethiopia. Discussing these groups apparently risked legitimizing them and, consequently, further deteriorating Mengistu's political strength. In fact, the EPLF and the TPLF were major forces in shaping Ethiopian politics. Their military activities contributed to the food crisis, but they also carried out essential relief initiatives of their own.

Leland's failure to recognize these groups' roles handicapped him and other food aid advocates in Washington during the second half of the 1980s, particularly as the TPLF's and the EPLF's military fortunes increased. These groups shaped the famine experience for average Ethiopians and the government. As a pan-Africanist, Leland chose to work directly with Mengistu, but it was politically expedient for him not to engage with TPLF and EPLF leaders. Leland would have known through Hunger Committee reports that rebels and a strong, mostly exiled, political opposition had confronted the Derg since its inception. Mengistu tried to dance around the insurgencies in the north and the famine from a public relations standpoint. The two issues were interrelated; indeed, the one fueled the other.

For this reason, Leland's avoidance of Ethiopia's political and military conflicts stifled his effectiveness in truly bringing an end to the food crisis.
Though he did not demonstrate an appreciation for the nuances of the
TPLF, the EPLF, and government relations, he must have been aware of
them. Yet he made no effort to effectively incorporate them into his initiatives. During the late 1970s, a foundation for famine was built through the
combination of drought and civil war between the Derg and the Ethiopian
People's Revolutionary Party (EPRP), an outgrowth of factions from the
student movement. The situation was further complicated by Somalia's
irredentism in the predominantly ethnic Somali Ogaden region, whose
boundaries roughly correspond with those of the province of Hararghe.
More striking than Leland's almost complete silence on the civil war is
his public acceptance of Mengistu's narrative of the domestic antifamine
initiatives. His unwillingness to critically engage both Ethiopia's food crisis
and Mengistu's human rights record did not serve Leland well during congressional debates on white-minority rule in South Africa.

The Derg violently purged leftist opponents and used indefinite deten-
tion, forced exile, intimidation, assassination, and other forms of violence to
permanently silence the political opposition. Derg officials named this policy
of domestic political violence the "Red Terror." Amnesty International estimated that as many as five hundred thousand people were killed during 1977
and 1978. The Red Terror was a human rights problem for the government,
but Mengistu and his officials took full advantage of the political crisis to
consolidate power and assert authoritarian rule.[90] Thousands of young intellectuals and activists escaped into exile in the United States, Canada, and
Europe. EPRP members remaining in Ethiopia regrouped in Tigray, where
they built a rebel movement and waged a war on the federal government that
continued until 1991. With Mengistu at its helm, the Derg completed its
consolidation of power in December 1979. They inaugurated the Commission for Organizing the Party of the Working People of Ethiopia (COPWE).
Mengistu reorganized it in 1984 as the Workers' Party of Ethiopia.[91]

The Red Terror worsened the already deteriorating relationship between
Ethiopia and the United States. The U.S. ambassador to Ethiopia publicly
criticized the young regime's extreme tactics. Mengistu's frustration with
the United States surged as he continually failed to receive positive
responses to his requests for stronger and more flexible military assistance
from the Americans.[92] The State Department had reduced its military support for Emperor Selassie during his offensive against ethnic Somali rebels

in Ethiopia's Ogaden region in 1973, but arms and equipment sales ticked upward after 1974, when the military aid total stood at $10 million. By 1977 it had grown to $135 million.[93] In addition, the United States provided $5.3 million in grant economic aid and $6.6 million in Public Law 480 (also known as "Food for Peace") food sales and grants.[94] Yet Mengistu considered these levels unsatisfactory. The Food for Peace program's largest and most successful component was its arrangement for the sale of surplus food products by the U.S. Department of Agriculture to developing countries. The terms included payment in local currency and a substantial rebate in the form of loans and grants.[95]

The United States amassed an unprecedented agricultural surplus during the decades after World War II. Meanwhile, the government experimented with agricultural policies as Cold War weapons. The goal was to secure the loyalty of recently independent African and Asian nations by subsidizing the modernization of their agricultural sector. Post-1945 aid programs emphasized the importation of mechanized farm equipment, higher yield techniques, and mass-marketing strategies.[96] Agricultural diplomacy failed, however, as a tool to secure Global South countries' opposition to communism. From the 1950s to the 1970s, U.S. agricultural foreign policy was a peaceful initiative that steadily increased food supplies. The shift toward food aid from agricultural technologies occurred during the second half of the 1950s. Public Law 480 transformed U.S. Cold War agricultural diplomacy. Over the course of the next three decades, it would evolve from a bulk distribution or "surplus dumping" program into a sophisticated, global development program that established greater agricultural parity between developing and developed nations.

In addition to further damaging U.S.-Ethiopian relations, the events of the Red Terror inspired the growth of the TPLF and the EPLF. Meles Zenawi was among the most controversial and in many respects the most politically successful of the new rebel leaders. He was born Legesse Zenawi but adopted Meles to honor Meles Tekle, his schoolmate from Addis Ababa University whom Mengistu's government executed in 1975.[97] Meles Zenawi had been a medical student, but he gave up his studies to help found the TPLF and fight against Mengistu's Derg in Ethiopia's civil war. Meles was a serious student of Marxist theory, and he organized the Marxist-Leninist League of Tigray.[98] He did not assume the TPLF's top leadership position until 1989. Once in command, he made the group more ethnically and regionally inclusive, and then absorbed it within his newly branded political organization, the Ethiopian People's Revolutionary Democratic Front (EPRDF).

In the Tigrayan-dominated province of Eritrea, leftist and religious leaders organized the Eritrean Liberation Front (ELF). The ELF's members launched its armed secessionist movement in 1960. A decade later, a core group of its more radical, secular members broke away and founded the EPLF. Considering the EPLF's progressive origins, the repression that characterized its rule two decades later is striking. At its founding it was revolutionary and relatively egalitarian. Thirty percent of the EPLF fighters were women. It operated a relief organization to address famine-related issues and strived to remain truly self-sufficient. Initially, the EPLF partnered with the ELF, but the former demonstrated that it was militarily and politically superior. There is little doubt that the TPLF and the EPLF would have welcomed financial and military assistance from the United States, and there are unsubstantiated reports that the United States provided the TPLF with financial support.[99] Struggles in Ethiopia and elsewhere in Africa were distractions for President Ronald Reagan, who had entered the White House in 1981 with a strong sense that Africa was fundamentally irrelevant outside of gaining a geopolitical advantage over the Soviet Union.

The EPLF and the TPLF gained momentum from their northern strongholds against Mengistu's government. Thus, Mengistu faced two Marxist rebel movements fighting separately, for the most part, but simultaneously. Cold War geopolitics framed Ethiopia's evolving military scenario, but the presence of competing Marxist, revolutionary movements within a single country went against the traditional Cold War political dichotomy. The USSR and its communist allies put their support firmly behind the Ethiopian federal government, while the EPLF relied heavily on the ingenuity and generosity of the Eritrean diaspora and the Sudanese government's hospitality. The strength of all three sides intensified already ferocious fighting and rendered farming impossible for hundreds of thousands of peasants. By the end of the 1970s, Ethiopians faced a toxic mix of drought, political authoritarianism, and civil war. Mengistu lacked the resources and political flexibility to effectively respond to the famine that evolved from this crisis. No viable non-Marxist political alternative existed in the country. The region did hold strategic significance, although it had declined considerably after the United States installed a satellite communication station and a naval base on the Indian Ocean island of Diego Garcia. Kagnew Station was no longer essential. The unusual relationship between the

United States and Ethiopia never turned adversarial, even after the two countries broke off diplomatic relations.

Mengistu's government ran its famine relief initiatives through its Relief and Rehabilitation Commission (RRC). It operated with relative independence from the central government and had a sufficient budget for its administrators to effectively collect and disseminate information and coordinate relief programs.[100] The RRC's programs during the early stages of the 1983–85 famine belied simplistic descriptions of Ethiopia as neglecting the peasants' conditions and being dedicated solely to the single-minded destruction of international opposition. RRC chairman Dawit Giorgis and his officials achieved noteworthy success in building a famine relief operation in Ethiopia, considering the resources they had at their disposal.[101]

As U.S.-Ethiopian relations worsened, the United States secured its foothold in the strategically significant Horn of Africa by strengthening ties with Somalia's Siad Barre, a dictator who had formerly allied himself with the Soviet Union and declared his political project part of a Marxist-Leninist revolution. His project was also nationalist, which explains his claim to Ethiopia's predominantly ethnic Somali Ogaden region and his subsequent irredentist war. Barre, who was born in Ogaden and served in the Italian police force in Somalia, was not deterred by Cuban and Soviet support for Ethiopia. As early as 1976, Iran and Saudi Arabia counseled the Carter administration to establish its presence in Somalia to counter Cuba's and the Soviet Union's growing strength in the region. U.S. officials guaranteed their Ethiopian counterparts that the United States accepted Ogaden as Ethiopian territory, and no aid would go toward assisting Somalian irredentism.[102] While Carter denounced Barre's war to seize Ogaden, he found the United States had little choice in light of what he labeled "this new threat to security in the Persian Gulf and south west Asia."[103]

Washington remained in a wait-and-see mode until 1977, when Andrew Young, the U.S. ambassador to the United Nations and icon of the civil rights movement, stepped forward to change U.S. alliances in the Horn. More will be said of Young and his efforts to change U.S. foreign policy toward African countries in the following chapter, but it is worth briefly noting that Young helped persuade President Carter to secure U.S. influence in the region by building an alliance with Barre against the Soviet and Cuban presence in Ethiopia, despite Barre's irredentism. Young advised the president to reduce U.S. support for Ethiopia to the absolute minimum and to turn instead to Sudan and Somalia with support.[104] On April 19,

1977 President Carter leaned toward informing the Ethiopian government that his administration would close the Kagnew communications center, withdraw military advisors, and suspend all military aid.[105] Several key advisors insisted that this move would diminish U.S. importance in the region. While members of the Carter administration debated its next steps, Mengistu ordered the United States to end all of its cultural, medical, consular, and military operations.

Despite rising tension, the United States did not become openly hostile toward Ethiopia with these geopolitical shifts. In contrast with other regions, the United States had openly antagonistic relations with few African countries. It is also important to note that U.S. conflicts with Libya were only indirectly related to the Cold War, in contrast to its support of rebels in Angola, which was distinctly Cold War related. The United States provided financial backing for mercenaries and the South African Defense Force to counter Cuba's political, material, and military support of the Marxist government in Angola, as well as that country's support of military rebels battling South Africa's apartheid regime.[106] Like Angola, Ethiopia hosted Cuban troops and military advisors. It also hubristically celebrated its close ties to the Soviet Union. Perhaps no African government had a closer relationship with the Soviets than the Derg. Despite these ties, neither President Carter nor President Reagan took steps to intervene directly in Ethiopian politics.

Mengistu bet that Soviet economic and East German economic and military support would secure his political position, and that defying the United States would boost his revolutionary credentials at home and in the Global South. He did not anticipate how long and politically damaging Ethiopia's civil wars would be or how the famines of the 1980s would alter Ethiopia's national identity, weaken its sovereignty, and undermine its status within international politics. The United States refrained from exploiting Mengistu's ever-weakening position to undermine his regime. Even during President Ronald Reagan's first term, from 1981 to 1985, when containing Soviet influence at all costs and decreasing it where possible were high priorities, the United States did not take steps to fund opposition groups, directly undercut Mengistu's authority, or weaken Ethiopia's economy. One explanation for the hands-off approach to Ethiopia was, again, the lack of options: the opposition groups that would serve as a potential alternative to the Derg—the TPLF and the EPLF—were Marxist. A second explanation was Ethiopia's economy, already weak and on a precipitous decline. From the standpoint of State Department officials, it was cost-effective, politically and financially, to allow the Derg to wither on the vine. During Ethiopia's war with Somalia, the United States had an opportunity to strike a blow against the Mengistu regime by backing Siad Barre, the Somali leader. Although the United States supported Somalia, it did not intervene on its behalf, despite the estimated twelve thousand Cuban soldiers fighting for Ethiopia in Ogaden.

These Cold War dynamics expanded the Ethiopia-Somalia conflict into an international crisis, but the United States did not exploit it to intervene directly in Ethiopia. Indeed, events in the Horn of Africa throughout the 1970s and 1980s make it impossible to offer a straight Cold War narrative for political events in the region. Political and military alliances were established on both sides for reasons that had little to do with Ogaden or Somali ethnic nationalism. Libya, Israel, South Yemen, and Kenya joined the Cubans and the Soviets behind Ethiopia. On the Somali side, the United States added to existing support from Iraq, Syria, Egypt, and Sudan. In terms of global politics, there was no rationale for these alliances, and the Cold War alone did not explain them. Anticommunist Kenya and Marxist South Yemen, for example, were on the same side. Kenya's alliance was explained, in part, by the fact that Somalia had the same irredentist claim on Kenya as it did on Ethiopia's Ogaden region. In the end, Cuba helped Ethiopia prevail over Somali irredentism in 1978, supported by Soviet military technicians and military equipment.[107]

By March 1978, the Somalian invasion had failed. Mengistu capitalized on the momentum moving in his favor to launch an offensive against the TPLF and the EPLF in Eritrea. Castro did not deploy Cuban troops to help defend against northern rebels, perhaps because the Ethiopian conflict was not ideological, geopolitical, or Third World related. All parties involved, moreover, were Marxist, or at least claimed to be. Therefore, Cuban soldiers did not participate directly in combat. Cuban and Soviet military advisors did, however, provide Mengistu with certain strategic advantages. The Ethiopian army relaunched its assault on northern rebels in April and by November had routed the ELF; captured Keren, the territory's third-largest city; and pushed back the EPLF.[108] Cuban soldiers and military advisors remained in Ethiopia, but by 1986 their numbers were down to 3,700 to deter any Somali reinvasion.

On April 23, 1978, Ethiopia declared Kagnew Station, the U.S. Military Assistance Group, the U.S. Naval Medical Research Unit, and the U.S.

Information Service closed and ordered their foreign staff to leave Ethiopia within four days. Mengistu justified his hostile move toward the Americans as necessary for Ethiopia to remain true to scientific socialism and its foreign policy of nonalignment.[109] There were more than four thousand U.S. personnel in Ethiopia. The United States subsequently reduced the number of American officials in the country to seventy-six plus five U.S. Marines. Those remaining guarded the U.S. embassy and the Agency for International Development office in Addis Ababa.

This political environment—with its mix of domestic and regional conflicts deepened by the geopolitics of the Cold War—incubated Ethiopia's historic famine. During the 1960s, most African nations produced sufficient food for their populations. The 1970s did not exactly mark a turning point, but many African countries moved away from agricultural self-sufficiency and toward food crises. During the 1980s, geopolitics combined with the food crisis to redefine African dependence and spur the rise of humanitarian aid as we know it today. By 1984, roughly 140 million of the continent's 531 million people depended on foreign grain to meet basic food needs.[110] In 1973 and 1984 in Ethiopia, the international public initially focused on drought to the neglect of the domestic and international economic and political factors behind famine. Meanwhile, African governments were dealing with an array of Western economic, political, and humanitarian intrusions into their domestic affairs. Humanitarianism, economic aid, so-called military assistance, and myriad additional sources of Western involvement limited African nations' capacity to be truly sovereign. Food crises in the Sahel and the Horn became justifications for intrusion by the United States and Europe. African governments ill-equipped to deal with the region-wide drought allowed humanitarian intervention as a salve. The absence of a real choice and the desperate need for aid obliged them to open their borders to Western humanitarian relief organizations.

Thus, the Horn of Africa's political environment and economic situation were extremely complex at the start of the 1980s. This decade ushered in a new era of African American involvement in U.S. foreign affairs, U.S.-Africa relations, Cold War politics, and humanitarianism. Ironically, Mickey Leland downplayed the broader geopolitical contexts for events in the Horn. Instead, he adopted a streamlined, humanitarianist outlook toward the region that emphasized the depth of the food crisis and the effective delivery of multilateral assistance. His black radical sensibilities were in accord with humanitarianism's mandate to avoid criticizing African heads of state. As the decade progressed and the role of international relief organizations gained increased prominence at the center of multilateral responses to humanitarian crises, the political dimensions of crises and humanitarian assistance became difficult to ignore. Leland was deeply immersed in his political and ideological milieu. He successfully aligned black radical politics and humanitarianism, but his experiences throughout the 1980s demonstrate that both were of only limited usefulness in helping him achieve his domestic and international political goals.

Chapter 2

Redefining Black Politics

The Third World Spirit and Black Internationalism in Congress

> *I don't know how many times I rededicated myself since I have seen and witnessed what problems there are, to doing all that I can, not only as a member of Congress and not only as a US citizen, but as a citizen of the world.*
>
> —Mickey Leland

In 1972, with renewed optimism for black political power after his travels in Africa, Leland decided to enter the race for the Texas state legislature. The upcoming election presented an unprecedented opportunity for African Americans to win seats in the Texas House, after the commissioners of Harris County (which included Houston) had drawn new legislative districts. Leland and his close friend Anthony Hall devised a plan to organize African American candidates to pool their campaign resources and run in adjoining districts. They recruited Craig Washington, Cecil Bush, and Russell Hayes to join them as candidates. Touted as the "Big Five" and the "People's Five" in black Houstonian politics, they were widely regarded as among the most promising and talented leaders of their generation. Three of the five—Washington, Hall, and Leland—won their elections, but the team succeeded in its overall mission. And with Leland's victory, de Menil realized his dream for his unlikely protégé. Unfortunately, he would not live to witness Leland's second act as a U.S. congressman. John de Menil, Leland's patron, mentor, and friend, died of cancer at age sixty-nine, not long after Leland took his seat in the State House. "I can't even begin to repay their kindness," Leland said of de Menil and his wife ten years later. "But someday I will, I will."[1]

Although he had achieved his goal of winning elected office, Leland began his first term in the legislature with neither the interest nor the acumen to cultivate support from his colleagues for the issues he cared about. He wanted to be an advocate for affordable health care, lower prescription drug costs, and affordable housing, among other issues. But he found it difficult to adjust to his role as a lawmaker in a political system that for more than a decade as an activist he had philosophically and morally opposed. It was some consolation to be in the legislature with Anthony Hall and Craig Washington. Hall's politics were more in the mold of a traditional Democrat than those of his two friends, while Leland and Washington early on proved to be the most reliably liberal legislators. Outside of a small group of liberal Democrats, Leland had little respect for his white colleagues and, consistent with the black radicalism of his time, equated compromise with capitulation. These are among the reasons he had no tangible legislative success during his first term.

Leland's political path is fascinating for how swiftly he turned to insisting that the U.S. political and economic system, and the government specifically, had an obligation to rectify the injustices African Americans faced, after years of railing against the system for its antagonism toward African American economic and political interests. During his first years in the legislature, Leland learned how he might gain the rewards for his community that came from his working within the political establishment. As a start, he toned down his black radical rhetoric. But to Leland, change in tone did not come with a change in passion and conviction. "While I have always been a so-called radical," Leland said in 1975, "I probably do fit in with the definition of a revolutionary. I am an advocate of the whole system of the United States government being—if not overturned—at least reoriented. I did not believe in the system at all. I did not think that a person like me could operate in the system."[2] However, he said, "After being in the legislature for a while I found there are certain things that can be gained through being in the system." Compromise was an imperative, a recognition of the pragmatic nature of working for political change. Nonetheless, Leland maintained clear limits on how much he was willing to concede and what ideological lines he would not cross. "Of course," he declared, "there are some things—like moral issues—I would never compromise. I would never compromise my principles."[3] As he immersed himself in mainstream politics, he acquired no fondness for it. "My primary job here," he said, "is to get as much for my people as possible. I might be beating a dead horse and that too brings about a great deal of frustration. I try to maintain a great degree of humbleness. I'm not proud of being a state representative. It's because my people are proud. That it helps them a lot. They see that maybe something can be done."[4]

Leland represented the overwhelmingly African American Eighty-Eighth District. It comprised the area Houstonians continue to call the Fifth Ward, even though city officials dismantled the ward system in the first decade of the twentieth century. In the late 1970s a *New York Times* reporter described Houston, the South's most populous city, as "a vast, politically liberal, potentially powerful island of racial and ethnic diversity in a sea of white, middle class Texas conservatism."[5] Deep, concentrated poverty was the Fifth Ward's distinguishing characteristic, together with persistent municipal neglect. Unemployment affected 8 percent of the district's residents, compared to the city's overall rate of 3 percent. The sewage system lay in disrepair, and the city erratically collected garbage. Municipal malfeasance and racist housing codes discouraged real-estate investment. These were the domestic issues Leland tried to bring to the fore in the legislature, but he often encountered resistance in the conservative-dominated State House. "Since my constituency is predominantly black and near northeast Houston my priorities have been and will continue to be the development of the community," Leland said. "However, generally, I have been and will always be an advocate for poor people and deprived communities all over Texas."[6]

Leland wanted his legislative actions to reflect his political philosophy. In 1973, he lobbied his colleagues to support one of two "People's Bills," while Craig Washington prepared to introduce the other. Leland's bill would require pharmacies to list the prices of the one hundred most commonly prescribed medications so consumers could compare costs. Washington's bill would force the state to provide attorneys for juvenile inmates in Texas reform schools.[7] Their colleagues voted overwhelmingly against the two bills, but the opposition he faced did not deter Leland. He continued to push similar "People's Bills" on an array of issues, from blocking the construction of new freeways that would intersect poor communities to advocating low-cost health maintenance organizations throughout Texas.[8] With this strategy, he believed, he remained true to his political principles, continuing to confront the obstacles everyday people faced rather than serving the interests of corporations and special-interest groups.

Leland also made his political statements with the clothes he wore. He used both legislation and his fashion sense to affirm his identity as a man of the people and a political radical. "In the 1960s," Leland explained, "I learned to hold on to my African-ness dearly, as many others did during that time. I was part of the movement to rename us [as] we wanted to be called, as opposed to negro, coloreds or nigras." He stood with his dashikis, cowboy boots, and an Afro hairstyle during his first two terms in the Texas House. In the Texas State Capitol Building, he frequently sported Nehru jackets with a high mandarin collar and spoke unflinchingly of black pride in the presence of his white colleagues. As Leland's friend Gene Locke recalled, "Many people applauded him, others thought he was crazy, yet he was a man of conviction."[9] His stylistic choices were meant to convey the authenticity of his pan-Africanism and black radicalism, even as he began to conform to the protocols of the legislature. But his expressions of solidarity reached beyond his own community and Africa. "I appreciate this country and the good that it has done. But I'm not a patriot. I'm a citizen of the world. I respect the value of human life in North Vietnam and South Vietnam. In China and Africa. We're all kin to each other. There's no document that can divide us. No national boundaries can divide us."[10]

Many of Leland's colleagues considered his personality rather than the substance of his politics as instrumental to the support he gained for his projects during his six-year tenure in the legislature. As Leland began to get to know his white and more conservative colleagues better, he discovered how to successfully use the political process for progressive aims. He softened his rhetoric and presented the veneer of one growing into his role as a traditional politician, and he soon began to harbor ambitions for higher office. Leland had a friendly, jocular folksiness that drew people to him. As his political star rose in Houston, he asked that people continue to call him "Mickey," even when working in the Capitol Building in Austin. Representative Jack Fields, a conservative Republican from Humble, Texas, had little in common with Leland politically, but they grew to be very close friends through Leland's magnetic personality. "Mickey charmed my staff to the point that they would do anything he asked them to do," Fields said.[11]

Leland's opportunity to break into national politics arrived in December 1977, when Congresswoman Barbara Jordan announced she would not seek reelection. Jordan had served in Congress since 1972 representing Houston's Eighteenth Congressional District, which included Leland's Eighty-Eighth Legislative District. Her rise to political prominence inspired younger African Americans, like Leland, Washington, and Hall, and demonstrated that African American lawmakers could be effective through hard work, mastering political rules and process, and remaining connected to local constituents and local organizations.[12] When she entered Congress, Jordan, Andrew Young of Georgia, a civil rights activist who had been a close advisor to Reverend Martin Luther King Jr., and Harold E. Ford of Tennessee were the only African Americans representing southern districts, with Parren Mitchell representing the border state of Maryland. Jordan gained national attention as a member of the House Judiciary Committee and for her stirring, eloquent, and sagacious speech during the hearings that led to President Richard Nixon's resignation in August 1974.[13] Her constituents knew of her gift for oratory, but she received wider praise and reached greater political prominence during and after the Watergate hearings. Jordan's iconic status in Houston politics heightened the significance of the race to elect her successor.

Leland was one of seven candidates on the Houston Democratic Party's 1978 primary ballot to succeed Jordan; the others were Anthony Hall, Jack Linville Jr., Judson Robinson, Harrel Tillman, Al Vera, and Nathaniel West. Leland, Hall, and Robinson, all close friends, were known as the "Big Three" within this group, as they were the most widely known and politically active. Robinson was a prominent Houston businessman and the first African American elected to Houston's city council, where he was completing his seventh year. Anthony Hall had joined the Texas legislature with Leland in 1972. Of the three, Leland was the least polished linguistically and politically.

But of all the candidates Leland was the most politically progressive and most firmly rooted in working-class social and political issues. Leland had endorsed Frances "Sissy" Farenthold in her campaign against incumbent governor Dolph Briscoe for the Democratic Party nomination in 1974. He received praise from feminist organizations and earned the respect of many veteran politicians for taking this principled risk so early in his political career.[14] He had a reputation as an independent-minded, people-centered politician. He also had loads of charisma, firm progressive convictions, support from grassroots leaders and women's groups in the Eighteenth District, and, as always, the financial backing of the de Menil family. One of his campaign slogans, "I'm Taking the People to Congress!" captures Leland's goal to position himself firmly in the grassroots of local politics as the people's candidate. "I'm more of an activist than an intellectual. But I'm an

Figure 4. Mickey Leland and Congresswoman Barbara Jordan at Wheatley
High School Alumni Day at *The De Luxe Show*, Houston, Texas, 1972.
Hickey-Robertson. Used by permission. Courtesy of the Menil Archives, Rice
University.

activist with intellectual aspirations," he said lightheartedly.[15] He won the election, but not before a runoff election against Anthony Hall on June 5, 1978. The district was overwhelmingly Democratic, so the winner of the primary had a clear path to victory in the November general election.

In his victory speech, Leland wove in a new liberal Democratic theme of inclusion. Just a few years earlier, he spoke of dismantling the U.S. political system and called himself a revolutionary, but now he spoke of reform rather than revolution. He called for a fundamental change within the U.S. government so that it would serve the interests of its citizens regardless of their background. "America has not yet met its promise to all of its people," Leland told the large crowd of supporters. "The Constitution of the United States has not yet been exercised to its fullest. Many people are still unequal in this country. Black people still exist at the bottom rung of the economic ladder, as does the Chicano community and even the poor white community, and we have to equalize the circumstances of their lives in order that they can provide a comfortable survival for their folks—for our folks."[16] After the election, Leland continued to insist that he was just an activist from Houston's Fifth Ward and that everyone must call him "Mickey," but eight years in the Texas state legislature had modified his approach to politics and to what he might achieve through participating in the political system.[17] Nonetheless, he continued to regard himself as a political radical, philosophically and morally predisposed to serve the interests of the socially and political marginalized in U.S. society and around the world.

Congressman Ronald Dellums, Leland's mentor and close friend throughout his time in Congress, told an amusing story about meeting Leland for the first time. It captures much of the unique character both men brought to Congress as well as the bond that quickly formed between them. When he was elected in California in 1971, Dellums said, "The shot that was heard across America was, 'afro top, bell bottomed, radical black dude from Berkeley wins election.' Eight years later, my colleagues walked up to me and they said, 'You know Ron, you're not alone any longer. Fifth Ward of Houston sent an afro top, bell bottomed radical dude to Washington.'" When he saw Leland's photograph, Dellums continued, he was elated by Leland's radical look. "Goatee and dashiki! And, they said he's radical and militant. I said, 'that's my kind of brother!'" When he encountered Leland at a Congressional Black Caucus weekend gala before Leland moved to Washington, he sent his young radical soon-to-be colleague a note. "Mickey Leland," he recalled writing, "let's take it all the way to the max!" Dellums then turned around to look at Leland, who responded, "Let's do it!"[18]

During the 1980s, Leland and Dellums endeavored to fundamentally change U.S. society through Congress. Similar to his early experience in the Texas state legislature, it took Leland time to find his political footing in Congress. His initial plan was to continue to work on the issues he had championed in the Texas legislature, including health care, education, labor, and law enforcement. As a congressman he now had the opportunity to also work on a variety of international issues, but his involvement in African affairs progressed slowly. There were already a number of African American lawmakers actively working on African and Caribbean issues, principally Detroit, Michigan's Charles Diggs and Dellums of Oakland, California, but also John Conyers Jr., who had joined the House in 1965, representing Detroit; Harlem's Charles Rangel, who succeeded the legendary Adam Clayton Powell Jr.; and California's Julian Dixon.

William H. Gray III, an African American congressman from Pennsylvania, entered Congress with Leland and quickly proved himself as a skilled legislator and commanding figure on the issue of apartheid in South Africa. He was a thirty-three-year-old pastor of Mount Hope Baptist Church in Philadelphia when he first ran for Congress in 1976. He lost to Robert N. C. Nix Sr., who entered Congress in 1958 and was the first African American to represent Pennsylvania. Gray succeeded at his second attempt two years later.[19] Leland and Gray developed a strong bond around shared interests but were a study in contrasts. Gray exhibited a more conciliatory, less strident, and certainly less radical style than did Dellums and Leland. He was a smoother, steadier public orator than Leland and in the mold of a more traditional Democrat. There were no revolutionary aspirations lurking in his political closet. Moreover, while Leland suffered through the protocols of legislating, Gray immersed himself in congressional rules and procedures and would quickly rise through the leadership ranks to become chair of the influential House Budget Committee by 1985. He held moderately liberal positions on most social and political issues, and he successfully positioned himself early on as a leading voice in the Congressional Black Caucus. Unlike Leland, and Diggs and Andrew Young before him, Gray accepted anticommunism as a legitimate strategy and foreign policy position, and he saw Soviet expansion as a threat the United States should take seriously.

Dellums earned his colleagues' respect for his passionate speeches from the floor of the House against military interventions, the ballooning military budget, U.S. aid to dictatorships, and in support of imposing sanctions on the apartheid regime in South Africa. Leland and Dellums fit within the tradition of black radical internationalism with their commitment to advancing the cause of global black empowerment, disregard of anticommunism, and their amicable relationship with the Cuban government. In this way, they followed in Congressman Diggs's footsteps. His political model synergized government policy and local activism. Until the late 1970s, Diggs was most often the lone African American voice on foreign affairs. Despite their similarities, he only overlapped with Leland for one year in Congress.

Diggs was part of the first generation of African American politicians to work from a decidedly African American perspective within government and as ambassadors in international governing bodies on foreign policy.[20] Unlike elected officials, who in theory speak on behalf of their constituents, ambassadors represent the interests and views of the government or institution that appoints them. Be that as it may, Ralph Bunche at the United Nations and Ambassador Andrew Young, the U.S. representative to the United Nations in the Carter administration, who were Diggs's contemporaries and occasional political collaborators, reflected the consensus on anti-imperialism and white-minority rule that was the bedrock of black internationalism. Diggs, Young, and Bunche set a precedent of applying elements of black internationalism in mainstream politics. Members of the Black Caucus would later build on this approach during the 1980s to challenge Reagan's domestic and foreign policy agenda and elevate the Caribbean and Africa within U.S. politics. Leland, Dellums, and Gray, did not explode onto the political scene during the early 1980s with legislation to impose South African sanctions, mass anti-apartheid demonstrations, and challenges to the prevailing paradigm of anticommunism as effective foreign policy toward Global South nations. They benefited from and built on the work of a generation of African American political leaders, organizations, journalists, and academics who cultivated a strategy around a consensus on apartheid in South Africa to change U.S. foreign policy toward the continent. Diggs, Young, and Bunche exemplify the early institutional wing of this movement.

Andrew Young represented Atlanta's Fifth Congressional District in 1977 when President Jimmy Carter appointed him U.S. ambassador to the United Nations. Young was elected to Congress in 1972, the same year as Barbara Jordan. As UN ambassador, he was the first African American to represent the United States to the world community. His ambassadorship marked the starting point of African American influence on U.S. foreign policy from the higher echelons of the foreign policy establishment.[21] In this capacity, he did not lack influence with the president and elsewhere within the Carter administration. In fact, he stirred up controversy on several occasions by stating his support for sovereignty, human rights, and antiracism in the Global South.[22] Despite the vigilance of conservative skeptics, during his two years as ambassador Young managed to tilt Carter's approach to Africa in a more country-specific direction and to take a more critical stance toward white-minority rule in southern Africa. Young influenced Carter's choice to make a definitive statement in support of democracy in South Africa.[23] Carter's critics took note of Young's positions and accused him of being too inclined toward a Third World perspective.[24]

When he spoke with Dan Rather on the CBS television show *Who's Who*, Young discarded the U.S. government's decades-long practice of condemning Cuba and communism. He offered Cuba's military presence in Angola as an example of one of the island nation's positive contributions in global affairs. When Rather suggested that Cuban troops would aggravate guerrilla warfare in Angola, Young responded, "There's a sense in which the Cubans bring a certain stability and order—to Angola, for instance." He went on to explain that he did not see communism as a real enemy of the United States. Again, he spoke not only as a U.S. government official but self-consciously as an African American and a member of a global black community. "Most colored peoples of the world are not afraid of communism," he explained to Rather. "Maybe that's wrong but communism has never been a threat to me. I have no love for communism. But—it's never been a threat. Racism has always been a threat—and that has been the enemy all of my life."[25] Members of Congress, particularly Republicans, responded with outrage to Young's statements, but what he said squared with the Carter administration's goal to decenter U.S. foreign policy from a singular, narrow focus on the bipolar Cold War.[26]

Ralph Bunche had a different approach to international affairs from Young. Both men were skeptical of the rise of black radical politics as a positive influence on the African American struggle for social and political equality and engagement in Global South affairs. But, in contrast with Young, Bunche championed the "go slow" approach of working within the political establishment toward social and political change, whether in Africa, the United States, or elsewhere. He was at odds with the emerging class of black internationalists for his lack of faith in the efficacy of protests and cultural nationalism. Nonetheless, his work on behalf of African decolonization helped to align African and African American affairs. During his time as a student in London, he developed close friendship with future African and Caribbean leaders, such as Jomo Kenyatta, Peter Mbiyu Koinange, C. L. R. James, and George Padmore.[27] He became an expert on peacekeeping and decolonization, which in 1960 made him indispensable to Dag Hammarskjöld, UN secretary-general and Bunche's close personal friend. He fulfilled his duties as ambassador as a self-conscious African American and believed that doing so provided an important role in African affairs. In 1960, Bunche was optimistic about the future of Africa, a future he had worked hard to ensure would develop around political and economic stability.

Young and Bunche shaped the context in which white politicians and policymakers would begin to distinguish African issues as distinct from European and Cold War politics. Yet more than any individual of the period, Charles Diggs built the mold for black internationalism within U.S. institutions and the mechanism for African Americans to influence U.S. foreign policies toward Global South nations during the 1980s. In 1955, thirty-one-year-old Charles Diggs joined Powell and Chicago's William Dawson as the only three African Americans in Congress's 435-member House of Representatives. During the previous ten years, Powell and Dawson had been the only African American lawmakers in Congress. Diggs had a freer hand to play in international affairs than his colleagues who were ambassadors because he answered to his Detroit constituents, whereas Young spoke on Carter's behalf and Bunche answered to Dag Hammarskjold.

Congress was a bastion of sexism and white supremacy in the 1950s and 1960s. A young African American lawmaker had no real influence on domestic policies. However, Diggs seized upon opportunities for leadership and influence within Congress and applied the resources of office toward initiatives in African American communities. Early in his tenure, he learned that many of his congressional colleagues would accept relatively radical stances on U.S. foreign policy but would not exercise similar tolerance for such an approach to domestic issues. He acquired this political wisdom from Adam Clayton Powell Jr., the iconic Harlem lawmaker, who embraced Diggs as his protégé.[28] Powell was among the first African American leaders to employ the term "Black Power" to articulate the goal of economic and political strength. In contrast to the younger generations' use of Black

Power, Powell envisaged African Americans exercising this power from within mainstream institutions.[29]

Diggs also addressed African issues self-consciously as an African American with the belief that African Americans had a unique role to play in U.S. involvement on the continent. His initiatives, like Leland's and Dellums's in the 1980s, reflected the promise of black radical political syncretism. During the 1960s, however, Diggs's unabashed anticolonialism and support for African sovereignty was unique among lawmakers. Powell arranged for Diggs to attend Ghana's independence celebration in March 1957 and the inauguration of that country's prime minister, Kwame Nkrumah. On the heels of this momentous event, Diggs lobbied for a seat on the House Foreign Affairs Committee. He aspired to be an advocate for African interests.[30] Once on the committee, Diggs worked to be a voice within U.S. policy making circles, particularly with regard to U.S. assistance to newly independent countries and policies toward the territories under Portuguese and white-minority rule.[31] In ways similar to Ambassador Young, Diggs preached about the pitfalls of blind anticommunism and that it was a distinct disadvantage to U.S. global leadership to marginalize African affairs. "The United States is in danger of losing the present advantage it holds in Africa to the Soviet Union," he told journalists in 1959. "Our nation needs to be educated on the tremendous significance of development in Africa."[32]

Diggs was the first U.S. lawmaker with a consistent commitment to African affairs, and remained one of only a handful of representatives with even a passing interest in the continent during his quarter of a century in Congress. As a result, he was known as "Mr. Africa."[33] Most African Americans in positions of influence were preoccupied with domestic economic issues rather than foreign affairs.[34] Many African American leaders and intellectuals with a strong sense of connection to Africa and deep interest in African affairs during the 1960s and 1970s had a healthy skepticism of mainstream politics and elected officials, even as increasing numbers of African Americans joined voting rolls and won elected office. Some argued that to participate in electoral politics was to accept the U.S. political system and abandon aspirations for radical or revolutionary change. Diggs welcomed this debate. He understood that community organizing, mass protest, the ballot, and elected office collectively were important tools for black radicals to achieve their shared goal of community control and assert a voice in U.S. foreign policy toward Africa and the Caribbean.

His unique political style was most visible in his engagement with the ongoing Black Power, Black Arts, and pan-Africanist movements. He saw no boundaries dividing congressional and community affairs, as would be true for most members of the Congressional Black Caucus during the 1980s. He partnered with African American activists on a variety of issues. These figures included the writer Amiri Baraka (LeRoi Jones), one of the most influential proponents of Black Power and the Black Arts Movement during the late 1960s and early 1970s, and pan-Africanist Owusu Sadaukai (Howard Fuller). Diggs also capitalized on the expanding network of African American elected officials who aimed to bridge radical and electoral politics, including Gary, Indiana's Richard Hatcher, who in 1963 became the first African American elected mayor of a large U.S. city.

Diggs was part of Sadaukai's first African Liberation Day, a three-day-long celebration and display of solidarity with African liberation movements that culminated in a march and demonstration on May 27, 1972. Sadaukai was an African American who founded Malcolm X Liberation University in Greensboro, North Carolina, and the African Liberation Support Committee.[35] He and Mickey Leland traveled in Tanzania during the same year, but there is no reason to believe that their paths crossed. Yet, like Leland, Sadaukai returned to the United States full of inspiration. In the summer of 1971, he was back in Africa. Sadaukai traveled to Mozambique with Robert Van Lierop and photographer Robert Fletcher to film a documentary on FRELIMO.[36] Samora Machel, leader of the Mozambique Liberation Front (FRELIMO; Frente de Libertação de Moçambique), welcomed Sadaukai and other black internationalists to witness the liberation struggle and life in the liberated areas.[37]

Sadaukai's experience with FRELIMO inspired him to launch African Liberation Day in 1972 in Washington, D.C., and, simultaneously, in thirty other cities across the country. Among the more than fifteen thousand people in the D.C. march were well-known African American leftists such as historian Vincent Harding, Black Panther leader Erica Huggins, and scholar and activist Angela Davis.[38] As activists marched through Embassy Row toward the Washington Mall, they paused to protest in front of the Portuguese, Rhodesian, and South African embassies. When they arrived at the Mall, marchers declared the Washington Monument renamed as Lumumba Square in honor of Congo's first prime minister.[39]

Sadaukai invited Diggs to be one of speakers at the event. His address fused the cultural nationalism that had gained currency within Black Power circles to African American radical internationalism. He told the crowd that he hoped that the three days of events for African liberation would foment a reawakening to African nationalism among African Americans. He also hoped, he said, to shine a spotlight on the "cozy" relationship between the United States and white-minority regimes in Rhodesia, South Africa, Angola, and South West Africa.[40] He told his audience that it was imperative, "for people in America and the Caribbean to see that our African past is connected to the African future." He declared the movement for justice in the United States to no longer be confined within U.S. borders. The shared African and African American movement would no longer "stop at the water's edge."[41] As he said, "I believe that 1972 will be a landmark year in awareness on the part of black Americans to the problems of African liberation and an awareness as well of recent US policies in Africa."[42] Diggs sent a message of solidarity and common cause between radical black activists and lawmakers by appearing beside radical activists that day, including poet Baraka and writer Haki Madhubuti.

Diggs and Baraka were more in sync than one might suspect. Baraka made a remarkable, but seldom recognized, mark on the success and substance of African American electoral politics, most notably through his work to make electoral politics acceptable and respectable among grassroots activists.[43] He never sought elected office, but had a strong political following in Newark and was active and influential in African American politics nationally. He and Diggs were both bridges between Black Power and electoral politics, and they both capitalized on Congressman Powell's strategies for African American political power. Powell spent over a year organizing the National Conference on Black Power, which he scheduled to open on July 20, 1967 in Newark. His goal for the conference was to attract younger radicals, such as those within and who closely followed SNCC, into mainstream political institutions.[44] This goal reflected the disconnect between his brand of black power and that which most young activists embraced. Three days of revolt had erupted in Newark just before the conference, so Powell did not attend. Baraka stepped into this leadership void and facilitated dialog between the array of civil rights, black nationalist, and labor organizations at the conference and oversaw the publication of the conference's official statement, *Black Power Manifesto*.[45] Through the remainder of the 1960s and the 1970s Baraka was a principal organizer of black political conventions, similar to the 1967 gathering.

With de jure political rights secured by landmark civil rights Supreme Court cases in the 1950s and 1960s, African American activists grappled with how to best protect and enforce those rights and define American citizenship, or reject it, if they chose to, on their own terms. These were among the concerns when Baraka and Diggs, along with Mayor Richard Hatcher of Gary, Indiana, organized the National Black Political Convention in 1972 and 1974, the first major gatherings of African American activists, artists, and lawmakers of the period for the purpose of establishing a united black political front. The conventions, and the organizing meetings surrounding them, were instrumental in launching the political careers of countless African Americans during the late 1970s and early 1980s.[46]

While Diggs shared Powell's vision of absorbing young activists into the Democratic Party and shifting it further to the political left, Baraka envisioned an independent black political party as the logical conduit for young, activist-minded, aspiring politicians to win elected office without conceding to the capitalist-controlled platforms of the Democratic and Republican parties.[47] The question of political independence was among the most politically divisive of the black political convention movement, but building a black political party to influence domestic and foreign policy had been a major goal of the Black Power movement.[48] Baraka's strategic partnership with mainstream politicians was a political model for radical activists and community organizers. Through his community development organization, the Committee for a Unified Newark, which he founded in 1968, he worked with Newark, New Jersey's first African American mayor, Kenneth Gibson, to win city contracts to build low-income housing for African American residents.[49]

There are similar examples of alliances between black activists and black politicians throughout the country during this period. In Oakland, California, the Black Panther Party operated voter registration drives and get-out-the-vote campaigns in 1974 to elect Jerry Brown governor and in 1977 to elect Lionel Wilson mayor of the city of Oakland in return for public sector contracts and, by extension, jobs for African American residents. In addition to Wilson in Oakland, activism for expanded access to and control over city resources propelled the rise of a host of African American urban mayors, including Gibson in Newark, Maynard Jackson in Atlanta, Marion Barry in Washington, D.C., Harold Washington in Chicago, and Coleman Young in Detroit.[50] For many black radicals, activism through mainstream politics became either an attractive alternative or a complementary strategy.[51] The interface of activism and electoral politics shows that traditional, civil rights–era style protest and community organizing were insufficient to achieve Black Power activists' goal of community empowerment and control.

Diggs spearheaded several initiatives in 1969 that set the stage for these changes. To draw attention to African issues in Congress he successfully pushed for a subcommittee on African affairs within the House Committee on Foreign Affairs, and he became its founding vice-chairperson. Prior to Diggs's initiative to push Congress to support sanctions legislation, the sanctions movement had been confined to the political margins, mostly kept alive during the 1950s and 1960s by the American Committee on Africa (ACOA), the Council on African Affairs (CAA), the National Association for the Advancement of Colored People (NAACP), and the National Council of Negro Women (NCNW). Each of these organizations worked to influence United States policy toward South Africa and to tap into and develop the network of South African activists working to end apartheid from exile.[52]

ACOA submitted a recommendation to Congress in October 1962 to impose sanctions on South Africa. In ACOA's statement, "South African Crisis and United States Policy," the organization presented South Africa and apartheid as vestiges of a dead imperialist system: "The South Africa issue is symbolic of the last and the greatest struggle for freedom and equality in Africa. If the US can take the leadership in ending the reign of apartheid, it will be the greatest possible step toward establishing the US as the champion of equality and freedom."[53] The previous year, the UN General Assembly had debated sanctions, but the United States opposed trade restrictions in favor of formally censuring the apartheid regime for its racist policies.[54]

Diggs had a keen understanding of the relationship between political narratives and policies. In preparation for his push to change U.S. policies toward white-minority regimes in southern Africa, Diggs tried to change how his colleagues understood and discussed the U.S. role in the region. He also organized nine African American colleagues that year as the Democratic Select Committee, a forerunner of the Congressional Black Caucus. They were galvanized by their opposition to President Nixon's position on health care, welfare, social services, and other programs that directly affected African American communities.[55]

In the year he became the subcommittee vice-chair, Diggs introduced the first anti-apartheid legislation in Congress. The bill would impose sanctions on South African sugar. But even with these modest aims, the bill did not gain traction.[56] Most of his white colleagues remained committed to President Nixon's policies toward the white-minority regimes that maintained the status quo.[57] Diggs's effort was monumental nonetheless: he made anti-apartheid sanctions a legislative issue.[58] He also organized an official fact-finding mission to Nigeria, as that nation drifted into a war-induced famine.

During the Nigerian Civil War, which began in 1967, it did not take long for the Nigerian army to gain the advantage over ethnic-Igbo separatists of the self-declared independent Republic of Biafra in oil-rich southeastern Nigeria. The secessionists were on the precipice of defeat before the government's blockade of rebel-held territory led to a humanitarian crisis that caught Western journalists' attention. Both sides used the international media to bring their political and moral cases to the world.[59] Biafran leaders were eager to attract the attention of intermediaries and supporters in the West. They actively promoted the plight of civilians in Biafra suffering from food and medicine shortages. Biafran leaders appealed to religious groups and humanitarian organizations to intervene, which precipitated the first international humanitarian relief effort couched in the rhetoric of humanitarianism and political neutrality.[60] In reality, neutrality was a conceit that suggested relief organizations only focused on those in need and not the political circumstances that gave rise to the need. Just as Leland would seek to use the historic response to Ethiopia's famine to force a paradigm shift in U.S. foreign policy toward Africa, Western relief workers in Nigeria in 1969 and 1970 failed to turn the humanitarian campaign for Biafra into an international network of human rights activists in the aftermath of the Biafran famine.[61]

Diggs hoped his fact-finding mission to Nigeria would raise enough awareness of and interest in the Nigerian conflict to generate broader interest in the entire African continent, particularly among African Americans. He believed that if African Americans citizens and political leaders were more vocal African issues Africa would gain relevance within general U.S. foreign policy.[62] While Diggs was in Nigeria, Biafran officials attempted to appeal to him through racial politics. Lieutenant Colonel Chukwuemeka Ojukwu, the Biafran leader, presented Biafra as "the true awakening of the African man." He described Biafra as comprising black men fighting for their dignity. Rather than accept the colonial boundaries Europeans designed to ensure European neo-imperialism, the black men of Biafra had defined their borders and determined for themselves what constituted a truly sovereign state. Ojukwu tried to tap into the very essence of African American political links to the continent: the right to self-determination and racial unity. Diggs did not visit rebel-held territory. He chose to remain in Lagos, the Nigerian capital, to meet with government officials rather than see rebel-held territory for himself. It seems, in fact, that Diggs had determined in advance of his trip that he would not support Biafra. He turned a blind eye to the federal government's alleged human rights abuses and the unfolding humanitarian crises in Biafran territory to declare his support for the integrity of a whole, sovereign Nigerian state.[63] Diggs's staunch support of African sovereignty limited his receptiveness to a nuanced position on the Nigerian Civil War, much as Leland's politics enabled him to turn a blind eye to Mengistu's actions during the 1980s.

Diggs's most outstanding and long-lasting achievement in Congress was his founding of the Congressional Black Caucus, beyond the ways in which he influenced African American lawmakers to craft U.S. foreign policy and help his colleagues gain a better understanding of distinct issues in African countries. In March 1971, with thirteen African American members of Congress, he formed the Black Caucus from the existing Democratic Select Committee. Diggs ensured that Africa was part of its agenda from its inception. African American lawmakers slowly built their case against U.S. support for white-minority rule in Africa and contended with colleagues' sympathy toward the ruling white-minority in southern Africa. They also had to contend with well-financed lobbying firms and interest groups that worked in Washington on behalf of governments in Rhodesia, South Africa, and Portugal.[64]

Diggs returned to Africa in August 1971 on a fact-finding tour of South Africa and Portuguese-held Guinea-Bissau and Cape Verde. He also tacked a second visit to Nigeria onto this trip. He was the first African American member of Congress to visit South Africa.[65] The trip crystallized for Diggs the urgent need for African Americans to challenge ongoing white supremacy on the continent. He was convinced that South Africa would change only when U.S. policies changed and corporate investment ended. As he said not long after his return, "American business must either justify its presence in South Africa by an equitable sharing of its enormous profits with the majority of the people or be called upon to disengage."[66]

Diggs could not rely on legislation to effect change to U.S. policies toward South Africa and Portugal, with a majority of his colleagues firmly against sanctions. His strategy was to establish an organization outside of Congress that would work in coalition with the Black Caucus to influence how members of Congress understood African issues. This was a radical move, as it targeted the bedrock of U.S. policies in Africa: anticommunism and white supremacy. At the center of his method for change was African American activism, issuing policy statements, building a network of allied organizations outside of the U.S. government, and submitting legislation to change U.S. policy toward southern Africa.

Diggs launched his Africa program with the National Black Conference on Africa, a gathering of African American political leaders, journalists, and academics that the Black Caucus convened in Washington on May 25 and 26, 1972. Diggs issued a policy statement at the conference, later published as "An Action Manifesto on US Policy Toward Africa." It presented fifty-five recommendations for changes to the U.S. approach to human rights, self-determination, and private enterprise in Africa.[67] He also called on President Nixon to support liberation movements in white-ruled Rhodesia and an end to apartheid in South Africa.[68]

Diggs tried to respond to the limited backlash that President Nixon faced when the president unilaterally lifted the ban on U.S. companies trading with South Africa and Rhodesia. He submitted a bill, cosponsored by twenty-three House colleagues, aimed to combat "participation by US businesses in the exploitation of labor and racial practices in southern Africa."[69] By the end of the year, Diggs, with support from his colleagues in the Black Caucus, had submitted an additional eleven sanctions bills, although none passed.[70] Again, Diggs was aware that these bills stood little chance of passing in the House, but by making his case for them he challenged the soundness of Nixon's position and could gauge the level of support he had from his white colleagues.

When Diggs founded the Black Forum on Foreign Policy in 1975 it marked a major turning point in African Americans' influence on U.S. foreign policy. Events in southern Africa in 1974 and 1975 were auspicious for the end of white supremacy. Angola, Mozambique, and Guinea-Bissau were victorious in their wars of liberation against Portugal and declared their independence. In July 1975, Cape Verde was the last Portuguese territory to claim its independence. The end of Portuguese imperialism raised the stakes for South Africa, Namibia, and Rhodesia as the continent's remaining territories under white rule.[71] White supremacy in Africa appeared to be approaching a violent end. Congressman Diggs counseled

Figure 5. Charles Diggs, Shirley Chisholm, and Ronald Dellums, press conference of African American lawmakers, 1971. Bettmann Collections. Getty Images.

President Gerald Ford, who succeeded Nixon in 1974, to officially recognize Angolan independence and the legitimacy of the MPLA-led government, rather than collude with South Africa to install a puppet and expand white supremacy in Namibia.[72] The question among African American leaders was: What role would they play in the final liberation of Africa and in the continent's future? Diggs intended the Black Forum on Foreign Policy to provide the answer.

To gather information on these fast-changing events in Africa and to work toward establishing African Americans' role in African affairs, in 1975 Diggs established the Black Forum. It brought African American lawmakers and activists together to develop strategies to shape conceptions and discussions of African affairs.[73] In September 1976, three months after the South African police shot down students in Soweto while they peacefully protested the enforcement of the Bantu Education Act, Diggs and Congressman Andrew Young, before he became UN ambassador, used the Forum to convene the Black Foreign Policy Forum Leadership Conference on Southern Africa in Washington, D.C. This was a historic gathering of national African

American civil and civil rights organizations, including leaders from the NAACP, Operation PUSH (People United to Save Humanity), Africare, the Black Economic Research Council, and the National Council of Negro Women, to strategize on how to build African American influence on foreign policy.[74] The fall of Portugal's African empire had implications for white-minority rule in Rhodesia and South Africa. The approximately 120 attendees, leaders from labor, business, civil rights, religious groups, and government, work toward a consensus on U.S. policies.[75] They adopted an eleven-point foreign policy agenda. They criticized President Ford for failing to objectively assess the changing political environment in southern Africa and continuing to stand on the side of the settlers and colonists rather than with liberation movements.

The conference produced two significant outcomes. One was "The African-American Manifesto on Southern Africa" that three members of Diggs's staff—Randall Robinson, Herschelle Challenor, and Willard Johnson—produced based on the general consensus among conference attendees as to the direction that U.S. foreign policy should take. "The African American Manifesto" boldly declared African Americans' duty as "the descendants of Africa" to "proclaim our unswerving commitment to immediate self-determination and majority rule in Southern Africa." It condemned the president for imposing anticommunism as a foreign policy in southern Africa. To do so, it read, "in the Southern African context is to confuse the issue and to align the United States once again with the racist forces of reaction and totalitarianism against the advocates of self-determination and progressive change."[76] Among its more concrete proposals was a call for the United States to impose economic sanctions on Rhodesia and South Africa, support liberation movements in those countries, recognize the MPLA-led government in Angola, and endorse its admission to the United Nations. "The normalization of relations with the Angolan Government will facilitate any U.S. involvement in bringing about a just peace in the region."[77]

Hidden among the document's declarations is a clear call for African Americans to address southern Africa and the white-minority regimes' exclusive hold on power through violence as the consensus priority issue in foreign affairs. "The escalating conflict in Southern Africa, and the real possibility that this situation could lead to a wider war if appropriate action is not taken, makes a black American consensus on U.S. policy toward Africa all the more urgent."[78] Although "The Manifesto" did not receive much media attention, it set the tone and the language through which African Americans would address issues in southern Africa. It also made prioritizing southern African a settled matter. The region and the challenge of ending white-minority rule is where they would channel their energies and resources.

The conference's second major outcome was an ambitious plan to establish an African American foreign policy lobbying firm and think tank: TransAfrica Forum. Randall Robinson chaired a taskforce to develop the plan for TransAfrica as an institutional vehicle through which black Americans could express to the Congress and the president their views on U.S. foreign policy toward Africa and the Caribbean.[79] He became its founding executive director the following year. TransAfrica Forum quickly became the most active, influential, and effective lobby on Caribbean and African affairs and remained so through the 1980s. It joined the Black Caucus and other U.S. political organizations in the "movement of movements" against apartheid in South Africa.[80] Its political orientation resembled that of earlier African American organizations that focused on African affairs, like the NAACP, the Council on African Affairs (until 1941 called the International Committee on African Affairs), and the American Committee on Africa. But it had the distinct advantage of the Black Caucus, a body of African American lawmakers with a powerful network of white colleagues and influence over legislation and congressional hearings. It also benefited from having been formed when the media and, therefore, the U.S. public began to pay attention to events in southern Africa. TransAfrica expanded the formula Diggs established: direct action combined with internal pressure on the White House from African Americans in positions of power. It became a distinctive synthesis for African American politicians and activists during the 1980s.[81]

Diggs did not radically change U.S. policies toward Africa and the Caribbean, but Leland, Dellums, Gray, and their colleagues in the Congressional Black Caucus continued with this approach and built on it to gain unprecedented influence in foreign affairs. They had the advantage of a large Black Caucus and members with a commitment to African affairs.

When Leland arrived in D.C. in 1979, Houston was home to 1.3 million residents—one-third of whom were African American—making it the nation's sixth-largest city. It was one of several cities with a growing African American political class that increased the number of African American representatives in municipal and state governments. The most prominent members of this group were mayors, most notably Carl Stokes of Cleveland (1968–71); Maynard Jackson of Atlanta (1974–82); Coleman Young of Detroit (1974–94); Harold Washington of Chicago (1983–87); and Richard Hatcher of Gary, Indiana (1968–87). Most members of this new cohort of African American elected officials were liberal Democrats, but many rose to power in response to public outcry over police, violence, targeted assassinations—Fred Hampton in Chicago and Carl Hampton in Houston—and municipal neglect of African American communities in the wake of white flight to the suburbs. A small group of radicals among them had the political skills to wield considerable weight in the debates on domestic issues related to education, welfare, homelessness, and unemployment. Leland's radical praxis and outlook in domestic and international issues brought together seemingly disparate initiatives—homelessness, global hunger, health care, and apartheid—as a cohesive project.

President Ronald Reagan was the most significant obstacle to Leland's and other African American lawmakers' agendas throughout the 1980s. Post-Diggs, the Black Caucus and TransAfrica continued to raise the profile of Africa and the Caribbean, often in opposition to the Reagan administration's policies, practices, and positions. As Ronald Dellums said, their activism was galvanized and energized by "the black community's distaste for Reagan's ideology."[82] He wasted no time implementing his radical agenda. In February 1981, one month after he entered the White House, Reagan proposed cuts to domestic and international assistance programs, including close to $500 million from USAID for fiscal year 1982, which would reduce it to 20 percent below what it had been under Carter.[83] The new president planned to request $5.4 billion from Congress for major aid programs, a $1.8 billion reduction from existing funding levels.

In the Black Caucus statement to the president on March 26, 1981, William Gray advised Reagan to consider more than austerity and the Cold War when crafting his foreign policy. "Our analysis differs profoundly from that of Reagan," Gray wrote. "The administration sees our problems in foreign policy as primarily East vs. West; therefore, the administration poses military solutions. . . . We find the assumption that the Soviet Union and Cuba are all controlling forces in the Third World misses the major thrust of positive Third World policy and is extremely dangerous. We view the most effective weapon against Soviet imperialism as a policy which emphasizes our inherent strengths—our economic and our technological expertise and our commitment to the democratic process and human rights. When our foreign policy has emphasized these strengths through tenacious and creative diplomacy, the results have been significant and positive."[84]

President Reagan rebuffed the Black Caucus's attempts to dialogue with him. He met with its members in February 1981 then ignored them entirely for the duration of his presidency. Reagan's cold shoulder solidified Leland's belief that the president was a racist. "Black people in this country believe," Leland said in September 1982, "whether he denies the allegation or not, that he is racist."[85] Indeed, the president had, in the least, signaled to racists an indication of his low regard for African Americans in 1980 when he launched his presidential campaign in Philadelphia, Mississippi, where in 1964 three young civil rights activists were famously murdered by members of the Ku Klux Klan. Reagan won the 1980 election with negligible support from African American voters. He felt no pressure to address African Americans' domestic or foreign policy concerns, and his advisors wagered that Reagan stood to lose little if he angered African Americans because, more than any other group, they voted overwhelmingly for the Democratic Party.[86] Leland insisted that the president robbed himself of the benefit of their counsel by ignoring the Black Caucus. "He's missing the opportunity to be privy to hearing from some of the best minds in Congress by his unwillingness to meet with us," Leland told journalists.[87]

African American lawmakers were a well of knowledge and experience on Africa and issues in African American communities, but the president did not equivocate on his approach to Global South nations. To the extent he considered them at all, he viewed them through a narrow Cold War frame. Governments and movements whose policies, philosophy, and political praxis did not align with U.S. interests were dangerous. His administration took steps to either weaken or wholly subvert the leftist governments of Nicaragua and Cuba, as well as leftist guerrillas in El Salvador. Black Caucus members tried to counter Reagan's positions toward Central America and Cuba with their own set of policy proposals, which extend their political activities beyond issues of race and putative cultural and historical ties to Africa and the Caribbean.

Leland's interest in U.S. relations with leftist regimes in Latin America brought human rights issues more directly and deeply into his political orbit. Latino Americans were a growing demographic in Leland's district, and he had advocated forming coalitions between African American and Latino organizations since his activist days in college; building those coalitions was personal rather than political for him. He spoke of Cuba and its revolution in a reverential tone, and he respected Cuba's leadership within the Third World. Economic support from the Soviet Union, in the form of nearly $2 billion per year in loans, development aid, and sugar subsidies, empowered Cuba to support wars of national liberation in Africa and South and Central America.[88]

Human rights had not yet become a major foreign affairs issue in the early 1970s, despite Carter's attempts to bring it into the American political lexicon. Its definition remained vague during the 1970s.[89] Had Leland lived into the next decade and confronted the genocide in Rwanda and the violence in Darfur, Sudan, he might have absorbed the language and ideals of human rights. But even today, "human rights" is not a popular term in the African American political lexicon, in part because the political right has used human rights to attack governments not aligned with the United States. In the 1980s, the Reagan administration redefined human rights to be indistinguishable from anticommunism.[90] Nations that were not communist did not factor into Reagan's human rights calculus. Therefore, human rights discourse was negatively tied to geopolitics.

Nicaragua was Reagan's priority in Central America where several small groups fought the ruling Sandinista National Liberation Front, which came to power in 1979 during the revolution that ousted the right-wing dictator Anastasio Somoza DeBayle. The Sandinistas held the Cuban revolution up as a model for their own success. There was great sentimental value to the Cuban revolution among radicals throughout the world, even in the United States. However, conditions in Nicaragua were not suitable for Cuba's revolutionary model.[91] Still, to propel the Sandinistas' social revolution forward, the Cubans provided a wealth of resources, from fertilizer to doctors and construction brigades for highways, schools, and houses.[92]

Reagan defined the Sandinista regime as totalitarian based on its human rights record. Ostensibly, human rights violations distinguished "totalitarian" regimes, such as Fidel Castro's Cuba, from more palatable "authoritarian" regimes, such as those of Zaire and Saudi Arabia. Some political analysts and scholars have called this approach "the Kirkpatrick Doctrine," after Jeane Kirkpatrick, Reagan's ambassador to the United Nations.[93] Based on her rationale, the United States supported "authoritarian regimes out of 'national interest,' but not 'totalitarian' ones, also in accord with US interest."[94] A close look at how the administration applied the Kirkpatrick Doctrine does not show human rights as the most significant determinant for whether a country was totalitarian or authoritarian. Reagan approached

Marxism and Leninism—and any combination or variation of the two—as rigidly antithetical to human rights. A major problem, from his standpoint, was that their ideologies were fixed and, therefore, could neither be swayed nor forced to align with U.S. geopolitical and economic interests.

According to Sergio Ramirez, whose memoir provides details about this period, after the Sandinistas' victory in the 1979 elections they were destined for conflict with the United States. They regarded the superpower to the north as the source of many of Nicaragua's problems throughout its history.[95] Reagan continued this legacy of U.S. intrusion in Nicaraguan affairs throughout the 1980s. He threatened invasion but never followed through. Instead, he armed and financed the Nicaraguan Democratic Front, the "Contras," which had previously been armed by Argentina. The Reagan administration was determined to overthrow the Sandinista government, and by 1981, Reagan's illegal aid to the Contras had become their lifeline.[96] By the time the war ended, thousands had been killed, disabled, or displaced, and the conflict damaged the economy. Moreover, as Ramirez argued, it sabotaged the revolution's transformational potential.[97]

In April 1981, Leland wrote "The United States and Central America," the Black Caucus's position statement in response to Reagan's policies on the Global South. He presented a sharp critique of Reagan's continued support of the white-minority regime in South Africa and the "barbaric regimes" in Guatemala, Chile, Argentina, and Haiti. "We feel that this spells out a foreign policy blatantly insensitive to human rights and human suffering," Leland wrote. "A foreign policy which tries to turn the clock back on history; a foreign policy which in no way represents the interests and fundamental values of our nation. We believe there is an emerging consensus in the United States and in the world that a return to the politics of counter-insurgency and gun-boat diplomacy has no place in the foreign policy of our nation in the 1980s."[98] In contrast to Reagan's hard line against the Sandinista government, Leland's expressed solidarity with them, which was not an entirely uncommon position among the political left in the United States at the time. In honor of the sixth anniversary of Daniel Ortega's Sandinista People's Revolution, for example, Dellums sent Ortega an official letter of congratulations. "Your successes and accomplishments in providing for the enrichment and enhancement of the quality of life over the past six years stand on their own merit and must be commended," he wrote. "On this day of festivity and celebration I join you in spirit and solidarity."[99]

The Reagan administration, however, saw no grounds for celebrating the Sandinistas. The president believed there were no areas in which the two governments had shared interests. The president also justified his support for the Contras by labeling the Sandinista regime totalitarian and describing its political success as a springboard for a communist insurgency in Central America. For evidence, he pointed to Soviet and Cuban support of the Sandinistas and leftist rebels in El Salvador. To Reagan, this support defined the Sandinistas as a threat to U.S. security and meant that the entire region was vulnerable to the spread of Soviet influence. "I do not believe that a majority in Congress or the country is prepared to stand by passively while the people of Central America are delivered to totalitarianism," Reagan told a joint session of Congress. "And we ourselves are left vulnerable to new dangers."[100]

Later that month, Alexander Haig, Reagan's secretary of state, spoke to members of the Black Caucus regarding the administration's position on authoritarian and totalitarian regimes. The question to the Reagan administration from the Black Caucus was regarding the president's support of the white-minority government in South Africa. Black Caucus members wanted the administration to explain its paradoxical embrace of the apartheid regime, a gross violator of black South Africans' human rights, while it attacked the democratically elected Sandinista government. Haig explained that the president justifiably supported some authoritarian regimes because they had the potential and requisite openness to evolve. Totalitarian regimes, on the other hand, would not and could not be changed. "Human rights," he said, "should be a fundamental aspect in the formulation and assessment of our foreign relations." But this policy had an important caveat that superseded any consideration of a regime's human rights record: close allies must never be isolated. This position reveals the Reagan administration's privileging of human rights as a pretense for marginalizing regimes that the United States had difficulty influencing and protecting those that supported U.S. interests. That is the precise argument that Haig presented to the Black Caucus: "Isolating traditionally friendly countries leads to further excuses. Dialogue conducted quietly leads to greater results."[101]

Reagan was uncompromising in his decision to support the Contras. The rebels lacked popular support within Nicaragua, but Reagan portrayed them as patriotic freedom fighters. In direct response to Reagan's efforts to fund the Contras, the Democratic-controlled Congress approved three amendments between 1982 and 1984, collectively known as the Boland amendments, that banned U.S. assistance to the Contras if the aid was for the purpose of overthrowing the Nicaraguan government.[102] Latin American and African affairs overlapped through Reagan's two terms. Leland continued to work on Latin American issues after 1983 when global hunger and African affairs became the focus of his foreign policy initiatives. But his desire was for a signature issue that people would identify with him and his leadership. "I came to Congress to pursue health issues. I got on the Energy and Commerce Committee. I got on the Health and Environment Subcommittee. But I found it very difficult to carve a niche for myself in the arena of health per se. Primarily because before I'd gotten to Congress there were other people who had done just that and thought pretty clearly the same as I did. It was very difficult for me to identify health as an issue that was mine."[103] He chose to redouble his commitment to global hunger. Ethiopia offered the best option to demonstrate the U.S. government's capacity to look past ideological differences in order to respond to a nation's humanitarian need. Beyond Ethiopia, hunger was a window into other critical issues, such Sudan's civil war, conflicts in Angola and Mozambique, and food insecurity in the Frontline States stemming from the South African apartheid regime's destructive policies toward its neighbors. Hunger, moreover, was a problem throughout the United States. Therefore championing U.S. government attention to global hunger allowed Leland to combine his interests in domestic and international affairs.

Leland's timing for his mission to change how the U.S. government officials conceive of hunger and humanitarian relief was unfortunate. He found it difficult to convince his colleagues of the importance of his humanitarian relief initiatives because austerity had become popular in Congress. Increased government spending on social welfare programs and international aid was a difficult sell. Public opinion also did his cause no favors. A good portion of the U.S. public believed that hunger resulted from individual failings rather than the country's culture and economic system. Many others did not believe it existed. Leland tried to change public opinion on the scope of the hunger problem and the necessary steps the government needed to take to address it. "Hunger in America is real and far more widespread than imagined. According to recent statistics, more than 35 percent of Black Americans and 30 [percent] of Hispanic Americans are unable to meet their basic needs for nutritional sustenance," Leland said in an interview. He argued that Reagan's policies had led to an increase in the malnutrition rate in the United States.[104]

Media coverage of the 1983–1985 famine in Ethiopia and humanitarian relief organizations' unprecedented response to it lent urgency to Leland's mission to end hunger. It also shaped how Western powers discussed African development. In 1984, Western governments would make famine in Ethiopia emblematic of hunger in Africa. The country's crisis, as journalists represented it, inspired Leland's belief in the imperative to discuss hunger as a global problem. The Ethiopian famine was part of a broader food crisis in the Horn of Africa that included Somalia, Sudan, and Kenya, and across the Sahel to Chad, Mali, Niger, and Mauritania and to Angola Mozambique, Zambia, Zimbabwe, and Tanzania in southern Africa.[105] In May 1983, Edouard Saouma, director of the Food and Agriculture Organization (FAO) of the United Nations, called on Western nations to respond to the crisis: "I am hopeful that you will generously respond to my appeal for increased assistance to these really needy countries."[106] International humanitarian relief organizations raised their commitments in the region on an unprecedented scale. Because Ethiopia was just one of as many as two dozen countries that needed assistance, it was easy to ignore Ethiopia's famine and the unique political and economic circumstances surrounding it. Agricultural productivity in Ethiopia had declined from previous years, but not every region faced a shortage. The crisis affected roughly one-fifth of the population of over seven million people, mostly in Wello, Tigray, Eritrea, and Shewa. Food production was also down in Bale, Hararghe, Sidamo, and Gamo-Gofa in the south and Gondar in the west.[107] Ethiopia faced the most severe food crisis, which, coupled with the journalists' close attention to it, placed Ethiopia at the heart of the international relief campaign for Africa. The Ethiopian regime's close ties to the Soviet Union were not a characteristics of a country with which to demonstrate the strength of U.S. government-led humanitarianism.

Leland condemned President Reagan's political response to famine in the Horn of Africa, which limited humanitarian assistance to Marxist Ethiopia and denied direct aid to its government. Leland hoped for politically neutral action from the White House. But Reagan's approach was consistent with the history of U.S. internationalism since the start of the Cold War, although he adopted an extreme iteration of this practice. U.S. presidents have always leveraged humanitarian aid to compel vulnerable, weaker nations to support their international interests. Other objectives behind food aid had been to expand overseas markets for U.S. agricultural products and to support economic and social development in recipient countries that supported U.S. policies. Finally, the U.S. government aimed its aid at helping end food emergencies.[108]

Reagan's predecessors had both provided and denied food aid as a tool to bend Global South governments to align with U.S. interests. The cases of Central America and South Asia during the 1970s illustrate this practice. In 1973, Salvador Allende, Chile's Marxist head of state, formally requested a large purchase of wheat on credit from the U.S. Strategic Wheat Reserve. President Ford was aware that Chile's crisis would grow more severe without U.S. assistance. The country had exhausted its foreign reserves, opening the door to a national food shortage. When Ford denied Chile's requests for assistance, he allowed the country's economic crisis to worsen. By ignoring the country's humanitarian crisis Ford helped ripen its political environment for a coup that would end Allende's socialist government.

The following year, the U.S. government delayed a ship carrying food aid to Bangladesh, even though the government maintained friendly relations with the United States, to punish it for having sold jute to Cuba.[109] The United States might even punish a nation desperate for foreign cash reserves if it fell on the opposing side of political alliances. In 1974, Secretary of Agriculture Earl Butz described food as "one of the principal tools in our negotiating kit." Similarly, in 1980, John Block, a former Illinois farmer and Reagan's nominee for secretary of agriculture, told reporters, "I believe food is the greatest weapon we have for keeping peace in the world." He went on to say he envisioned America sending its agricultural surpluses to hungry nations in return for "more stability in the world." He later changed "weapon" to "instrument." Still, Block echoed established U.S. policy.[110] Meanwhile, the United States continued to sell increasing amounts of wheat to the Soviet Union, which it had begun doing in the early 1960s through the 1970s.

The question remained, then, what moved Reagan to approve humanitarian relief for Ethiopia, which within a year grew into the largest U.S.-sponsored relief initiative in U.S. history? The answer lies in the complex of issues that defined the turning point in U.S. policies toward Africa: the decline of anticommunism, the rise and expansion of international food aid, and the growing number of African Americans in Congress. Reagan had a strictly anticommunist foreign policy during his first two years in office. In 1982, and increasingly in 1983, he gradually shifted to promoting democracy rather than doggedly pushing anticommunism.[111] Communism remained a threat in the Global South from Reagan's perspective and to many U.S. politicians in general. Until the decade's end, racism and anticommunism were central features of U.S. foreign policy. But by the end of 1983 and, to an even greater extent, at the start of his second term in 1985 the president managed to see past many of his ideological differences with the Soviet Union to build common ground and work toward a lasting peace. Reagan no longer had the partisan and ideological constraints of a first-term president and proved to be less doctrinaire.[112] Yet open-mindedness does not fully account for Reagan's shift on large-scale humanitarian assistance.

He softened his opposition to direct and indirect aid for Marxist Ethiopia in part because of media and public responses to the famine. He also grew to appreciate the short- and long-term political benefits of humanitarian relief. Peter McPherson, director of USAID during the Reagan administration, explained that the president conceived of U.S. assistance in purely humanitarian, non-ideological terms.[113] Here, the tactical shift in the president's politicization of food aid is evident, despite his efforts to position himself above politics. He would approve limited assistance, while he and other officials used this purportedly nonpolitical act to weaken Mengistu and the Soviet Union and stave off critics from the political left who called for ever-larger levels of U.S. assistance. The president routinely and strategically added minor increases to congressionally approved aid levels to remain beyond rebuke by liberal critics. In one instance, for example, he approved adding $3 million to a preexisting commitment of $3.7 million that USAID would distribute to partnering humanitarian relief organizations.[114]

Leland also wanted to change the way Americans generally conceived of hunger, malnutrition, and food aid. He joined with Congressmen Ben Gilman of New York and Tony Hall of Ohio, fellow Democrats deeply committed to ending global hunger, to plan the details for a new committee, the Select Committee on Hunger. Before they settled on the idea of a select committee, their first plan was to establish a caucus within Congress to shape the discourse on hunger and promote effective legislation to help end hunger.[115] They were fortunate to have the sympathetic ear of Congressman Tip O'Neill, Speaker of the House. He had the power to present proposed committees for a vote in the House. O'Neill, a liberal Democrat from Massachusetts, had a strong, progressive record, but he had earned high marks for compromising with the Reagan administration and his Republican colleagues in the House. Rodney Ellis, Leland's chief of staff, explained that

Leland worked through Chris Matthews, O'Neill's chief of staff. "Mickey was persistent," Ellis recalled. "He kept working it, kept pushing. So eventually he got them to create that select committee on world hunger."[116]

Leland and Hall sponsored the legislation to create the Congressional Select Committee on Hunger. "We believe that a Select Committee on Hunger," Leland said from the House floor in April 1982, "can be the appropriate vehicle to best address and focus on the problem both on the domestic and international front. The select committee would serve as a mechanism for assessing hunger issues in a comprehensive manner—issues that currently cut across the jurisdiction of a number of standing committees."[117] Leland faced an uphill battle in convincing Republicans to support the measure. They disliked new committees and were inclined to reduce the number of existing committees. Moreover, there were already several committees addressing hunger-related issues, including Agriculture, Appropriations, Foreign Affairs, and Ways and Means. Leland and Hall had to win over several of their Republican colleagues. Representative Bill Frenzel, a Republican from Minnesota who remained dubious of the proposed Hunger Committee's capacity to make any headway on the task that Leland had set for it, predicted the new committee would not, as he said, "help the hunger problem at all, but certainly will add to the staff level of the House." Rather than relief for the starving, he complained, "we will only create a well-fed staff."[118]

Even with the strong Republican opposition to adding new congressional committees, when O'Neill called for a final vote on February 22, 1984 Congress had approved its first committee devoted exclusively to hunger, with 309 representatives in favor and 78 opposed. There was concern among Republican leaders that Democrats would use the new Hunger Committee to paint a negative image of the president's position. They assigned Congressman Bill Emerson and Congresswoman Marge Roukema, a fellow Republican, to the Hunger Committee. They were tasked with tempering what they anticipated would be the new committee's liberal bias. Emerson had been a Hunger Committee skeptic and had joined the committee as a watchdog for Republican leaders in the House. He explained that he had opposed not antihunger initiatives in principle but creating more committees: "I didn't think that Congress needed a different committee. We could do a better job if we had fewer committees. Where I have changed my opinion is that until Congress reforms its structure, the Hunger Committee provides a very useful oversight function."[119] Before long, the Republican members grew enthusiastic for the committee's work. Emerson even served as the committee's vice-chairman. He became a convert to the mission to end global hunger.

As a select committee, it could make proposals to the various preexisting standing committees, hold hearings on relevant issues, and conduct investigations on policy issues related to hunger throughout the world, including the United States. As chair, Leland took both responsibilities seriously and saw them as sufficient to shape political narratives and influence public opinion. He used the committee's meager resources to cement its position as a clearinghouse for issues related to domestic and international hunger and poverty. The committee's accomplishments during Leland's tenure as chair silenced most of its critics and demonstrated its political relevance. His staff gathered information, held hearings, and lobbied members of Congress on hunger-related issues. Their efforts were as small as launching campaigns in poor communities to provide women and children with fresh fruits and vegetables as part of the WIC (Women, Infants, and Children) program.[120] They conducted research other standing committees' staff were not willing or did not have time to complete. And they tackled more politically sensitive issues that standing committees did not want to take a stand on. Leland managed to garner high attendance at his hearings, while other committees struggled to attract attendees. He attended many of his colleagues' hearings and persuaded them to support Hunger Committee causes.[121]

In his antihunger campaign, Leland followed in the footsteps of African American leaders who addressed food crises in Africa and elsewhere in the world as a political issue prior to the approval of his Hunger Committee. Through Operation PUSH, for example, Jesse Jackson in 1973 advocated a U.S. response to the famine in the Sahel, where an estimated one hundred thousand people died. Jackson and his associates solicited food from major food processors and supermarket chains to send to the Sahelian nations of Chad, Mali, Mauretania, Niger, Senegal, and Burkina Faso. He also communicated with ambassadors from the affected countries and secured promises from the mayors of several large U.S. cities, including Chicago, to support the humanitarian initiative. Jackson also received support from the Nation of Islam, which hosted a fund-raiser that boxer Muhammad Ali and entertainers Stevie Wonder and Lola Falana attended, and raised $10,000 for Operation PUSH and $100,000 for UNICEF's Sahel drought relief campaign.[122] Congressman Diggs also led a famine-relief campaign. He and sociologist Elliott Skinner founded Relief for Africans in Need in the Sahel (RAINS) in July 1973 under the umbrella of the Interreligious Foundation for Community Organization (IFCO). Mindful of humanitarianism's deleterious effects on African sovereignty, RAINS apportioned its funds directly to African governments in the Sahel.[123] Diggs also received congressional support for famine relief, through an amendment to the Foreign Aid Bill in 1973 to provide an additional $30 million above existing levels in relief aid for the six countries in the Sahel affected by severe food shortages.[124]

In light of these precedents, Leland's vision for U.S. food aid to help African countries achieve long-term economic self-sufficiency was radical only because USAID had moved away from its original goal to lift "those people in the huts and villages of half the globe struggling to break the bonds of mass misery" out of poverty. Leland might have endorsed this goal, as set by President John F. Kennedy in 1961, but for the fact that he distinguished between communist and noncommunist nations. Foreign aid would, according to Kennedy, work miracles in addressing the problems of the noncommunist world.[125] But the president wanted a program that was not self-consciously anticommunist. Rather than viewing aid as an instrument against communism, he envisioned, at least rhetorically, aid "for constructive economic and social advancement."[126]

The 1980s and humanitarian action toward the Horn were part of an exceptional era of humanitarianism that began after World War II.[127] Leland's posture toward aid and his belief in the efficacy of humanitarian relief for African crises show the extent to which his thinking was in sync with the contemporary discourse on humanitarianism. When Leland urgently called for neutral humanitarian assistance for Ethiopia and the southern African Frontline States, he spoke in the 1980s lexicon of humanitarianism. Like the strands of black radical politics and black internationalism in his political ideology and praxis, Leland's approach to humanitarian relief had a broader context and genealogy grounded in post–World War II humanitarianism. The most influential relief organizations involved in various crises of the 1970s and 1980s had their start addressing the needs of the victims of World War I and World War II. Following World War II, they focused on reconstruction, development, and tending to the wounded and displaced. Relief organizations' influence grew in the 1970s as the media exposed Western publics to the depth of crises in Cambodia, Nigeria, and Ethiopia and to the work of humanitarian relief organizations.

Figure 6. Ethiopian famine, 1985. Joel Robine, Agence France Presse. Getty Images.

Britain, Sweden, the United States, the Soviet Union, the German Democratic Republic, and the Republic of Germany directed close to half of their humanitarian aid through UN agencies. In 1988, for example, 45 percent of such aid was channeled in this way. These governments directly funded NGOs like Oxfam, Christian Aid, and the Catholic Fund for Overseas Development during the 1970s and 1980s. The British relied on NGOs to manage 50 percent of its relief to Ethiopia and 70 percent of its aid to Sudan by the mid-1980s.[128] These numbers dropped precipitously in the following decade, and unilateral direct assistance and military intervention began to define humanitarianism.[129]

Multilateralism was the practical reality of humanitarian aid during the 1980s. It also explains Leland's and other humanitarian actors' insistence on political neutrality, lest politics stand in the way of saving lives and maintaining access to lives in need of saving. Maintaining access to and mobility within countries that faced humanitarian crises were key relief organization strategies during the period; it secured their position as intermediaries for humanitarian relief. Eschewing critiques of leaders' domestic policies helped Leland cultivate close, direct contact with political leaders in crisis zones, including Sudan's Gaafar Nimeiry, Sadiq al-Mahdi, and Omar al-Bashir, the Sudan People Liberation Army's John Garang, and Mengistu of Ethiopia.

Images in the media and stories of famine victims and the tireless work of humanitarian workers persuaded the government and public to support large-scale humanitarian assistance. But Leland and others failed to account for the myriad political forces that compounded the effects of natural disasters and prolonged the famine. They limited their cause to short-term relief and exposed themselves to critiques from political partisans who continued to view these crises through a Cold War lens. Mengistu also deflected blame for the food crisis. After the 1974 revolution, Derg officials tried to establish legitimacy for their regime by addressing the country's food crisis. Their first step was to blame it on Emperor Selassie. Then they claimed victory over the crisis, purporting to have "ended forever" the "permanent hunger" of the Haile Selassie regime.[130] In 1983, almost ten years after the revolution, the Derg again confronted a famine. Rather than draw public attention to it as Mengistu and fellow officers did in 1973 and 1974, he seldom addressed it publicly and channeled the lion's share of his country's meager economic resources to his military campaigns against the TPLF and the EPLF rather than the food crisis. Leland did not criticize Mengistu's handling of the famine. He seems to have believed that to include civil war, irredentism, and disastrous economic and agricultural policies in his framing of the Ethiopian crisis would cross the line into interfering in Ethiopia's domestic issues. Focusing on the decisions and actions of Mengistu and rebel leaders, Leland thought, would weaken Ethiopia's already tenuous sovereignty. It was easier to point to failed rains than failed policies.

Chapter 3

"Horrendous Are the Hard Times"

Western Food Aid and Ethiopia in the Age of Reagan

> *Horrendous are the hard times,*
> *That evil day saddled me with,*
> *I brought my water-carrying pot,*
> *Right out of my back room and sold it.*
>
> —Anonymous Amhara poem

The oral poetry of northern Ethiopia provides valuable insight into aspects of Ethiopian highlanders' famine experience. Little of the caricatured victimization and helplessness common in Western narratives of famine in Africa are present in these verses. Amhara highlanders in Shewa commonly referred to the 1983–85 famine interchangeably as Agurtachäw and Seventy-Seven, the year in the Ethiopian calendar that corresponds to 1984. Dubbalä is the name highlanders in northern Shewa used for the 1973 famine.[1] A Shewa poem translated by Fekade Azeze employs both terms:

> I am Agurtachäw, Dubbalä's brother
> I am still in the marketplace,
> I have yet to enter your house[2]

The poetry describes the peasants' movement through distinct phases of the crisis. Livestock flooded the market as families sought immediate cash to purchase food; then the price of cattle dropped precipitously and people migrated en masse from rural areas. In the final phase, peasants recalled their crisis and expressed remorse for their suffering and loss.[3] The first phase is nicely represented in the following stanza of a different poem and exhibits the irony common in Amarinya:

> Let us not mention this Seventy-Seven!
> I parted with my pregnant cow,
> For a mere two days' lunch[4]

A stanza of another poem, included as the epigraph for this chapter, evokes similar irony and remorse. Parting with a water-carrying pot would further impair one's capacity to survive famine. The struggle to survive, however, is a most rational response to adversity, regardless of its form. The above verses, and others like them composed in the 1970s and 1980s, reflect not futility and the inevitability of death but the tenacious quest to endure, if only incrementally.

A very different famine narrative came from Western media and humanitarian relief organizations during the Ethiopian famine of the 1980s. The crisis was the most noteworthy example of the Western media's power to shape conceptions and responses to humanitarian crises.[5] Images of Ethiopia misrepresented who Ethiopians were and how they dealt with chronic hunger. Highlanders' complex experiences conveyed in their poetry are absent from the Western narrative. Western journalists flattened Ethiopia's environmental, political, and economic circumstances to fit preconceived, paternalistic notions of the West's role in African affairs. The starving thousands in Ethiopian feeding camps were a small, tragic piece of the famine crisis, but Western media, relief organization officials, and interested politicians, including Leland, portrayed Ethiopia's in feeding centers as the famine's main feature and upheld food aid as an instrument to resolve the crisis. Moreover, Ethiopia was one of several countries that experienced varying levels of food shortage during the 1970s and 1980s, including Somalia, Niger, and Mali. But none captured international interest and affected the discourse on humanitarianism like Ethiopia.

What about Ethiopia's famine turned it into *the* famine? How did Ethiopia become the site of "the African famine"? Ethiopia, Leland said in a television interview in 1985, is "the place where the news media dramatized the famine itself. Ethiopia became Africa to a lot of people outside of the continent."[6] British journalist Graham Hancock wrote at the time that the apparent dignity and fortitude of the starving Ethiopians "appealed most directly to the imagination, conscience and sympathy of the West and that set in motion one of the great emergency aid efforts of modern times."[7] Images of Ethiopians, calm and stoic in the face of unavoidable death, made the scenes uniquely tragic. Most reports reduced Ethiopians to stereotypes of pathetic dependency and were composed of certain stock features.[8] The emaciated child at the feeding center usually cried or lay lethargically near its mother. Invariably, the mother's shrunken breasts were clearly exposed. A second essential element was the white aid worker. In most famine reports, women dominated this role. The visuals and accompanying reports depicted European and American men and women fighting against all odds to save as many people as possible.[9] Occasionally an Ethiopian doctor or relief worker described the enormity of the challenge, but for the most part black faces belonged to victims, helpless sufferers in passive resignation and silent despair.[10] These images made the famine digestible for the Western public. Ethiopia became synonymous with the helpless and desperate Global South and reinforced a sense of the imperative of benevolent white intervention.[11]

Accordingly, the famine became a uniquely African tragedy, with the people and governments of the West as natural, logical redeemers. A quarter century removed from 1960, the "Year of Africa," Ethiopia's crisis, as viewed from the West, exposed the shortcomings of African sovereignty and revealed Africa as ill-suited to deal with even its natural disasters.[12] The convenience of the Western famine narrative was that the victims and the villains were black, unlike with apartheid in South Africa. Most important, the heroes of the African famine, as cast by the Western famine narrative, were white. The allure of the Ethiopian crisis in the West highlighted the links between racial, Cold War, and, in striking ways, domestic politics. Indeed, the Ethiopian crisis as a media sensation made it politically expedient for President Reagan to support large-scale U.S. aid after he initially opposed all but limited, largely symbolic assistance. In response to the U.S. humanitarian relief program, U.S. politicians celebrated American moral authority, demonstrated by their country's generous, unprecedented food aid initiative for Ethiopia.

Political, economic, and environmental factors within Ethiopia produced the famine, but foreign interventions' early stages willfully ignored the famine's political dimensions. Nonetheless, the climate and environment played an evident role in the crisis. Two consecutive *belg* (normal seasonal) rains failed to arrive in 1983 and 1984 in the Ethiopian lowlands.

This short rainy season in March and April follows a long dry season. The lack of rain left the soil too dry to cultivate in preparation for the main growing season. An infestation of stalk borers, larvae that feast on sorghum and maize, made matters worse. Crops failed, and many oxen died from lack of nourishment. These conditions were extreme forms of the historical stresses and risks inherent in Ethiopia's existing farming practices that rely on the ox plow and rainwater.[13] In most circumstances such conditions would have been manageable, but in Ethiopia during the 1980s they were insurmountable, given Mengistu's focus on military matters. By 1984, more than six million people in Ethiopia were estimated to be "in serious distress" because of the famine, with one million of those under the age of four.[14]

Leland entered this environment during his first official trip to Ethiopia in March 1983 to visit the feeding centers and to assess the success of foreign relief initiatives in the region. He was member of Congressman Howard Wolpe's three-week, six-nation fact-finding delegation to Africa that included six other colleagues: Robert Garcia, Ted Weiss, Parren Mitchell, Katie Hall, Jim Moody, and Gerald Solomon, the only Republican. Among members of Congress, Wolpe, a Michigan Democrat, was most extensively and consistently involved in African political issues. In contrast to Leland, he was not an activist. For Wolpe, policy was paramount. Before entering politics, he had been a political science professor at Western Michigan University and the University of Michigan's Institute of Public Policy Studies. He wrote a book on politics in Nigeria but would gain notoriety within academia for his article in the World Policy Journal in 1998, "The Other Africa: An End to Afro-Pessimism."[15] During his fourteen years in Congress, Wolpe was rarely absent from a major hearing on African affairs. He shared Leland's desire for the United States to approach African issues on their merits rather than with a Cold War litmus test. These shared interests fostered a close friendship between the two men.

Wolpe's itinerary for the delegation was ambitious. In addition to Ethiopia, the delegation visited Algeria, Morocco, Zimbabwe, Zaire, and Cote d'Ivoire. But Ethiopia affected Leland most deeply. He saw firsthand the country's food crisis and its toll on the people, especially in the famine-stricken areas of Wello, Tigray, and Eritrea. The experience affected him profoundly and permanently. The scenes Leland took in at the feeding centers in northern Ethiopia affirmed that it was imperative for U.S. humanitarian relief programs to have a greater presence in African countries. "It was one of the most grueling experiences I have ever had," he said shortly after he returned to the United States. "I must say though it was also the most eye-opening experience and it gave me a rededication to working for the humanity of people everywhere."[16] The group's meeting with Mengistu convinced Leland that the Ethiopian government approached the famine with utmost seriousness and concern. He accepted Mengistu's contention that nature, far more than his policies and the civil wars, precipitated the famine. Leland tried to remain strictly outside of politics when it came to famine relief.

The difficulty for Leland was that generally speaking aid was overtly political in the United States and in Ethiopia. The Mengistu regime's famine-relief initiatives combined humanitarian and military tactics. At times, however, the two worked at cross purposes. He mixed politics, agricultural policy, and famine relief in ways that changed the relationship between the peasantry and the state.[17] In the United States, President Reagan did not intend to work directly with the Ethiopian government on humanitarian relief and he sought to approve the minimum possible assistance. The Michael Buerk and Mohamed Amin reports from Korem were among several catalysts for changes in U.S. food aid to Africa. The public and private responses to the BBC reports compelled the president to shift his public position, at least rhetorically, to embracing U.S.-sponsored aid to Ethiopia.

Buerk of the BBC and Amin, Africa bureau chief for Visnews, produced two reports for the BBC about the Ethiopian famine. The first report became iconic soon after it aired on October 23, 1984, and quickly became a model for famine reporting that journalists replicated into the twenty-first century. At the same time, the report solidified the powerful, enduring, and influential narrative of famine that colored how Westerners viewed starvation and African food crises, and how politicians, policymakers, and relief workers discussed them. The BBC report and the countless others that followed affirmed a popular conception of Ethiopia and, therefore Africa, as a land of starving masses trapped in a desiccated, decontextualized feeding camp.

Korem is located on the main road between Addis Ababa and Asmara, the country's second-largest city at the time (it would become Eritrea's capital after 1995). Typical of Ethiopian towns in the highlands, Korem had an Orthodox church, a market, and several of what journalist Peter Gill described at the time as "extraordinarily scruffy hotels."[18] When Buerk and

Amin visited Korem, it had a population of approximately seven thousand. Amin's choice to only capture footage of people in the feeding centers introduced a distorted image of the town to the world. Through his lens the town in its totality was in dire straits because he did not include footage of people in the town itself, and, as far as the viewer can tell, Buerk did not reach out to them to record their perspectives on the crisis and the thousands of people it brought to their town. Amin also chose not to capture footage of the hundreds of families in the camps with relatively healthy children; viewers saw few smiling, playing children because they did not evoke the same profound sympathy and pity as images of the suffering.[19]

Buerk tailored his monologue that accompanied Amin's footage from Korem and Mekelle so that viewers would derive a sense of what he called "a biblical famine in the 20th century" and "the closest thing to hell on Earth." If not hell, the millions who viewed the story certainly saw a human tragedy unlike any they had witnessed before: a seemingly endless mass of emaciated people who were experiencing the end of the world as they knew it. Deprivation was the context: parched land with a mass of brown, bone-thin bodies clad in beige rags. For an intense sixteen seconds, Amin fixed his camera on a mother and child. Her skeletal body draped in thin cotton cloth, she sits lethargically but tries to console her crying, emaciated child. She appears resigned to her inability to provide the child—screaming yet lying limp in her arms—any comfort. The next scene is similarly unsettling. A small, apparently lost child with large eyes and a wide, open mouth that issues a faint cry stands searching, while Buerk implores viewers with grim statistics: "Fifteen thousand children here now: suffering, confused, lost. Death is all around. A child or adult dies every twenty minutes." If one were to only read those words or hear them narrated with no accompanying images, they would seem improbable, impossible to believe. But the people who sit and lie on the ground behind Buerk as he speaks appear so close to death as to make his grim figures sound conservative. Buerk describes a scene his viewers would find unacceptable: "The relief agencies do what they can. Save the Children Fund is caring for more than seven thousand babies." And then the call to action: "There's not enough food for half these people. . . . Rumors of a shipment can set off panic. As on most days, the rumors were false. For many here there will be no more food again today."[20]

To close the segment, Amin captured a three-year-old child splayed lifelessly on a cloth with an IV attached to his arm. During the few seconds that Buerk described the state of the child's health, Amin filmed the child's death. Amin described it as the most touching scene he had ever filmed. "I cried when I was editing this film," he told his friend, the writer Graham Hancock. "I actually broke down and cried."[21] In Buerk's words, the scenes "are by far the most influential pieces of television ever broadcast."[22] But for aid workers in Mekelle and Korem, Amin and Buerk's visit was unmemorable. It is likely they would have forgotten it if not for the flood of attention the report received from around the world. As Claire Bertschinger, a field nurse for the International Committee of the Red Cross (ICRC), recalled, "For me, their appearance was just a blink in the day. . . . It didn't occur to me that their visit would make any difference."[23]

Buerk and Amin's seven-minute report aired October 23, 1984, on *News Afternoon*, BBC1's lunchtime program. It had its greatest impact when it aired on the *Six O'clock News* later in the day. Over half of the program focused on Ethiopia. Sue Lawley, the show's anchor, offered detailed context for the story and warned viewers of the potentially upsetting scenes they were about to air. NBC partnered with the BBC at the time and was the first U.S. network to air the footage. After NBC executives initially turned down the report, sight unseen, Joe Angotti, head of NBC News, battled to air it. Angotti, on his own initiative and against NBC executives' orders, put the Korem report on the regular satellite feed into the NBC newsroom in New York. Normally the staff did not watch the feed, but on that day, veteran NBC anchorman Tom Brokaw recalled, "the entire newsroom came to a stop. Not a breath was taken. I think people were washed in their own thoughts, deeply moved by what they had seen."[24]

The timing of media outlets' initial broadcast of the report contributed to its considerable effect. There were few international news stories to compete with the famine. In the United States, the political contest between President Reagan and Walter Mondale, his Democratic challenger for control of the White House, failed to captivate U.S. audiences. By October the outcome was a foregone conclusion. "Buerk's report," Robert Kaplan wrote in 1988, "had arrived at the perfect moment. Had US Marines still been in Lebanon; had Konstantin Chernenko died a few months sooner, bringing the fascinating Mikhail Gorbachev to power in the Soviet Union in late 1984 instead of in 1985; or, had South Africa exploded a bit earlier, those unforgettable images of starving Ethiopian children might have had much less impact than they subsequently did."[25] The report originally broadcast on a midday program for the BBC ultimately aired on 425 television stations worldwide and reached an audience of more than 470 million.[26]

Although the Buerk-Amin report was evocative and impactful, it perpetuated a myth. The public saw Ethiopia as comprising hordes of starving women and children and perceived the communist dictator, Mengistu, as intent on capitalizing on the ravages of a ceaseless drought to starve his own people. This duality—starving people/ruthless communist dictator—anchored debates in the Reagan administration over the appropriate response to the crisis. Leland and the American left also embraced this duality but distanced Mengistu within the evolving famine narrative.

Within ten days of the broadcast, planes loaded with food arrived near major feeding centers. Relief workers in Mekelle had to build additional warehouses to accommodate the sudden spike in food supplies. The ICRC doubled the number of people its program accommodated at feeding centers.[27] The United States also vastly increased its aid after the program aired. In 1983, the United States had contributed $11 million to food aid in Africa, compared with $111 million contributed by the European Community. In 1984, before the Ethiopian famine became a major news story, the United States donated $32 million. Between November 1984, a few weeks after the report, and early 1987, the United States committed over $500 million to famine relief in Ethiopia and delivered over 800,000 tons of food, one-third of the total private and public disaster aid given to Ethiopia during this period.[28]

Britain witnessed what was arguably the most active public humanitarian giving. Leland embraced the famine narrative to promote public funding for humanitarian initiatives, but in Britain the Buerk-Amin report ignited a push for food aid that Reagan would likely have regarded as a more appropriate response than Leland's. Individual donations to private relief organizations skyrocketed in Britain during the so-called Band Aid phenomenon. Band Aid consisted of a series of massive fund-raising events organized by celebrity humanitarian and musician Bob Geldof.[29] Between April 1984 and September 1985, the British public donated close to £100 million to relief organizations, including £34 million directly to Band Aid. Five organizations grew rapidly during this period with an influx of income: the British Red Cross, Christian Aid, the Catholic Fund for Overseas Development, Oxfam, and Save the Children.[30]

In addition to driving up funding for humanitarian relief, the famine reports spurred U.S. politicians to get directly involved in the push for even more government resources to support famine relief. Jesse Jackson and Senator Edward Kennedy scurried to organize separate trips to Ethiopia to be a part of the famine relief story and raise awareness of the plight of starving Africans. But Reagan administration officials, ever vigilant to remain on the offensive in the discourse on U.S. famine relief, ensured that high-level administration officials were the first to visit the Horn in the wake of the report, and scrutinized Mengistu's policies.

One example of these policies was the government's highly controversial "resettlement" scheme. The government forcibly moved whole groups of people to more fertile areas in the southern part of the country from the famine zones in the north and west, where the land was severely denuded, to create collectivized-farming villages.[31] The United Nations and the United States supported Mengistu when he initially launched the program. Its basic premise was sound. But it turned out to be overambitious, ill-timed, and brutal. Mengistu initially proposed to relocate 1.5 million people, anticipating this number would eventually grow to 7 million. In drawing up his plans, Mengistu did not consult ecologists, agronomists, horticulturalists, economists, or anthropologists. Moreover, the government did not share resettlement plans with the settlers or the host populations. Instead, from the outset, the government carried out the resettlements whimsically and by fiat. When Leland's delegation met with Mengistu, he presented the resettlement scheme as a means to save lives. He conceded that it would not fully resolve the problem of chronic hunger.[32] The government may have been well intentioned, and some families did benefit from resettlement, but how the government executed the program exposed Mengistu's view of the food crisis as secondary to his military challenges. He was trying to survive as the TPLF and the EPLF gained strength and territory. But the Westerners who poured into Ethiopia as humanitarian workers and observers scrutinized his policies and weaknesses. As the famine relief initiative grew more politicized, Reagan labeled the resettlement program an unacceptable human rights violation.

Other famine relief initiatives were less controversial. The Relief and Rehabilitation Commission (RRC) was a liaison for Western relief agencies and governments seeking access to Ethiopia. Dawit Wolde Giorgis, the RRC's director, was Leland's and other foreign officials' principal government contact in Ethiopia. Leland often based his retorts to his colleagues' charges that Mengistu was ignoring the famine on his conversations with Dawit. The Derg established the RRC after the revolution. Derg officials were eager to prove the monarchy's complicity in the food crisis of 1973–74 and disregard for the people's needs, and part of the RRC's mandate was to document peasants' famine experiences in the northern provinces and Hararghe. RRC officials worked closely with Catholic Relief Services (CRS), an organization with a long history of involvement in Ethiopia. USAID channeled most U.S. "Food for Peace" aid through the CRS, in addition to UNICEF and CARE.[33] CRS had remained active in Ethiopia throughout the revolution and was the first to partner with the Ethiopian government. The partnership would have been stronger had Mengistu made famine relief a priority and had the military not soaked up national resources and Mengistu's attention. Still, Mengistu and the RRC mounted a significant, yet controversial and complicated, response to the famine.[34]

Ethiopia's civil wars posed an existential threat to Mengistu's regime and therefore were more pressing to him than the famine. To secure a military victory and hold onto power, he built Ethiopia's army, already the largest in Africa, into a colossus of three hundred thousand men. His return on this investment was a prolonged struggle with the TPLF and the EPLF. Mengistu had initial military success in the early 1980s, but this was followed by a string of military setbacks and, ultimately, failure toward the end of the decade. In the end, his massive, well-equipped army could not prevail against the EPLF's and the TPLF's well-organized guerrilla tactics. The rebels also possessed significantly higher morale and commitment to their struggle, which gave them an advantage over the federal soldiers.[35] But the rebels' military success came with high costs. Eritrea devolved into a veritable internally displaced persons' camp, and by 1984, more than half a million Eritreans had fled to Sudan.[36] Many Eritreans eventually returned to Eritrea and added to the population in EPLF-operated camps, which grew to nearly two hundred thousand people. The population of dispossessed precipitated a drop in agricultural production to close to half the normal level and dramatically worsened the existing food crisis.[37]

Even in the face of Mengistu's decisions to prioritize his military goals and hastily carry out his resettlement scheme, Leland avoided criticizing him. Not speaking ill of African governments had been a hallmark of black internationalism during the 1970s, but in the 1980s this practice would ultimately prove to be a political weakness for Leland. His argument that the U.S. government must be open to dialogue with Global South governments with which it had ideological differences, including Marxist Ethiopia, was far more effective. "A first step in increasing the United States response, both private and public," he said, "is to look at conditions and to talk with leaders of the Ethiopians and donor nations." He continually returned to the theme of dialogue throughout the decade, along with his conviction, shared among humanitarian relief organizations, that political neutrality must be maintained among relief workers, relief organizations, and donor nations during a humanitarian crisis. He outlined part of his position in a press statement his office released a week after the Buerk-Amin report aired on the BBC: "I have said repeatedly that political differences must be put aside to get to starving people. Private agencies need the support of a government to government structure. We should not castigate the political system espoused by the Ethiopian government or dwell on the inadequate Soviet response while people are dying."[38]

Leland's Republican colleagues would use his push for dialogue against him during congressional debates on sanctions and constructive engagement toward South Africa. Although issues and events in South Africa and Ethiopia at the time were distinct, the Cold War and political divisions within the United States joined them within a common debate. Leland would argue that apartheid in South Africa was a human rights issue and Ethiopia was humanitarian crisis. But his colleagues delineated Mengistu's policies and practices and held them up for comparison with South Africa's record.

In the meantime, Leland hoped to capitalize on the growing popularity of food aid for Ethiopia. In early November 1984 Leland's Hunger Committee announced that it would sponsor a congressional delegation to Ethiopia. He appreciated the Buerk-Amin report and the generous public responses to it. He saw it as a turning point for food aid. Leland understood the difference between hearing about a crisis and seeing it: "Knowing is not the same as seeing and feeling which happens when the camera brings us face to face with awful human devastation. Looking at a father holding a starving child or starving people kept from meager rations by a wall, gives the crisis a new urgency . . . and requires a new assessment of need."[39]

Assistant Secretary of State Chester Crocker and Peter McPherson, director of USAID, traveled in advance of Leland to Addis Ababa, where they met with Dawit Giorgis to discuss a comprehensive relief program to be spearheaded by the White House. Leland did not depart with his delegation to Addis Ababa until November 23. By then, Reagan had outflanked Leland and food aid advocates a second time with his pledge of fifty thousand tons of grain to go directly to the Ethiopian government, rather than channeling the grain to Western relief organizations through USAID. This pledge was in addition to the government's existing commitment it made a year earlier when Dawit met with McPherson and Crocker to provide direct and indirect food assistance. In all, the U.S. effort totaled $60 million in food aid.[40] With the United States providing large humanitarian relief packages, the question was no longer whether the United States should send significant humanitarian relief to Ethiopia. Still, for Leland and his colleagues the debate remained unsettled and the U.S. contribution remained insufficient to end the famine and help build Ethiopia's food security infrastructure to ensure the current famine would be its last.[41]

The fact remained that after the Buerk-Amin report and the waterfall of media coverage of the crisis in the Horn, the Reagan administration quickly pivoted to championing famine relief. Media-defined public moralizing did not easily move Reagan, however. His intransigence on apartheid in South Africa demonstrated this fact well. He had to consider the public responses to media-driven famine stories when he formulated his policies toward aid. He considered left-leaning members of Congress and the relatively generous public contributions to private relief organizations in Britain. The European Economic Community, the Soviet Union, and the United Nations had quickly established food aid programs for Ethiopia. The president did not want U.S. allies and adversaries to peg him as privileging Cold War politics over saving lives.[42] Officials in his administration understood the positive optics of the United States contributing humanitarian aid to Marxist Ethiopia, whose leader had made lambasting the United States and celebrating his alliance with the Soviet Union into a policy.

The Reagan administration seized the moral high ground and immediately tried to reshape the famine narrative. At the center of their highly political version was the Soviet Union ignoring Ethiopia's crisis while the United States floated above politics to address the needs of the suffering. McPherson debuted the administration's narrative when he announced the U.S. aid package. "The United States recognizes that the Ethiopian Government has become a Soviet ally," he explained to journalists. "But we say a hungry child knows no politics and cannot blame a child for what the government does."[43] McPherson was the first Reagan administration official to use the phrase "a hungry child knows no politics," but it originated with Bread for the World, a U.K.-based NGO, whose officials had used the line repeatedly. Reagan employed the phrase in a manner that made him appear to stand above politics as he approved food aid.[44] The slogan itself, however, was wholly political. Reagan claimed to look past ideological differences while he actively used humanitarianism to undermine Marxist regimes.

Much to Leland's chagrin, while the rise of Ethiopia in Western media coverage forced the Reagan administration into action, it did not provoke the Black Caucus to mount a sustained response. Leland regarded the tragedy of war, famine, and the Cold War for the Horn of Africa as an opportunity for African Americans to utilize the economic resources at their disposal and establish a model for political affairs and food aid in Africa from the outside. In editorials Leland urged African Americans in a humanist tone to change their relationship with Africa to one based on substance and knowledge rather than emotion and imaginings of the past. It was important to him that Americans take the lead, particularly African Americans, because of their economic and political strength. "We can start by being much better informed," he said of African American leadership in African affairs. "By aggressively seeking information on what is going on: war, famine, division. Then we must speak out, frankly and courageously, no matter where the problem originates. Although the problems are not simple and will not yield to simplistic answers, we must start somewhere, and African Americans must take the lead."[45] African Americans were the constituents who would keep Africa on the American political agenda. But they had to be informed to be able to do so. "We must establish ongoing dialogues with the peoples of Africa, and African American leaders, intellectuals and journalists must conduct their own fact-finding missions to Africa and keep the plight of these citizens before the world," Leland proclaimed. In this regard he held himself up as a model.[46]

Certainly many Black Caucus members supported Leland's initiatives and attended his hearings on hunger issues. But his staunchest supporters and partners in the fight for sustained U.S. aid for famine relief were his white colleagues. Black Caucus members rose in defense of Ethiopia when conservatives criticized Mengistu and his policies, and some participated in delegations to the Horn, but famine failed to emerge as a Black Caucus issue, even during Leland's term as Black Caucus chair. It was no match for the South African consensus. Therefore, Leland failed to transform food aid into a moral obligation or to galvanize African Americans to join his crusade. But Ethiopia was an example of how self-governing African countries fractured African Americans' opinions on African issues. Independence made Africa a far more complex continent. Rather than unravel the vast assortment of cultural, political, and religious dimensions in various countries, most African Americans engaged with ongoing white supremacy and resistance to it in southern Africa.[47]

Leland planned a trip to Ethiopia for November 1984 that he hoped would promote long-term U.S. support for the country rather than aid to meet its short-term needs. He also wanted to keep media attention on the crisis so that the president would be forced to act. "The most obvious requirement for addressing the difficulties in Africa," he said, "is long-term commitment."[48] The delegation was composed of eight members of Congress—William Gray, Gary Ackerman, Edolphus Towns, Marge Roukema, Bill Emerson, Thomas Foglietta, Peter Kostmayer, and Leland—and their staffs. Before departing, Gray called the president's response unacceptable. "NBC, CBS, and ABC have just caught up with the problem now; everybody is caught up [on] it," Gray said angrily. "For 18 months, people have been starving. If we had responded in 1983, the tragedy would not be of the magnitude that it is today." He accused the president of willfully remaining on the sidelines of the international response even though Reagan was aware of the magnitude of the problem. "The administration, even though now responding," he said, "failed to respond adequately for two years."[49]

The group's small size did not detract from making the trip a turning point for Republican members of the Hunger Committee, Roukema and Emerson, who initially opposed creating it. For that reason, Leland worked hard to ensure that Emerson joined the 1984 delegation.[50] It was Roukema's and Emerson's first exposure to extreme hunger and poverty, and they were deeply moved. After the trip Emerson went from being part of the committee's internal opposition to being a hunger relief devotee. Miranda Katsoyannis, the Hunger Committee's chief of staff and a member of the delegation, explained that "when the Republicans who went on the trip saw catastrophe for the first time in their lives, that's how some of the allies were made."[51]

From Addis Ababa, the group traveled to Assab, a small port town on the Red Sea coast in the province of Eritrea, to observe the off-loading of food aid. They then traveled overland along the route the unloaded aid would follow to feeding centers in Tigray, Wello, and Gamo-Gofa provinces. Their stop in Korem, two days after arriving in the country, provided the most talked-about event of their trip. The town had acquired some resonance with the U.S. public since Buerk and Amin's report a month earlier. To get to Korem, the group first flew to the city of Alamata, then endured a rough, ninety-minute bus ride to Korem. Days before they arrived, the federal soldiers had recaptured the town from the TPLF. Planes ferrying aid to Korem had been suspended, and the U.S. embassy warned of security threats. Leland decided to press ahead with the trip as planned. Chris Matthews, assistant to House Speaker Tip O'Neill and future host of a popular American television news program, wrote in an article in the *New Republic* soon after he returned from the trip that the treacherous terrain rivaled the fear the rebels inspired: "When our bus left open country, and began the 8,000-foot ascent, our fear of ambush was quickly nudged aside by a starker fear: that of the mountain itself. The road was unpaved; the hairpin turns had no guard rails; our driver was in a hurry. With each grind of the gears, I focused on the next heart-stopping turn, deciding each time whether to look down at the awesome drop below and count the number of tumbles I could imagine the bus taking before reaching the canyon below."[52] As their bus moved into town, people along the side of the road cheered, and a Land Rover, holding two young men wielding AK-47s, pulled alongside them as an escort. At the top of the plateau, long rows of government-built corrugated dwellings housed the "immobile," those who had starved to the point of incapacitation. Beyond these worst of cases, the "mobile" were housed in white military tents spread over an acre. As Matthews recalled, the air smelled like a butchery, "the kind where meat hangs for days, unrefrigerated, in the summer heat. Here, in Korem, there were no animals. Yet the smell of rotting meat was everywhere. The horror began to penetrate."[53]

Leland immediately connected with a group of children by improvising a game of call-and-response. "Mick-ey, Mick-ey," Leland shouted and pointed to himself. "Meek-key, Meek-key," the children shouted in answer. Then "Dis-co! Dis-co!" from Leland. "Dees-koo! Dees-koo!" the children yelled back toward Leland.[54] The scene Leland created astonished Congressman Gary Ackerman, Leland's close friend and colleague from New York. "It was something that we'll never, never forget," Ackerman told a journalist shortly after the delegation returned to the United States. "I'll always remember the smiles of the children at the camp."[55] "They had fun and I had fun," Leland said in a speech the following year. "[I hoped] that I had given them a happy moment in an otherwise unhappy time. We all need to remember that the hungry are not a faceless mass, but individual people who can laugh and joke with us, who need our loving attention."[56] Leland searched for scenes of life amid the suffering, he said later.

Ethiopia's famine attracted hundreds of foreigners to Addis Ababa. The city's pleasant atmosphere contrasted with common perceptions in the West of African cities. The city hosted the Organization of African Unity (OAU) headquarters and had good, relatively clean roads. The Hilton Hotel rested at the city's center, and, at least for the foreign community, it was generally regarded as one of the best-managed, most conveniently located Hiltons in the world. It remained overbooked throughout 1984.[57] On their final day in the country, the group met with Mengistu Haile-Mariam at Emperor Selassie's former palace. The emperor had built the grand château, surrounded by gardens, in 1955 as his main residence and named it Jubilee Palace. The Derg seized it during the revolution "on behalf of the people." Mengistu granted few Westerners an audience at the former palace, but this visit would be Leland's second. The group gathered around two parallel tables, with the Americans sitting opposite Mengistu's ministers. Mengistu entered and sat in the middle of his ministers. Leland opened with some brief remarks, then Mengistu embarked on a fifty-minute monologue, translated in a trembling voice by a visibly nervous older man. During much of his talk, Mengistu pushed the benefits of the resettlement scheme.

Leland was concerned more about the crisis's human dimension than the legal, ideological, and geopolitical aspects of it. On November 28, the day after his delegation returned to Washington, D.C., he held a press conference to describe what he had witnessed in Ethiopia. The fact was, he said, the enormity of the tragedy had drained him and left him feeling helpless.[58] "Never, ever, had I seen anything like this," he said. "It was so difficult to take, that I couldn't help but wonder 'why am I here?'"[59] The events during the trip and what he had seen changed him. "I don't know if I can convey what this has done to me as a human being," Leland told the journalists. "It was like going to the end of the earth, to the worst place I could imagine." He was struck, he said, "by the sea of humanity that was suffering so badly."[60] Alison, Leland's wife, described his state of mind upon his return to Washington and Houston after trips to the Horn as fraught with feelings of guilt and helplessness. "We would go into a grocery store," she remembers, "and he would be overwhelmed. Leland would see other children and he'd be overwhelmed." He believed, she said, in the significance of his work, and his failure to produce fast and palpable results frustrated him. "He couldn't reconcile the fact that he had a voice in Congress, this country has all the resources that it has to offer, and yet he couldn't fix this," Alison recalled.[61]

Although the trip had taken an emotional toll on Leland, it also affirmed his commitment to a U.S.-government-sponsored humanitarian initiative as the only truly viable way to end famine. U.S. food assistance to Ethiopia had grown to a historic level after a meager start in the spring of 1983. For the United States to support a broader European and U.S. combined initiative rather than spearhead its own was unacceptable. Leland wanted a major U.S. push to end the famine, not simply to provide for food relief. Evidently he was unaware of the direct talks between USAID and RRC officials for a large-scale U.S. initiative. Still, since the Buerk and Amin report aired, Leland had been optimistic about the potential for U.S. foreign assistance. Perhaps he thought Ethiopia's crisis was the last great famine. He considered the current program a stopgap measure to allow Ethiopian farmers to recover from the drought. It amounted to a pittance compared with what the United States might provide if pushed to do so. Leland decried the relatively low level of U.S. aid as a crime against morality and pressed the administration to utilize the Strategic Wheat Reserve to expand the U.S. initiative. "Each day when we were there," he said in January 1985, "and every day since then, more people, usually infants and children fell to the deadly combination of inadequate food and medical care."[62]

In December 1984, members of the delegation received an unexpected invitation from President Reagan to meet at the White House to update him on their experience in Ethiopia; a rare note of congeniality from the president toward a Democrat-dominated congressional group. But the gesture likely included a bit of strategy on the president's part to remain current on the Hunger Committee's humanitarian activities. Leland had made only one prior visit to the White House when the Black Caucus met with the president. Leland welcomed this second visit as an opportunity to call on the president to use the Strategic Wheat Reserve to buttress U.S. food aid to African countries. He also asked the president to reconsider his plan to encourage the private sector to take the lead in U.S. humanitarian relief efforts. Leland supported private-sector famine relief initiatives but did not see it as an either-or debate. He considered the private sector essential to the success of U.S. foreign assistance in Africa and elsewhere, a view he expressed to the president in a letter asking him to alert his Advisory Council on Private Sector Initiatives of ways its members might become involved in Ethiopia. Leland felt that the private sector, however, should complement and not replace the federal government's efforts. Reagan and Leland disagreed on these two points.

The meeting with the president planted the faintest hope that Reagan was open to making concessions on food aid for Ethiopia. "I was really happy, for the first time proud that President Reagan was our president," Leland said after the meeting. "He was far greater concerned than I had seen him on any issue dealing with human beings. That was a rare occasion, I might add."[63] Leland would not allow his favorable assessment to stand without a caveat. He said it was uncharacteristic of Reagan to be so amenable to humanitarian requests, and he reproached him for not meeting with the Black Caucus after its members sent numerous invitations. Leland went from expressing pride in Reagan to deep resentment toward him. He saw the slight toward the Black Caucus as a true reflection of the president's character. To ignore the Black Caucus, he said, was "past being just insensitive. It is an evil character who refuses to spend time with people who have a deep abiding concern about humanity when we are in severe jeopardy."[64]

Leland's case for U.S. food aid for the Horn of Africa remained compelling, so long as he used the "need" and "suffering" of the people to support it. But there were limits to humanitarian arguments. By mid-decade, Leland's famine narrative collided with an aggressive push by his conservative colleagues who were less willing than Leland to ignore Mengistu's actions for the sake of advancing the cause of U.S. international benevolence. Leland's failure to properly contextualize the food crisis and prescribe a comprehensive U.S. response, both political and humanitarian, opened space for the White House and Leland's Republican colleagues to deploy human rights to undercut his food aid campaign and, with some ingenuity, slow the Black Caucus's anti-apartheid initiatives.

Similar to the ways in which Buerk and Amin's documentary established the model for European and U.S. reports on famine in Africa, early in the U.S. humanitarian initiative, Republicans in Congress developed a narrative of humanitarian relief centered on the United States' singular magnanimity, human rights, and the general iniquity of Mengistu and his communist regime. The strength of this narrative, including the requisite duality of good and bad, U.S. and foreign, exposed how profoundly domestic politics and events in both countries shaped U.S.-Ethiopian relations and U.S. relations with Global South nations generally. Leland's narrative centered on the "suffering" and the U.S. obligation to respond. The emerging counternarrative centered on U.S. exceptionalism for having responded. "Looking back on the complex operation to import and distribute humanitarian relief in Ethiopia," Ambassador Robert Houdek, U.S. chargé d'affaires in Addis Ababa, said several decades later, "it was difficult to overstate how exceptional it was. International organizations coordinated in a Marxist-ruled nation that simultaneously fought several civil wars."[65]

Houdek concluded that the relief operation was an impressive display of U.S. moral and global leadership. Leland hoped that a compulsion to further this initiative with the goal to end hunger worldwide would accompany such an assessment. But in downplaying the famine's political dimensions Leland allowed the famine narrative to get away from him before he successfully employed it in his mission to end global hunger. In the United States the narrative evolved beyond famine as a natural disaster to center on U.S. exceptionalism, human rights abuses, and theft of humanitarian aid by the Mengistu regime. A subtheme emerged: the crisis of famine had been tackled through the exceptional generosity, moral superiority, and technical might of the United States and its people. By the winter of 1985, less than four months after the famine took center stage in the U.S. media, American politicians had begun to preface formal statements about food aid in Africa with a congratulatory statement on American generosity and moral authority.

Leland's goal to use U.S. resources and global leadership to end global hunger led him to distinguish between the Ethiopian regime's political ideologies and its ongoing humanitarian needs. For the wealthiest nation in the world to deny or debate whether to provide food aid to poor nations to score political points against the Soviet Union was immoral, he argued. "We should not castigate the political system espoused by the Ethiopian government or dwell on the inadequate Soviet response," Leland said, "while 6,500 people are dying of starvation every day."[66] These were the ingredients, Leland believed, for a humanist consensus on both sides of the political divide in the United States on food aid. U.S. humanitarian initiatives elicited a different and, for Leland, wholly unexpected political response. Much to Leland's chagrin, Republicans, and not a few Democrats, used Ethiopia's humanitarian crisis to make the case against communism and the Soviet Union, even as the Soviet Union reduced its role in African affairs.

USAID officials and Republicans in Congress elevated human rights in the discourse on humanitarian relief, and both sides celebrated the U.S. response to the famine. They projected an image of the United States leading the world with historic humanitarian action in Ethiopia, despite Mengistu's Marxist policies. The champions of this narrative presented U.S.

action in Ethiopia as part of its Cold War victory. When U.S. leaders spoke of the virtues of America's global reach, their words reflected U.S. Cold War political culture. The U.S. national security apparatus provided the basis for political analysis and ideological warfare.[67] The ideology trickled down from national security personnel to Congress and to the American people, though officials and politicians accepted and presented their strategies as non-ideological.[68]

It became a common feature of the U.S. response for government officials to announce new aid packages and increased funding for ongoing initiatives toward the Horn of Africa and to frame the news in a self-congratulatory fashion and include sharp rebukes of Mengistu, the Soviet Union, and communism. One example of this was the Reagan administration's response on October 31, 1984, to the Buerk-Amin report. White House spokesman Larry Speakes announced that the president had "taken a personal interest in the famine situation in Africa, particularly the current crisis in Ethiopia," and approved more funds for humanitarian relief.[69] As Speakes presented it, Reagan's reaction to Ethiopia's crisis did not rest with supporting humanitarian assistance. The president, without citing the Ethiopian regime's humanitarian work to date, criticized Mengistu for "paying little attention" to food needs and recommended that the Ethiopian president show "a more cooperative attitude" in getting help to his starving people. From the outset, as this example shows, the U.S. famine relief initiative was rooted in U.S. lawmakers' and policymakers' conception that aid should help celebrate the United States and denigrate Ethiopia. USAID's early involvement in Ethiopian famine relief offered an additional example of celebration and denigration. At the end of October 1984, Peter McPherson, USAID director, announced the U.S. government's pledge of $42 million to hunger relief in Africa, with $9 million slotted for Ethiopia. The United States also pledged $11.5 million to the ICRC's Africa program. McPherson praised the United States and chided the Soviet Union for its "callous indifference," despite the fact that the Soviets had pledged to send three hundred trucks, twelve planes, and twenty-four helicopters to distribute food to the feeding centers.[70] On a later occasion he would describe U.S. humanitarian assistance in Africa as arriving faster and remaining longer than that of any other donor nation or institution.[71]

U.S. politicians and government officials suggested that it was difficult to quantify the vastness of U.S. generosity. McPherson characterized the U.S. initiative as a product of its moral exceptionalism: "I believe the US, speaking generally of the drought, can be enormously proud of the leadership role and the bipartisan leadership role. I would quickly add we, the US citizens, and the United States have been viewed as clearly having a leadership role in the world."[72] Capitalism had so thoroughly prevailed over communism that capitalist nations were obliged to intervene and rescue the starving Ethiopians from the ravages of Marxist policies.

Leland did not anticipate this counternarrative on food aid would prove to be so compelling and persuasive. He had envisaged that images of the Ethiopian crisis would foster bipartisan agreements in Congress to help a starving people. He did not have an effective rebuttal for the counternarrative. He struggled to balance his advocacy for a stable humanitarian program and support for Ethiopian sovereignty, while he continued to try to distance himself from Mengistu's domestic policies, particularly after the Ethiopian leader restricted relief workers' mobility in the country. Leland encouraged his colleagues to appreciate the broader political and economic context of Mengistu's actions, but this argument was not convincing. Leland was more persuasive when he emphasized that it was imperative for relief workers to have unrestricted access to famine areas and therefore Western governments could not afford to ostracize the Ethiopian government. He also understood the challenges that relief workers' freedom of movement through Ethiopia's famine zones would pose for Mengistu's capacity to assert his authority amid the country's humanitarian, military, and economic crises. "It's an issue of sovereignty," Leland argued to journalists in February 1985. "It's the same as in Nigeria when the government froze out all outsiders to feed Biafrans. [But] my own plan is for the International Committee of the Red Cross to be allowed into northern Ethiopia from the South."[73] For most of his colleagues, however, even those not committed to U.S. food aid, the U.S. response to the Ethiopian crisis was a testament to the country's singular greatness and extraordinary generosity.

Soon after he returned from a tour of feeding centers and refugee camps in Sudan and Ethiopia, Senator Edward Kennedy criticized the Soviet Union for failing to consistently provide humanitarian assistance to Ethiopia, its Marxist ally in Africa, and continuing to provide military equipment: "This is something, quite frankly, that I think we have every right to take a sense of pride in, and we have every right to point out to the world community that it is the United States that is responding to this human crisis in a way that no other country in the world is responding to and with a sense of generosity exceeding what any other country is doing, and we ought to challenge both our friends and adversaries around the world who speak about the matters of human concern to demonstrate their willingness to join in this undertaking."[74]

Similarly, Congressman Howard Wolpe declared it "nothing short of miraculous to see the impact of the international relief assistance effort, particularly that of the American effort in not only Ethiopia but throughout the African continent."[75] Leland neither discounted nor contradicted U.S. exceptionalism. In fact, playing to notions of U.S. exceptionalism was key to the argument for U.S. humanitarian relief. He characterized the exceptional nature of the United States as lying in its outsized control over wealth and resources. These facts, not its moral standing in the world, obligated the United States to respond to crises, particularly in Africa. Leland said during a Hunger Committee meeting in July 1985, "I am proud of the fact that the American Government and the American people have, indeed, contributed more than any other donor nation in the world to this emergency." He customarily accompanied praise for the United States' benevolence by declaring its obligation to lead in humanitarian assistance. "While we have contributed more, and we have been most generous," he argued, "with our vast resources we can even be more generous."[76]

Republicans welcomed the focus on human rights in Ethiopia. For them, Ethiopia's crisis presented a perfect example of a Global South nation imploding from unworkable communist policies. The issue of human rights allowed Americans to define what America stood for in foreign relations. Human rights became tied to American identity.[77] In addition, claiming the mantle of the virtuous nation added no cost to the humanitarian relief budget and conveniently shifted critical gaze away from U.S. domestic crises. Mengistu's blustery anti-Americanism gave the right a straw man for anticommunism and the inefficacies of Soviet support for its Global South allies. It was less a government priority to deliver food aid to those in need in Ethiopia than to employ U.S. largesse to compel the Ethiopian government to account for exploiting the food aid to fight a civil war. "We think that starving people simply cannot be pawns," Senator Richard Lugar declared. "We are stating that consistently and, frankly, I expressed this quite forcefully to the Ethiopian Government."[78] Wolpe chided his colleagues for failing to scrutinize the human rights records of U.S. allies as thoroughly as they did Ethiopia's. "It seems to me that US human rights policy would be far more credible and effective," he said during a hearing, "if the Reagan administration was as strong and unequivocal in criticizing the countries that we support. Zaire and Chilé would be a good start."[79]

New York Republican congressman Gerald Solomon, who had visited Ethiopia with Leland in 1983, responded that human rights abuses and tyranny were at the root of the famine. Solomon stated that when politicians ignored the government's role in the crisis, they neglected the heart of the problem and focused instead on the symptoms. A true humanitarian approach to Ethiopia, Solomon argued, would involve eliminating "the vicious despotism that preys on innocent people, and consigns them to a lifetime—however abbreviated it may be—of starvation, disease, and degradation."[80] Though Solomon and Leland were deeply affected by what they had witnessed during the 1983 mission, they drew strikingly different conclusions from the experience. Their contrasting assessments reflected their conflicting ideologies. For Solomon, combating tyranny was on par with addressing famine, whereas Leland saw U.S. food aid as America's principal moral obligation, regardless of the domestic policies and ideologies of the countries in need. He did not dispute accusations of human rights violations by Mengistu's regime, but he separated critiques of the Ethiopian government's politics and policies from the moral imperative to provide food for those who lacked access to it.

Leland did receive support for his effort to disentangle Cold War politics from U.S. food aid from several members of the Black Caucus who were wary of their colleagues' Cold War triumphalism. Congressman George Crockett Jr., for example, echoed Leland's arguments. The Michigan Democrat and Black Caucus member was elected to replace Congressman Diggs in 1980. He was active in his own right on African affairs, particularly through his seat on the Foreign Affairs Committee and his annual seminars on American policy in Africa.[81] Crockett insisted that Cold War politics and moralism should not drive the debates on U.S. humanitarian assistance initiatives. He called on his colleagues to refocus on Ethiopia's food crisis and to resist the temptation to wage the Cold War through humanitarianism. "I thought we were calling a hearing here to discuss the famine in Ethiopia and not to put on trial the kind of government the people of Ethiopia might have decided they wanted," Crockett thundered. "I think it is unfortunate how we allow the East-West controversy to cloud our judgment when we come to deal with humanitarian problems."[82] Despite the strength of Crockett's argument, it went against the sense of moral superiority and exceptionalism that undergirded U.S. engagement in the world, particularly in the Global South.

Ethiopian officials tried to counter the U.S. humanitarian narrative and critiques of their government. Ethiopia's ongoing civil wars made it imperative that the federal government mount a rhetorical defense. Dawit Wolde Giorgis, head of the RRC, warned McPherson of the consequences of rhetorical attacks on Ethiopia and Mengistu during McPherson's visit to Ethiopia in November 1984. Dawit understood that members of Congress and USAID leveled their critiques expressly to hurt the regime and its Soviet sponsors. He and Mengistu recognized this link between higher levels of U.S. aid and greater rhetorical hostility toward the Ethiopian government. "American rhetoric, particularly from USAID," Dawit wrote, "was inflammatory in the extreme. I reminded the State Department, Congressmen, and Senators on various occasions that this only polarized relations and hindered relief efforts. I told them that the conservatives in the Reagan administration were playing into the hands of the hardliners in Addis—creating, in fact, an unintentional alliance between them."[83] Ethiopia lacked the political leverage to stifle accusations of malfeasance.

Mengistu repudiated U.S. politicians' and policymakers' accusations that his regime misused relief aid and committed human rights abuses. He also contended that relief organizations had benefited from Ethiopia's crisis. "In many countries, they started large fundraising campaigns in aid to Ethiopia," Mengistu told the pro-government *Ethiopian Herald* in March 1985. He accused American and European governments and relief organizations of demonstrably insufficient appreciation of the famine-based boon in prestige and, among relief organizations, donations that they enjoyed. "They used Ethiopia's name for this purpose. But I must say that we have not been the full beneficiary of that assistance, of that fund raising campaign which has been conducted in our name," he stated.[84] For Mengistu, famine relief provided a cover for international subversives and northern rebels, "terrorists, brigands and robbers," financed by "anti-Ethiopian forces."[85] Mengistu defended his handling of famine relief in this manner, reiterating the many obstacles that his country faced on its road to self-sufficiency and the fact that the famine was but one of those obstacles.

Mengistu denied that he tried to conceal the famine. He contended that hiding food crises had been the previous regime's tactic. By contrast, he claimed to have paid unprecedented attention to the situation in the north: "It is the fact that the people in the north had in the past been completely abandoned in terms of assistance that led the people, the Ethiopian revolutionaries and patriots, to rise against the previous regime that followed a policy of concealment. . . . Everything was done to ensure that the inhabitants of the area were cared for. It was, by the way, the revolution that revealed to the world the hidden hunger. The effort exerted to render assistance to them was tremendous."[86] Nonetheless, the number of Mengistu's critics in Washington grew during 1985 and 1986, and his image declined to the point of being a caricature of despotism in Africa. As the level of U.S. assistance to Ethiopia increased, so did condemnation of the Ethiopian regime's human rights practices and socialist policies. In dealing with these contradictions, Leland portrayed the limits of his Third World outlook with its call to support rather than criticize putative nonaligned regimes. His own position hamstrung him and exposed him to charges of hypocrisy as he increased his attacks on South Africa's apartheid regime.

U.S. criticism of Ethiopia did not necessarily weaken the Ethiopian regime's position in the international community, but for many foreign observers it affirmed preconceived notions of African political and economic ineptitude and moral degradation. Mengistu did mount a program to address the effects of famine in his country, but the fact that the assertions that he callously ignored the crisis easily rang true with so many speaks to the tenacity of colonial-era notions of African politics and political leaders. A palpable sense of moral exceptionalism fueled these narratives, compounded by evidence that the Soviet Union provided Ethiopia with planes and other military equipment rather than grain.

Reagan administration officials hoped to leverage humanitarian assistance to Ethiopia, whose regime Reagan labeled totalitarian, to gain support for U.S. aid to Nicaraguan rebels fighting a Central American regime the administration labeled totalitarian. The White House and members of Congress attached amendments to aid the Contras to popular legislation and budget proposals submitted by the opposition. Unpopular amendments had the potential to stall otherwise popular bills. In March 1985, the president proposed to Congress a $90 million food aid package for African countries. Republicans in Congress proposed $150 million, which pleased Democrats, but the Republicans quietly attempted to attach an amendment to provide funds for insurgents fighting against the Farabundo Martí National Liberation Front, a leftist guerrilla group in El Salvador, and the Contras in Nicaragua. Congressman Tip O'Neill denounced the president's tactics and accused him of holding food legislation hostage in order to get Congress to approve aid to the Contras. "It is a sad thing to say, but this administration has shown that it is ready to starve Africans so that it can kill Latin Americans," O'Neill said.[87] These critiques did not stop Reagan.

The bill languished in the Democrat-controlled House of Representatives without being voted on until Senator John Danforth, a Republican from Missouri, attached funds for African food aid to a bill subsidizing heating oil for American households that ultimately passed. When the president signed the bill, U.S. support for relief operations in Africa topped $235 million, with $11 million for relief operations in Ethiopia.[88] This level of aid was higher than that previously pledged by any nation to deal with the Ethiopian food crisis.[89] These were major victories for food aid advocates, and Leland intended to capitalize on them. The consensus on U.S. food aid for Africa helped normalize other foreign policy issues, from aid to the Contras in Nicaragua to constructive engagement in South Africa.

While Republican policymakers and lawmakers capitalized on the politics of famine relief, and civil war in Ethiopia continued to foment the food crisis, Leland tried to stay clear of both issues. He had wanted to stick to a simple, people-centered narrative of U.S. food aid for Africa in which the government altruistically allocated funds in cooperation with African governments and lives were saved. He hoped to establish an ongoing pipeline of assistance from the U.S. government. In May 1985, Leland met with Dawit Giorgis in Washington to discuss the U.S. role in Ethiopian development beyond the current food crisis. Leland envisaged long-term Ethiopian agricultural development with U.S. assistance. The two spoke about strategies for improving agricultural practices in Ethiopia and ways the Hunger Committee might assist the Ethiopian government toward that end.[90] Leland planned to introduce a bill in Congress to provide financial assistance to Ethiopia to boost its agricultural capacity. The bill did not materialize but plans for it speak to Leland's sense of the U.S. response to the Ethiopian famine as a first step in a longer journey toward African development. Leland's ambitions were theoretically sound, but he failed to account for the Ethiopian government's short- and long-term goals. Mengistu hoped to increase Ethiopia's agricultural capacity, but he was preoccupied with how to stop the EPLF's and the TPLF's progress.

Not long after the famine and government-sponsored food aid gained traction as major policy issues and held wide public attention, they faded. The crisis, it seemed, had grown too complicated. When Americans were bombarded by images of people starving in an exotic land due to an act of God, their sympathies were charged. The media held their fire on the war and the government's famine-sustaining policies. It is unlikely that if the media had presented the full dimensions of Ethiopia's crisis the United States and other governments would have been moved to carry out large-scale humanitarian relief initiatives. When stories of rebels raiding feeding centers and diverting aid and of Mengistu forcefully resettling northern peasants in the south reached U.S. viewers, they were crowded out by news of the rapidly escalating struggle against apartheid in South Africa, civil war in Nicaragua, and the intensifying civil war in Angola.[91]

The UN Food and Agricultural Organization and the U.S. Department of Agriculture estimated that the twenty African countries facing a food shortage collectively required 6.8 million metric tons of cereal grain from the 1984–85 growing season. The international entities that were cooperating to meet this need included the United States, Canada, the European Economic Community, the World Food Program, India, and China. The United States provided close to half the needed amount, with 3 metric tons at a cost of $1 billion, and an additional $156 million in nonfood relief.[92] On the heels of the apparently successful international relief effort, Leland called for the international community to partner with African governments to confront the causes of famine. With millions of Africans living on the margins of starvation, it was inevitable that food crises would erupt.

Leland wanted the United States to lead a multilateral African development effort. "The urgent task at hand," he wrote to his congressional colleagues in May 1986, "is to see that the donor community, African governments, and the private agencies better address the underlying causes of the famine, which was not caused by drought alone." Leland described an effort akin to a Marshall Plan for Africa, but he did not suggest an obligation among partnering governments and agencies to contribute to the effort. In his subtle campaign for African development, he sold the notion that the response to the 1983–85 famine had succeeded. The logical next step was to ensure that these crises would not happen again. He wrote to his colleagues using language that spoke to the supposed American ethos of personal responsibility: "Much can be done to help people help themselves improve food security, increase crop production, raise their incomes, improve their health standards, fight desertification and environmental decline to avert famine in the future."[93] By the mid-1980s, largely through Leland's efforts, humanitarian relief had secured an elevated status in U.S. politics, but not to the extent of shifting the paradigm in U.S. policies toward Global South nations, let alone adopting Leland's goal to end hunger in the world.

The reflexive nature of humanitarian action increased after the Cold War when the United Nations and NGOs assumed oversight of human rights. They were no longer national rights. Human rights violations became the justification for calls for humanitarian intervention and evolved to be defined primarily as the use of military force rather than food aid and medical assistance, as was the case in the 1990s.[94] Thus the humanitarian action toward the Nigerian Civil War in the late 1960s, Cambodia in 1978, and continually in Ethiopia since the late 1960s differed in significant ways from international interventions in Somalia's warring factions during the 1990s.[95] As relief organizations became more involved in crises, many of their officials examined the causes of and enduring solutions for them. Many turned to development rather than short-term emergency aid. The changes in Leland's posture toward aid mirror those of the broader humanitarian and NGO community.

This period was followed by more aggressive efforts to tackle the root causes of humanitarian crises. Humanitarian relief organizations came to view traditional humanitarian relief—sending food parcels and blankets and granting asylum to refugees—as problematic for its singular focus on immediate needs and the absence of concern for human rights.[96] Leland's brand of humanitarian action came to be seen as merely acting in the face of tragedy while avoiding the far riskier commitment of addressing the roots of a crisis.[97] Ironically, this position justified the use of military intervention to defend human rights goals, particularly by the United Nations. These were among the significant differences between the definition of humanitarianism in the 1980s and 1990s. In the 1980s, international organizations sought to save lives in the short term. In the following decade, they pursued longer-term goals through military action to protect human rights.

As the major tenets of humanitarianism changed, South Africa moved to the center of the international debate on human rights and minority rule in Africa. The shift in support of democracy in South Africa evolved in parallel with the expanding U.S. humanitarian initiative for the Horn of Africa. Reagan had all but ignored African affairs, allowing Leland and other progressives in Congress to lead the White House in shaping other areas of foreign policy toward nations on the continent. U.S. disengagement from South Africa, which accelerated between 1984 and 1987, provided an opportunity for U.S. leaders to claim moral authority. Yet the general U.S. population's embrace of anti-apartheidism, a defining position of the Third World movement, materialized only after debates and protests led largely by former Black Power radicals in Congress. Anti-apartheidism in Congress challenged the viability of anticommunism as foreign policy. Not surprisingly, then, Ethiopia entered congressional debates on South Africa as conservative policymakers and politicians sought to highlight liberal opposition to South Africa's staunchly anticommunist and U.S.-allied white-minority regime while simultaneously supporting dialogue with Mengistu, an avowed Marxist and Soviet ally. Caught squarely in the conservative crosshairs were members of the Congressional Black Caucus. Indeed, the mid- to late 1980s, as seen through U.S. involvement in Africa, marked the high point of African Americans' political effectiveness as an ethnic bloc in foreign affairs.[98] African American members of Congress not only effectively forced changes in U.S. foreign policy toward African countries but continued to be essential to the general debates on anticommunism that defined the winding down of the Cold War.

Chapter 4

Activists on the Inside

The Black Caucus Battles White Rule and U.S. Anticommunism in Southern Africa

I believe you can be part of the solution to the problems faced by our brethren in Africa. I think that you can and must for humanitarian reasons certainly, but also for very selfish reasons. I am convinced that the fate of African Americans in this country is very closely tied to the fate of the people of the nations of Africa.

—Mickey Leland, 1989

During the Ninety-Ninth Congress (1985–87), the Black Caucus, with Mickey Leland as its chairman, was the most powerful African American political collective on foreign policy in U.S. history. The 1980s marked the first time that activism in response to the grand civil and human rights issues of the day—including apartheid in South Africa—emanated from a sizable cohort of African Americans inside Congress. Non–African American organizations were an essential component of this campaign, particularly the American Committee on Africa, the Interfaith Center on Corporate Responsibility, and the American Friends Services Committee. Although the twenty-one African American representatives in Congress were fewer in number than during the preceding session, an unprecedented number of them now held leadership positions. South Africa was their foreign policy priority for a variety of reasons, not least of which was that the ruling National Party modeled apartheid on post-Reconstruction segregationist laws and practices in the United States and that the United States was South Africa's most important political and economic partner.[1]

As part of the Congressional Black Caucus's initiatives to undermine the relationship between South Africa and the United States, Leland helped coordinate the bills Black Caucus members sent to the House of Representatives to impose economic sanctions on South Africa. His office also investigated U.S. corporate investments in South Africa and developed a disinvestment strategy. He remained largely out of the media spotlight during the buildup to the vote on sanctions legislation, but his work on disinvestment helped enforce existing sanctions and strengthened the case for broader, more comprehensive restrictions. Ronald Dellums and William Gray were the most public anti-apartheid lawmakers, but they remained key behind-the-scenes coordinators of sanctions legislation, while being the main faces of the movement within Congress. As head of the House Budget Committee, Congressman Gray held the most powerful position among Black Caucus members. Dellums maintained the highest political profile and was the most politically savvy among Black Caucus members. He skillfully navigated a series of complex procedures en route to Congress passing the first piece of legislation that imposed comprehensive sanctions on South Africa.

Dellums's sweeping anti-apartheid bill that passed in the House of Representatives was the culmination of decades of activism to end U.S. government support of South Africa's white-minority government. African Americans constituted the core of this movement in the United States. Prominent leaders included Martin Luther King Jr. and members of the American Committee on Africa (ACOA).[2] The ACOA, King, and Malcolm X, among others, defined conditions in South Africa as similar and related to those of African Americans in the United States. But the fight against apartheid in South Africa was international, and it grew into the largest and most successful political dissent campaign of the 1980s. The internal and external struggles against South Africa's system of apartheid were part of one broad transnational and international campaign.[3]

The anti-apartheid movement within South Africa provided a platform and global network for activism around the world. As a global phenomenon, the anti-apartheid movement conditioned the U.S. trend toward anti-racism at home and abroad. Post–World War II radical internationalism sets the anti-apartheid movement in an even broader context, including labor movements, solidarity movements, student movements, women's movements, and peace and green movements.[4] Many activists involved in decolonization, African and Asian nationalism, the international student movements of the 1960s, and the domestic and international anti–Vietnam War protests were also involved in the anti-apartheid movement.[5] Britain had the oldest international anti-apartheid movement organization, the International Defence and Aid Fund, formed in 1956 to provide legal support for individuals in South Africa prosecuted for violating apartheid laws and to support the families of political prisoners. The protest movement followed in 1959 with a small group of South African expatriates and their British supporters and grew to a mass movement that peaked in the mid-1980s, as Prime Minister Margaret Thatcher's policies further motivated anti-apartheid organizations to take action.[6] By 1990, more than 184 groups had become affiliated with the British Anti-Apartheid Movement.[7]

Anti-apartheid activists inside and outside South Africa targeted South Africa's economy, primarily through sanctions, disinvestment, and strikes. Well before Western Europe and the United States officially turned against apartheid, the domestic campaign to fundamentally change the country centered on its economy. For two decades after the National Party officially mandated apartheid the law of the land, South Africa had a strong economy. The country had a thriving gold industry, productive local manufacturing, and an abundance of cheap, black laborers who possessed neither the legal recourse nor the capacity to negotiate the terms of their employment. South Africa's burgeoning economy required an increasing supply of skilled African laborers. African high school enrollment expanded fivefold between 1965 and 1975 as the industrial economy sought more educated labor. Black students continued to be subjected to inferior curriculum, inferior job opportunities, and limited space for legal political expression. Rapid urbanization and the expansion of education were the seeds of apartheid's unraveling, as African urban culture and an increasingly sophisticated political leadership could not be contained by apartheid laws.[8]

External pressure combined with slow but steady internal concessions from the South African government. South African prime minister P. W. Botha, who took office in 1978, was keenly aware of the power of political messaging, as Cold War politics grew increasingly marginal and the world paid ever more attention to events in his country. In 1979, the government legalized African trade unions and allowed Africans to reside in urban areas. Still, unrest intensified. In 1984, his government abolished the office of prime minister and replaced it with an executive presidency, his title changed, and he held that office until 1989. The new constitution that created the presidency in 1983 also established two new houses of parliament, a House of Representatives for Coloureds and a House of Delegates for Indians. But the racially distinct bodies had jurisdiction over their respective communities. Botha clearly intended for this Tricameral Parliament to foreclose on political alliances between Indian, Coloured, and black political leaders. Actual power remained in the white chamber. It was a shrewd move aimed at signaling to international critics that the white-minority regime was capable of reform and appealing to blacks to exercise patience. The following year, parliament granted black South Africans the right to form legal trade unions and lifted restrictions on managerial positions in the mining sector previously reserved for whites.

However, Botha's reforms failed to stem the tide of activism because they did not do away with the system of apartheid. If anything, these measures fanned the flames of black resistance. Blacks flocked to the trade unions and as a result, according to a CIA report, unions grew increasingly militant and demanded more concessions from the government and business community.[9] The United Democratic Front (UDF), a nonracial alliance of workers, religious groups, students, and civic organization, came together in 1983 to challenge Botha's superficial political reforms. By the mid-1980s, South Africa was on the precipice of revolution. Students, journalists, black trade unionists, and guerrilla movements prepared for the overthrow of the white-minority government. Large-scale popular protest augured well for a successful rebellion.[10] On July 20, 1985, the government declared an indefinite state of emergency throughout large parts of the country, for the first time since the Sharpeville massacre in 1960. A year later, on June 12, 1986, President P. W. Botha declared a national state of emergency. The government placed the entire country under martial law.

The nature of the resistance to the apartheid state that began in 1985 was different from that of preceding years. For example, black activists had sustained myriad forms of civil unrest, protest, and sabotage throughout the country that began in the Vaal townships south of Johannesburg, where 450 people were killed during rioting that began on September 3, 1984. The rioting quickly spread to other townships around Johannesburg, the western and northwestern Cape, and Durban. Perhaps government officials could not conceive of another option, but the state of emergency exposed the government's weak hand to urban activists and PAC and ANC freedom fighters. Government officials intended the declaration to restore enough order in the townships so as to demonstrate to whites and their European and U.S. allies that their "reforms" were yielding success. But rioting increased and the death count went up daily. With each black leader that the government arrested, the possibility that activists would abandon the tactic of civil unrest to join apartheid leaders at a bargaining table was further diminished. Bishop Desmond Tutu assessed the weak hand the government had dealt itself: "They are not in control of the situation, and they do not know where they are going, which is a very dangerous state of affairs. If they lift the state of emergency, it will seem as if they are giving in to pressure."[11] Two elements converged in this new phase of the black resistance movement: growing confidence and defiance among Africans in the townships, and a crisis of confidence in the white community.[12]

The official state of emergency gave South Africa's police and military nearly unlimited power to search and seize property in the townships, to make arrests without formal charges, and to hold individuals indefinitely without access to legal representation. The decree limited African mobility in designated areas and placed urban residents under a curfew. But these tactics were met with violent protests that made the government obsolete in the townships. In addition, the schools were virtually inoperable, and local governments could not collect garbage. Many black local officials whom the government sponsored and relied upon abdicated, fearing for their lives.[13] In 1986, the government finally abolished the pass system. Meanwhile, COSATU and the UDF offered democratic, peaceful alternatives. The South African regime lost its ability to persuasively justify its policies. Ten years after the Soweto uprising, the South African government's violence attracted attention from governments around the world and widepsread condemnation.

The U.S. Congress was unique among Western government bodies in its response to the events in South Africa. While other governments responded to public pressure for action against repression in South Africa, some members of Congress were critical of the anti-apartheid movement. Others viewed themselves as part of the international fight against white supremacy. Black Caucus members targeted the financial relationship between the United States and South Africa, arguing that U.S. investments subsidized South African oppression.

There had long been concern within the U.S. State Department that African American interest in the movement against apartheid within South Africa carried with it the potential to fan the flames of dissent within the

United States. In 1964, en route to accept the Nobel Peace Prize in Oslo, Norway, the Reverend Martin Luther King Jr. spoke of sanctions as a moral duty:

> It is in this situation, with the great mass of South Africans denied their humanity, their dignity, denied opportunity, denied all human rights; it is in this situation, with many of the bravest and best South Africans serving long years in prison, with some already executed; in this situation, we in America and Britain have a unique responsibility. For it is we, through our investments, through our Governments' failure to act decisively, who are guilty of bolstering up the South African tyranny. Our responsibility presents us with a unique opportunity. We can join in the form of non-violent action that could bring freedom and justice to South Africa—the action African leaders have appealed for—in a massive movement for economic sanctions.[14]

In a 1978 National Security Council memorandum, policymakers considered the consequences of an alliance between African states opposed to apartheid and African American activists protesting U.S. policy toward South Africa. "These factors taken together," the report read, "may provide a basis for joint actions of a concrete nature by the African nationalist movement and the US black community."[15] The National Security Council feared "attempts to establish a permanent black lobby in Congress including activist leftist radical groups and black legislators; the reemergence of pan-African ideals; resumption of protest marches recalling the days of Martin Luther King Jr.; [and] renewal of the extremist national idea of establishing an 'African Republic' on American soil."[16]

These warnings of the perils of African nation-building for the United States were misplaced, but the report was accurate regarding a pan-Africanist resurgence in the United States and the fact that black legislators, if only a small group among them, would help lead that cause. African American pan-Africanism predated and would continue long after the high point of the anti-apartheid movement of the late 1970s and 1980s. But the anti-apartheid movement as it evolved in the United States came in the wake of Black Power and the Black Arts Movement, and the rise of African American electoral influence sparked multifarious expressions of identification with Africa, from popular culture to politics, grassroots organizations, the arts, and children's names. African American leaders easily drew political, ideological, and material connections between the struggles for racial justice in South Africa and the United States. This strategy of solidarity successfully positioned African American activists at the heart of the U.S. anti-apartheid movement. African American lawmakers were united in their opposition to apartheid and the Reagan administration's inaction toward undermining it. They focused specifically on Reagan's policy of constructive engagement. Apartheid formed the bedrock of the African consensus among African Americans on U.S. foreign policy. But their hyperattention to battling apartheid in South Africa turned the country into an entity larger than the continent itself. South Africa became Africa or, at least, symbolic for all of Africa in many circles, which foreclosed drawing sustained attention to other issues and events elsewhere on the continent. Rallying around South Africa, however, provided African American lawmakers with the focus and unity to bring a sufficient number of their white colleagues into their cause.

Black lawmakers' tactics in the anti-apartheid movement straddled formal and informal arenas and continued Congressman Diggs's strategy of a decade earlier to build coalitions within the community and across international borders, use civil disobedience tactics, and introduce anti-apartheid legislation.[17] The Black Caucus's use of protests, boycotts, sit-ins, picketing, coalition building, and formal styles of political influence reflected the black radical political tradition.[18] Black Caucus members worked closely with grassroots and registered lobbying organizations, particularly TransAfrica and the Free South Africa Movement, groups they had helped found. Ronald Dellums and William Gray, Leland's close partners in the caucus, along with Washington, D.C., congressman Walter Fauntroy, were deeply involved in crafting legislation and orchestrating public protests that would ultimately bring the United States into a position of global leadership in the fight against apartheid in South Africa. They did not merely oppose apartheid in South Africa; they purposefully sought to dismantle all economic and political links that enabled the white supremacist regime.[19]

African American lawmakers understood that their presence in Congress alone was not enough to bring fundamental change to domestic and foreign policies. There were many routes to shaping U.S. foreign policy, and African American lawmakers had little access to them. The Senate lacked a single African American member. Without solid allies in the Senate, any legislation African American lawmakers managed to get passed in the

House would be blocked in the Senate. Coalitions shaped political narratives. Aware of their limited political capital, Black Caucus members had established the Free South Africa Movement (FSAM) in 1984. African Americans' political clout contributed to the tremendous success of TransAfrica and the FSAM in galvanizing support for the push for U.S. sanctions against South Africa and for overall changes to U.S. policies toward southern Africa.

The Free South Africa Movement was the most public manifestation of the anti-apartheid alliance in the United States, and the movement exhibited the most explicit return to 1960s-style demonstrations, marches, and police arrests. On Wednesday, November 21, 1984, the evening before Thanksgiving, Bernardus G. Fourie, South Africa's ambassador to the United States, welcomed several high-profile individuals to the South African embassy to discuss U.S.-South African ties: TransAfrica director Randall Robinson; Congressman Walter Fauntroy; Mary Frances Berry, a member of the U.S. Civil Rights Commission; and Eleanor Holmes Norton, a Georgetown law professor and former Carter administration official. They spoke with the ambassador for forty minutes on a range of issues, including the South African government's treatment of protestors, its exclusion of blacks from parliament, and apartheid more generally. Finally, they presented the ambassador with an ultimatum and refused to vacate the office until he accepted it. Among their demands was that South Africa's government release all political prisoners and immediately abolish apartheid. In coordination with the meeting inside the ambassador's office, TransAfrica staffers organized approximately fifty demonstrators outside the embassy chanting, among other slogans: "Freedom yes! Apartheid no!"; "The people united will never be defeated!"; "Free Nelson Mandela!" As Mary Frances Berry recalled, "Ambassador Fourie looked out the window and seemed astounded. He couldn't believe what was happening. He looked at Walter Fauntroy to ask whether, as a member of Congress, he would help to quell the protest. But Fauntroy responded that he was present because he had devoted his life to racial justice, and that cause had brought our group there."[20] Police arrived and arrested Robinson, Berry, and Fauntroy just after Norton left the room to brief the international press. After one night in jail, the activists announced the launch of the Free South Africa Movement.[21]

Civil rights leader Jesse Jackson's two presidential campaigns, in 1984 and 1988, were extremely important to the U.S. movement for sanctions against South Africa. He made anti-apartheid central to his campaigns, and as he traveled the country and made media appearances he spoke compellingly against the white-minority regime and Reagan's support of it. He turned opposition to apartheid into a mainstream political position. His campaigns made it easier for Black Caucus members to make their case for sanctions legislation. No presidential candidate prior to Jackson had prominently featured African affairs in his or her political platform or consistently spoke out against apartheid in South Africa.

On July 18, 1984, during the Democratic National Convention in San Francisco, Jackson delivered a powerful speech that addressed the relationship between U.S. foreign policies toward the Global South and the legitimacy of U.S. claims to moral authority. He referenced major Global South hot-spots and gestured toward his embrace of Third World solidarity. From the convention stage he preached of America's moral failings in the Global South. "Our nation at its worst, at its worst," Jackson preached from the stage, "will mine the harbors of Nicaragua; at its worst will try to overthrow their government, at its worst will cut aid to American education and increase the aid to El Salvador; at its worst, our nation will have partnership with South Africa. That is a moral disgrace. It is a moral disgrace! It is a moral disgrace! [Applause.] We look at Africa. We cannot just focus on Apartheid in southern Africa. We must fight for trade with Africa, and not just aid to Africa. We cannot stand idly by and say we will not relate to Nicaragua unless they have elections there, and then embrace military regimes in Africa overthrowing democratic governments in Nigeria and Liberia and Ghana. We must fight for democracy all around the world and play the game by one set of rules."[22] Four years later, at the Democratic National Convention in Atlanta, Jackson delivered a speech that even more directly called for policy changes in the U.S. approach to Africa. He demanded a complete reorientation of U.S. foreign policy: "We have already agreed as Democrats to declare South Africa to be a terrorist state. But don't just stop there. Get South Africa out of Angola; free Namibia; support the Frontline States. We must have a new humane-human rights consistent policy in Africa."[23]

Jackson's attack on President Reagan's policies was striking for a U.S. candidate for president during the Cold War. He presented a short blueprint for what was possible in a U.S. foreign policy based on democracy and human rights. His implicit statement, one of great significance, was that Africa mattered and how the United States behaved toward African nations mattered. He was a candidate for president, but his vision for the Global South was a Third World and black radical vision, certainly not a product of the American political tradition. He placed South Africa and apartheid beyond the pale. After Jackson's campaign, even conservatives in the United States found it nearly impossible to defend South Africa's policies without facing harsh criticism. Diggs, Dellums, and the Black Caucus elevated South Africa to a legitimate legislative issue, and Jackson made anti-apartheid a mainstream political issue.

For six years, President Reagan was the colossus that obstructed the path to reforming U.S. foreign policy toward South Africa. Before Reagan entered the White House, Chester Crocker's assessment of the former California governor's knowledge of Africa was less than flattering. "All Reagan knows about southern African is that he's on the side of the whites," Crocker is reported to have said.[24] In addition to white rule, it also mattered to Reagan that South Africa was purportedly anticommunist. During his first term, he avoided the issue of South African apartheid. He wanted to treat it as a domestic issue for South African leaders to resolve on their own terms. "South Africans certainly don't need us to tell them how to resolve their race problems," he declared soon after the 1980 election.[25] He expressed a similar sentiment during an interview with television news anchor Walter Cronkite in March 1981. "Can we abandon a country that has stood beside us in every war we've ever fought, a country that is strategically essential to the Free World in its production of minerals we all must have and so forth?" the president asked rhetorically. "I just feel that if we're going to sit down at a table and negotiate with the Russians," the president continued, "surely we can keep the door open and continue to negotiate with a friendly nation like South Africa."[26] Reagan's words to Cronkite betrayed a willful ignorance of South Africa. The South African anticommunism that Reagan took for granted targeted black resistance to the apartheid state rather than the socioeconomic system that Cuba and the Soviet Union championed and Reagan feared. Moreover, he overstated South Africa's history of support for U.S. interests. The National Party was pro-Nazi during World War II and actively opposed South Africa's participation in the war. "Friendly," moreover, was by no means a debatable adjective for South Africa and how it treated its nonwhite inhabitants. Anti-apartheid activists benefited from the fact that Reagan's imperative to ignore human rights and the political shortcomings of U.S. allies out of Cold War pragmatism eased during his second term, in large part because East-West ideological and economic tensions had waned.[27] But during his first term, anticommunism formed the core of his foreign policies toward Global South nations.

The president refused to alter his position, even as the Washington political establishment and the U.S. public coalesced against apartheid in South Africa. Leland believed that when Reagan expressed concern for events in South Africa, he was being insincere. Reagan had no desire to let African affairs tie up his foreign policy. Generally, he did not want Africa to distract from his broader foreign policy centered on Latin America, Eastern Europe, and the Soviet Union. Anti-apartheid activists continually highlighted the evident double standard in Reagan's stance on human rights in Eastern Europe and South Africa. The president frequently celebrated the "courageous" fight waged by those who "have been betrayed by their own governments," citing as a prime example the brave and vibrant opposition to Poland's communist government. "How can [the Polish government and its allies] possibly justify using naked force to crush a people who ask for nothing more than the right to lead their own lives in freedom and dignity? Brute force may intimidate, but it cannot form the basis of an enduring society," the president stated in an address from the Oval Office in December 1981. He went on to state emphatically and unequivocally that if the Polish government remained on its current course, the United States would respond. "Make no mistake," Reagan warned, "their crime will cost them dearly in their future dealings with America and free people everywhere." He proposed a political, economic, and humanitarian answer to Polish repression. He repeated his charges against the Polish government in an address the following year.[28]

Black Caucus members used President Reagan's strong rhetoric against the Polish government's record on human rights to highlight his political inconsistencies and encouraged him to view the situation in South Africa as he had that in Poland. Leland and a few of his colleagues wrote a letter to Reagan in July 1983 demanding greater consistency on human rights from his administration; it stated in part, "We urge you to stand as clearly for human rights in South Africa as you have in Poland, and to review US policy towards South Africa to reflect more clearly the determination of our people to effect basic democratic changes by the South African government."[29]

The Free South Africa Movement held daily demonstrations in front of the South African embassy in November 1985 that attracted political, labor, and religious leaders. Congressmen Ronald Dellums and Charles Hayes protested in front of the embassy and were among the first members of Congress to be arrested protesting against apartheid in South Africa. Hayes served the Chicago district formerly represented by Harold Washington before Washington became Chicago's first African American mayor in 1983. Hayes had been a union organizer and worked closely with Dr. Martin Luther King Jr. and the Southern Christian Leadership Conference during the 1960s.

Randall Robinson wanted to make it publicly known that the arrests at the South African embassy were not the start of a new movement but, rather, an extension of centuries-old African American involvement with Africa. "The Free South Africa Movement," he said, "is an expression of a black American interest in and concern about Africa that is as old as our presence on this continent."[30] What was new was African Americans had a strong influence on the anti-apartheid narrative. He presented the Free South Africa Movement's goals as threefold: gain press coverage in the United States to educate the public on South Africa; dramatically change U.S. policies toward South Africa; and use changes in U.S. policy to influence other Western countries' policies toward South Africa.[31] Robinson was confident that changes in South Africa and in U.S. policies were inevitable: "You have variables that come together in combination to make the force for change simply irresistible and have a lot to do with the continued development of urban military capacity on the part of the African National Congress, the continued growth and political strength of black labor unions in South Africa; the continued deepening of consciousness and activity of young people throughout South Africa, all coupled with increased pressure from without." Robinson pointed to the factors previously discussed as fueling the imminence of apartheid's fall: "When these come together in a kind of requisite chemistry, then you will see South Africa fundamentally changed. One can't say with any preciseness when that will happen. I'm confident having said that that we will see change in the foreseeable future. We are closer to it now than we have ever been."[32] Together, the Free South Africa Movement, TransAfrica, and the Black Caucus vowed to continue their demonstrations until Congress passed a bill to impose comprehensive sanctions on South Africa. Anti-apartheid protests from late 1984 through 1986 commanded more public attention than any others in the history of the anti-apartheid movement.[33] Local activists and university student organizations around the country protested, rallied, and launched disinvestment

Figure 7. Randall Robinson, Rosa Parks, and Mickey Leland protesting in front of the South African embassy, Washington, D.C., 1985. *Washington Post.* Getty Images.

campaigns to garner media attention for apartheid and U.S. relations with the apartheid regime.

Activists targeted the Reagan administration's constructive engagement policy as a cynical ploy at best and evil at worst.[34] They sought to replace constructive engagement with comprehensive sanctions. Chester Crocker developed constructive engagement as a medium by which South Africa could move toward political reforms. Gradually, according to this plan, state-driven change would protect U.S. investments. Anti-apartheid activists argued that the policy defined a goal for U.S.-South African relations in ways that avoided forcing or providing specific guidelines for South Africa to enact actual economic or political reforms. Administration officials wanted to blunt criticism and forestall proposals from the Democrat-controlled Congress that might economically and politically hurt the South African government.

The Black Caucus's goal was to cut economic ties between the United States and South Africa. Members criticized financial transactions between the two countries, calling them subsidies for white-minority rule and the repression of South Africa's black majority that, therefore, marked the United States as complicit in perpetuating South Africa's racist system.[35] Leland helped lead the attack on U.S. corporate investment in South Africa, while he pressed U.S. humanitarian relief and sanctions against South Africa specifically as altruistic initiatives. However, partnering with South Africa on humanitarian relief tainted U.S. moral authority. Leland had recently learned that the U.S. government had contracted with South African vessels to transport a portion of U.S. food aid to African ports. The discovery disturbed him, primarily because it integrated South Africa directly into U.S. humanitarian initiatives and, consequently, normalized it. Worse still, South Africa stood to benefit financially from its partnership with the United States. "I find it offensive that the humanitarian assistance offered by our great nation could be marred by leasing transport ships from a government which has demonstrated no humanity and decency in the treatment of the overwhelming majority of its people," Leland stated.[36]

When he learned that it was legal for U.S. corporations and nonprofit organizations to work with the South African government, Leland decided to change those laws, even if doing so compromised U.S. humanitarian relief.[37] In the spring of 1985, Leland submitted legislation to Congress that would bar USAID from leasing South African ships for humanitarian relief. "It is morally reprehensible for the United States—the major donor to the World Food Program—to use South African vessels to transport any amount of food aid when other vessels are available,"[38] he said from the House floor in an attempt to persuade his colleagues to support his cause. His bill failed to make it to the full House for a vote; still, his effort remains worth noting because it was part of the coterie of tactics of organizing, lobbying, and agitating to shift U.S. discourse on South Africa toward human rights and democracy.

Forging ties with leaders in the Frontline States—Zimbabwe, Mozambique, Namibia, Botswana, and Angola—was another component of the Black Caucus strategy. In August 1986, Leland asked President Robert Mugabe of Zimbabwe to participate in an open discussion with other heads of the Frontline States on ways the Black Caucus might assist in ensuring their strength and stability as they contributed to the fight against white-minority rule. "The 30 million Black people in the United States of America are demonstrating an expanding interest in the peoples of Africa," Leland wrote. "To many of us, this is a welcome and long overdue development. The emergence of the Free South Africa Movement, the leadership of many

Blacks in the recent drought relief efforts and the Black community's valiant efforts to prevent the sending of US military assistance to UNITA are the more visible examples of this enhanced interest."[39] The South African government aided the National Union for the Total Independence of Angola (UNITA; União Nacional para a Independência Total de Angola) to destabilize Angola's ruling Popular Movement for the Liberation of Angola (MPLA; Movimento Popular de Libertação de Angola). Considered in its political and historical context, Leland's letter to Mugabe represented a push for racial solidarity and a commitment to international human rights but also a sense of Third World spirit.

The majority of African American political leaders active and vocal on United States policies toward southern Africa were firmly against Savimbi and UNITA, but that was not the only view. Small, but well-connected, groups of politically conservative African Americans expressed a strong interest in battling communism in Africa. One such group was Black Americans for a Free Angola, led by Maurice Dawkins, Clarence McKee, and Gregory Simpkins. In a statement published in the *Baltimore Afro-American* on July 5, 1986, Dawkins complained of African American political leaders and journalists' shortsightedness toward communism in Angola and Mozambique. African American leaders' opposition to the UNITA leader, Dawkins insisted, was racist. "If Savimbi, whose UNITA controls 1/3 of the country and has the support of over 50 percent of the total Angolan population, were fighting a white oppressive regime, the black press and black politicians would be cheering him on!"[40]

Dawkins either purposefully exaggerated or was misinformed on the extent of Savimbi power and popularity in Angola. Nonetheless, his underlying premise was that alternative viewpoints within the African American community were essential, particularly those grounded in religious beliefs and avowed faith in capitalism as the natural system by which African Americans will raise their standard of living. "To me, Dr. Savimbi represents a positive alternative to the Soviet strategy which pits black Africans against black Africans in a growing design to make the continent of Africa an instrument in [the] hands of Moscow and a strategic part of the geopolitical plan to make communism an imposed way of life all over the world." His religious argument is one that likely resonated more broadly within the African American community. But it was the profession of atheism within communism rather than the substance of its political components that was problematic. Dawkins, however, casts communism in opposition to Christianity and, therefore, as unacceptable. "Since I prefer democracy as a way of life because it is more consistent with my Christian philosophy and the theology of Jesus, I am unequivocally and categorically opposed to a communist takeover of Africa."[41]

African Americans speaking on Savimbi's behalf helped present him as a credible alternative to José Dos Santos and the MPLA. African American support for Savimbi was low, but their voices were enhanced by the fact that the president had a similar message regarding Savimbi. And the president matched his words with action. In 1986, his administration acknowledged that it had funneled up to $50 million annually in covert aid to UNITA rebels through Zaire.[42] The MPLA had the support of the activist core of the Black Caucus, but no formal presence in Washington. Yet the Black Caucus strongly opposed aid to UNITA and advocated the president's formally recognizing the Angolan government.[43]

Again, Poland also factored into the debate on U.S.-South African relations. Leland targeted Reagan's double standards on Poland and South Africa. The Civil Aeronautics Board (CAB) provides a useful case in point. It approved South African Airways' petition to continue service between Johannesburg and Houston. Leland reminded the board that it had suspended Soviet and Polish airlines' permits in response to increased political repression in Poland. With an eye on Reagan's firm position and statements regarding political developments in Eastern Europe, Leland's position was that the CAB must remain consistent and not contravene its "own precedents in other cases involving foreign policy issues" that did not serve the public interest. He accused the board of ignoring "the normal standard of reciprocity—getting a concession of value in return for extraordinary granting of such air rights."[44]

Leland's tactics bear the mark of Congressman Charles Diggs's legacy, particularly his practice of linking protests with legislative affairs within Congress. As head of the Black Caucus in 1973, Diggs had joined with civil rights organizations to oppose South African Airways' plan to create additional air routes between Johannesburg and New York. The airline had established regular flights between New York and Johannesburg in February 1969. On February 23, the day of its inaugural flight, ACOA organized a protest in front of the airline's Manhattan offices and the Harry W. Graff advertising agency, which ran the airline's ad campaign.[45] In April 1969, Diggs's House Subcommittee on African Affairs held hearings on the legality of South African Airways' New York route. The Black Caucus failed to stop the airline's expansion but secured its officials' guarantee to desegregate passengers on domestic U.S. flights.[46] An added minor victory was that Graff responded to the negative publicity by dropping the airline as a client.[47]

Leland asked the CAB to respond similarly to South African Airways, considering the escalating violence and repression.[48] The board defended itself against Leland's accusations that it colluded with the apartheid regime by highlighting the fact that its decisions complied with Reagan's policy toward South Africa and that it had acted at the behest of his administration. Leland failed to block the airline's flights from Houston, but his effort strengthened his and his fellow anti-apartheid legislators' arguments for sanctions. Activism within and outside Congress eased the path to successfully passing legislation to sever economic ties between the United States and South Africa. The Black Caucus moved forward with its strategy to introduce multiple bills simultaneously, with only modest differences between them, to build momentum toward a comprehensive sanctions law. Then the lawmakers would gauge which bill showed the greatest promise of garnering support from their white colleagues.

Much as Reagan had used economic and other incentives to force the Polish government to enact political reforms, the Black Caucus found sanctions to be a useful, digestible cover for their push for sweeping economic, political, and social reforms in South Africa. Leland contributed to this effort by continuing to identify companies doing business in South Africa. He created the Black Caucus's Disinvestment Task Force and named Ronald Dellums as chair, with the charge of finding out the names of such companies. The task force began with U.S. companies that invested both domestically and in South Africa. Representative Charles Rose, a Democrat from North Carolina and chairman of the Subcommittee on House Systems, agreed to work with the Black Caucus to identify companies with investments in South Africa that also had contracts with the U.S. Capitol, including Congress, the Capitol police, and the postmaster.[49]

The United States was South Africa's largest source of foreign currency exchange, its chief source of political support in the international arena, and its primary military partner. South African economic and political stability mattered to Reagan more than human rights or the geopolitical consequences of standing by the apartheid regime. The president did not want to act in any way that might destabilize or otherwise compromise the country's ability to protect its interests. For the United States, its economic investment in South Africa was not large, accounting for only 1 percent of total U.S. overseas investment, but from the South African point of view, the investment was quite large. Nearly one-fourth of all foreign investment in South Africa originated in the United States.[50] Most U.S. investments in South Africa were concentrated in transportation, energy, and information technology. U.S. business investment totaled close to $10 billion and bilateral trade was close to $4 billion.[51] South Africa's mineral wealth—particularly platinum and chrome—was the cornerstone of its economic and strategic importance to the United States. Indirect investment—mainly holdings in South African gold-mining companies—amounted to $2.5–33 billion. In addition, U.S. corporations paid $200 million a year in corporate taxes to South Africa.[52]

In a speech in August 1981, Assistant Secretary of State Chester Crocker listed several reasons why it was desirable for the United States to sustain a white regime in South Africa. One was to ensure that dynamic democratic capitalism remained strong in the country. South Africa's economic strength reverberated domestically and throughout the sub-region.[53] Crocker argued that the United States had moral, political, and economic interests in not only continuing but accelerating investment in South Africa. In a bold statement of how far his economic support of the South African regime went, and over the objection of some members of Congress, Reagan pushed through a $1.1 billion International Monetary Fund loan to South Africa.

Proponents of constructive engagement backed up arguments against sanctions by insisting that economic penalties would most adversely affect black workers. However, black employment in sectors that benefited from U.S. investment totaled only 1 percent of workers. Leland and the Black Caucus dismissed Reagan's assertions that constructive engagement catalyzed social and political progress in South Africa. "Constructive engagement has not worked, does not work, nor will it ever work," Leland declared from the floor of the House. To suggest otherwise was delusional, he said, because the situation had deteriorated while U.S. business with the white-minority regime had increased. Sales of computers to South Africa and of nonlethal goods to its military and police had risen during this period of quiet diplomacy. "What do these actions tell the world about the morality of the United States?" Leland asked. "How can we claim apartheid is repugnant and continue to do business with those who perpetuate this repugnant system?"[54]

The Black Caucus and Rose's subcommittee investigated companies that sold office equipment in South Africa. They zeroed in on IBM and XEROX. The Disinvestment Task Force promoted a boycott of these companies and publicly removed the equipment they made from their own offices.[55] Their efforts did not result in changes in policy, but they did raise general awareness of the extent of U.S.-South African economic ties. Equally important was that the task force's work contributed to cementing in mainstream thinking the notion that U.S. companies should not conduct business, directly or indirectly, with South Africa.

There were more than two sides in the sanctions debate. The ironic contrasts between views from the political right and left on Crocker and his prescriptions for constructive engagement with South Africa shaped the evolving national narrative.[56] Constructive engagement included allowing financial investments and loans and defending against sanctions. Liberals generally supported sanctions, but they continued to wrestle with how strong and broad to make them. They treated constructive engagement as a conservative policy, symptomatic of all that was wrong with Reagan's approach to southern Africa. This perspective flattened a highly fraught endeavor among conservatives to confront apartheid's moral failings while continuing to support the white-minority regime and avoiding accusations of racism from the domestic and international left.

Several influential members of the president's staff held views on sanctions that were farther to the right than his. They regarded Chester Crocker as insufficiently conservative and opposed constructive engagement as a negative attack on the South African regime's policies and sovereignty. A group of stridently conservative members of Congress called for Reagan to fire Crocker because he had indicated a need for changes to the U.S. relationship with the South African regime.[57] Pat Buchanan, the White House communications director, represented this perspective within the White House and believed that he channeled the true spirit of Reagan. Buchanan's position was that the president must support the anticommunist, white-minority regime no matter the cost. Secretary of State George Shultz was on the opposing side of this debate. He recognized the advantages of a more critical stance toward the South African government and wanted the president to avoid squandering political capital with Congress and becoming mired in African issues, especially when the United States had gained distinct economic and political advantage over the Soviet Union.[58]

As his first term progressed, Reagan became less rigidly ideological and, therefore, less predictable to liberal lawmakers. He entered office with a Manichaean understanding of superpower relations, but his outlook on U.S.-Soviet relations and the potential for mutual understanding evolved in 1983.[59] The president reevaluated what he had accepted as the Soviet leaders' rationale for building up their colossal nuclear arsenal. He had erroneously believed that they were motivated by a desire for global revolution. He realized that rather than striving for global dominance, Soviet leaders amassed their nuclear arsenal to protect themselves from what they perceived to be an impulsive president.[60] Apprised of the factors behind the Soviet position, Reagan feared an accidental war and recognized the necessity for change in U.S.-Soviet relations.[61] The president's fear of nuclear fallout caused him to reassess U.S. relations with the Soviet Union. He recognized that the so-called Reagan Doctrine's focus on containing and shrinking Soviet influence and maintaining the American edge over the Soviet Union in the arms race was not a recipe for peace. But, he continued to interpret human rights goals in Latin America and Eastern Europe as coinciding with the narrow interests of Cold War anticommunism.[62] The shift necessarily forecast changes to U.S. policies.

On January 16, 1984, in an address to the nation, Reagan outlined the steps he would take to build closer ties between the United States and the Soviet Union; but he spun his turn toward reconciliation as an outgrowth of U.S. strength and ideological steadfastness. "I believe that 1984 finds the United States in the strongest position in years to establish a constructive and realistic working relationship with the Soviet Union," the president said. "We've come a long way since the decade of the seventies, years when the United States seemed filled with self-doubt and neglected its defenses, while the Soviet Union increased its military might and sought to expand its influence by armed forces and threat."[63] The president tasked the country with establishing common ground with the Soviet Union and opened the way to greater nuance in deciphering Cold War foreign policy. Reagan's outlook and policies remained conservative, and he clung to simplistic, often racist conceptions of affairs in the Global South. But as he stepped subtly, albeit perceptively, away from the straitjacket of Cold War anticommunism, alternative approaches to U.S. foreign policy became possible. His political shift toward peace through dialogue cleared space for U.S. lawmakers and activists to advance their cause to bring the living conditions and political status of black South Africans into U.S. policy debates.

Reagan wrote General Secretary Mikhail Gorbachev a note soon after this address to invite him to a summit meeting on nuclear disarmament. This proposed meeting was not whimsical on Reagan's part. Gorbachev entered the international political arena at a moment when the U.S. president was becoming increasingly concerned about the consequences of nuclear fallout.[64] Reagan said later that watching the ABC drama *The Day After*, which depicts the town of Lawrence, Kansas, following a nuclear attack, "left [him] greatly depressed." In his 1984 State of the Union Address, Reagan turned directly to the Soviets with his appeal: "People of the Soviet Union, there is only one sane policy, for your country and mine, to preserve our civilization in this modern age: A nuclear war cannot be won and must never be fought. The only value in our own nations possessing nuclear weapons is to make sure they will never be used. But then would it not be better to do away with them entirely?"[65] Leland would not have found fault with much of Reagan's statement. One of the myriad problems Leland had with the president was that his policies toward Global South nations changed more slowly than his policies toward Europe. Reagan did not extend his reevaluation of the Cold War to Africa, the Caribbean, and Central America until Leland and his congressional colleagues persuaded the president to do so.

The president's two January 1984 addresses to the nation showed his awareness of the Soviet Union's limited capacity to assert its strategic interests in global affairs. Its influence in Africa, never what the United States envisioned it to be, had waned considerably throughout the 1970s. Yet the South African Communist Party and individual communists, particularly Joe Slovo, Ruth First, and Chris Hani, did indeed play a critical role in building and sustaining the opposition to the apartheid regime as partners to and, in some instances, members of the African National Congress and the South African Congress of Trade Unions. Yet communists neither led the movement nor were they in a position to lead in the future.[66] With regard to communism's external influences in southern Africa, Cuba, rather than the Soviet Union, played a direct and consequential role in Angola and gave logistical support to the African National Congress operating in exile in Lusaka, Zambia. Reagan continued to use anticommunism to justify his opposition to recognizing the legitimacy of black antiapartheid activists, but toward the end of his first term and throughout his second, anticommunism lost its political potency. He issued a more nuanced explication of his position on resistance to apartheid that grounded his support for the status quo in South Africa in economic interests and visions of the white-minority regime's march to racial equality and in respect for South African sovereignty. African American lawmakers homed in on the evident contradictions in on Reagan's revised approach to communist Europe and the Marxist governments of the Global South.

Bishop Desmond Tutu's visit to the White House in December 1984 exposed the deep holes in Reagan's arguments against sanctions. President Reagan and Republicans in Congress spun sanctions as detrimental to black South African workers and, therefore, a poor strategy to improve their condition. Tutu had accepted the Nobel Peace Prize two months earlier in Zurich for his role as a champion of dialogue against and nonviolent resistance to the apartheid regime. On December 4, during his visit to Washington, D.C., the bishop testified in front of Congress's Committee on Foreign Affairs on U.S. sanctions against South Africa. Not everyone in Washington believed that South Africa needed to change. Some members of Congress, and officials from the Reagan administration, praised the South African government for taking steps toward a more inclusive government through its new constitution that granted limited political participation to Indians and Coloureds. They advised the White House to encourage this trend rather than punish the government with sanctions. However, the new constitution excluded black South Africans entirely, while it allowed separate legislative bodies for Indians and Coloureds. "The new constitution is an instrument of the politics of exclusion I referred to earlier," Bishop Tutu told the Committee on Foreign Affairs. "Seventy-three percent of South Africa's population, the blacks, have no part in this constitution, which mentions them quite incredibly only once. How could this be regarded as even remotely democratic? Its three chambers are racially defined. Consequently, racism and ethnicity are entrenched and hallowed in the constitution."[67]

For Bishop Tutu and the Black Caucus, violence in South Africa—among black partisans, anti-apartheid demonstrators, and the government—affirmed constructive engagement's failure as a policy and exposed it as a mere facade for Reagan's continued support of the white-minority regime. Although it was a violation of South African law to call for sanctions against the government, Bishop Tutu remained undeterred and continued to advocate for sanctions upon his return from his three-week tour through the United States and Britain. South African media attacked his pro-sanctions stance, but he was defiant: "It won't help the anti-sanctions lobby to vilify me. Even if they were to liquidate me, what I say is true: apartheid is filthy, it is vile, it is immoral, it is violent, it is vicious, it is evil, it is un-Christian."[68] The bishop's tour was a resounding success and accelerated the momentum in Congress toward the passage of sanctions legislation.

During Bishop Tutu's visit to the White House on December 7, he and President Reagan could not have held positions on apartheid and economic sanctions in South Africa more fundamentally at odds. Reagan praised the South African regime for, as he described, moving in a positive direction. He posited that constructive engagement was a motivating force behind this positive trend. He argued that his critics had failed to bring about substantive change in South Africa. The demonstrations and protests in front of the South African embassy in Washington and in other cities across the country by the Free South Africa Movement, he argued, had shown no tangible results.[69] Reagan officials pointed to South Africa's revised constitution as evidence that president's constructive engagement positively contributed to South Africa's reforms.

In his address to Congress, Bishop Tutu directly rebuked Reagan for his position on sanctions. He labeled constructive engagement an unmitigated disaster and an instrument in support of evil. "Apartheid is evil, immoral, is un-Christian, without remainder," he stated clearly before Congress. "It uses evil, immoral and un-Christian methods. If you had supported the Nazis against the Jews, you would have been accused of adopting an immoral position. Apartheid is as evil and immoral and un-Christian in my view as Nazism[;] in my view, the Reagan administration's support and collaboration with it is equally immoral, evil and totally un-Christian, without remainder." He warned his audience that they possessed the power to act on the right side of history. "I hope this great country, with an extraordinary capacity sometimes for backing the wrong horse, will for once break from that record. Will you please for a change listen to the victims of oppression? We shall be free, and we will remember who helped us to become free."[70] The anti-apartheid movement in the United States could not have asked for a more positive endorsement.

Three days after his meeting with Bishop Tutu, Reagan delivered a major speech on South Africa. He expressed his abhorrence of racism and urged the government and the people of South Africa to move toward a more just society. Rather than inspiring patience among his critics, however, the speech was seen by his political allies as evidence that Reagan had no grasp of how politically dire South African apartheid had become as an

issue. By standing against sanctions, with no alternative proposals for forcing the South African government to move toward full, multiracial democracy, the president accepted the legitimacy of apartheid, despite his rhetoric
to the contrary. To stifle the opposition and preempt action in Congress,
in September 1985 Reagan signed an executive order that imposed limited
sanctions on South Africa. The order restricted loans to the South African
government and banned sharing nuclear technology and all computer technology with the South African military. Although the president's order had
the potential to negatively affect South Africa, its importance lay in the fact
that it established the first direct sanctions the U.S. government imposed
on South Africa.[71] It did not produce Reagan's desired outcome of slowing
the momentum toward sanctions legislation, however.

After two years of activism, lobbying, and legislative setbacks and minor
victories, Black Caucus members achieved a historic win with the passage
of the Anti-Apartheid Act of 1986. Dellums had introduced a bill to impose
economic sanctions on South Africa each year during the 1980s leading up
to his successful bill in 1986. As part of the Black Caucus strategy to introduce multiple anti-apartheid bills, Dellums and Gray both introduced sanctions legislation. Dellums's would mandate full U.S. disinvestment from the
South African economy. Few had faith that his proposal to completely iso-
late South Africa economically would pass Congress, let alone the Senate
and get past Reagan's desk without a veto. Gray's colleagues considered his
anti-apartheid legislation to be the more reasonable of the two and the one
with the greater potential to gain traction in Congress, because it was less
comprehensive.[72]

The vote in the House came on June 5, 1986, and the tally was 295 to
127 to approve Dellums's legislation that would impose a trade embargo
and complete economic disinvestment. Congress passed Dellums's bill by
voice vote as an amendment to William Gray's weaker bill. Fifty-six Republicans joined their Democratic colleagues to support the legislation. It
would block only new investment from the United States and bank loans.
Representative Mark Siljander approved the amendment, hoping that it
would kill the Gray bill in the Senate. The Speaker of the House called
Dellums's bill up for vote before Gray's because it was widely expected to
fail. Republicans hoped that if it passed in the House, the bill would prove
so unpalatable to the Senate that it would not bring it up for a vote, thus
killing it. House leaders opted to subject it to a quick voice vote and awaited
its defeat in favor of Gray's more moderate bill. But it passed. The legislative

victory was the high point of Dellums's sixteen years in Congress.[73] In a failed strategic move, antisanction forces in Congress voted for the bill. This legislation marked a point of transition for the U.S. anti-apartheid movement and the high point of African American activists' involvement in U.S. foreign affairs.

The House vote in favor of radical sanctions did not deter President Reagan in his opposition to economically punitive measures against the apartheid regime. During a televised address on July 22, 1986, the president reiterated his case against sanctions and praised white South Africans' recent social and political achievements toward a more inclusive society. The president had demonstrated his capacity for creativity in his efforts to build common ground with the Soviet Union. He showed similar imagination in his support for the solidarity movement in Poland. But bewilderingly, in the case of South Africa he remained trapped in a pro-white-minority regime mind-set. He appeared either incapable or unwilling to acknowledge the parallels between the resistance movements in Poland and South Africa or the common characteristics of the brutal regimes the resisters confronted. With the draft of a presidential speech addressing the new anti-apartheid legislation, Chester Crocker tried to nudge the president closer to the emerging consensus on South Africa. Reagan rejected the draft that Crocker's deputy, Chas Freeman, had prepared in favor of a speech that Pat Buchanan had apparently reworked. Freeman's draft included criticisms of apartheid and white-minority rule. "That speech went to the White House pretty much the way I had written it," Freeman recalled. "And exactly two lines of it survived the pen of one Pat Buchanan, who was the speechwriter for Reagan, and who, himself, has very definite views on racial issues and on Africa, about which he knows nothing."[74]

In the speech, Reagan declared sanctions immoral and "utterly repugnant."[75] He continued to praise South Africa for its achievements and excused its government from negotiations "on the future of the country" with the ANC, "or with any organization that proclaims a goal of creating a communist state and uses terrorist tactics to achieve it."[76] What Reagan depicted as communist-inspired anti-apartheid activism in South Africa had no basis in fact. The ANC's platform did not endorse communism, nor did it imply any sympathy for the communists' ideology or movement in South Africa. Notwithstanding the president's erroneous political characterizations of the ANC and the pace of social change in South Africa, his address marked a final stand of sorts for the politically conservative approach to white-minority rule. Widespread and detailed coverage of black political activism in South Africa and the material conditions in the townships definitively shifted popular opinion in favor of multiracial democracy.

Many conservatives praised the speech, but other Republicans found the president's position on U.S.-South African relations untenable. He delivered it three months prior to the midterm elections. Secretary of State Shultz had to perform damage control for the White House, as the president was sitting on the verge of a major foreign policy defeat. Shultz sat before the Senate Foreign Relations Committee the day after the speech to assure senators of the president's outrage over the situation in South Africa. Shultz informed the senators of the administration's intentions to be a mediating force in the country by reaching out to the opposition, stating, "We intend to raise the level and frequency of our contacts with the South African Government's black opposition, including, among others, the African National Congress."[77]

The House bill called for a near-complete break in business ties between South Africa and the United States, but the Senate's bill was more limited. It banned new investment in South Africa and prohibited trade in agricultural products, steel, and nuclear supplies. Jesse Helms, a conservative Republican from North Carolina, successfully inserted an amendment into the Anti-Apartheid Act of 1986 that categorized ANC activities in South Africa as "terrorist" and stipulated that the United States must encourage the ANC to disavow such tactics and "re-examine their ties to the South African communist party."[78] The Senate bill banned new investment, terminated South African landing rights, and prohibited the import of iron, steel, uranium, coal, and agricultural products from South Africa, among other measures. The Black Caucus strategized on what position to take on the Senate's bill. They hoped for a bill closer to that of Dellums, but Senator Richard Lugar, chairman of the Foreign Relations Committee, promised to defend the legislation in the face of a presidential veto.

On August 15, all forty-seven Democrats in the Senate voted in favor of the Anti-Apartheid Act. Rather than debate the differences between the House and Senate versions of anti-apartheid legislation, the House leadership agreed to support the Senate's milder bill. The Senate's version had a better chance of getting the president's signature. Thirty-seven Republicans joined the Democrats. In the House of Representatives, the legislation passed by a lopsided margin of 308–77 on September 12. Close to half of all Republicans in the House voted for the legislation.

The legislation's key sponsors in the House believed, perhaps erroneously, that compromise on its content was necessary for the Anti-Apartheid Act of 1986 to pass and to avoid a Reagan veto. The bill's language regarding the government's prerogative in negotiating with the ANC was posed to lessen its impact.[79] "We made a statement to P. W. Botha and to the world," Representative Leland declared. "But we realize that this sanctions bill is not a cure-all for the problems faced by black South Africans."[80] The political terrain had quickly shifted beneath Reagan. Even members of his cabinet struggled to spin the president's position as defensible. A remarkable groundswell of support for sanctions emerged in the Senate, where lawmakers embraced a diluted version of the Dellums bill. The Anti-Apartheid Act was among a suite of laws imposing sanctions on South Africa that foreign governments passed in the fall of 1986. The same month that the House voted on the sanctions bill, the European Economic Community approved comparatively less stringent sanctions on South Africa. The following month, Canada imposed trade sanctions on the apartheid regime. Scandinavian governments imposed the most sweeping sanctions. In 1986 Denmark, Norway, and Sweden banned trade with South Africa, with Finland following suit in 1987.[81]

The process that led to anti-apartheid legislation in the United States was unique, because it was championed by a racial minority, and it was notable as an example of the public pressing Congress to act. African Americans' strength as an electoral bloc increased political organizations' capacity to effect change. There were two million African American registered to vote in 1968. By 1988 the number had increased to nearly four million. The number of African Americans holding key political offices quadrupled between 1970 and 1985 to over 6,000 from 1,500.[82]

Reagan's fellow Republicans implored him to accept the Senate's bill, but he pushed forward with his veto of sanctions legislation. Once again, the president's defense of his headstrong yet severely weakened position on sanction rested on anticommunism. Despite the preponderance of evidence against strong Soviet or even communist influence over the antiapartheid movement, he continued in his role of faithful Cold Warrior and misrepresented the choice of policies toward South Africa as for and against Marxism in South Africa. The sanctions legislations, he suggested, was a victory for the Soviet Union. The implication was that he vetoed it for the good of the free world. "Not only does this legislation contain sweeping punitive sanctions that would injure most the very people we seek to help, the legislation discards our economic leverage, constricts our diplomatic freedom, and ties the hands of the President of the United States in dealing with a gathering crisis in a critical continent where the Soviet Bloc—with its mounting investment of men and arms—clearly sees historic opportunity." The president did not mince words, but he was vague on which he considered the greater threat: Marxism or apartheid. "Any unyielding opposition both to the unacceptable doctrine of apartheid as well as the unacceptable alternative of Marxist tyranny—back by the firm determination that the future of South Africa and southern Africa will belong to the free."[83]

In September 1986, the Senate overrode Reagan's veto 78–21. For only the third time in the twentieth century, Congress overrode a U.S. president's veto on a foreign policy issue.[84] It was an unquestionable political defeat for the president. After six years of vehement and consistent opposition to sanctions, he adroitly shifted to support sanctions. On the day of the Senate's scheduled vote to override Reagan's veto of the Anti-Apartheid Act of 1986, the president wrote to Tip O'Neill, Speaker of the House of Representatives, and Robert Dole, the Senate majority leader, to defend his veto and outline his revised position. "These sanctions," he wrote, "directed at the enforcers not the victims of apartheid, encompass measures recently adopted by many of our allies, as well as many elements of the original Senate Committee version of the bill. They are incontestably necessary in today's circumstances." The president's letter suggests that the debate over sanctions succeeded in making him conscious of the immorality of racial oppression. "My intention," he continued in his letter, "is to make it plain to South Africa's leaders that we cannot conduct business-as-usual with a government that mistakes the silence of racial repression for consent of the governed."[85]

His concern for democracy and racism in South Africa in 1986 was a far cry from his position in 1980 that "South Africans certainly don't need us to tell them how to resolve their race problems"[86] Yet, he continued to oppose legally enforcing sanctions. After the historic vote, he stated that his administration would implement the sanctions, but he feared the punitive sanctions "will not solve the serious problems that plague that country."[87] Myriad forces aligned to bring about a fundamental change in U.S. policy toward South Africa. Activism, legislation, lobbying, and coalition building all came together to force the United States to reevaluate its policies and disentangle itself from South Africa economically. Passing the Anti-Apartheid Act of 1986 had not been the goal. The bill was a means to bring about an end to U.S. support of apartheid in South Africa, but to be effective, the sanctions law had to be enforced.

The disinvestment campaign accelerated after the Comprehensive Anti-Apartheid Act passed. Two years earlier it would have been unfathomable that General Motors Corporation, with 3,056 employees in the country, would pull up stakes. It was the largest of the ten major corporations that disinvested in 1986, along with IBM, Carnation, VF, General Electric, Blue Bell, Navistar, Computer Sciences Corporation, City Investing, and Coca Cola.[88] Official disinvestment did not necessarily mean the companies severed ties with the country. General Motors and IBM, for example, ensured that their products remained available in South Africa through licensing and franchise agreements.[89] Activists were well aware of this scheme, so they continued to target these companies. Other companies recognized the short and long-term damage that continuing to conduct business in South Africa could do to their brand, and quickly moved to sever all ties.

Companies remained unmoved by protests throughout the first decade of the disinvestment campaigns. Escalated violence in South Africa in 1984 and the Free South Africa Movement's success in drawing public and media attention to the U.S. relationship with the apartheid regime through daily, around-the-clock demonstrations outside the South African embassy in Washington tainted the profits that U.S. companies made in South Africa. Activists and leftist politicians were not alone in the disinvestment campaign. Numerous Republican politicians, particularly those with sizable Democratic constituents, advanced the call for disinvestment and submitted legislation to make it law. By the end of 1986, approximately 116 colleges and universities, 19 state governments, and 83 cities and counties reportedly passed anti-apartheid measures that required a total of $22 billion worth of stocks and bonds in U.S. corporations and banks invested in South Africa.[90] Still, by the end of the following year, although ninety-six companies had pulled out since the previous year, 167 U.S. firms remained with direct investment or employees in the country.[91]

Congressman Leland marked the passing of the U.S. anti-apartheid bill as a watershed moment in U.S. political and economic history. Sanctions on South Africa had real economic consequences for U.S. businesses, though they did not threaten the U.S. economy or even force corporations to shed jobs in great numbers. But it did cost some jobs. His support for comprehensive sanctions bears witness to the strength of his convictions. As one of the leaders within Congress calling for sanctions, Leland faced a potential backlash in his home district where Shell Oil Company had its North American headquarters. The anti-apartheid legislation prohibited South African companies from drilling for oil, natural gas, or any minerals on U.S. property. It placed a similar ban on U.S. companies in South Africa. After Dellums's legislation passed in the House, Shell executives lobbied Leland before the Senate's vote in anticipation of the financial costs of South African sanctions. Shell operated domestically, while its parent company, Royal Dutch Shell, operated internationally, including in South Africa. Leland had little sympathy for Shell, and he came close to saying as much to the company's executives. Charting the proper moral, political, and economic course for the U.S. approach to South Africa was of greater importance than the economic health of Texas's "more prominent corporate citizens," he said. "Would you put our economic and strategic interests over and above 26 million human beings in South Africa who suffer?" To shield himself politically, Leland searched for ways to address Shell's dilemma without weakening the sanctions bill but concluded that the bill was his priority.[92]

Most critics of the anti-apartheid legislation spoke of its drawbacks by highlighting that it was economically detrimental to black South Africans, but its potential damage to domestic corporations was also an important issue. Leland largely dismissed short-term financial losses as minor relative to the long-term political and moral gains. "The cost of sanctions," he said in 1989, "are [sic] minuscule when compared to those of a prolonged violent struggle. By acting now, we prevent the continued loss of property and lives that are falling victim to black South Africans' struggle for freedom and equality. South Africa will change. What emerges from this change will be determined by our willingness to impose sanctions aimed at effecting timely change or remain silent as the degree of violence increases."[93]

Leland monitored corporate entities with either suspected or potential ties to South Africa. Legislation alone was not enough to sever economic ties between the United States and the apartheid regime. The global nature of investments allowed them to take advantage of loopholes in the Anti-Apartheid Act to invest in U.S. markets. One way that large South African corporations did this was to transfer their investments from the South African market to the more stable and profitable U.S. market. Ninety-six U.S. companies pulled out of South Africa by the end of 1986, but nearly half of them continued to allow their products to be manufactured and sold in the country.[94] Despite a wave of disinvestment from South Africa, ongoing indirect ties blunted the effects of sanctions on the South African economy. These setbacks in the campaign notwithstanding, sanctions were a major development in U.S. corporate history. Even prior to the sanctions bill, companies disinvested from South Africa, an allied country with a strong economy, without being directed to do so by the federal government. As Michael Isikoff wrote in the *Washington Post* in November 1986, never before had the U.S. business community seen "significant US corporate flight from an economically advanced and until recently profitable foreign market."[95] In fact, the Reagan administration worked purposefully to stop disinvestment. But the prospect of tarnished brands and diminished profits in other locales motivated a host of multinational corporations to disinvest.

Leland, ever determined to block all channels for South Africans to profit from apartheid, submitted legislation, the Apartheid Profits Disincentive Act, to close existing loopholes and completely ban South African corporations from the U.S. market. Speaking from the House floor in September 1987 in support of his bill, Leland detailed the way companies generated profits in South Africa despite existing sanctions. "It is clear to me that the profits generated in South Africa through the apartheid system are, under our very noses, being invested in the United States capital markets." South African investments demonstrated for Leland the success of economic sanctions in weakening South Africa's economy. But sanctions were not universally enforced. South African businesses redirected their capital to more stable markets. In doing so, they diminished their share of the pain from sanctions. They attempted, as Leland said, "to dilute their exposure to the political and economic pressure that the free countries of the world are bringing to bear on the apartheid system." The legislation he proposed but failed to pass would have barred South African mining companies from U.S. capital markets and from investing in U.S. corporations until apartheid practices ended at their mines.[96] Mining accounted for 15 percent of South Africa's GNP, and mining corporations benefited from low wages and loose regulations in South Africa.

He homed in on two corporations, Newmont Mining Corporation, an American company, and South Africa's Anglo American mining company. Newmont was on track to establish itself as the largest gold producer outside South Africa. Anglo American owned a minority stake in Newmont but exercised de facto control through a web of intermediary companies.

In South Africa, Anglo American employed 40 percent of black miners and produced roughly 40 percent of South Africa's gold. Recent attacks on striking black mine workers, numbering upward of 350,000 miners, drew attention to labor conditions in South Africa and the fact that black South Africans worked under dangerous conditions for far less than their white counterparts and had little means for recourse. Once Consolidated Gold Fields, a British company owned by a South African mining conglomerate dominated by Anglo American, took over Newmont, it would control global gold production.

The Newmont Mining Corporation opposed Leland's legislation. Richard B. Leather, Newmont's executive vice president, said in his testimony before Congress that Leland's legislation, if passed, "would mark a radical departure from the long-standing American policy in favor of an open economy and the free movement of investment capital across national borders." He said he feared the effects of increased executive and legislative power over investments in the United States. "As an American company that invests overseas," he said, "Newmont is also concerned about the prospect of retaliation. Ore bodies occur throughout the world and Newmont needs maximum ability to find and develop them."[97] A counterargument came from American oil tycoon T. Boone Pickens. In his statement before Congress, he expressed support for sanctions but insisted that they did not go far enough to block South African investments in the United States. He described U.S. sanctions legislation as unintentionally providing South African corporations with an economic advantage, since they had the freedom to invest in U.S. markets but U.S. corporations could not do the same in South Africa. "As an American investor," he said, "I am prohibited by US law from investing in South African companies. This law discourages investment in a country that allows discriminatory labor practices. I respect this law. As a businessman, I recognize that the purpose of this law can be evaded, as Anglo-American is attempting to do here."[98]

Although his bill failed, Leland made the case to his colleagues that passing the sanctions bill did not resolve the debate on United States corporate ties to the apartheid regime. His watchful eye on U.S. and South African corporations was a small part of the anti-apartheid movement, but it demonstrates its dynamism and the challenge of reinventing the relationship between the two countries. Leland's work also shows that the U.S. anti-apartheid movement involved more than a series of protests that culminated in a landmark sanctions bill. Like the civil rights and Black Power movements, behind the demonstrations against U.S. ties to the white-minority regime were countless individuals and groups that conducted research, issued policy recommendations, and coordinated communication between the U.S., British, South African, and other activists around the world. But Leland's work sent the additional message that investments and profits from the United States must not be used to subsidize oppression and the continuance of white supremacy in South Africa.

As the political winds turned in support of sanctions, Leland continued to seek to leverage the unprecedented prominence of African affairs in the media and on the U.S. political radar to gain traction for humanitarian relief and development in the Horn. In October 1984, in a keynote speech at the Congressional Black Caucus's Annual Legislative Weekend dinner, Leland spoke passionately, in his characteristic blistering style, of the moral failing of international responses to the famines in the Horn of Africa. "The signs of the coming tragedy were present in Africa long before 1984," he exclaimed, regarding the famine in Ethiopia. "But they were ignored—ignored by callous governments, ignored by ideologues who would not aid starving people because of political differences with their leaders."[99] Few at the time would have missed this swipe at Reagan. Leland amply used his platform as chairman of the Black Caucus to outline for Reagan and all of America what he regarded as the failure of the president and his congressional allies to act against apartheid, global hunger, and poverty in the United States. "Ultimately," he argued, "the media brought the human devastation into the living rooms of the world and individuals everywhere responded with compassion. In Britain and the United States concerned entertainers sustained and channeled that momentum. Literally millions of lives were saved because people instinctively know that the death of another human being diminishes us all."[100]

Lawmakers and Reagan administration officials frequently evoked Ethiopia as a foil to South Africa in U.S. policy debates. Leland acknowledged South Africa as the foreign affairs priority. "Our highest priority on an international scale now," he said on C-Span, "is what are we going to do as a body, as a Congress, as a country, as a government to assist the poor, desperate, suffering people of South Africa. That's our highest priority on our international, foreign policy agenda."[101] South Africa had an outsized significance in U.S. policies toward Africa, but Leland did not believe it should crowd out hunger, refugees, agricultural development, and other pressing issues.

On the surface, Ethiopia and South Africa lacked any tangible connection apart from the global media attention they garnered. On March 12, 1986, during a morning hearing of the Subcommittee on Africa on "Recent Developments in South Africa," Congressman Toby Roth, a Republican from Wisconsin, brought up Ethiopia. "I do not know any other nation in the world or combination of nations where we have that type of holocaust occurring today," he said of the Ethiopian government's resettlement program. "If we are going to have 20/20 vision out of our right eye, then we cannot be blind out of our left eye. While there are members of this congress who understand how to oppose dictatorships that are pro-American, when they see a leftwing, pro-Soviet dictatorship, they are blind."[102] Democrats on the committee perceived Roth's comments as unnecessary tangents to the issue at hand. Roth, on the other hand, charged that the difference among the U.S. approaches to South Africa and all other African governments was of overriding importance to the debate.

Howard Wolpe presented the case in a slightly different manner but with the same sentiment in mind: "Occasionally I hear complaints from some quarters that the [Subcommittee on Africa of the Committee on Foreign Affairs] has focused more attention upon human rights violations in such countries as South Africa, Zaïre, and Liberia than such countries as Ethiopia, or Mozambique and Angola. It should be noted, however, that there is more to be done in terms of US policy in the first group of countries, where heavy US military and security assistance, political support, private investment and, in some instances, economic assistance, as well, falling to governments that have these dictatorships in place, creates a powerful impression that the United States condones human rights abuses." Wolpe shared many of his colleagues' critiques of the Ethiopian regime's human rights record, but he insisted that the United States would have greater moral sway in global affairs if its officials offered more balanced critiques of regimes' human rights records. "It seems to me," he argued, "that US human rights policy would be far more credible and effective if the Reagan administration was as strong and unequivocal in criticizing the countries we support. Zaïre and Chile would be a good start."[103]

The matter was more straightforward for conservatives. They compared South Africa to governments in other countries, principally Ethiopia, regarding domestic policies and human rights. Congressman Mark Siljander, a Michigan Republican, described Ethiopia's treatment of its citizens as far worse than South Africa's, and he argued that racial bias skewed his colleagues' perspective and objectivity toward South Africa. "Unlike South Africa, where the issue is political rights, Ethiopia's is also of basic survival. Why hasn't there been a louder cry in the Congress and in the world community? I think possibly the silence is because of confusion caused by disinformation. But I am sad to say also that I think racism is a major factor. When the South African government kills three people in a township riot, it is reported all over the world. In all the major international media, it is on the front page. But millions are dying because of the Ethiopian Government in that nation. Our State Department needs to put a foot down on it." Conservatives could not defend their position through anticommunism alone, so they hid it behind human rights and racial rhetoric. "Our State Department has said that Ethiopia's policies are not starving its people and are not deliberately engaged in this activity," Siljander argued. "But somehow, a white murder of 600 is worse than a black murder of 6 million. We are led to believe that we can't expect as much from a black government as we do from a white government. I say that's racism, and I don't like it any more than you do. We need to be willing to stand up and speak out the truth firmly." In his description of the Ethiopian government Siljander used language similar to that used by anti-apartheid legislators in describing the situation in South Africa. "I say that Hitler shouldn't have been trusted, Pol Pot shouldn't have been trusted, and definitely not the Government of Ethiopia," he said. "I say, instead, that the regime is in the world's horror story list and we should try and help put the Mengistu story to an end. The Ethiopian Government is criminal, and I don't want to be an accomplice to their murderous activities."[104]

Racism in southern Africa dominated the political discourse on Africa in Washington, but anti-apartheid advocates' attacks on Reagan's constructive engagement and white-minority rule provided ammunition, however limited, for their critics. During the 1970s military coups, suspension of constitutions, one-party rule, and outright dictatorship disenfranchised 85 percent of Africans, but the House Subcommittee on Africa held most of its hearings on white-ruled states—South Africa, Rhodesia, and Namibia.[105] Repressive, white supremacist regimes garnered greater attention from Congress. The anti-apartheid movement was said to have strengthened binaries of power/resistance and whiteness/blackness "in such a way that the experiences of real South Africans were oversimplified."[106]

Reagan administration officials' most effective argument in support of the contention that anti-apartheid activists were racist came from Alan

Keyes, assistant secretary of state for international organizational affairs and an African American. As Keyes accused liberals of racism, his tone combined personal insult and incredulity. He suggested that liberals held "black-ruled" nations to a lower human rights standard than they did white-ruled South Africa and doing so was an affront to U.S. progress on racial issues and stifled African development. He described the United Nations' and most members of Congress's soft stance on human rights issues in the majority of African nations repugnant because they held South Africa to a unique standard. Keyes argued that it was racist to have different standards for black and white governments on human rights. He went on to say, "In adopting this posture, the UN has refused to challenge the reluctance of many donor governments to speak out or take action regarding the reported human rights abuses." Keyes's statement was consistent with other Reagan administration officials' and representatives' responses to critics of its South Africa policy. Their remarks commonly referenced Ethiopia and what they argued was the United Nations' weak response to the country's human rights abuses. Rather than offer robust support to the Reagan administration's defense of the apartheid regime, Keyes's actual strategy was to disarm Reagan's critics: "Those who condemn the white government of South Africa for its injustice against blacks, but who do not even wish to verify the injustices that may be perpetrated by Ethiopia's government against its people obviously imply that a higher standard of human rights is to be applied to whites than to peoples of other races or colors. We reject this implication. If it is racist not to care when black people are denied their rights, then it is racist not to care when black governments deny them."[107]

By putting South Africa in the same light as Ethiopia, Keyes conceded that support for the apartheid regime was untenable. "Those who excuse the actions of the Ethiopian government because the country is undeveloped, the people poor, uneducated or unfed also imply by their excuses that the poor, the uneducated and the unfed must also be unfree. We reject this implication too. As a government that stands by the universal creed of our declaration of independence, as human beings who respect the universal scope of the UN's Declaration of Human Rights, we believe that rich or poor, black or white, ignorant or learned, skilled or untrained or unfed—human beings as such deserve their human dignity and all are entitled to be free. This means of course that governments everywhere, white, black or red, must be held to a standard which respects the rights and dignity of their citizens no matter how trapped or powerless those citizens may be."[108] Through this line of argument, Ethiopia emerged as an issue for conservatives in the South Africa debate. Conservatives like Keyes and Siljander highlighted the differences between Addis Ababa and Pretoria, as liberals and a small but growing group of more right-leaning congressmen turned aggressively and systematically against the apartheid regime. Considering Ethiopia's power grab, corruption, and disregard for human rights, conservatives labeled those who criticized South Africa as racist, hypocritical, and unpatriotic.

Even though Leland could not dodge the blowback from his problematic relationship with Mengistu and his frequent meetings with the Ethiopian leader during trips to the Horn, he remained focused on his agenda. In addition to continuing to address problems of hunger in the United States, Congressman Leland targeted hunger in the Frontline States. He implicated South African policies and military incursions into these countries that exacerbated protracted hunger, even when some of his constituents in the Eighteenth Congressional District, where his popularity remained strong, complained of his travel schedule and what many considered a disproportionate concern for global rather than domestic hunger. His acute awareness of these criticisms did not deter him. Yet he did defend his involvement in activities overseas by arguing that conservatives were more likely to support aid for poor communities at home and abroad if they spent time in them and saw firsthand the residents' everyday challenges. These trips, he added, fostered camaraderie among members of Congress who might otherwise find little common ground. "A fiscally conservative member may be more inclined to vote increased funds for medical facilities after traveling many miles to a clinic on an Indian reservation," he wrote. "Network coverage in Mississippi means millions of people have seen that, despite progress, harsh poverty persists in rural America in 1987. Members appreciate the time and effort such trips entail."[109] Leland described congressional trips abroad and to generally overlooked areas within the United States as essential to confronting Reagan's policies. The effort pulled Leland away from Washington and his Houston district, but he was adamant that his travels did not mean he neglected his obligations to his constituents. He believed he had a responsibility to open his colleagues' eyes to the realities of poverty: "I knew the realities of poverty in Houston before I brought the [Hunger] Committee here to talk with homeless families at the Star of Hope Mission and to hold a formal hearing. But until there were hearings in New York, San Francisco and reams of publicity, Congress was unable to rally public support and pass substantial legislation to aid the homeless."[110]

Reagan did not veer much from his position that South Africa had a right and a responsibility to resolve its domestic problems. Until the closing months of his second term in office, the president refused to support a democratic solution for South Africa. If he had endorsed and pushed for a democratic solution it would have radically altered the South African and international debate on apartheid. As news of violence in South Africa played out almost nightly on U.S. television, Reagan viewed the violence black dissidents committed and government violence as moral equivalents. To the president, the South African problem, at least rhetorically, was a failure in communication and understanding. Government claims that its measures were antiterrorist or anticommunist carried a hollow ring in the face of clear evidence of police torturing and executing anti-apartheid leaders, outlawing legitimate opposition organizations, and the mass arrest of church leaders, including Bishop Tutu. Leland referred to the white-minority regime's violent efforts to retain exclusive claims to power "affronts to man's civility."[111] Nearly a decade of international pressure had failed to force the regime to enact viable reforms. In 1988 apartheid remained entrenched in the character of South Africa's social, political, and economic spheres. Leland insisted that South Africa had "tightened its repressive grip on basic freedoms." The only solution, then, was representative, multiracial democracy. "The Administration continues to resist further legislation which would usher overdue reforms. Indeed, one cannot help but to question our President's understanding of apartheid when he, in a news conference, referred to apartheid as more of a 'tribal' situation. I ask you, how can we not question his commitment?" Leland exclaimed.[112]

The anti-apartheid movement benefited from the growing power of the television news media, particularly evening news programs. Just as the images of police officers beating children and spraying them with hoses in the U.S. South to end their protests for the free and unhindered exercise of their rights as citizens had shocked Americans, images of mass protests in South Africa moved a significant portion of the American public to sympathize with anti-apartheid activists. The Black Caucus had many nongovernmental allies to help sway the government toward a more progressive position on South Africa. With TransAfrica and the Free South Africa Movement, the coalition signaled a turning point in the role of African American leaders in U.S. foreign policy. The crowning irony of freedom in South Africa was that it eroded African American leadership in African affairs.[113]

Chapter 5

Ending Hunger in Africa

Humanitarianism Against Austerity

> *National boundaries are imaginary lines drawn for a matter of convenience. That matter of convenience is fine but on the other side of those imaginary lines are people just like us, and we have to see them as sacred. That's the essence of my philosophy.*
>
> —Mickey Leland, 1989

During the first week of December 1984, a few days after he returned from the Horn of Africa, Leland began a campaign that he hoped would force the U.S. government to use the U.S. Strategic Wheat Reserve for humanitarian relief initiatives it sponsored in Africa. He made his case in letters to newspapers, the president, and colleagues. In the way he laid out the case for a larger role for the government in U.S. humanitarianism, an early rendition of what will become his argument for the United States to lead a transnational initiative to end global hunger is evident. He described it as an insult to justice and morality for the United States to strategically store, at taxpayers' expense, food that was unlikely to be used in the domestic market while people of the Sahel and Horn confronted a historic famine. Leland asked Reagan to approve tapping into the U.S. Strategic Wheat Reserve to complement the aid package the president had approved. He reasoned that using a portion of the reserve would reduce the cost and time involved in delivering food to famine zones in Africa.[1]

In a letter to the *Baltimore Afro-American*, to make the public case for his cause, Leland described it as unconscionable "that people on the other side of the globe should die of starvation while mountains of food . . . pile up in our warehouses."[2] He made a compelling case, but Leland continually underestimated the president's capacity to shrewdly appropriate narratives of the United States as leading the international humanitarian imperative in Africa to deflect criticism of his administration and present himself and the United States as embodying moral leadership. He wove these narratives to his own advantage. Reagan had reason to abide by his faith in his political instincts. The president was enjoying rising popularity after a sluggish start to his first term, and 1984 was an election year.[3]

Congressman Leland faced more obstacles to seeing his plan come to fruition than merely doing political battle with an incumbent president during an election year. He wanted to energize the advocacy of humanitarian relief and development in Africa in a way similar to the anti-apartheid movement, but he had little success. Reports of starving women and children quickly grew trite. Rather than those experiencing famine, relief workers acquired exalted positions. Rather than a movement, Leland was part of a lobbying campaign, buttressed by events such as delegations traveling to the Horn to report on the efficacy of U.S. aid and keep the issue of famine in the media. He struggled to avoid being overtaken by the domestic politics of international food aid. There were three areas where the politics of food aid were particularly evident: in the debate over use of the U.S. Strategic Wheat Reserve, the public sector's role in humanitarian relief, and debates over U.S.-Soviet humanitarian partnerships in delivering assistance.

Reagan initially dismissed pressure to link the Wheat Reserve and food aid for Africa. His officials argued that the wheat would be wasted in Africa because corn and millet, not wheat, were the primary staples. Besides the basic illogic of supplying wheat, they contended that doing so would undermine the legislation that had established the reserve. They claimed that it was strictly designated by law for domestic emergencies only. "We feel that use of the Emergency Wheat Reserve is not appropriate to meet this emergency situation," read a White House statement.[4] Congress established the reserve as part of the Food for Peace program (Public Law 480) after President Carter placed sanctions on the Soviet Union in response to its invasion of Afghanistan in December 1979.[5] Ultimately, however, authority over the reserve rested with the president, who determined when and how it would be used. So, to succeed, Leland had to give Reagan clear incentives to use it. Leland countered that the White House's argument was only partially accurate. He reminded the president that the legislation that created the reserve in 1980 stipulated that it existed to stave off a food crisis in the United States or an "exceptional need" anywhere in the world.[6]

Fortunately, Leland benefited from his like-minded colleagues and a host of interested journalists who brought the debate to the public's attention. Representative Tony Hall, a Democrat from Ohio and chair of the Hunger Committee's International Task Force, also asked the president to change his position. Following his own fact-finding mission to the Horn he was convinced that the United States had a moral obligation to use the Wheat Reserve and that it was essential for famine relief. Hall echoed Leland's demand that the United States must not stockpile food that could be used to help save others from starvation.[7] He quietly called on the president directly to change his position, while publicly Leland organized protests and continued to issue press releases to criticize the president's policies. The pressure on the president, negative and positive, prevailed, as there was no rationale for him to block the use of a stockpile of wheat that was unlikely to be consumed domestically, while reports of starving and malnourished children in Africa continued unabated. The upside for the president was that releasing a portion of the reserve was his prerogative. The positive media response would be aimed at him and his administration.

At the end of the first week of December 1984, Reagan announced what to Leland certainly would have sounded like a victory: The United States would tap the Strategic Wheat Reserve. NGOs partnering with the government would incorporate the supply into ongoing U.S. humanitarian initiatives in Africa.[8] Leland benefited from the fact that on matters that the president regarded as minor, and most nonpolitical African issues certainly counted among them, he avoided firm ideological positions that placed him on the political defensive. In other words, he would rather send wheat to Africa than force his officials to continuously justify allowing potential food aid to sit unused when images of starving Africans remained fixtures on the evening news.

Reagan claimed the victory for himself. The White House staff choreographed the president's capitulation to make it appear that the new policy originated with the president rather than being one he only belatedly embraced. During the signing ceremony for the program, White House officials ensured favorable optics and expressed candidly their aim to present the president as the driving force behind the U.S. humanitarian initiative in Africa. It was an opportunity, as one White House official noted, for the "president to take credit for the largest food aid program in the world, and to receive deserved credit for the very generous US response, and counter attempts by members of Congress to blame loss of life on the Administration."[9]

The ten-minute ceremony brimmed with praise for U.S. food aid initiatives. The motley assemblage of legislators and USAID officials—Peter McPherson, Robert McFarlane, Robert Dole, Leland, Jesse Helms, Bill Emerson, and William Gray—gathered behind the president for the official signing. In his remarks, the president again sought to outflank relief advocates in Congress. He did not mention Leland. The president briefly summarized U.S. achievements in response to the famine and outlined a five-point plan to accelerate U.S. delivery of emergency food aid. He purposefully paid tribute to private-sector responses to the Ethiopian famine. He described private volunteer organizations as "America at its very best."[10] Reagan went a step further than the reserves and announced that he would make an additional $50 million in food aid available to distribute to private volunteer organizations in Africa. For White House officials, the signing ceremony demonstrated that the president and his administration remained committed to famine relief. They wanted to "counter criticism in some quarters that we are not doing enough."[11] Reagan also hoped to send the message that although government was involved in the relief initiative, the private sector remained the more important player.

Leland had little choice but to appear to applaud the president's leadership on the issue. Leland stood to gain from the president staging the Wheat Reserve source as his idea. It aided his case for a strong government role in African humanitarian relief. Leland supported a role for the private sector, but he held to the view that the federal government had an obligation to act as the primary supporter of U.S. humanitarian assistance.

With his lobbying the White House about the Wheat Reserve over, Leland moved to a more ambitious campaign. In early December 1984, Leland called on the U.S. government to set aside $1 billion to fund a global initiative to end hunger. He was still energized by the success of his congressional delegation to Africa and the president's about-face on using the Strategic Wheat Reserve. He appeared to have momentum on his side to demonstrate the strength of the public sector leading U.S. humanitarian relief initiatives. He wanted to keep the pressure on the president and the issue alive in the media. On December 8, he held a rally on the Capitol steps with five Democratic colleagues, several African ambassadors, heads of relief agencies, and American actor Cliff Robertson to demand the funds for the global hunger relief program.[12] Leland continually argued against political ideologies factoring in decisions to deliver humanitarian assistance. But he showed that foreign aid was deeply political. "While it is unarguable that providing humanitarian assistance promotes the interests of the US," Leland said, "it is equally unarguable that aid delivered in a nonpolitical manner makes the greater contribution to our nation's credibility." Advancing one country's security in an increasingly interdependent world by withholding from neighbors the fundamentals of life was not only morally wrong but also politically counterproductive.[13] As had been the case with the Anti-Apartheid Act of 1986, humanitarian assistance represented a redirection for the United States. There was a political dimension at each step of his campaign to transform the status of humanitarian relief in the U.S. government.

They were not successful, but their demonstration advanced the argument for an unprecedented relief initiative. It also paved the way for the African Famine Relief Act of 1986, a more than $800 million relief package for African countries. Releasing supplies from the Strategic Wheat Reserve set a precedent for Leland to broaden U.S. humanitarian relief in Ethiopia. He wanted assistance to go directly to the Ethiopian government, because it operated most of the feeding centers and displaced persons camps in the country. He also wanted to shift toward development aid. Leland's narrative defined U.S. aid as indispensable in the global fight against hunger, starting with Ethiopia, but his Republican colleagues painted a different image. They spoke frequently of Ethiopian malfeasance, food aid diversion, and human rights abuses. In speeches and policy statements, the president painted a convincing picture of the United States as a nation that spent beyond its financial means, often wastefully.[14] He also shifted the focus of U.S. foreign aid to military assistance instead of traditional developmental aid.[15]

Even though Leland believed the U.S. government should be directly involved in providing humanitarian assistance, he also believed private voluntary organizations (PVOs) had a big role to play in the effort. Leland cited InterAction and its director, Peter Davies, as evidence of the strengths of PVOs and his support of them. InterAction was a coalition of more than one hundred private voluntary organizations working in developing countries.[16] Leland hailed it and other PVOs as "the heroes of the African crisis." Leland recognized many private organizations' strengths in humanitarian initiatives, but he insisted that they could not "fully meet the requirements of the hungry and malnourished throughout the world and in our own country." The problem was far too vast. "Food assistance and a new commitment to attacking the conditions which allow such hunger in a world of plenty by our national government are clearly required," Leland wrote to Reagan.[17] Leland believed that the U.S. government had an obligation to mount an effective response to the crisis. As he said at a Senate hearing, "Every single person has the responsibility to see to it that innocent children do not die from starvation or suffer the consequences of malnutrition. "Hunger in a world of plenty is simply unacceptable to all of us." To attain the goal of eliminating hunger in the world, he declared, would "require the leadership, the resources and the full commitment of the U.S government working with the United Nations, the World Bank, other donor governments and host governments to attack the underlying conditions which permit— even encourage—the epidemic of hunger to linger with us."[18]

During an interview that aired on C-Span on December 16, 1985, Leland once again placed the United States at the center of Ethiopia's prospects for social and economic advancement. He argued that it was essential for the United States to provide direct development assistance to the Ethiopian government. "Things have changed for the better to a very limited extent in Africa," he said. "But at the same time," Leland continued, "we have to recognize that we have to be forever vigilant about the problem because we still have not implemented that sort of long-term development support to Africa that is necessary in order for us not to see a repetition of what happened in the last year in those countries that have been suffering so gravely." Leland regarded himself as Congress's moral conscience on world hunger. He won his colleagues' support for food aid for the Horn, but he did not anticipate the extent of "famine fatigue" in Congress and among the public. He was concerned that Ethiopia would slip back into "the same cataclysmic famine" of the previous year.[19]

Leland's first, most obvious goal for the U.S. response to the Ethiopian crisis was to deliver food aid to save lives. He also wanted U.S. food aid to evolve into effective government assistance. His ultimate, longer-term objective was to eliminate the factors that caused hunger in Ethiopia, other parts of Africa, and the rest of the world. Changing conceptions in the United States of the role of humanitarian assistance in saving lives was critical to achieving this goal.

In a February 1985 speech he had argued that if Western nations possessed adequate political will they would eliminate hunger within a generation: "In less developed nations the causes of hunger are multiple—national poverty, lack of training, desertification, poor agricultural policies—to name a few. Nevertheless, given the political will, hunger can be ended worldwide in our generation."[20] Leland's inclination to separate Mengistu's personality and policies from Ethiopia's food challenges was an additional complicating factor. Rather than leverage his relationship with Mengistu, he looked past him almost entirely. He prescribed U.S. development assistance almost as if African leaders did not exist. "We've placed our priorities primarily in the area of emergency relief," he said during the C-Span interview, "but we need to reorient our priorities to long-term development relief, wherein we teach farmers how to make money from their own crops."[21] It was also imperative that African governments be prepared for food shortages. When Leland enumerated the causes of widespread famine in Africa during a congressional hearing, he included "an initial failure on the part of African and donor community government officials to detect impending famine."[22]

His prescription to end hunger in the world included making the realities of people's experiences with daily hunger clear to the public, outside of the well-publicized famine crises. Absent images he used numbers to dramatize the depth of the problem: "The fact is that every day, without famine or civil war, more than 40,000 men, women and children—primarily children—die from lack of adequate diet. 40,000 deaths per day means that this year, just as last year, 15 million people—again primarily children—will die from hunger."[23] When Leland described what he called "the daily reality of hunger" he presented a simple, streamlined assessment. He avoided complicating the picture he painted with civil wars and politics. This was, of course, a political choice on his part. He insisted that the central underlying cause of hunger was poverty. Therefore, hunger would be eradicated through wealth redistribution. "People are hungry," he insisted in an address at the University of Houston in 1987, "because they are poor—too poor to produce or to purchase adequately nutritious food."[24]

Leland envisaged U.S. humanitarian assistance expanding beyond food supplies and financial support to U.S. agricultural and economic expertise. He believed, for example, that U.S. farmers were global models for food production. He felt that the absence of a program for U.S. agricultural experts to share techniques with their African counterparts was similar to hoarding. He called U.S. farmers "a great brain trust." Their success and high productivity were evidence that the United States possessed the expertise to solve Africa's food crisis. Leland said in the C-Span interview:

The president deserves some good marks in the area of African famine relief and the emergency crises in those twenty-eight countries in Africa. I pay special tribute to USAID and Mr. McPherson in that effort. I have some areas of concern even in that effort, but I will give them good marks. The fact of the matter is we spent a pittance of money even though we provided about half of Africa's needs in that crisis. The fact of the matter is we should not wait for other donor nations when in fact we have the resources to help in a greater sense. We spent about $800 million out of our [congressional] budget on African famine relief. That's a pittance when you consider that we raised the military budget by upward toward $300 billion. We can take a few of those $5, 6, 10 billions of our nation's resources to target those problems of hunger in this country and the world.[25]

Leland wanted long-term engagement to allow for gradual but sustained economic growth. Leland foresaw an African future shaped by U.S. investment. The shift in his view of the United States was not subtle. Previously he had advocated reforming the United States entirely, if not seeing it completely destroyed. He now envisaged using its tremendous wealth for the greater good of the world. Africa's rise would extend from a combination of African initiatives and U.S. support for long-term development programs. He highlighted four particular investment points for the United States: primary health care, agriculture programs, basic education, and ending apartheid. "Those of us in the US who care passionately about Africa," Leland said during the African-American Conference in Gaborone, Botswana, "must be encouraged and optimistic. The answers to the great problems facing Africa today will not come easily. Progress on some fronts will not be immediate, as you know. But the direction is clear, the outcome is now certain. Only the timing is unknown."[26]

Leland presented ending hunger as an attainable goal, achievable only with collective engagement: "We could solve the problem if there was the political will, and if we were really ready to put our money where our mouths are." He considered the president's posturing on hunger as wholly inadequate. He insisted that for both humanitarian aid and development to fulfill their potential, nations that provided assistance must disentangle aid from politics. Therefore, diplomatic ties and long-term development aid went hand in hand. He conceived of the U.S. role in African development as having a strong redistributive aspect. As the famine appeared to be ending,

Leland intimated that nation building was an American obligation: "We have to look into the long-term solutions now," Leland said. "Unless we solve the long-term problem we'll have a perpetual short-term problem on our hands. We can provide all the food in the world to countries like Ethiopia today, but if we don't go in there and retrofit the agricultural infrastructure for the long-term, those we've fed today will be starving tomorrow."[27]

Leland argued that his strategy would help both U.S. and African farmers, but this approach had little support in the United States. Again, he pointed to the lack of political motivation and of a real understanding of African crises that might advance effective development. "The political will we don't have," he said on a local Houston television news program in 1987.

> There are some of us who want to bring those factors together so that we can help to feed the rest of the world and ourselves for that matter. We have millions of tubs of grain in silos just wasting away. We pay farmers billions of dollars in subsidies not to grow crops on their land. We have family farmers suffering a plight that none of our people should be suffering, because for years they have in fact fed the American people; they helped build this incredible infrastructure we have. This incredible economy we're booming from even though we have a problem with our federal spending, our budget deficit and so forth. It was the family farmer who fed America and gave us the ability to do so. By that example, we can go and translate that in other countries and help other countries to do the same thing. But we have not yet married those respective factions together so we can help to produce food to feed the rest of the world.[28]

Political will and knowledge of Africa remained in short order in the United States; however, the list of obstacles to Leland's goal of a dynamic movement to end hunger was long. While he argued his case that food aid was the appropriate response to chronic hunger in Africa, stories proliferated in the U.S. media about recipient countries misappropriating aid, with some even funneling it to sustain their war efforts. With regard to Ethiopia in particular, these news stories affirmed a widely held suspicion in Congress that the humanitarian initiative was grossly mismanaged at a minimum and at worst buttressed the Mengistu regime through his theft of aid.

Though Reagan issued a statement on September 9, 1985, that the State Department found the government of Ethiopia was not "at this time conducting a deliberate policy of starvation," media reports of mismanagement continued.[29] Reagan's statement did not stop the attacks of Congressman Toby Roth, Congressman Gerald Solomon, and their colleagues on the Ethiopian government's credibility and their questioning of its role in creating and sustaining the famine. Roth, a Republican from Wisconsin, proposed legislation that would require the president to confirm that Mengistu did not channel humanitarian relief to his military and political operations before Congress would appropriate additional food relief funds.[30] The bill ultimately passed in Congress.

Mengistu gave the Relief and Rehabilitation Commission (RRC) fairly broad latitude to carry out famine relief in cooperation with foreign NGOs and PVOs. He also did not concede to accusations, mostly foreign, that his policies and personality contributed to the ongoing food crisis. He chose to view it as a recurring issue in Ethiopia's history. In one revealing response, Mengistu advised the RRC chairman not to "let these petty human problems that always exist in transition periods consume you. There was famine in Ethiopia for years before we took power—it was the way nature kept balance. Today we are interfering with that natural mechanism of balance, and that is why our population has soared to over 40 million." According to Dawit Wolde Giorgis, Mengistu described the crisis as cultural and agricultural but in no way political. Primitive agricultural practices had exhausted the soil of its undulating terrain. "Consequently," Mengistu explained, "the land is badly eroded."[31] His expressed priority was to achieve the regime's political objectives.[32] Famines, like wars of secession, for Mengistu and for most of Ethiopia's preceding monarchs over the centuries were part of Ethiopian life. Of greater significance, from Mengistu's standpoint, were national defense and agricultural reforms rather than squandering precious resources on an issue that time itself would solve. As food aid from the West amassed on the Ethiopian coast and finally made it to those who needed it, from February to May 1985 Mengistu launched a major offensive on the TPLF.

Waging war on the TPLF and the EPLF, rather than on his country's chronic food problem, exposed Mengistu to accusations that he was ignoring the crisis and that his regime was responsible for human rights abuses and redirecting humanitarian assistance for military purposes. Leland had been defending the Ethiopian government against such allegations since the start of the large-scale U.S. relief program in 1984. In September 1986, in one of his office's many press releases on the subject, Leland insisted that it was dangerous to undermine the credibility of the relief initiative with baseless allegations against the Ethiopian government. "It is a real disservice to the people of this country and certainly to the people of Ethiopia to imply that these relief efforts were futile or mismanaged or inappropriate," Leland argued.[33] However, as part of his ongoing political assault on Mengistu, in January 1987 Toby Roth cosponsored "The Promotion of Democracy in Ethiopia Act of 1987" with William Gray. The bill called for sanctions against the Ethiopian government if it failed to "respect the human rights of its people, grant basic civil rights, terminate and dismantle its forced resettlement program, free all political prisoners, establish laws that protect citizens and ensure their participation in a free society."[34] The region's critics in Washington also charged the Ethiopian government with diverting humanitarian aid as a means to support its military campaigns in the north. Leland did not support the bill, fearing that the successful propagation of this narrative would potentially halt, or at least severely reduce, the relatively free movement of relief workers and aid in Ethiopia.

Leland linked these accusations to the president's broader politicization of humanitarian relief: "The government of Ethiopia has a political agenda with which a lot of us involved in the relief program have great differences. The parties making these allegations have their political agenda, however. To advance it, they are apparently willing to cite numbers which have no basis." He insisted that only 50,000 of the 800,000 tons in U.S. food aid were delivered through the RRC. And all the food aid deliveries were monitored by USAID and reached their intended recipients.[35] Ambassador Robert Houdek's position was that all sides had diverted food aid. Relief organization officials, he recalled, referred to the groups from the government army and the rebel groups that blocked and diverted humanitarian relief as "wheat militias." The United States was aware of the relationship between these militias and the EPLF, the TPLF, and the Ethiopian army.[36]

The discussions of aid diversion and human rights, for Leland, distracted from the more pressing problem of immediate aid and long-term development in Africa. He believed diplomacy was an essential conduit for both. Rebuilding diplomatic relations between Ethiopia and the United States would ease the flow of humanitarian assistance and generally benefit Ethiopians. President Mengistu also wanted to renew ties with the United States with the hope of receiving larger amounts of direct aid, but he had no desire to be the first to extend an olive branch, and he had not fully come to terms with the economic and political importance of the United States for his regime's survival. He preferred to conceive of citizens of European and American countries, not their governments, as the driving force behind humanitarian action. So, he expressed his gratitude to the people of the United States rather than President Reagan and Congress. After all, he said, citizens were responsible for "bringing pressure to bear on their governments to send emergency famine relief to this country. . . . We are touched by the humanitarian outpouring which the people of these countries demonstrated."[37] By 1987, the African political climate had compelled Leland to more forcefully and directly address the African country's political issues. He traveled to the Horn in February 1987, his first trip to Ethiopia since November 1984, specifically to study the country's political situation.[38]

In addition to Mengistu's seeming inability to recognize the depth of his country's food crisis and the magnitude of the U.S. response, there were legal hurdles in the United States to restoring full U.S.-Ethiopian diplomatic ties. The Hickenlooper Amendment, which was attached to the 1962 Foreign Assistance Act, prohibited aid to countries that expropriated property owned by the U.S. government or its citizens. Congress had to deal with this legislation before any plans for revived diplomatic relations with Ethiopia could even be considered. To avoid being the target of the amendment's sanctions, Ethiopia had to compensate the American government and owners of private properties it had seized after the 1974 revolution. Leland had been optimistic. "I feel that the government of Ethiopia is close to coming to an agreement with us on Hickenlooper," he said after he met with Mengistu in December 1984, despite little evidence that this was in fact the case. To achieve this would have been no small task, and neither Congress nor the president had indicated that it would jump-start diplomacy between the two countries. Leland appeared to be getting ahead of the issue with the hope that reality would catch up to him. "All they have to do is make a good-faith effort," Leland posited.[39]

Leland pushed for diplomacy, while political change in the Soviet Union added an additional layer to Mengistu's economic and political troubles. Perestroika sent shock waves throughout Eastern Europe and the Global South, as Mikhail Gorbachev rapidly repositioned the Soviet Union's economic and political stakes in foreign affairs. While the Soviet leader's reforms created a crisis for leftist regimes reliant on Soviet assistance, Gorbachev's earnest desire to reinvent U.S.-Soviet relations was an opportunity for Leland and other U.S. politicians who had long rejected Cold War policies in international affairs. At last, it seemed to Leland, ideology would no longer serve as a barrier to U.S. assistance for Mozambique, Angola, and Ethiopia. Even as he established a more central role in laying the groundwork for U.S. policies in post-Soviet Africa, he would continually be disappointed by the persistence of political ideology in the president's and his colleagues' views of the Global South.

In 1985, Gorbachev foresaw economic and political calamities for Ethiopia under Mengistu, who would not have survived EPLF and TPLF offensives to that point if not for foreign assistance, particularly from the USSR. But the Soviet Union's domestic reforms had little room to accommodate international patronage in the Global South. Many historians have credited Gorbachev's bold reforms in 1985 as signaling the end of the Cold War. Beginning as an obscure member of the Politburo, Gorbachev rose to the premiership and led a remarkable turnaround from the ruinous policies of the three preceding premiers, Leonid Brezhnev, Yuri Andropov, and Konstantin Chernenko.[40] Imperialist overextension had been the Soviets' problem. Soviet leaders had supported Marxist governments abroad regardless of the negative consequences for the Soviet economy.[41] The Soviet Union no longer had the credibility to stand as a model for Global South political and economic development.[42]

Gorbachev reined in the Soviet Union's overseas obligations from 1985 through 1990. He aimed to increase his personal political strength, achieve genuine rapprochement with the United States, and make serious progress toward mutual superpower disarmament.[43] Gorbachev wrote Mengistu in an attempt to persuade him to reconcile with the United States. "Let me be entirely frank," Gorbachev told the Ethiopian leader. "There simply is no alternative to a political solution, naturally within the framework of a united Ethiopian state."[44] Mengistu did not immediately warm to Gorbachev's proposal. He seemed to have always gained personal strength from his defiant challenge of U.S. interests in the region. When considering his approach to the United States, Mengistu was aware of the dramatic events taking place in Eastern Europe. Many political experts had predicted a different end to the Cold War. Some had envisaged the United States and the Soviet Union waging a major war that would, quite possibly, end in a nuclear exchange.[45] Instead of superpower confrontation, domestic movements in Eastern and Central Europe precipitated social, economic, and political reforms. For example, in Poland, the Solidarity Movement, led by

Lech Walesa, seized power in Poland's largest cities and demanded participation in the national government.

The contraction of the Soviet global footprint forced Mengistu to seek
alternative sources of military aid. He understood that one potential outcome of embracing U.S. assistance was scrutiny from the United States of
his regime's domestic policies. But there were no viable alternatives that
would ensure his regime survived internal and external threats. He did not
want to rely solely on the United States, so in a last-ditch effort Mengistu
turned to Israel for aid. In exchange for assistance, the Israelis asked Mengistu to agree to allow Ethiopian Jews to immigrate to Israel. But Israel
could not satisfactorily replace Soviet support. Since 1977, the Soviets had
provided an estimated $11 billion in aid to Ethiopia.[46] East Germany and
Czechoslovakia had given Ethiopia at least $12 billion in support, consisting
mostly of military equipment.

For two years after Mengistu broke diplomatic relations with the United
States in 1980, Premier Leonid Brezhnev had been Mengistu's lifeline. Premier Yuri Andropov maintained Soviet assistance to Ethiopia until his
death in 1984. The Soviets had provided Ethiopia with economic and military aid, but Gorbachev engineered radical political reforms in the Soviet
Union that created a potentially regime-ending scenario for Mengistu. As
secretary-general of the Soviet Union, Gorbachev did not regard buffer
states and proxies as a sustainable strategy for containing U.S. hegemony.
Rather than continue to compete with the United States, Gorbachev aspired
to steady the Soviet Union's declining economy and improve daily life
among its citizens. This restructuring included placing checks on military
arms proliferation. He wanted to work with the United States on building
peace in Angola, Mozambique, South Africa, and Ethiopia.

Strategic involvement in the Global South was costly and contradicted
Soviet interest in rapprochement with the United States. Anatoly Adamishin, the Soviet deputy foreign minister, developed the Soviet Union's new
policy toward African countries. He dismissed the Ethiopian revolution as
a lost cause on which the USSR continued to waste millions of rubles.[47]
Gorbachev supported Adamishin's position and agreed to shift Soviet
involvement in all liberation struggles to diplomacy, with limited economic
assistance and military support. Soviet leaders realized that the Ethiopian
people would face difficulties if the country's principal ally abandoned
them, so they agreed to propose a Soviet-U.S. effort to resolve "the Ethiopian regional problem."[48] They drafted a personal letter from Gorbachev to

Mengistu outlining the necessity of dialogue with combatants within the country and with the United States.

Gorbachev's goals for reforms included proposals to coordinate with the United States on peace and development in the Global South. A U.S.-Soviet humanitarian partnership in Africa had been one of Leland's long-standing goals. He hoped it would end the Cold War's East-West dichotomy and allow the United States to engage the Angolan and Mozambique governments beyond the confines of anticommunist policies. He developed an outline for a joint program and sent it to House Speaker Jim Wright, who was preparing for a congressional delegation to Moscow to discuss the Soviet proposal to eliminate medium-range nuclear missiles. As he had for U.S. food aid to Ethiopia, Leland had politically neutral, people-centered goals for the joint humanitarian initiative. "I believe that any serious proposal should incorporate collaborative efforts on the part of the Soviet Union and the United States," he wrote to Wright, "and should be seen as primarily benefitting African and other Third World people [sic]."[49]

Leland hoped that the Soviets would agree to persuade representatives from Angola's ruling Popular Movement for the Liberation of Angola (MPLA; Movimento Popular de Libertação de Angola) to enter into peace negotiations with Jonas Savimbi, leader of the National Union for the Total Independence of Angola (UNITA; União Nacional para a Independência Total de Angola), without preconditions. The peace conference would take place under the auspices of the United Nations, with the United States and the Soviet Union acting as sponsors. To end the civil war, Leland envisioned concessions from the United States and the Soviet Union. The United States would end aid to Savimbi and secure guarantees from South Africa against further interference in Angola.[50] For their part, the Soviet Union would end aid to the MPLA and Cuban forces would withdraw from the country. Leland was knowledgeable about the political situation in Angola. He traveled there twice in 1987 to gain firsthand information on the political situation and civil war.[51]

His plans for U.S.-Soviet cooperation in Mozambique were wholly humanitarian and focused on internally displaced in Mozambique and Mozambican refugees in Zambia. He proposed that the Soviets supply trucks, barges, and helicopters to transport food stocks provided by the United States, the United Nations, and the European Community. Leland believed that Mozambique would be acceptable to cold warriors in the

White House and Congress because, despite FRELIMO's professed Marxism, the country maintained relatively friendly relations with the United States.[52]

For the third component of Leland's proposal to Wright, he borrowed from Cuban medical internationalism to outline his vision for an international health service corps, a network of health-care teams sent to developing countries around the world.[53] It would be a joint health service corps, "a humanitarian people-to-people program to send joint U.S./Soviet health teams to developing countries around the world." He envisaged U.S. volunteers being recruited through a loan forgiveness program.[54] He explained to Wright that it would "provide an opportunity for both countries to use their physicians and other health personnel to deliver care, teach and enhance public health systems in countries where they are needed.[55]

For Leland, the initiative was a historic chance for both countries to demonstrate goodwill and be seen as humanitarian forces.

> Supporters of the proposed US/Soviet International Health Services Corps would see it as an opportunity for cooperation between the two countries on a truly humanitarian level. The presence of health personnel from both countries working together on a person-to-person basis would project goodwill and the hope of more substantive progress toward peace. Opponents of such a venture would be concerned that the United States would end up carrying the administrative and financial burden of a program that would give the Soviets substantial favorable publicity around the world.[56]

The proposal evidently impressed Wright. He invited Leland to join his congressional delegation to the Soviet Union scheduled for March 1987. It would be Leland's first trip to the Soviet Union. Wright included him specifically to present Soviet leaders with his plan for the joint humanitarian relief program.[57] The trip was the highest-ranking congressional delegation ever to the Soviet Union, and the congressmen met with the highest-level Soviet officials.[58]

During their six days in Moscow, the bipartisan group of lawmakers met with several top Kremlin officials, including Eduard Shevardnadze and Mikhail Gorbachev. Shevardnadze embraced Leland's proposal and offered Soviet civilian cargo planes to fly to the United States, load surplus U.S.

grain, and fly to Mozambique. Leland was so delighted by the prospect of collaboration that his "spine tingled with excitement."[59] It was precisely the cooperation he had yearned to achieve. If successful, it would cement the efficacy of peaceful U.S.-Soviet cooperation in Africa and quickly address a worsening food crisis.

There were obstacles to bringing all parties involved to a point of agreement, but Leland was optimistic that the two superpowers working together on outreach to Mozambique marked the beginning of an era of true humanitarian relief in Africa. "I think if it works," he mused, "it can work within a year and the two big powers can begin similar programs throughout Africa jointly, so that we can shift our emphasis toward humanitarian goals."[60] It must have seemed like a simple yet unattainable goal to Leland over the previous four years. Cold War politics had posed a formidable obstacle to truly effective humanitarian assistance. He does not appear to have foreseen obstacles to joint U.S.-Soviet humanitarianism within Congress. Mozambique was a logical recipient choice because its government was positively disposed toward the West and demonstrated eagerness to forge closer ties with the United States. It also faced a food crisis that had left an estimated 4.5 million people on the verge of famine. The United States was already involved in Mozambique, having pledged $75 million in indirect relief aid, mostly in the form of 200,000 tons of grain.[61]

When Wright met with Assistant Secretary of State Chester Crocker to update him on the bipartisan delegation and Soviet support for Leland's proposed initiative, he learned that President Reagan would not accept a humanitarian partnership with Moscow, despite Gorbachev's strong backing of the program. Reagan was unwilling to normalize relations with Mozambique's Marxist government, which was battling a self-described anticommunist insurrection. Leland was astonished that Cold War politics, again, had foiled an initiative intended to help bridge the political divide between the Soviet Union and the United States, and he lamented that he had support from all corners except his own government. He had pushed to target Mozambique for the pilot humanitarian project with the Soviets precisely because it was a Marxist country with relatively good relations with the United States.[62] The United States, however, was not heavily invested in the civil war in Mozambique. Apparently Reagan administration officials perceived no real political gain from the humanitarian initiative; they had already approved food aid. A joint initiative in Angola, on the other hand, could be leveraged to facilitate Cuba's withdrawal from the region, so Reagan officials floated the possibility of a joint program there predicated on the departure of Cuban troops.[63]

Politically, peace in Angola would do Savimbi no favors. Drawn-out civil war was to his advantage, and he had managed to stall peace talks by insisting upon preconditions. This tactic allowed him to avoid meeting MPLA leaders. As long as the civil war dragged on, Savimbi benefited from Washington-based financial and political support. He was, arguably, the Reagan administration's favorite African leader. U.S. support of Savimbi began under President Carter but increased under Reagan.[64] On June 11, 1985, the Senate repealed the Clark Amendment, which had prohibited covert operations in Angola for almost a decade. The House voted similarly on July 10. When Savimbi visited with President Reagan in January 1986 during his ten-day visit to the United States, the president had already committed a small amount of covert aid to the Angolan rebel. Savimbi wanted to increase the president's support for UNITA and gain broad support from Congress and the U.S. public.

The *Wall Street Journal* styled Savimbi as "the favorite anti-Communist hero of American conservatives." Yet beyond anticommunism, fighting the Marxist MPLA, and securing U.S. assistance, Savimbi's political goals were hard to discern. "Who is Jonas Savimbi?" Robert Greenberger asked. "To American conservatives he is, at long last, a romantic revolutionary, a Ché Guevara of the Right complete with beard and camouflage fatigues, who fights communism."[65] From the politically conservative standpoint, Savimbi had no peers among Global South leaders. Though Reagan supported the Contras in Nicaragua, they did not have a charismatic leader. Both Carter and Reagan had embraced the mujahideen leaders in Afghanistan, but they were shadowy, exuberantly conservative in their Islamic beliefs, and showed no love for the United States or capitalism. Savimbi presented himself as the model Third Word rebel. He told President Reagan and Republican leaders what they wanted to hear about Western-style development and communism, and he did so in fluent English.[66]

Leland blamed the State Department for spoiling the momentum toward cooperation between the superpowers: "The State Department's attitude is we need to embarrass the Soviets into giving more money through the United Nations. . . . They don't want to get involved in something where they think the Soviets might get more credit than they deserve." He called this approach ridiculous and detrimental to real human lives.[67] Leland did not abandon plans for Mozambique, however. He urged his colleagues to support his project, but as the Soviet Union moved rapidly away from a Cold War framework for global affairs, a sizable contingent within Congress remained as determined as ever to achieve a full, uncompromised Cold War victory. This position was ironic because of the president's previous statements about wanting to build common ground with the Soviet Union. The Global South remained fully enflamed in the Cold War. Rather than encourage greater reforms in countries like Mozambique that had relied heavily on Soviet economic and military assistance, Republicans enacted legislation to hobble these governments. One example was proposing amendments to a bill meant to increase total U.S. aid to African countries to $585 million for fiscal year 1988. The series of amendments would restrict aid to Frontline States in southern Africa—Botswana, Lesotho, Malawi, Tanzania, Swaziland, Angola, Zambia, Zimbabwe, and Mozambique. If one of the proposed amendments had succeeded, it would have stopped aid to all of the Frontline States except Botswana. Leland argued, "If the United States restricts or eliminates its assistance, it will be limiting its future influence in a region of vital significance." He insisted that the United States had to work with these countries to bring an end to apartheid in South Africa. "Only when the Frontline States are strong and independent will they be able to provide the necessary pressure for change in South Africa," Leland said.[68]

A group of Republican representatives proposed an amendment to ban aid to countries that received three-fourths of their military aid or more than fifty-five advisors from the Soviet Union. If successful, this measure would have excluded Mozambique from receiving U.S. aid. These radical amendments had no grounding in the political realities of the moment. Even Reagan had previously complimented Mozambique's economic and political reforms, but when the time came to formalize relations, these reforms were claimed to be insufficient. Leland called on Reagan to follow Britain's example, where Prime Minister Margaret Thatcher, hardly a moderating force, allowed her country to broaden its ties with Mozambique. The prime minister, Leland argued, was "clearly a democratic capitalist by anyone's definition," and she was "expanding economic and military assistance to Mozambique." When the amendments to the aid bill failed, Leland complimented his colleagues for rejecting Cold War politics: "Today people are literally starving because of the destabilization efforts of South Africa in Mozambique and adjoining territories and related food transport problems. We can be proud that Congress did not raise ideological barriers to the humanitarian aid and economic support the people of the region so desperately need."[69] Still, he and Wright failed to get support for the U.S.-Soviet humanitarian initiative in Mozambique, afterward blaming it on Congress's ignorance of African affairs.

Leland concluded that his colleagues' ignorance of even basic facts concerning Mozambique allowed Reagan officials to easily sway them to oppose the joint humanitarian initiative. This reflected a common lament among the black internationalist left in the United States about the extent of American ignorance on issues and affairs in the Global South. Randall Robinson frequently detailed the dire consequences of an under- and misinformed American public. "We are a sadly parochial country," he said to the Cleveland City Club in November 1982. "A congressman recently in a position to know told me he didn't think there were more than twenty members of Congress who could name three African countries. Perhaps he exaggerated, but the likelihood is that he did not. The question is, how can we afford as a nation to know so little about a continent on which this nation grows increasingly dependent?"[70]

Leland approached Jim Wright about creating a task force on Africa dedicated to educating the Democratic congressional leadership on African affairs. He hoped that with more information, his colleagues would take political positions closer to his own on African issues. How could they have a firm position on events in the region without basic knowledge of those events? His goal, he said, was "to inform them of the differences, for example between Ethiopia and Zaire. To deal with the nuances of politics among the different countries of Africa and the common interest that most of the nations of Africa have. As opposed to responding at times of crises in Africa I feel that members should become more aware of what Africa is about."[71] He cited Iran as an example of the level of misinformation prevalent in Congress and how detrimental this lack of knowledge was to U.S. foreign policy. During the first Iranian crisis, Leland contended, members of Congress knew nothing of Iranian culture, religion, or history. "I have found that members of Congress are even more ignorant about Africa. They believe that Africa is a jungle where black people run around in loincloths," he said. This ignorance, he argued, was the reason his proposal for Mozambique failed. He said his colleagues had supported earlier famine relief initiatives because hunger in Africa was easy for them to comprehend, because it fit their expectations for Africa. Dynamic issues such as East-West collaboration on hunger relief, however, were a greater challenge for them:

"When you get into the nuance of the difficulties of working in Mozambique you understand there is an East-West nuance. Mozambique worked with the Soviets for a long time, but we have an evolving relationship. It's not a competition. We need to educate members of Congress about Africa and I have that charge."[72]

Famine returned to northern Ethiopia and the Ogaden region in early 1987, while the political scene grew increasingly complex, as the TPLF and the EPLF gained the upper hand over the Mengistu regime. The rebels' growing strength, an evolving Soviet role in Ethiopia, and Mengistu's deepening political desperation forced Leland to grapple with more than aid as a solution to the Ethiopian crisis. The renewed crisis challenged Leland's faith in the possible end of famine but not his faith in the efficacy of U.S. government assistance. As he had done during the 1983–85 famine, Leland stressed to his colleagues in the House of Representatives the essential role of the United States in famine relief as a moral leader in the world. If the United States failed to set an example in the crisis, he contended, "Ethiopians will once again be forced to leave home and go to relief camps for food, and we will have failed." He implored his colleagues to not allow policy questions to dictate the U.S. response because, as he argued, responding to those in need was an American tradition. Therefore, Marxism "should not limit or slow our aid to innocent victims of hunger. That essential policy question was settled in 1984."[73]

Leland was frustrated that the United States had to be cajoled into action by public support for aid and food aid advocates. He feared that the slow start had allowed countless Ethiopians to die. He traveled to Ethiopia in April and August 1987. From these two trips, he concluded that the West was moving too slowly to provide aid in time. "The looming disaster in Ethiopia, caused by drought, is clearly understood by Ethiopians who have asked for international aid," Leland said after he returned from his August trip. "The donor community cannot move slowly and lose a million lives as we did three years ago." Leland, once again, put the onus on the donor community and Western governments, and rather than take on the intricacies of African politics, he was careful to emphasize that the current famine was "caused by drought."[74]

On October 23, 1987, the EPLF raided an emergency food convoy in northern Ethiopia, destroying sixteen UN trucks and seven Council for Responsible Nutrition trucks. In all, 446 tons of food aid for the Eritrea and Tigray provinces were destroyed. Those supplies had the potential to feed more than thirty thousand people for one month. In communication with rebel leaders, EPLF representatives took full responsibility for the raid. "We have made it clear that there is no explanation, no excuse, for actions which directly threaten the lives of thousands of innocent people," Leland responded. "There was no military escort with the convoy. The trucks were moving out of the conflict areas. The trucks were carrying the UN flag."[75] This was a rare reference to the EPLF and the TPLF from Leland.

One or two years earlier, Leland would not have used strong language to criticize an African government or organization, but he recognized the limited power of Western aid to end famine. It had grown clearer to him that African leaders—within governments and rebel movements—contributed to fomenting food crises. "I am horrified at this senseless raid on a relief convoy," Leland wrote in an op-ed. "Throughout the difficult periods of 1984 and 1985, when Ethiopia was on the brink of genuine catastrophe, we avoided this kind of incident. Neither side in the civil war in northern Ethiopia participated in these activities. The relief groups succeeded in getting food to the people. This incident raises grave questions about the ability to repeat that feat. I am fearful of where we go from here."[76] Already hampered by an acute shortage of transport vehicles, the relief effort was further hindered by this newest raid, which destroyed 20 percent of the existing transport fleet in northern Ethiopia.

After ten years on the defensive, in late 1987 the EPLF achieved success in its offensive against the Ethiopian military. The biggest victory in twenty-seven years of fighting came in March 1988. In a three-day battle in and around Afabet, the EPLF reported that they killed or captured eighteen thousand Ethiopian soldiers, seized fifty tanks, and seized three Soviet military advisors to the Ethiopian army. EPLF rebels also killed one Russian military advisor. They were known to exaggerate achievements, but the numbers suggested a lopsided victory. The rebels launched their offensives from their stronghold along the 217-mile stretch from the Eritrean town of Nakfa south and inland to the town of Hahlal. During the previous two weeks, the TPLF had elevated its attacks on the Ethiopian military, destroying six brigades and taking two thousand prisoners.[77]

As the war intensified, famine in the north worsened. Half of those affected were in Tigray and Eritrea. On April 6, 1988, Mengistu ordered all non-Ethiopian workers to leave the Eritrea and Tigray provinces to allow the RRC and local charities to control famine relief operations. The government needed to cleanse the north of "bandits" and ensure the safety of relief workers and displaced people.[78] In actuality, the government was losing its two-front war, and thus Mengistu was eager to remove journalists and relief workers from Tigray and Eritrea. Fighting had been intense over the previous two weeks and government losses had shocked Mengistu. He ordered the United Nations, ICRC, and Catholic Relief Services to hand over operations to Ethiopian agencies. The "evacuations" coincided with intense fighting and a series of Ethiopian military setbacks.[79] The international community interpreted Mengistu's "precautions" as a cover to gain control of the narrative and launch an effective offensive beyond the purview of the human rights vigilance of relief workers and journalists yet continue to receive Western aid.

In November 1988, Mengistu delivered his annual report to the Central Committee of the Workers' Party of Ethiopia. He openly stated that the country was facing major agricultural failures. He had not publicly acknowledged the food crisis before this address. Agriculture supported 89 percent of the population and accounted for 40 percent of GDP. Still, Mengistu allocated 50 percent of the federal budget to the military; Ethiopia had the third-largest army in Africa.[80] Mikhail Gorbachev encouraged Mengistu to pursue diplomacy to end the civil wars in his country and to soften his posture toward the United States. The Soviet premier addressed the UN General Assembly on December 7, 1988, declaring, "We have entered into an era when progress will be shaped by universal human interests." He advised that world politics should be guided by "universal human values." This reorientation, this move toward progress, as he described it, was "only possible through a search for universal human consensus to move forward to a new world order." The address signaled a paradigm shift for the Soviet Union. "Our country is going through a period of truly revolutionary uplifting," Gorbachev said. He reiterated his commitment to democracy and human rights and reaffirmed the Soviet Union's dedication to resolving international challenges through the United Nations, the Conference on Security and Cooperation in Europe, and the International Court of Justice at The Hague.[81] The following February, the Soviets halted military supplies to its key African allies, Angola, Mozambique, and Ethiopia.

Anticommunism also lost its veneer of credibility. Leland and other U.S. politicians had spoken of anticommunism during the early part of the Reagan presidency as hollow and detrimental to U.S. moral authority in global affairs. Their struggle to render anticommunism politically impotent continued in Europe until the opening of the Berlin Wall in 1989, and in

Africa until South Africa's multiracial elections in 1994. Reagan and his fellow conservatives held stock in the erroneous notion of exported revolutions—the myth that Moscow, Peking, or Havana produced revolutionary movements in the Global South rather than local circumstances.[82] There were, in fact, no examples of revolutionary movements that did not emerge from local circumstances and initiatives.[83]

During the second half of the 1980s, the Cold War slowed to a halt, and the Soviet Union withdrew from international affairs. Leftist regimes throughout the Global South found themselves struggling to keep their economies afloat and prevent rebel groups from taking the capital. In this environment, Reagan's anticommunism was superfluous and ultimately inconsistent with U.S. claims of promoting human rights and democracy. It appeared that the pretense of anticommunism as a basis for supporting rebel groups to oppose regimes that did not endorse U.S. interests would no longer suffice. Similarly, it was insufficient to support a repressive regime on the grounds of anticommunism.[84]

Leland had some of his greatest success in pushing forward the cause of humanitarian relief in Africa. But in achieving a high national profile and high-level involvement in Global South affairs he drew criticism from among his colleagues. Some accused him of neglecting constituents for the sake of pursuing his international pet projects. He even drew a formidable, long-shot challenge in the 1988 Democrat Party primary from Elizabeth Spates, a Houston School Board trustee. She pelted Leland with questions regarding the benefits of his friendships with political leaders and celebrities to the poverty-stricken residents of his district.[85] Leland responded, "There are always those who accuse me of neglecting home, while I run off to other parts of the world. I make no apologies for my concern for humankind, but I assure you that I have not forgotten the unfortunate in this country or in this city. As chairman of the House Select Committee on Hunger, I deal with the horror stories daily and we are working on solving these domestic problems. But I think we can work on both, we must work on both."[86] Leland certainly wanted to win elections, but he often said that he viewed himself as representing a global community. "I am as much a citizen of this world as I am of this country. . . . To hell with those people who are critical of what I am able to do to help save people's lives."[87]

Chapter 6

"Flying in the Face of the Storm"

Ethiopia, the United States, and the End of the Cold War

Mickey was always flying in the face of the storm. To feed the children.
To liberate the captives. That was his mission.

—Jesse Jackson, August 1989

Mickey Leland was glad to see the end of President Reagan's second term. President George H. W. Bush, the new president, was not a Democrat but had verbally committed to being less fixated than his predecessor on anticommunism to guide his foreign policy. Toward that end, he announced that he would end the Reagan era policy of constructive engagement. He also stated that his administration would assess the U.S. role on the African continent on a country-by-country basis. Leland genuinely liked Bush and saw him as the best Democrats could hope for in a Republican president. The two knew each other personally, having met when Leland was in the Texas legislature and Bush was a congressman. They were also linked by Bush's embrace of Houston as his second home.[1] Leland's expressions of global citizenship and affirmations of his links to Africa notwithstanding, he was a proud Houstonian and Texan. He had significant political differences with Bush, but he respected him.

Soon after Bush took office, Leland sent him proposals for how the new administration might positively change U.S. involvement in the Horn. One of his suggestions was for the president to send a high-ranking government official to Addis Ababa to meet directly with Mengistu and John Garang, of the Sudan People's Liberation Army (SPLA), which would be a gesture that would resonate throughout the continent and declare that the new administration intended to take a balanced approach to African affairs. Leland also anticipated several tangible benefits from his plan. For one, the SPLA's humanitarian relief organization was based in Addis Ababa, and the organization's operations in southern Sudan were an important link in the relief initiatives. Direct dialogue with SPLA officials had the potential of leading to a direct partnership on humanitarian relief and affirming U.S. moral leadership over the SPLA. A U.S. official working with the SPLA, Leland argued, would "send a signal that the legitimate political concerns of the South are of interest to the United States."[2]

Whether or not Leland ignited Bush's actions on Africa, the president's actions aligned with Leland's script. In an indication that the Horn was important to his Africa policy, Bush sent Herman Cohen, his assistant secretary of state for African affairs, to Khartoum, Sudan and Addis Ababa in May 1989. But Cohen had to postpone the Ethiopia portion of his trip due to an abortive military coup against Mengistu, who had been on an official visit to East Germany.[3]

Bush did not respond as favorably to Leland's request, sent on Mengistu's behalf, to accept Tibabu Bekele as Ethiopia's candidate to be ambassador to the United States. "I think we should have full diplomatic relations without preconditions," Leland told reporters. He described the advantages of a stronger U.S. role in the region as Soviet influence declined.[4] Leland also wanted to prove that dialogue with Mengistu was an absolute necessity for the success of the humanitarian effort in the region. Leland was adamant that change in the short term was imperative to the long-term goal of achieving a paradigm shift in U.S. foreign policy. "When the priority is getting food through Ethiopia into Sudan to save lives," he wrote to the *New York Times*, "it is necessary to talk to Col. Mengistu." Leland argued that foreclosing on dialogue did nothing to advance good governance or save the lives of Ethiopians: "I would urge greater communication. The United States should establish diplomacy with Ethiopia. The present (since 1980) 'no aid and no ambassador' policy has not improved the human rights status of Ethiopians."[5] Leland argued that the change in U.S.-Ethiopian relations need not be dramatic or compromise putative U.S. principles. "We're not endorsing a regime by exchanging ambassadors," he said. "We have an ambassador in Moscow and we don't endorse that regime."[6]

Within Ethiopia, Mengistu spun the prospect of diplomatic reconciliation with the United States as mutually beneficial so as not to diminish his political standing. The *Ethiopian Herald* editorialized that the rapprochement between the two governments was not based on Mengistu's need for support, but, rather, he remained "prepared to strengthen bilateral relations with the United States so that the peoples of the two countries would work together for common prosperity."[7] In reality, his desperation was palpable.

The State Department let Mengistu's candidate for ambassador languish without a response, leaving the Ethiopian government no choice but to withdraw his name.[8] Some Bush administration officials were determined to keep the door firmly closed on diplomacy with Mengistu. They saw isolating Mengistu as the most effective means of forcing change in the country and, ultimately, removing him from power. "The US is not particularly eager to normalize (because) we don't think this particular leopard can change his spots," one administration official told journalists.[9] Despite the continued absence of formal diplomatic relations, the Bush administration opened direct channels of communication with the Ethiopian regime.

Cohen returned to the continent in August, just days before Leland arrived in Addis Ababa with his delegation, to follow through on his planned meeting with SPLA leaders in Ethiopia. Cohen sat down for talks with the SPLA and the Sudanese government, and he called on them to work together to ensure that U.S.-sponsored food aid reached those in need in the south as well as in other parts of the country.[10] Additional changes in the U.S. approach to Africa followed in quick succession. On his way back to Washington from the Horn, Cohen stopped in Rome to meet with Anatoly Adamishin, the Soviet Union's deputy foreign minister. The two discussed strategies for U.S.-Soviet initiatives to resolve regional conflicts.[11] The Bush administration had embarked on an international partnership that Leland and Jim Wright had attempted to establish two years earlier, but that Congress and the State Department had blocked. Now, with a new administration, Leland was optimistic that the United States was poised to pursue a post–Cold War foreign policy.

Leland was also committed to a strong United Nations. He signed on to support its Operation Lifeline Sudan (OLS), the United Nations' large and complex $132 million scheme to rapidly transport hundreds of tons of food aid via truck convoys to famine-stricken southern Sudan from the port at Mombasa, Kenya, and across the southwestern corner of Ethiopia. Ideally, multiple nations and organizations would be coordinated under the auspices of the United Nations to achieve this remarkable operation. As part of this initiative, Leland wanted to prove that the United Nations had the capacity to devise, implement, and manage a major multistate humanitarian project. It was the first time he would participate in an internationally mandated relief operation to assist a civilian population under rebel control.[12] To promote OLS and ensure that East African leaders helped make it a success, Leland organized a delegation to travel to the region in March 1989. It was his tenth trip to Africa as a member of Congress. The delegation included of Leland; Representative Bill Emerson, vice-chair of the Hunger Committee; Representative Michael McNulty, a Democrat from New York; Julia Taft, director of Foreign Disaster Assistance; and Alma Newsom, Leland's press secretary. A key part of their mission was to sell regional leaders on the United Nations' "Corridors of Tranquility." To succeed, the entire operation had to be completed before the start of the rainy season in May. Once the rains began, the already barely traversable roads of northern Kenya, western Ethiopia, and southern Sudan would render the delivery trucks useless.[13] To further complicate matters, the scheduled convoy routes passed through hot spots in the civil war areas of Sudan and Ethiopia. UN officials had neither the time nor the resources to devote to resolving the conflicts. Their mission was to deliver humanitarian relief. Therefore, they focused their efforts on working with regional leaders to build "Corridors of Tranquility" for the safe passage of the humanitarian relief, toward the ultimate goal of a "month of tranquility," a cease-fire in southern Sudan to allow relief workers a period of intense activity.[14] If successful, OLS would move more food in a single month than had been done during the peak months of the 1983–85 famine in Ethiopia.[15] With $72 million in material and financial support, the United States was the leading donor nation for the relief effort in southern Sudan.[16]

They traveled together to Rome on March 25 en route to Nairobi. While in Rome, they met with Tun Myat of the World Food Program to discuss conditions in southern Sudan and received a briefing on UN initiatives, particularly the plans to establish a "month of tranquility." The group had an audience with Pope John Paul II two days later and departed for Mombasa that evening.

In Kenya, the delegation met with President Daniel arap Moi and toured the Port of Mombasa where the United Nations would bring in the supplies for OLS.[17] Moi assured the delegation of his government's assistance in the relief operation to the extent of its capabilities. From Mombasa, on March 29 the group flew to Addis Ababa for meetings with Ethiopian government officials. Leland did not see the success of the initiative as a foregone conclusion. Mengistu was facing domestic challenges that constrained his full participation in OLS. Securing support from Moi and Mengistu were markedly different projects. Ambassador Robert Houdek, U.S. chargé d'affaires in Addis Ababa, met Leland and his delegation at the airport and later briefed them on the current political and economic environment in Tigray and Eritrea, the regions where the civil wars were most intense and chronic hunger most severe. He escorted them to meet Berhanu Gebray, Ethiopia's minister of economic affairs and a member of Ethiopia's State Council, the permanent body of the Ethiopian parliament. Berhanu provided similar information as Houdek had but from an Ethiopian perspective, especially on evolving Ethiopian-U.S. relations.[18]

That evening, the delegation and Ambassador Houdek met with Mengistu at Jubilee Palace, where the Ethiopian president reportedly delivered a nearly three-hour lecture on Ethiopian history, including a lengthy description of what he called the Arab and Islamic threat to Ethiopia from the time of the Crusades to the present over claims to the Red Sea. He rounded out his remarks with details of his five-year plan for "rapid development of production forces" in Ethiopia.[19] Mengistu expressed his gratitude to the government and people of the United States for their humanitarian assistance. When Leland initially asked Mengistu to pledge his support for OLS, the Ethiopian president said that when he received word from Prime Minister Sadiq al-Mahdi of Sudan as to how the two leaders should approach the UN program, he would relay his decision to Leland. Members of the delegation pushed him for his immediate support so as not to delay the program. He ultimately said he would give his support but would have to work out the details with SPLA leader John Garang.[20]

Mengistu had a request of his own. Dealing with the current population of refugees emigrating from Sudan and Somalia to Ethiopia was a tremendous burden on the government. Mengistu doubted his government had the capacity to participate fully in OLS. Although there were refugee crises more severe than Ethiopia's (more than five million mostly Pashtun refugees from Afghanistan were divided between Iran and Pakistan), relatively speaking, Ethiopia's crisis was costly because it was unexpected and the camps of Sudanese and Somali refugees were isolated.[21] "There is in fact a perverted irony in the refugee situation in Ethiopia," Leland said later, "if you can imagine people leaving Sudan and going to Ethiopia looking for food. Think about what that means. 800,000 refugees in Ethiopia. You know it must be bad if people are looking to Ethiopia as a haven."[22] Ethiopia was already struggling to accommodate more than four hundred thousand Somali refugees in Ogaden. The Somalis were crowded into remote camps around Hartisheik and Aware. Jijiga, the regional capital of Ogaden, was the closest major town. The United States contributed $20 million of the food and transportation costs for the Somali camps. Mengistu hoped to gain an increase in U.S. assistance for Ethiopian government programs for refugees in Ogaden. The camps lacked resources, including adequate surface water, to support a large population.

Mengistu also appealed to the delegation to push for U.S. diplomatic relations with Ethiopia. He noted that tension between the United States and Soviet Union had been easing recently. In light of this development, he hoped that similar easing of tension might take place with the Soviets' allies in Africa.[23] For their part, the delegation asked Mengistu to arrange a meeting with John Garang in Ethiopia instead of in Sudan. As a State Department employee, Julia Taft could not travel to SPLA-held territory. Mengistu obliged, and Garang agreed to travel to Addis Ababa for the meeting.

During Leland's visit, Mengistu delivered a surprising televised address in which he publicly acknowledged Ethiopia's decade-long civil wars. He had no choice but to do so. The federal army was losing to the TPLF and the EPLF at enormous financial cost. The latter he admitted, but he remained reticent on the spectacular military setbacks. Though Mengistu would continue to portray the Ethiopian military as engaged in offensive campaigns, it was struggling to exist. The EPLF victory at Afabet emboldened the TPLF leadership to challenge the Ethiopian army at Indasilase, Shire, in February 1989. This victory opened the central highlands to the rebels. From there, the rebels prepared to seize Addis Ababa. They would commence their final march to victory two years later.[24] The Ethiopian army was left shocked and in disarray. Eritreans captured town after town, leaving tens of thousands of military and civilian casualties. More than 50 percent of the national budget went to funding the war, but the regime could not retain control in the war regions. It had lost its grip on Tigray, Wello, and northern Gondar outside of cities and towns. Economically distressed peasants swelled TPLF and EPLF ranks.

During his address, Mengistu did not describe his military setbacks. He also downplayed the humanitarian costs of the war. As in the first years of the 1980s, the effects of the military conflict on civilians were compounded by a worsening drought in Eritrea, Tigray, and parts of Wello during the

summer of 1989. The ravages of the 1983–85 famine had returned. Mengistu did tacitly concede that international relief workers in Eritrea and
Tigray impeded the government's offensive in the conflict zones. They
hampered effective offensives because relief workers were potential eyewit-
nesses to the wars' inevitable horrors. His solution to the conundrum of
foreign relief workers and journalists in the Ethiopian war zone was to
order all organizations except UNICEF out of Eritrea and Tigray, claiming
that it was for their own safety.

On Saturday, April 1, via private plane, the group departed Addis Ababa
for Khartoum, where they met for more than two hours with Prime Minister Sadiq al-Mahdi. Leland conveyed the American people's deep concern
for the military and humanitarian crisis in southern Sudan. Al-Mahdi
defended the government's position, stating that he wanted to pursue peace
in the south and respect Sudan's religious and cultural pluralism as an
essential principle. Al-Mahdi refuted allegations that the delegation presented to him. One was that the government used the population in Juba,
the largest city in southern Sudan, as a human shield against the SPLA. He
called the allegation ridiculous, saying that people migrated to Juba for
their own protection and the military blocked their passage south for the
same reason. Regarding his ties to Libya, he described his position as non-
aligned. The Nimeiry regime was hostile to Libya because his policy was to
regard enemies of the United States as enemies of Sudan. Sadiq said Sudan
and Libya were not neighbors by choice, but it was a geopolitical reality
and Libya had showed itself to be a good neighbor.[25] On the question of
his government using local militias to attack Dinka and Nuer villages, he
insisted that these militias were retaliating for SPLA attacks against them
and that the government was trying to control the militias. Al-Mahdi gave
his support to OLS but shared his concerns for security.

Leland's delegation arrived in Ethiopia on April 5 to meet with Garang
and SPLA leaders and was, once again, accompanied by Houdek and UNI-
CEF regional director Richard Reid. It was an important meeting for Garang and the delegation. The SPLA leader had traveled one thousand miles
from southern Sudan to attend. He was leading the SPLA against a putative
anticommunist government with close ties to the United States. The SPLA
promoted the idea of a "New Sudan," free of religious, ethnic, and racial
discrimination, after the government announced its plans to implement
sharia law. By 1989 the SPLA controlled roughly 90 percent of the southern
half of the country. Civil wars, famine, and displacement in Ethiopia and

Sudan had intertwined to the point where the substance of the crisis was lost on many Western aid donors. Moreover, international relief organizations could not reach the laudable goal of political neutrality while in a conflict zone. After six years of intense guerrilla warfare against the Sudanese government from bases in southern Sudan and Ethiopia, Garang had reinvented himself as a political leader with diplomatic leverage on the world stage and in Sudanese politics.

With some success, Garang courted leaders in Washington to support his cause. The previous June, Garang had made a successful trip to Washington, where he met with Ambassador Herman Cohen, then traveled to Atlanta to meet with former president Jimmy Carter at the Carter Center. UN officials and international relief organizations had already lobbied Garang to support OLS, so Garang agreed to cooperate with UN officials and allow food aid to enter southern Sudan. The delegation members began the meeting by urging Garang to end the fighting. He would not, however, agree to a cease-fire with Khartoum and warned the government against airlifting food aid from Khartoum to the government stronghold in Juba. Garang said he would support "corridors of tranquility" consisting of non-conflict areas where relief workers and aid materials would be safe. He warned that relief convoys must have SPLA escorts during their initial trips through SPLA territory because not all soldiers would be aware of the corridors. "I will guarantee," Garang assured the delegation, "food will be distributed to where it is intended."[26]

Western journalists accused the Sudanese government of blocking food aid that was supposed to be delivered to residents in Wau, Juba, and other southern famine-stricken towns. Like many towns in southern Sudan, Wau was deep in SPLA territory but remained under government control. It had over one hundred thousand residents, 50 percent of whom were displaced persons.[27] Leland wanted the group to witness the conditions in these towns. He also wanted to ascertain whether the government, as a U.S. ally, was acting responsibly toward its residents. The delegation was to visit one of the four feeding centers in Wau established by Sudan's RRC and run by the ICRC. From Wau the Americans hoped to fly to an additional feeding center near the town of El Aglab, and then to Khartoum to meet with Prime Minister Sadiq al-Mahdi before returning to Addis. Flying into government-controlled towns in southern Sudan was extremely dangerous. SPLA soldiers were known to try to shoot down any planes entering the area. Leland asked Garang about the safety of traveling to southern Sudan because he was concerned about the group's well-being and knew that Garang's word might provide some guarantee of protection. Garang consented to Leland's plane flying into the area, on the grounds that it was clearly marked as a relief agency plane. Nonetheless, the group still remained a potential target as it traveled from Addis to the southern Sudanese town of Wau in an Ethiopian government aircraft. The Sudanese civil war made it difficult to enforce agreements and ensure the safety of well-intentioned outsiders.

There was a real possibility that SPLA soldiers would mistake the delegation's plane for a Sudanese military aircraft and attempt to shoot it down. The risk was great enough that U.S. embassy officials in Khartoum informed Leland prior to his group's departure to Wau from Addis that it could not guarantee his party's safety once their plane entered Sudanese airspace. "After receiving the cable, I had taken the precaution of alerting the other congressional members of the delegation," Leland explained. "I had told the staff I would not knowingly endanger them and gave them the option of remaining in Addis Ababa. No one took me up on the offer." Leland was aware of the danger and the unique opportunity that came with flying into southern Sudan. As he said, "No aircraft, other than the relief planes, had been allowed to fly into the town in two years. Col. Garang's troops were poised to shoot down everything else. I looked at each of the faces around me on the plane. We were all on edge. Our five planes—which carried congressmen, staff and embassy personnel—were to be the exception."[28]

Conditions in Wau shocked the delegation members. Leland regarded the residents' dire state as a sign of an impending broader food crisis. "We were lucky," Leland said. "We landed and took off again without incident, both from Wau and then El Muglad. But what we found in those towns, and in the other towns we visited, gave us no reason to rejoice."[29] He warned, "Unless we get some food in there, we will have the same crisis as last year."[30] Once again, Leland's faith resided squarely in U.S. aid. He used the situation in Wau to support his case that the United Nations was incapable of effectively addressing the needs of those the drought left vulnerable. After their visit to southern Sudan, members appreciated the urgency of the situation. "Roughly 170,000 metric tons of food must be placed in southern Sudan before the heavy rains start in May or thousands of people, many of them children, will die. Last year, the death toll was a quarter of a million," Leland said. "Mother nature is not cooperating: the rains appear to be starting much earlier, thus narrowing considerably the window of opportunity for relief supplies to be put into place. When the rains come all access to the towns will be washed out. There will be no airfields for the planes to land; there will be no roads for the trucks to bring food in. The rivers will be too swollen to safely navigate. The area will be effectively cut off from relief for six to eight months."[31] When Leland returned from Sudan in April, the image of Sudanese children's faces haunted him. He admitted to being depressed over having no solutions to war and famine in southern Sudan.[32]

During the first week of April 1989, a few days after Leland returned to Washington, the House Foreign Affairs Subcommittee on Africa issued a highly critical report on the Kenyan government's human rights record. Its timing, as well as its content, disturbed Leland. He had never been fond of making a political spectacle of denouncing African leadership. But this report had the potential to damage not only President Moi's political standing in the West but also the tremendous diplomatic achievements of Leland's delegation. If Moi took the proposed legislation as an insult, he might back out of the agreement. This development could have undermined the support the delegation had secured from Mengistu Haile-Mariam, Prime Minister Sadiq al-Mahdi of Sudan, and John Garang.

Leland feared that his diplomatic faith building, together with the trust it engendered, would evaporate because of this largely symbolic vote in Congress. "I am concerned that at this delicate time in the relief effort, such strong negative language could jeopardize our efforts to speed relief to the victims of the war in the Sudan," Leland argued in a letter to Donald Payne, a member of the Subcommittee on Africa and one of the bill's sponsors. "I would be very grateful if you would try to work with Howard [Wolpe] and the rest of the Subcommittee to tone down the language concerning Kenya in the bill and report, and perhaps work to see that it is balanced in some way with positive language. I believe that in light of Kenya's help with the relief efforts, we should be expressing our gratitude rather than criticism."[33] It had been Leland's goal to stay clear of politics during the trip. Despite the bipartisanism represented on the trip, members had to filter out domestic politics. Leland also did not want members discussing issues with leaders in the region from a geopolitical or Cold War angle. "Throughout the trip the delegation was conscious of a position of neutrality," Leland said. "The United States must remain impartial in the midst of a civil war which is being waged both militarily and impeding access to food. It is the tradition of this country to assist with open hands and hearts the innocent victims of natural disasters and war regardless of the ideologies of their leaders."[34]

Leland was of two minds on the trip's success. He was proud of the diplomatic ground the delegation made regarding OLS, but he was pessimistic about the fate of those in the country who needed immediate relief. The problems were not poverty and nature, as Leland frequently suggested in his public addresses and during hearings. Rather, civil war stalled food aid deliveries. If deliveries were not completed before the rains began they would not be possible again for months.[35]

On June 30, 1989, Sadiq al-Mahdi was removed from office by a coup d'état, and Omar al-Bashir took power. There were concerns in the international humanitarian relief community about what this change in leadership might portend for OLS and the crisis in southern Sudan generally. James Grant, executive director of UNICEF, candidly conceded the limits of the operation's chances for success, during an interview on the U.S. television news program *Nightline*: "Even without the civil war, never before in history have we tried to move such a massive tonnage, over 100,000, in such a difficult logistical situation. Starting almost from scratch to do it in six weeks."[36] It required cooperation among eight countries, including Kenya, Ethiopia, Sudan, the United States, and the USSR, as well as the United Nations and more than thirty-five NGOs, and ran at a cost of more than $1 million per day. UN officials knew OLS would be the most expensive and expansive humanitarian operation in the world. It was also the lengthiest.[37]

Leland returned to the United States without visiting Pinyudo, the largest of four camps run by the UN High Commissioner for Refugees (UNHCR) in Fugnido. He had intended to go to Pinyudo when the group was in the town of Gambella, a short distance away, but they spent too much time on the ground there. Gambella was an arena for regional and Cold War politics, as an SPLA base and a site of numerous UN-sponsored refugee camps. Garang had established SPLA's base at Assossa in 1985, and from there fighters infiltrated the border into the Blue Nile region of Sudan. The Sudanese army's counterinsurgency, beginning in early 1987, included burning villages and forcing victims across the border into Ethiopia.[38] By 1989 tens of thousands of young boys, mostly ethnic Dinka, had streamed across the Sudanese border and into refugee camps in southeastern Ethiopia. These are the boys Leland would travel to see in Fugnido that August. During the first three months of 1988, more than thirty thousand Sudanese had trekked to Ethiopia.[39] Together the four camps in Fugnido accommodated three hundred thousand refugees from Sudan's civil war. Taking responsibility for these refugees exacerbated Ethiopia's existing dilemmas of famine and civil war.

The conditions in Sudan and Gambella forced Leland to address the political dynamics behind famine. Sudan's famine did not evolve from an absence of food but rather from restricted access to it. While the famine in the south worsened, the government continued to export large quantities of grain. A total of 446,000 metric tons of sorghum went to Europe in 1988, and another 34,000 metric tons to Saudi Arabia, while 250,000 people in southern Sudan starved to death. The paradox of exporting food products while huge swaths of the population died from the absence of food was undeniably a political choice on the part of the Sudanese government.

Six weeks into the United Nations' official timeline to complete OLS, 32,800 of the planned 120,000 metric tons of food aid had reached southern Sudan.[40] Leland was disappointed with what appeared to him to be the UN officials' lack of organization and poor planning around OLS. He complained that they prioritized their public image at the expense of effectively managing their programs. During an appearance on *Nightline* on April 10, 1989, Leland rebuked the United Nations for not setting a reachable goal and for using the facade of a robust and well-organized initiative to revive a tarnished reputation. "I would hope the United Nations would stop this public-relations [campaign]," he told host Ted Koppel. The aid moved but did so much too slowly. "I think the UN has the greatest of intentions," he said, "but I would just admonish them that they really need to get more into the substance, as opposed to the PR value of what this is all about. I'm hoping they get down to the nitty-gritty because there's no time left."

To Leland, Western nations and Japan lacked the political will to sustain the necessary momentum behind OLS. Their limited commitment confounded him. He and other members of the Hunger Committee feared that OLS would fail unless nations with the capacity to step forward with resources did so expeditiously and generously. Bill Emerson was similarly perplexed by the minuscule humanitarian response from the West and Japan. "I am puzzled as to why the countries of Western Europe and Japan have also not gotten on board," he told reporters in April.[41] The question was how much aid was sufficient to fully address the crisis. Paradoxically, OLS contributed to the conflict that perpetuated the humanitarian crisis. It was intended to feed civilians, but the government and the SPLA manipulated aid for their own benefit. Nonetheless, UN officials chose to continue

OLS. They decided that it was better to aid civilians who desperately needed it even though some of the aid was misused. As a result, the operation prolonged the situation that caused the suffering of the very victims it sought to relieve.[42]

OLS faced limits and constraints, but it managed to move massive levels of aid into southern Sudan. With Mengistu's support, the aid convoys moved through the pipeline during the final week of April. It was remarkable that the convoys moved at all, but the fact that the Ethiopian government provided half of the 125 trucks transporting the 7,000 tons of food to southern Sudan was astounding. Leland promoted the encouraging news concerning the Ethiopian government's participation. He capitalized on this positive development in the Horn to counsel the U.S. media to present a more balanced and nuanced portrayal of events in the region. He criticized the media for continuously painting a picture of the Ethiopian government as unwilling to cooperate with the UN operation. These reports, he said, had "unfairly painted Ethiopia as a villain in this very difficult situation."[43]

Operation Lifeline Sudan suffered from overambition, mismanagement, and inadequate resources. Moreover, the United Nations put OLS into place after the famine had already peaked in 1988. Nonetheless, it saved thousands of lives and demonstrated the United Nations' capacity to corral governments in conflict to act together on behalf of humanitarianism. The process also had positive residual effects for the conflict in Sudan. In the south, the SPLA endorsed a cease-fire from May to mid-June 1989, and the government unilaterally declared a truce for July of that year. The temporary peace provided the SPLA and the Sudanese government a rare opportunity to work together and to communicate on relief issues. Leland declared his delegation on behalf of OLS a success, having achieved most of the goals he set for it, including facilitating agreements and brokering commitments. "We were successful yet still people die because it's too little, too late. The only real solution is the cessation of war," he stated.[44]

Leland hastily planned a second delegation for that year to Africa for the first week of August, the start of Congress's summer recess. He wanted to build on the goodwill earned in the first trip and sustain Congress's and the U.S. media's interest in the region's humanitarian crises. This time, though, he wanted to arrive with a larger, more bipartisan group. In 1988 and 1989, the Anyuak people in and around Fugnido survived with limited resources, much of which they suddenly had to share with three large camps struggling to accommodate more than 365,000 Sudanese refugees. Pinyudo held 17,000 of them.[45] At its most dire moments, thirty to forty people died daily in the camps, while at its least dire, the figure fell to three or four per day.[46] Through the Sudanese refugees in southwestern Ethiopia, Leland believed he could draw the U.S. media's and U.S. government's attention to Sudanese government policies toward the country's southern regions. He wanted the United States to hold its allies to a higher standard; he also wanted to highlight the Ethiopian government's cooperation and generosity in their response to southern Sudan's humanitarian crisis.

The Ethiopian government's humanitarian program in Fugnido contradicted U.S. media descriptions and critiques from within the U.S. government that the regime had failed in its humanitarian obligations to the international community. The Ethiopian government had demonstrated its willingness to assist Sudanese refugees. Fugnido was not ideal for refugee camps, but it was the first town encountered when traveling east from Sudan and crossing the Akobo River marking the border with Ethiopia. It was extremely remote, and a single road passed through it. Dinka were not the first group driven to Pinyudo by a crisis, but the international media attention elevated the Dinkas' significance. A popular narrative emerged for public consumption in the West. Civil war had created the "Lost Boys" and an extreme food crisis for those who remained in Sudan. In 1984, civil war was marginal to the Ethiopian crisis narrative, even though it was the root cause. The civil war in Sudan, however, that lasted from 1983 to 2005 drew media attention.

Leland's trip to Fugnido for August 1989 would have to be short and he had limited time to plan it. He wanted a large delegation, but Congress's summer recess and Africa fatigue among his colleagues left him as the lone politician on the trip. It was Leland's sixth official delegation to Ethiopia but his least high-profile trip. The call he received from his wife, Alison, two days before he left Washington certainly made the journey more remarkable. She told him that she was pregnant with their second child. Initially, Alison had planned to tell him in person when he returned, but that would have required fifteen days of patience. What she did not know was that she was carrying twins. Immediately, as she recalled twenty-two years later, she detected a change in her husband's mood when she told him the good news. He felt, it seemed to her, that he should be with his pregnant wife. He confided as much to Rodney Ellis, his former chief of staff and close friend.[47] Nonetheless, he remained

Figure 8. Mickey and Alison Leland with their son, Jarrett, summer 1989. CQ Archive. Courtesy of Getty Images.

committed to leading the delegation to Ethiopia, with plans, at long last, to visit Fugnido.

On August 7, Leland arrived at Bole International Airport, where he and others in the delegation would board a plane for Fugnido. The group included three members of his congressional staff. Hugh Johnson was one of Leland's recent additions to the Hunger Committee staff as the international team leader. Hugh's wife, Patrice, and Alison Leland were best friends from their days together at Spelman College in Atlanta. Alison personally recruited Hugh for the Hunger Committee job from the Department of Energy, where he worked as an attorney.[48] Patrice Johnson was a thirty-five-year-old lawyer from Houston who had joined Leland's staff in April 1987 as his legislative director. She had recently taken on a new role as his top aide. Leland had personally invited Joyce Williams, a thirty-nine-year-old staff member for Congressman Ronald Dellums, because of her expertise in infant mortality, nutrition, and health-care issues. In the days before she left, Williams talked excitedly about the opportunity to witness the refugees' experience up close.[49]

USAID staffers traveled regularly to refugee camps in Ethiopia, including Fugnido. There were four USAID-Ethiopia officials on the trip: Thomas Worrick, Roberta Worrick, Gladys Gilbert, and Debebe Agonafer. Forty-eight-year-old Thomas Worrick had worked for USAID since 1974. His wife, Roberta, also forty-eight, was a contract employee with USAID who spoke fluent Amarinya. They had volunteered to serve in Ethiopia after severe drought returned. They knew the country well, having first served as Peace Corps volunteers in 1971. Gladys Gilbert, forty-three, also had a long relationship with both Ethiopia and USAID. She had been with the agency since 1977 and was an expert on refugee management. Debebe Agonafer, an Ethiopian agricultural economist working for USAID, was among the most renowned in his field.

Leland's close friend Ivan Tillem volunteered to join the delegation. He had been active in humanitarian relief, particularly that directed toward Ethiopian Jews. In recent years, he had raised money for and participated in a medical mission to Ethiopia and had been the director of the North American Conference on Ethiopian Jewry. For Tillem, famine relief and transporting Ethiopian Jews to Israel were part of the same mission. He personally underwrote the cost to establish Ethiopian synagogues in Israel. At age thirty-two, he was a star professor at Yeshiva University's Stern College for Women, where he was also a trustee—the youngest in the university's history.[50] Also on the trip were Robert Woods, a political-economic officer for the State Department on his first overseas assignment, and Yemisirach Tessema, the foreign affairs minister for the Ethiopian government. The United Nations was represented in the delegation by two officials: Aragaw Fetene, a refugee aid worker who was recruited for the trip to guide the Leland party through the refugee camp; and Melaku Asmare, a refugee analyst. The flight crew was led by Captain Assefa Gebre Giorgis, one of Ethiopia's most experienced pilots. He had received extensive flight training in the United States and had been a flight instructor while he was in the Ethiopian air force. He began work for the RRC in August 1985. His copilot was Captain Getachew Negash, who had also been a flight instructor in the air force of Ethiopia. He had worked for the RRC since 1978. Shimelis Amdebirhan was the technician onboard.

The delegation arrived at Bole at 8:00 A.M., an hour behind schedule, and the participants were to transfer directly to another plane for departure to Fugnido at 9:00 A.M.[51] For the ninety-minute flight to Fugnido and back, President Mengistu provided Leland with one of the government's RRC planes, a de Havilland Twin Otter Dash-6. August was the most inopportune time to travel in Ethiopia because of the long rainy season, called meher, that lasted from mid-June through September. It was common for rain, even hail, to continue incessantly for days and the skies to remain filled with thick clouds.[52] The vagaries of Ethiopia's weather and the country's treacherous mountainous topography honed Ethiopia's pilots into the most skilled in Africa. Leland was aware of the meher season when he planned the trip, but congressional breaks typically took place during the spring, summer, and December recess. He wanted his delegation's visit to follow quickly on the heels of his April trip and was resigned to deal with the rain and clouds of August.

Although the weather had forced the entire airport to shut down for several hours, Leland was determined to get his group in the air. Michael Beyene, the chief meteorologist at Bole International Airport, was described in the official accident report as having been "in continuous discussion with some RRC staff and the pilots themselves while they were waiting for the weather to improve." He told the pilots' chief engineer not to take off. Satellite images showed dense cloud cover as low as 400 feet west of Addis, in the direction they were scheduled to fly.[53] After several hours, there were reports of clearing skies around Jimma, 150 miles from Bole, but along the scheduled flight path. The flight crew waited by the aircraft; they did not review weather reports or satellite photos of the route. According to the accident report, this important information would have been available at Bole International Airport had the pilots requested it.[54] The flight crew felt very uneasy due to the high profile of the passengers, their tight schedule, and the weather.[55]

Captain Assefa informed the passengers and crew that they would only have two hours on the ground in Fugnido and that once in the air he even might have to turn back to Addis, depending upon the weather along the route. Small planes do not fly in Ethiopia at night, so they would have to return by 5:00 P.M. Leland reportedly responded, "That's more than enough time. Let's get going!"[56] Captain Assefa announced a 10:30 A.M. departure. The party quickly boarded the plane, escorted by Robert Houdek, who was disappointed that his schedule prevented him from joining them. Houdek bid the travelers a safe journey and helped close the plane's door behind them.[57] The plane left the ground at 10:47 A.M.; Captains Assefa and Negash reported to air traffic control at Bole when the plane had reached 12,500 feet.[58] At 5:00 P.M., officials of the UNHCR continued to wait in Fugnido to receive the Leland party. The weather during the rainy season commonly forced unscheduled or emergency landings, but officials back at Bole grew increasingly anxious. The time of 5:00 P.M. was a critical point in these events, because it was the landing curfew for all aircraft in Ethiopia. Officials at Bole no longer considered the flight delayed; it was missing.

Captain Assefa was scheduled to fly toward Jimma, where there were better weather conditions. He would land there to refuel and then continue to Fugnido. Evidently to save time, however, Assefa attempted to fly directly to Fugnido. It is common during the rainy season for the weather to further deteriorate around the mountains, with rain obscuring and often low clouds covering the mountains themselves.[59] Assefa flew his plane lower than the planned altitude of 12,500 feet to get below the clouds but remain higher than the mountains along the course. He would have had to balance a low altitude and navigate mountains of varying heights while keeping his eyes on the river that guided him to Fugnido. It was a perilous challenge. Had Assefa flown 300 feet higher, he might have managed to land on the far side of Mount Tullu Welel, where vast stretches of lowlands extended westward toward the Sudanese border. But evidently he simply could not see. The Ethiopian Civil Aviation Authority's crash report suggested that the pilots could see neither the mountains in front of them nor the ground beneath them.[60]

Mengistu applied all available resources to locate the plane. The seriousness of his direct involvement in the search undoubtedly shaped the congeniality between Mengistu and President Bush from the outset of the search for the Leland party. In one of Bush's messages to Mengistu, he graciously thanked the Ethiopian leader for his commitment to the rescue mission: "I know you share my fervent hope that our joint efforts succeed in rescuing our friend, Congressman Leland, his group and your countrymen who are accompanying them."[61] Mengistu's response to the U.S. president was equally magnanimous. "We are deeply concerned about the safety of Congressman Mickey Leland and his party, and all those on board the plane," he said. "We assure you Mr. President that this effort will continue to the end. Please accept, Mr. President, the assurances of my highest consideration."[62] Leland had been trying to achieve direct communication between the two governments for half a decade, only to succeed in death. "The paradox for the Ethiopians," Jane Perlez of the *New York Times* wrote, "is that [the Ethiopian government's] show of good will comes after the disappearance of Mr. Leland, their best friend in Washington, who wanted to restore full relations immediately."[63]

On Sunday, six days after the Leland party departed Bole for Fugnido, the joint U.S.-Ethiopian military search for the Leland party concentrated on an area near the town of Dembidolo, 60 miles north of Fugnido and 280 miles west of Addis. Villagers reported seeing a plane during the storm the previous Monday flying very low, below the thick cloud cover. It was an area of grasslands and forests and contained several refugee camps. Mount Tullu Welel, standing at 10,830 feet, dominated the landscape. There were several old airstrips northeast of Dembidolo that the ICRC had used during the famine in the mid-1980s. The plane reportedly descended as if to prepare to land, but then it suddenly flew higher and then away.[64] While Black Hawk helicopters searched from above, members of the Ethiopian police force, local farmers, and other volunteers conducted a search on the ground, despite the difficult weather.[65] At 1:18 P.M., while flying toward the village of Dembidolo, a Black Hawk pilot spotted pieces of aircraft along a steep slope of Mount Tullu Welel.[66] There was no doubt that the Leland party's plane had been discovered at last.

Sixty meters above the wreckage, a dark spot and scrub marks were visible on the terrain where the plane had collided with the mountain and exploded. It was near the crest of a steep cliff, thousands of feet above the muddy river but only 300 feet from the peak of the mountain. The plane appeared to have increased its altitude and rapidly accelerated to scale it, but it struck a tree that severed one of its wings; 250 feet later the plane hit a bolder then crashed into the mountain. "The plane went nose-first into the rocks," Congressman Gary Ackerman told reporters. He had flown to Addis Ababa out of concern that the search had been disorganized and halfhearted, and he had been aboard the helicopter that spotted the crash site. "The two wings were sheared off," he told reporters. The explosion instantly killed all onboard and destroyed the emergency transmitters that would have aided rescuers in locating the wreckage. From all appearances, the aircraft disintegrated in a fire that was so intense it melted the plane's two engines.[67] Upon impact, the craft fell 60 meters into a riverbank below.[68]

It was still early Sunday morning when the news of Leland's death reached most of Houston. The memorials commenced immediately. Leland's Houston office had remained open throughout the weeklong rescue mission to receive journalists, supporters, and well-wishers. Upon being notified of the crash, the office was emptied of all but its staff, who locked the doors for privacy while they absorbed the reality of Leland's death and grieved. Until that moment, they had believed his death to be impossible.[69] Congress put together a ceremonial delegation with Representatives William H. Gray III, Ronald Dellums, Bill Emerson, and Jack Fields to join Alan Wheat and Gary Ackerman, who had arrived in Ethiopia a week earlier. Other officials and military personnel went to Addis Ababa to assist the Ethiopian Civil Aviation Authority in investigating the cause of the accident.

President Bush cut short his weekend vacation and phoned Alison Leland to express his condolences. He held a press conference to formally announce Leland's death, commenting, "I have known, admired, and worked with Mickey Leland for many years. His sense of compassion and desire to help those in need has aided millions of people from Houston to Addis Ababa."[70] To reporters he said, "It's a sadness for everybody." Leland, he continued, was "an outstanding man, a man of great humor."[71] Houston and Washington moved in tandem toward memorializing Leland. The Ethiopian-U.S. collaboration to search for the Leland party and the collective national mourning in both countries for all who died in the crash gave the assumed ideological incompatibility of the two governments a palpable irrelevance. Returning the bodies to their respective hometowns was the third joint project that officials from both countries used to build common ground.

At midmorning on Tuesday, August 22, 1989, a ring of police surrounded Bole International Airport near Addis as a plane prepared to depart for Europe, en route to Maryland. Ethiopian soldiers escorted the caskets, each draped in a national flag: an American, next to an Ethiopian, then an American, and another Ethiopian. They were all together. An ensemble of U.S. Marines and Ethiopian color guards escorted the caskets to the center of the tarmac, toward the waiting plane. A small crowd of spectators, including family members, friends, and coworkers of the departed Ethiopians, gathered on the tarmac. "As the caskets came within sight," the *Houston Chronicle* reported, "the Ethiopian families began wailing, chanting and falling to their knees."[72] Ethiopian soldiers loaded the American caskets bearing their U.S. flags onto the plane, beginning the first leg of their journey home. In the United States, Leland's celebrity would continue to rise beyond his local constituents, celebrity friends, and colleagues.

Mengistu spoke freely of Leland's humanitarian activism with an ease that would likely have been absent had Leland been on his way to Mekelle or Korem to visit displaced Ethiopians rather than Sudanese refugees in southwestern Ethiopia. For Mengistu, the Ethiopian camps reflected his government's magnanimity. Mengistu was part of a uniquely African trend in the Global South. In contrast with Southeast Asia, it was not uncommon for African countries to open their doors to refugees.[73] While Leland did not try to sell the United States on Mengistu's magnanimity, he did try to spread a narrative of Ethiopia's humanitarian cooperation. He did not fully realize that goal, but in the aftermath of his death a more positive light shone on Ethiopia from the West. In this instance, Ethiopia stood proudly as a humanitarian partner with the international community, particularly with Leland, rather than as an accessory to the famine's spread. "Congressman Leland, a great humanitarian and statesman and an outstanding legislator, was a fighter for the cause of the hungry," Mengistu stated in a letter of condolence to President Bush and Congressman Foley, Speaker of the House. "That he should lose his life while on a humanitarian mission on behalf of refugees, for whose welfare he has so gallantly stood and fought, is a glaring tribute to his dedication to the service of humanity."[74]

Bush responded with similar words of kindness: "I very much appreciate your letter of condolences regarding the death of Representative Mickey Leland and those who were with him. I share the deep sense of loss you have expressed." The president contributed to the rapidly developing narrative of Leland's stature as a citizen and humanitarian leader for the entire world as he described Leland's constituency as formally based in the Texas Eighteenth Congressional District, "but in a wider sense his constituency extended around the world and included all who are hungry. On this issue, he was our conscience, and we will miss him profoundly." The international press and the discourse around the search for the missing had focused on Mickey Leland, to the neglect of the fifteen people with him on the plane. Conscious of this fact, perhaps, Bush included them in his statement to Mengistu: "I also wish to extend my deepest sympathy, and that of the American people, to the families of those Ethiopian officials and crew members who accompanied Representative Leland and who lost their lives in the crash. They were assisting a noble cause." Finally, President Bush closed with words that a year earlier would have been surprising from a U.S. president in reference to Marxist Ethiopia. He issued a clear statement of cooperation and goodwill between the United States and Ethiopia: "The continued devotion of our two countries to that cause [hunger] will help to ensure that they did not die in vain. Let me express again the gratitude of the American people for the assistance provided by the People's Democratic Republic of Ethiopia in the search for Representative Leland and his party. The selfless efforts of your people, in difficult and often dangerous conditions, are deeply appreciated. Please extend to the pilots and crew members, and to all the officials involved, our heartfelt thanks."[75]

In the weeks prior to Leland's death, the Bush administration had taken tentative steps toward reconciliation with Mengistu in the form of low-level talks between the two governments. On August 6, the day before Leland arrived in Addis, Ambassador Herman Cohen met with Mengistu and other senior Ethiopian officials. Cohen was in the country for three days to discuss a range of issues, including Ethiopia's civil wars and diplomatic relations between the United States and Ethiopia. He departed optimistic that the two countries were making great strides toward reconciliation. "I am leaving with a good feeling that the main problems facing Ethiopia today will be addressed in an expeditious fashion," Cohen remarked after the talks.[76] Still, he said strengthening ties between the two countries would require Ethiopia to settle its twenty-eight-year civil wars with Eritrea and Tigray, improve human rights practices, and launch major economic reforms. During the months that followed the plane crash, the State Department eased its position, saying that the Ethiopian government need not tackle all the problems at once but should demonstrate that it was taking positive steps.[77] The day after the U.S. military located the Leland party's plane, Houdek, Ackerman, and Wheat met with Mengistu in Addis. The table was set for the State Department to consider Ethiopia as an international partner and tone down its human rights critiques if not look past them.

Despite the efforts by Leland and many others to clear a path to a new political era, his aspirations were not fulfilled until after his death. That tragic event provided the symbolic turn that nudged the United States and

Ethiopia closer together. His death alone did not dismantle the Cold War framework of U.S.-Ethiopian relations. However, the search for Leland's plane, and the mourning of his death and the deaths of the fifteen others who traveled with him, provided a sliver of tangible, nonpolitical common ground for the two governments to build on.

Leland's death accelerated the gradual easing of tension between Ethiopia and the United States. It was not so much a turning point as an accelerant. The complex factors behind the Ethiopian tragedy were apparent. As with all modern food crises in Africa, this one also had the element of a military conflict. By the time of Leland's death, addressing the issues around the conflict was deemed essential. However, not all the news from the region was encouraging. In September 1989, the SPLA attacked villages in the area around Pinyudo and killed 120 people. Its spokesman claimed that the villagers had planned to rob the refugee camp. Fighting followed between the SPLA and the Anyuak militia in the Itang village of Akada. The government in Khartoum used OLS to move military supplies. In the final months of 1989, the government's attitude toward the SPLA hardened to the point that it declared it would rid the country of the SPLA in two months and halted relief flights for OLS.[78]

In 1987, Leland had put together a plan for a U.S.-USSR humanitarian initiative in Mozambique and Angola. This program would have saved countless lives and made the Cold War a moot point. Two years later, President Bush called on Premier Gorbachev to work with the United States to help resolve Ethiopia's military and humanitarian crisis.[79] The two governments issued a joint statement in 1990 on the political and humanitarian crisis in Ethiopia. They affirmed their shared commitment to working to achieve peace in Ethiopia: "Recognizing the continuing political and military conflicts that exacerbate the problems of starvation and recognizing also the lack of momentum on peace talks, the US and USSR will support an international conference of governments under the auspices of the UN on settlement of conflict situations in the Horn of Africa." They commended Ethiopia for agreeing to allow food aid to reach Tigray, Wello, and Eritrea. The Ethiopian government would allow aid to enter through the Port of Massawa under a UN program. It was an ironic turn of events. "In addition, to deal with the growing problems of starvation, the US and the USSR are prepared to work together and combine their assets," the statement read. "US food will be transported on Soviet aircraft to demonstrate our joint commitment to responding to this tragic humanitarian problem."[80] Tony Hall, who chaired the Select Committee on Hunger after Leland's death, and Rudy von Bernuth of CARE had both lobbied to include Ethiopia on the agenda for the U.S.-Soviet summit and welcomed the joint statement. "The promise offered by this statement," Hall wrote to Bernuth, "not just for Ethiopia, but for the entire developing world represents a turning point in East-West relations. President Bush and Gorbachev have put their combined clout behind an effort to save lives. I believe this represents a mighty victory for those of us who fight for humanitarian causes all over the world."[81]

Mengistu did not simply fall from power; he was pushed out and dragged others down as he departed. In 1989, a year after an attempted coup to topple his regime, he ordered the execution of twelve generals who had been implicated in the plot. For the moment he managed to hold on, but in doing so he deprived an already demoralized and disoriented army of its most skilled and experienced leaders. It was only a matter of time before the federal army would fall to Ethiopian People's Revolutionary Democratic Front (EPRDF) forces. Early in the year, TPLF leaders met with their counterparts in the Ethiopian People's Democratic Union. Together they formed the EPRDF. Its leader, Meles Zenawi, recognized the pragmatism of abandoning Marxism as an ideological centerpiece. "We are not a Marxist-Leninist movement," Meles stated. "We do have Marxists in our movement. I acknowledge that. I myself was a convinced Marxist when I was a student at [Addis Ababa University] in the early 1970s, and our movement was inspired by Marxism. But we learned that Marxism was not a good formula for resistance to the Derg and our fight for the future of Ethiopia."[82] In place of Marxism, Meles declared the movement's ideology as "Revolutionary Democracy." He asserted at the time that "our revolutionary democratic goals are the only guarantee for the survival of our country."[83]

The EPRDF catered to a broad coalition and quickly gained the U.S. State Department's attention as a prospective partner in the region. The movement against Emperor Selassie, and then Mengistu, was launched in a moment of seemingly limitless political possibilities but was concluding in a vastly different world. It was a postcommunist, post-Soviet world with no viable alternative to the United States and other Western powers as global partners. The government's offense-turned-defense against the TPLF and the EPLF turned the crisis of drought and the resulting food shortage into a disaster for millions of Ethiopians. Celebrating the end of these wars would have been fitting for those who advocated the end of hunger in

Africa. Hunger, however, was not a Black Caucus agenda item. A few of its members spoke eloquently and, in some respects, consistently on the U.S. government's obligations toward chronic hunger domestically and abroad. But Leland stood alone in his mission-oriented approach to chronic hunger. He failed to gain traction for humanitarian assistance because it lacked resonance with U.S. racial history and politics. As the revolution came full circle, and the former student-activist leaders closed in on Asmara in Eritrea and Addis in Ethiopia, African American leaders did not bring the United States into the ensuing political dialogue.

U.S. food aid to Ethiopia provided a basis for the U.S. role in Ethiopian peace talks. U.S. involvement began in earnest in 1991 when the outcome of the war had already been decided. Influential U.S. officials contended that the United States had squandered an opportunity to broaden its economic and political reach in the continent by failing to effectively intervene in Somalia and Liberia.[84] The final round of talks took place in London on May 27, 1991, with representatives of the EPRDF, the EPLF, and the Oromo. Tesfaye Dinka, the new prime minister, led the Ethiopian delegation. Herman Cohen mediated and surprised everyone by detailing a prospective political transition process that in no way resembled democracy but had the potential to secure Ethiopia and Eritrea as solid U.S. allies. He offered a clear indication that the United States would recognize an independent Eritrea. He advocated in his proposal "self-determination by the people of Eritrea."[85] He also recommended that the EPRDF establish itself in Addis Ababa and assume control of the government. U.S. support was now firmly behind the EPRDF. The United States established new partnerships in the region. Sudan, under Omar al-Bashir, pursued religious fundamentalism for the whole country and demonstrated a strong reluctance to speak directly with the SPLA. U.S. support for Sudan had ceased, apart from humanitarian assistance and the aid it channeled through the UNHCR. The United States also reduced its support for Kenya, as Daniel arap Moi demonstrated his dexterity in cracking down on pro-democracy activists. Ethiopia offered an opportunity for the United States to remake its role in the region.

In the West, Ethiopia became synonymous with famine and government policy failure, but the cocktail of crises in Sudan surpassed Ethiopia's dilemma, despite the unbalanced Western media coverage tilted toward Ethiopia and the fact that the United States had willfully turned a blind eye. Leland and his political career, particularly his championing of strong and consistent U.S.-government-backed humanitarian initiatives in the Horn of Africa during the weeks before and following his death, contrast markedly with his virtual disappearance from the history of African American politics and the U.S. response to hunger in Africa. The brief celebration of his political career hinted that Leland might join the pantheon of celebrated African American political heroes.

Outside of Houston and Addis Ababa, and the memories of his colleagues from Congress, Leland quickly faded into political obscurity, becoming known more for dying in a plane crash somewhere in Africa than for his unique political persona, humanitarian work, and a true reflection of black radical politics in the U.S. government. During one of several memorial services for Leland, the Reverend Jesse Jackson eulogized Leland for his "unselfish service to humanity." Jackson was not alone in his belief that Leland had attained a special place in the history of U.S. humanitarianism and foreign policy. He predicted that "they will be naming streets after Mickey, schools and highways and federal buildings."[86] During the week-long search for the plane, newspaper headlines honored Leland; one declared him a "Texas Maverick Who Built Lasting Bonds Between Minorities."[87] The *Christian Science Monitor* hailed Leland as a "champion of the hungry."[88] Journalists acknowledged the irony that the media discussed his signature issues after his death, while they paid little attention to them during his life. President Bush and Ambassador Houdek both noted that following the joint Ethiopian-U.S. search for the Leland party it seemed inevitable that the two countries would build a close relationship.

Nearly a quarter century removed from Jackson's heartfelt prediction of Leland's rise to iconic status, I found myself painstakingly attempting to explain to people who Leland was and to convince them of his significance in the history of humanitarianism and U.S. politics at the end of the Cold War. For those for whom a summary of the Leland story rang a bell, it was usually through the detail of his ill-fated flight to Fugnido. For most others, there was interest but no recollection. His name is absent within the scholarly literature on the U.S. response to the Ethiopian famines of 1983–85 and 1988. The histories of the Congressional Black Caucus and African American anti-apartheid activism ignore him as well, despite government documents and U.S. newspaper articles of the time testifying to his leadership and the active role he played in these issues. Outside of Houston, Leland's legacy remains strongest with Ethiopian Americans and Ethiopians in Addis Ababa, where a school and, until recently, Asmara Road were named in his honor. Even in Ethiopia, however, I found that most who recalled Leland did so through the details of his doomed flight to Fugnido from Bole.

Leland had attained celebrity status within Washington, within a select group of leftist Hollywood actors, and among African leaders, but he remained largely unknown elsewhere in the United States. Alison, Leland's widow, recalls Ethiopian taxi drivers in Washington, Dallas, and New York asking her where she was from, presumably because she could pass easily for Ethiopian. When she responded that she was from Houston, invariably the driver would ask if she had ever heard of Mickey Leland. She would most often simply respond affirmatively, but on occasion she would reveal that she was his wife. The drivers would react in shock and insist she not pay the fare. Some called their mothers or wives, with her still sitting in the back seat. "The first time it happened," she recalled more than two decades later, "I welled up. There is such love and affection for him."[89]

Conclusion

The Tragic Demise of Third World Politics in the United States

I don't know whether the Hutus or the Tutsis were correct. I couldn't tell anybody what I thought they should do. . . . A lot of people were like me; they didn't know crap.

—Congresswoman Maxine Waters, 1994

In July 2015, Ethiopia's prime minister, Hailemariam Desalegn, welcomed U.S. president Barack Obama to the National Palace in Addis Ababa. In his opening remarks for the occasion, the prime minister outlined his country's historic links to the United States and, notably, to African Americans. Expressing pan-Africanism and African diasporic solidarity, Hailemariam emphasized the notable African American intellectual and cultural contributions to global black political uplift, inspired, as they were, by Ethiopia "as the only surviving vessel of freedom and independence in Africa." He picked from a veritable pantheon of African American leaders, including Dr. Martin Luther King Jr. and W. E. B. DuBois, and connected them to the proud spirit of the Ethiopian people: "They saw the courageous struggle of Ethiopia as the symbol of the struggle of the whole community of Africa across the world for civil liberty, equality, and freedom." These were more than emotional and intellectual bonds. He acknowledged African American support for Ethiopia during the Italian occupation from 1936 to 1941 and Ethiopia's participation in the Korean War. "In this context," Hailemariam said, "let me also remember all those Americans who have given their lives to Ethiopia, not least the late Congressman Mickey Leland who worked so hard to build the relationship between our two countries based on dignity, faith and hope. He would have very much appreciated this visit as a symbol of the friendship that has been built up over the years, and which he did so much to encourage."[1]

At the time of the meeting, Ethiopia's economy, position within continental affairs, and relationship with the United States showed little resemblance to the Ethiopia of the 1970s and 1980s. The country's economic and geopolitical strength ensured that it was no minor stop on Obama's tour. Ethiopia had Africa's fastest-growing economy and had amassed an impressive state-driven development portfolio. The United States was an important military partner particularly within the context of the "war on terrorism." To that end, since 2011, the United States had maintained a drone base at Arba Minch airfield, in southern Ethiopia, to target designated "terrorist" sites on the Arabian Peninsula and in Somalia.

But the country's domestic politics were exceedingly complex. For many political observers Obama's visit was inopportune rather than auspicious. In Washington, during the week prior to the president's departure for East Africa, a group of Ethiopian Americans and Ethiopian expats protested in front of the White House. They wanted to send the message to Obama that his meeting with Hailemariam would confer legitimacy upon the Ethiopian prime minister.[2] Since assuming office following the sudden death of Meles Zenawi in August 2012, Hailemariam had drastically curtailed political freedoms and amassed a tragic record of political repression and ethnocentrism in favor of ethnic Tigrayans. His actions cast a dark shadow over Ethiopia's phenomenal economic growth. The Ethiopian government had a slim threshold for dissent even before Hailemariam came into office. Meles was known for his ironfisted control of the media and the Internet and a very narrow definition of free speech.[3] More journalists were jailed in Ethiopia than in any other African country.[4]

Hailemariam opened a deep political divide along ethnic lines, wider than at any point in recent history. The ethnic Oromo majority and the Amhara, the country's second-largest ethnic group, mounted the greatest, most sustained protests against Hailemariam and his Tigrayan-dominated government. The protests began in November 2015 in Oromia and spread to Amhara. No condemnation of its actions came from Washington, even after the government shut down the Internet across the country and responded to protests with police tactics that led to hundreds of deaths and thousands of injuries.

The African American community was silent as well. Its political tradition of aligning with Global South movements and peoples concluded in the 1990s. There was only one black radical lawmaker accompanying the first African American president to Ethiopia. Within government, Mickey Leland's was the final generation of self-consciously African American and internationalist lawmakers, ambassadors, and mayors for whom the Global South, and Africa particularly, was tethered politically to African American interests and aspirations. The Congressional Black Caucus had established a strong, although inconsistent, record during the 1980s and 1990s of holding America's allies' feet to the fire on democracy and political freedoms, but it issued no statements calling on the Ethiopian government to free imprisoned journalists and student activists in the 2000s. Indeed, since the turn of the twenty-first century, the Black Caucus has issued few official, substantive statements on African affairs and, moreover, its members have rarely had direct links with African governments. Its influence has waned partly because its members failed to reach a consensus on African affairs as they had on white-minority rule in Africa but also because of the dwindling number and diminishing strength of community-based and nongovernmental organizations with a political and emotional investment in Africa and the declining intellectual legacy of direct action and revolutionary change in the African American community.[5] The result was the demise of long-standing, strong leadership in Congress on African issues.[6]

Leland's political relationship with Africa provides insight into the factors that gave rise to a strong humanitarian and anti-apartheid impulse in Washington during the 1980s. It also gives some sense of why this impulse did not become the political norm. Key members of Congress who were most active and influential in putting African issues on the congressional agenda in the 1970s and 1980s retired from the Hill. Ronald Dellums retired in 1997, while other activist-inclined African American lawmakers departed earlier in the decade. Congressmen George Crockett and William Gray retired in 1991. Donald Payne Sr., who had entered Congress in 1989, died in 2012. Their careers demonstrate that the afterlife of radicalism, in which activists pursued their social and political goals without the benefit of a strong anti-imperialist and antiracism global network, was an ideologically transient period and added to the unique character of the leaders it had produced in the 1980s. They also show how, after a strong run through the 1980s, the fire of black radicalism died in Congress. Urban restoration and gentrification during the 1990s exposed the fragility of black radical community-building enterprises. Their demise removed an alternative form of civic engagement and means for them to define citizenship as penetrating the social and political mainstream.[7] There had also been powerful and senior white members of Congress, such as Steve Solarz, Howard Wolpe, and Gary Ackerman.

Obituaries for the Black Caucus had already begun to be written as early as 1989, well before the fall of apartheid. The caucus had built strength throughout the 1980s on solidarity, but by the close of the decade the promise of chairmanships and seniority on congressional committees led individual members to break rank. Power was the culprit. The balancing act involved being a caucus that defined itself by challenging the power structure, while its members moved into positions of power within the structure. By the end of the decade, Dellums was the third-highest-ranking Democrat on the Armed Services Committee. He represented one of the most liberal districts in the nation, but he established himself as an inside player by the close of the decade. In an article on changes in the Black Caucus at the time, Tom Kentworthy wrote in the *Washington Post* that Dellums's radicalism had become more rhetorical than real. "We're all growing older, we're all growing more responsible, we all recognize there are nuances," Dellums told journalists. "I came to Congress as a 100-yard sprinter. I'm now a marathoner."[8]

African affairs grew murky and difficult to pin down in the early 1990s, and African American lawmakers with an interest in Africa had a difficult job building a consensus. White-minority rule in South Africa had been a rallying point for African American activism like no other issue in African affairs. With democracy in South Africa, the last vestiges of explicit colonialism ended. As Randall Robinson, president of TransAfrica, predicted at the time, the end of the colonial era would lead to ambiguity over "rights and wrongs" on African issues.[9] Throughout the 1990s, Africa-interested groups remained active in the United States, and many in Congress continued to push Africa-related issues, but the deep engagement was gone. Congressmen Ronald Dellums, Alan Wheat, William Gray, George Crockett Jr., and Donald Payne, a New Jersey Democrat, remained exceptions to the trend away from African affairs, but rather than delegations to expose the horrors of hunger and political repression they worked relatively quietly, issued reports, and submitted legislation.

Congressman Payne was the Black Caucus's chief foreign policy spokesperson. He held a challenging position considering the group's lack of a foreign policy consensus. But on most international issues he was a one-man movement. As had Leland with his black internationalist paradigm,

Payne and his small group of colleagues were determined to ensure that African nations remained part of the U.S. government's foreign policies. They were particularly concerned about U.S. aid to Africa—that the United States provide aid regardless of the receiving nation's politics. It was imperative that aid to Africa and the Caribbean not function as a tool for political persuasion. Charity and altruism must not serve as a facade for political and economic interests.[10] There were reasons for them to remain vigilant.

The African American consensus was racial justice, and on the continent by the mid-1990s that justice appeared to have been served. South Africa and Haiti had fit the racial justice paradigm, while Rwanda, Somalia, Nigeria, and Sudan did not.[11] Africa, and the Global South generally, no longer enjoyed a constituency in the U.S. Congress centered on political, economic, and social strength. The new professoriate was careerist rather than internationalist and pan-Africanist, and overwhelmingly interested in either condemning African governments for their human rights abuses or in development through bank-centered capitalism.

Ronald H. Brown, President Bill Clinton's secretary of commerce, was an exception to the trend of dispassionate pursuit of U.S. goals in African affairs. He was an advocate of mutually beneficial relations between African countries and the United States. Brown served from 1992 until his death in a plane crash in 1996. Neither the civil rights movement nor the Black Power movement provided his political foundation, but still he spoke forcefully in support of African sovereignty and economic development. He criticized France's support of Zaire's Mobutu Sese Seko and genocide in Rwanda in 1994, championed investment in African companies, and helped establish the U.S.-Africa business roundtable.[12]

Humanitarianism had also evolved during the 1990s. Leland would have found the militarization of humanitarian interventions to be a grotesque contradiction. But the intersection of civil war, easy access to weapons, and humanitarian crises called for an international response beyond food aid. These dilemmas—in Somalia, Sierra Leone, Sudan, and Eritrea—had no easily discernible villains. They were fomented by neither nature alone nor white supremacists. A few Black Caucus members waded into Somalia's opaque political waters and chided U.S. and UN inaction in Rwanda, but Haiti was a more accessible, digestible political crisis than could be found in postapartheid Africa.

In the early 1990s there was evidence that black internationalism would continue to have a presence in Congress. In 1990, when Secretary of State

James Baker presented President George H. W. Bush's foreign policy priorities and budget requests to the House Foreign Affairs Committee, William Gray, a committee member, was alarmed by Africa's absence. Baker touched on specific issues throughout the Global North but mentioned Africa and the Caribbean only once. This was the erasure of African affairs, Gray complained in a March 2, 1990, memo to George Crockett Jr. It was conspicuous neglect, a throwback to the start of the Reagan administration. Bush's proposed budget allocated $617 million for Africa, compared with $5.1 billion for Israel and Egypt, $1.11 billion for Greece, Turkey, and Portugal, and $736 million for Central America. The Philippines alone was slated to receive $650 million. "What should be abundantly clear to us all," Gray insisted, "is that if we don't act soon Africa will receive less and less while more and more will be found for Eastern Europe, for Panama, and now for Nicaragua."[13]

Black Caucus members demanded increased aid levels for Africa and the Caribbean in Bush's 1991 budget. They held a closed meeting on March 12 with the Africa Subcommittee to devise a plan for the Black Caucus to take the lead in drafting a resolution for expanded funding for Africa and the Caribbean. The plan was for George Crockett Jr. to introduce the bill on April 3. It was the Mickey Leland African and Caribbean Act of 1991, or H.R. 4443 as it was known in Congress. The bulk of the resolution included development funds for Caribbean and African nations, $900 million for Africa and a total of $240 million for the Caribbean. The funds were to be directed to long-term development and to encourage local activities, particularly those geared toward economically integrating women. It mirrored Leland's vision of the form that U.S. foreign policy should take after the humanitarian crises of the 1980s. Leland held faith in the ability of an infusion of American financial assistance to spur widespread and varied development in the Global South to end the cycle of natural and political crises. The proposed budget was to be a burst of energy for the Black Caucus's attenuated Africa agenda, but the bill floundered for lack of support and ultimately failed.

The 1991 coup that removed Jean-Bertrand Aristide and the subsequent political violence in Haiti became a foreign policy priority for the Black Caucus and TransAfrica. It gained popular traction among African Americans in large part because it took on racial justice overtones. The U.S. responses to Haiti and Somalia reflect the extent to which racial justice had become the most significant part of the platform for popular African American political investment in African and Global South affairs. U.S. policy forced Haitians fleeing to the United States to be returned to the island, while granting asylum to Cubans fleeing a wealthier, more politically stable, and much less violent country. (The Cuban Adjustment Act of 1966 allowed any Cuban who reached the U.S. mainland to pursue residency within a year.) African American activists read the disparate treatment of Haitians, who were almost entirely black, and Cubans, most of whom were white, as racist.

In March 1994 thirty-nine members of the Congressional Black Caucus introduced a bill to tighten the economic embargo against Haiti, sever its commercial links to the United States, halt the summary repatriation of Haitian refugees picked up at sea, and block financial assets held in America by Haitian nationals. Later that month Randall Robinson galvanized the public with his twenty-seven-day hunger strike to protest Clinton's policies toward Haitian refugees.[14] Before the Black Caucus members' measure was considered for a vote, President Clinton adopted many of the provisions as his policy toward Haiti.[15] On September 19, the U.S. Army led a multinational force into Haiti that restored Jean-Bertrand Aristide to power in October. Congressman Donald Payne took credit on behalf of the caucus for changing the Clinton administration's policy. "We've made legislative suggestions in a number of areas and have had limited success in a number of areas," Payne told reporters. "I think we certainly have played a role in the changing of the policy."[16] But the caucus did not speak with one voice on military intervention.

The civil war and resulting humanitarian crisis in Somalia following the overthrow of Siad Barre by clan-based militias in 1991 erupted in parallel to the Haitian crisis, but these conditions did not attract the same level of attention from the United States, perhaps due to Somalia's geographical distance, complex political and cultural contexts, famine fatigue, or some combination of these issues and more. But for African American activists and politicians, the racial context of the U.S. approach to Haiti and the lack of a racial context regarding Somalia were defining distinctions. Representative Alcee Hastings commented, "In my constituency, I'm the first to admit that the primary focus is on Haiti. You have to remember that I come from south Florida, and . . . we have suffered the mega shocks of refugee influx. Africa seems so far away, and there is no vital interest that my constituency sees."[17]

Congressman Payne had supported U.S. intervention in Somalia from the outset of the civil war–induced humanitarian crisis. In November 1992, he traveled to Somalia to investigate the depth of the obstacles to effective humanitarian relief operations. He concluded that the best course to end the violence and provide sufficient food aid was a U.S. military intervention. When he returned he delivered a report on his trip to Somalia that sounded like something straight out of the Leland political playbook: "Many people may have forgotten that for ten years the United States supplied the aid and weaponry and so forth that is in the hands of these thugs and warlords. And so, I think as we talk about our foreign policy in the future, I think that we must be concerned about the past. There is something of a responsibility, I think, that is due, and I hope that we will be able to come up with a foreign policy that will certainly keep all of these points in mind."[18] Payne argued that sending weapons to support one side had the negative consequence of increasing the number of munitions in the region. It was better, he surmised, for U.S. Marines to enter Somalia, arrest Gereral Mohamed Aidid to end the war, and depart with their own weapons.[19]

President Clinton concurred with Payne's assessment and decided the United States would enter militarily into the Somali crisis because, as Herman Cohen explained, the existing relief operation had failed. "Someone had to fix it or tens of thousands more would die," he told the congressional committee. "Only we could do it. The United States and other international donors have massive quantities of food available to end famine in Somalia." Clinton believed the operation would achieve success within three to four months.[20] But as the United States fell deeper into a humanitarian and military quagmire in Somalia, by mid-1993 some members of the Black Caucus expressed their misgivings about the mission. There was no agreement within the caucus on the mission. In October Dellums, chairman of the House Armed Services Committee, wrote to Clinton to warn him of the dangers of continued U.S. military involvement in Somalia.

Days later, on October 3, a special unit of U.S. Army Rangers conducted a raid in an attempt to capture General Aidid. In the course of the ensuing firefight, a Black Hawk helicopter was shot down and one hundred Rangers were pinned down by Somali National Army (SNA) gunfire as they tried to protect the helicopter crew. At the end of the battle, eighteen Rangers were dead and seventy-five wounded. One American, pilot Michael Durant, was captured. Media coverage of the firefight was intense. Videotape of an apparently mistreated Durant and images of Somalis dragging a dead U.S. soldier through the streets of Mogadishu as crowds cheered shocked the American public.[21]

The final, large-scale African American–led initiatives in African affairs of note after apartheid were the pro-democracy movement in Nigeria and the humanitarian crisis in Somalia. The Black Caucus called for sanctions on the regime of Nigerian general Sani Abacha, who refused to hand over power to Moshood Abiola, who had close ties to members of the Black Caucus, when he was democratically elected. At the time, Nigeria was the United States' largest African trading partner. The United States purchased nearly 40 percent of the oil produced in Nigeria; oil exports constituted 90 percent of Nigeria's annual hard currency earnings and 80 percent of all government revenue.[22] For these reasons, TransAfrica and some members of the Black Caucus argued that the United States should use its economic leverage to sway the Nigerian government to enact democratic reforms.

Rather than foster the transition to a democratic republic, Abacha had Abiola arrested. Congressman Payne, with the support of most but not all of his Black Caucus colleagues, advocated oil sanctions on Nigeria. He introduced the Nigeria Democracy Act. This bill would have frozen American investments in Nigeria and embargoed Nigerian oil. But without the full support of his Black Caucus colleagues Payne's bill had little chance of passing.[23] Some of his colleagues defended the Abacha regime. Senator Carol Moseley-Braun of Illinois, the only African American senator, Representative William Jefferson of Louisiana, and other African American members of Congress spoke out against sanctions and in favor of a policy of "constructive dialogue" with the Abacha regime, a poorly named strategy that shows the disarray of the Black Caucus's postapartheid foreign policy. Minister Louis Farrakhan, of the Nation of Islam, and Moseley-Braun both visited Abacha during a "vacation" to Nigeria.

TransAfrica promoted the return to democracy in Nigeria, but this policy did not enjoy a groundswell of support from the media or from a strong corps of African American politicians. Abacha attracted western media attention after the assassination of Nigerian activist and journalist Ken Saro Wiwa in November 1995. Robinson penned a public letter to Nigeria's military leader. "We beseech you to expedite the restoration of democracy to Nigeria's 100 million people who yearn for it," he wrote. "To do less will result in incalculable damage to Africa' most populous nation and eventually global economic and political isolation of your regime."[24] Randall Robinson argued that U.S. corporations were enabling the Abacha regime to survive. In one of his many calls for sanctions, he said, "American companies have become the legs on which the monster of military dictatorship in

Nigeria stands. It is our responsibility here today to say to the U.S. Congress that we must pass legislation to prohibit any new investment, to freeze assets of these generals, to bring in line the conduct of these companies with the notions and values of democracy worldwide."[25]

In response to the threat of U.S. sanctions, Abacha hired American public-relations and lobbying firms in Washington, D.C., including Washington & Christian, a law firm supposedly run by liberal black Democrats, to wage an antisanctions campaign. If the United States imposed sanctions Abacha threatened to retaliate against American oil companies in Nigeria: Chevron, Exxon, and Mobil. Not surprisingly, the American oil giants questioned the benefits of a unilateral U.S. oil embargo and tirelessly reiterated their fears that European companies would move in to fill the vacuum. Senior American officials quietly dropped their previous threats of oil sanctions.

There were short-lived rallies of political interest in Africa, but African American public opinion was divided on most issues. The debate surrounding the African Growth and Opportunity Act of 2000 (AGOA) is an example.[26] The Black Caucus did not take an official position on AGOA, because of the deep split among its members.[27] African Americans in Congress had lost their internationalist fire. The Rwandan genocide and multiracial elections in South Africa both took place in April 1994 but received entirely different responses from the United States. The dynamic connections between activists in South Africa and the United States, extending back to the 1950s, had enabled the success of sanctions legislation. No other issues generated an international network even remotely similar to the one connected to the anti-apartheid movement. The complexity of the Ethiopian crisis did not inspire mass action, while the Rwandan crisis stunned and bewildered outsiders.

Indeed, Rwanda provides an instructive contrast with South Africa. In April 1994, while much of the world celebrated South Africa's first democratic elections, Hutu militias slaughtered more than eight hundred thousand ethnic Tutsi and sympathetic Hutu. Activists did not respond to Rwanda as they had to South Africa. The activist infrastructure of information, networks, and committed organizers had been dismantled with apartheid. The Clinton administration took their time labeling the violence in Rwanda "genocide." Donald Payne was one of the few members of the Black Caucus to even notice. He chided officials for not consulting the Black Caucus on Clinton's intended response and for failing to arrange a multinational intervention.[28] Payne's advocacy in support of African issues, however, was a minority voice among African American lawmakers. During the last years of the century, despite gaining influential positions within Congress, most of them adopted the mainstream Democratic Party foreign policy agenda and positions.

Barbara Lee, a Democrat from California, offers a glimmer of the Black Caucus's activist, internationalist past. Forty years after Leland's death, Lee is the exception in Congress. While she is not alone in working to represent African American interests in Congress, few others exhibit and express an ongoing commitment to shaping U.S. policies toward Global South nations. She is the last of the black internationalists. In ways similar to her predecessors, she positioned herself as tied to the *darker nations* of the world. In 1987 she wrote of African Americans' growing strength in U.S. foreign policy as a vehicle to affirm their connections with groups outside of the United States. "The growing emergence of Afro-Americans in international affairs and foreign policy offers the black community an opportunity to become a major, powerful participant in world affairs. In contrast to being relegated to a 'minority status' by virtue of its numerical and economic status in the U.S., Afro-Americans have become connected with the majority of the world, that is, to people of color who comprise over 60 percent of the world's population."[29]

Lee has kept her eyes on international affairs. She was the sole vote against the authorization for the use of military force in Iraq. She founded the Out of Iraq Caucus and the Out of Poverty Caucus. Since her election to Congress, she has authored or coauthored every piece of legislation related to global HIV/AIDS.[30]

In the absence of an African American political and ideological consensus on Africa, the religious right took the lead on U.S. influence in Africa. Many severely right-wing religious groups have enjoyed porous boundaries between religion and U.S. politics to leverage support from conservative senators and representatives to strengthen their footholds in countries like Uganda, Nigeria, and Kenya. For example, Senator Jim Inhofe, an Oklahoma Republican, and Governor Sam Brownback, a Kansas Republican, established close ties to the Ugandan regime through their involvement with Christian groups. A significant number of African Americans also began to focus on business investment on the continent. Doug Wilder, former governor of Virginia, organized a 1993 conference attended by twenty-five African heads of state and was intended to promote African development through the establishment of regional economic ties between African states and the former slave-holding areas of the United States. In 1995, several African American mayors traveled to South Africa to explore the opportunities inherent in establishing "sister city" ventures with black townships such as Soweto.[31]

Several African Americans had influential policymaking positions during the Clinton, George W. Bush, and Obama administrations. Constance Newman, followed by Jendayi Frazer, served as Bush's assistant secretary of state for African affairs from 2005 until the end of the Bush presidency in 2009. They helped advance a series of successful initiatives, most notably those centered on public health. The President's Emergency Plan for AIDS Relief included HIV/AIDS programs and tuberculosis and malaria treatment. The first commander of the United States Africa Command was General William E. Ward, an African American. His tenure began in 2007, during the Bush administration, but stretched into the second half of President Obama's first term. There were other African Americans active within President Bush's Africa-related programs, including Sarah Moten of USAID.

When President Obama met with Prime Minister Hailemariam Desalegn in July 2015, their discussion centered on regional security, specifically al-Shabaab, the Somalia-based jihadist terrorist group. The political and humanitarian crisis in South Sudan was also a major issue in conversations between U.S. and Ethiopian officials in Addis Ababa. Obama had a hand in making South Sudan's independence from Sudan possible. Ethiopia had been playing a leading role in efforts to resolve South Sudan's internal political crisis. During their talks, Obama referenced in passing Ethiopia's need for greater respect and protection of human rights in their own country. Ethiopian-U.S. relations had come full circle from the days of Emperor Haile Selassie. Security, stability, and economic interests trumped democracy and human rights.

On July 28 in Addis Ababa, Obama spoke to African heads of state in Mandela Hall. In introducing him, Nkosazana Dlamini-Zuma of South Africa, chairwoman of the African Union Commission, welcomed the U.S. president and said that the African Union claimed him as their own.[32] Obama's speech there marked the end of his five-day trip to the continent. He explicitly acknowledged the personal significance of the occasion: "I stand before you as a proud American. I also stand before you as the son of an African. Africa and its people helped shape America and allowed it to become the great nation that it is. And Africa and its people have helped shape who I am and how I see the world."[33] From this point on, his speech departed from the pan-Africanist spirit of the preceding generation of African American political officials, more inclined to reserve policy critiques and condemnation for closed-door sessions. Their primary concern had been U.S. moral correctness. Not only a sense of black solidarity but Cold War politics would have tempered broad, sweeping denunciations of African leaders. Obama's remarks reflect the assimilation of African American politicians and African leaders' political expendability.

Obama spoke of the importance of protecting journalists' freedom to carry out their important work and the significance of education and job growth in Africa. His speech touched all the important buttons, from trade, terrorism, and energy to human rights. U.S. antiterrorism in the region had been the policy focus since George W. Bush's second term. Obama expanded the U.S. military presence in the Sahel with drone bases in Djibouti and Ethiopia to address security concerns in the Arabian Peninsula and Somali. The Pentagon built bases in Niger to facilitate responses to issues in Mali and northern Nigeria. Issues of good governance and economic development have been sidelined.[34] The United States had an African American president and high-ranking African American officials, but it had lost strong voices in support of African interests separate from U.S. global aspirations.

Under Presidents George W. Bush and Barack Obama, African Americans held the highest positions in government for shaping foreign policy. Frazer was a prime example of the triumph of careerism over ideology. Bush appointed Colin Powell and then Condoleezza Rice as secretary of state, the highest-ranking cabinet position. Powell expressed a genuine interest and connection with Africa, but the policies of the conservative administration he served hamstrung him, along with his own limited sense of the continent's possibilities. In a trip to South Africa in May 2001, he affirmed his affinity with Africa and expressed his desire, as the first African American secretary of state, to build closer ties with African countries on behalf of the United States.[35] However, he withdrew from the United Nations World Conference Against Racism in Durban in September 2001 when the body issued criticisms of Israel's occupation of Palestine. African American leaders lacked the political sway that might challenge the administration to change its position. As Adekeye Adebajo wrote at the time, "This was the clearest sign, if any was needed, of how powerful the Jewish-American lobby is, in stark contrast to the powerlessness of the African

American lobby. In a global conference to discuss slavery, reparations, and racism—the issues closest to the hearts of many African Americans—the United States could not muster the will to send a representative to the conference."[36]

Leland's cohort was the end of Third World activism within the U.S. government in a period that extended back to Ambassador Andrew Young at the United Nations and Charles Diggs in Congress. President Obama has arguably been the most influential African American in history. Susan Rice served as U.S. ambassador to the United Nations under Obama and then as his national security advisor. Both positions have significance within the U.S. foreign policy establishment. There have also been numerous lower-ranking, but still influential, African American government officials over the last twenty-five years. The Obama administration demonstrated that an African American presence within the U.S. government does not necessarily translate into robust advocacy for African and Global South nations' interests. African Americans in government positions are part of the African American community in terms of identity, but politically they are just as likely to represent policies and perform functions that are antithetical to the dominant interests represented in that community.[37]

Notes

Introduction

Note to epigraph: Mickey Leland, "The Politics of Hunger Among Blacks," *Black Scholar* 21, no. 1, (January–March 1990): 2–5.

1. For a detailed outline of Sudan's civil wars and their historical and political contexts, see Douglas H. Johnson, *The Root Causes of Sudan's Civil Wars: Old Wars and New Wars* (New York: James Currey, 2016).

2. U.S. approaches to refugee crises offer additional examples of domestic issues, ideologies, and activism that shaped foreign policy. See Carl J. Bon Tempo, *Americans at the Gate: The United States and Refugees During the Cold War* (Princeton, NJ: Princeton University Press, 2008), 3.

3. During the Cold War, "Third World" had a meaning distinct from its current, largely pejorative connotation. Between 1955 and 1992, leaders of formerly colonized and soon-to-be-independent nations, dominated by India, Indonesia, Burma, Egypt, and Ghana, organized themselves as an alternative to the eastern and western blocs. These third-option, or Third World, political actors promoted the cause of antiracism, anti-imperialism, and anti–nuclear proliferation. In spirit, they crafted foreign policies for their postcolonial states that promoted international cooperation. They framed the political and economic disadvantages that their respective countries collectively faced as direct consequences of Western, imperialist exploitation. The Third World movement sought to protect the sovereignty and self-determination of Global South nations against the powerful gravitational pull of the Cold War powers. For the most sophisticated discussion of the rise and ultimate failure of the Non-Aligned movement, see Vijay Prashad, *The Darker Nations: A People's History of the Third World* (New York: New Press, 2008). Odd Arne Westad has also made an important contribution to understanding the challenges the Cold War posed for sovereignty and political stability in Global South nations, as well as the ways the Cold War elevated local and regional conflicts into international crises. See Westad, *The Global Cold War: Third World Interventions and the Making of Our Times* (Cambridge: Cambridge University Press, 2007). Also, on the role of the Cold War in internationalizing African crises, see Elizabeth Schmidt, *Foreign Intervention in Africa: From the Cold War to the War on Terror* (Cambridge: Cambridge University Press, 2013). "US Third World left" is the label Cynthia A. Young uses for this political phenomenon and period. See Young, *Soul Power: Culture, Radicalism, and the Making of a US Third World Left* (Durham, NC: Duke University Press, 2006), 7. On the 1955 Bandung Conference and the movement for Global South solidarity, see Prashad, *The Darker Nations*, 2008.

4. For radical black organizing during the latter years of the civil rights movement and the high point of the Black Power era, see Nikhil Pal Singh, *Black Is a Country: Race and the Unfinished Struggle for Democracy* (Cambridge, MA: Harvard University Press, 2005), particularly chap. 5; and Russell Rickford, *We Are an African People: Independent Education, Black Power, and the Radical Imagination* (New York: Oxford University Press, 2016). Cedric Johnson provides the most comprehensive discussion of the continuities and discontinuities between the civil rights movement, Black Power, and electoral politics. See Johnson, *Revolutionaries to Race Leaders: Black Power and the Making of African American Politics* (Minneapolis: University of Minnesota Press, 2007). Joshua Bloom and Waldo E. Martin Jr. demonstrate through the Black Panther Party the failure of the civil rights movement to bring about fundamental change in the daily lives of African Americans, particularly those living in the deindustrializing North and West of the United States. Black radicals filled this void with anti-imperialist, community-centered Black Power activism. See Bloom and Martin, *Black Against Empire: The History and Politics of the Black Panther Party* (Berkeley: University of California Press, 2016). Like Johnson, Ronald Williams II explains the conflicts among African American leaders on issues related to the global African diaspora as extending from increased access to mainstream sources of political power. See Williams, "From Anticolonialism to Anti-Apartheid: African American Political Organizations and African Liberation, 1957–93," in *African Americans in Global Affairs: Contemporary Perspectives*, ed. Michael L. Clemons (Boston: Northeastern University Press, 2010), 66–67.

5. On African American activism tied to African issues during the nineteenth and early twentieth centuries, see Wilson Jeremiah Moses, *The Golden Age of Black Nationalism, 1850–1925* (Oxford: Oxford University Press, 1978); Moses, *Alexander Crummell: A Study of Civilization and Discontent* (Amherst: University of Massachusetts Press, 1989). Penny Von Eschen chronicles the mid-twentieth-century African American movement to shape U.S. policy toward Africa in *Race Against Empire: Black Americans and Anticolonialism, 1937–1957* (Ithaca, NY: Cornell University Press, 1997).

6. Louis Sell suggests, not in a flattering tone, that Castro regarded himself as the "apostle of third-world revolution." See Sell, *From Washington to Moscow: US-Soviet Relations and the Collapse of the USSR* (Chapel Hill: University of North Carolina Press, 2016).

7. Odd Arne Westad defines the Cold War as a period in which the superpowers' views were skewed toward the absolute, in which "only one's own system was good. The other system was inherently evil." See Westad, *The Cold War: A World History* (New York: Basic Books, 2017), 2. Similarly, Cary Fraser describes the "bipolar paradigm" as an insufficient analytical tool for fully understanding the forces that reshaped the international order, particularly "the influence of longer-term historical processes and of other state actors." Fraser, "A Requiem for the Cold War: Reviewing the History of International Relations Since 1945," in *Rethinking the Cold War*, ed. Allen Hunter (Philadelphia: Temple University Press, 1998), 95.

8. "An Activist on Behalf of Humanity: Honorable Mickey Leland," *Modern Black Man*, March 1987.

9. The scholarship on African American political and cultural engagement with Africa in the post–civil rights period has experienced remarkable growth during the past decade. Kevin K. Gaines explores African American travels to and writings on Ghana in *American Africans in Ghana: Black Expatriates and the Civil Rights Era* (Chapel Hill: University of North Carolina Press, 2006); see particularly the second half of the book, in which he discusses experiences

during the period when Kwame Nkrumah ran the government. In *Proudly We Can Be Africans: Black Americans and Africa, 1935–1961* (Chapel Hill: University of North Carolina Press, 2002), James H. Meriwether takes a more geographically expansive view of African Americans and Africa than Gaines, but he does not extend his study through the civil rights movement. In *Middle Passages: African American Journeys to Africa, 1787–2005* (New York: Penguin, 2007), James T. Campbell reconstructs histories of Africans and African Americans traveling between the continent and the United States to argue that African American imaginings of and political involvement with Africa were largely determined by events and experiences in the United States. As I argue, the movement against apartheid in South Africa enabled African Americans to exert tremendous influence on U.S. foreign policy toward that country and enabled leaders and organizations to raise their foreign policy profiles. Yet there remains limited scholarship with a critical historical analysis of this connection. Francis Njubi Nesbitt relies largely on newspaper coverage of the anti-apartheid movement in the United States in his *Race for Sanctions: African Americans Against Apartheid, 1946–1994* (Bloomington: Indiana University Press, 2004). On community organizing, institution building, and Black Power that emphasized Africa, see Rickford, *We Are an African People*; Rob Skinner, *The Foundations of Anti-Apartheid: Liberal Humanitarians and Transnational Activists in Britain and the United States, c. 1919–64* (New York: Palgrave Macmillan, 2010); Schmidt, *Foreign Intervention in Africa*; Ronald W. Walters, *Pan Africanism in the African Diaspora: An Analysis of Modern Afrocentric Political Movements* (Detroit: Wayne State University Press, 1993); Brenda Gayle Plummer, *Rising Wind: Black Americans and US Foreign Affairs, 1935–1960* (Chapel Hill: University of North Carolina Press, 1996); Plummer, *In Search of Power: African Americans in the Era of Decolonization, 1956–1974* (Cambridge: Cambridge University Press, 2013); Mary L. Dudziak, *Cold War Civil Rights: Race and the Image of American Democracy* (Princeton, NJ: Princeton University Press, 2010); Thomas Borstelmann, *The Cold War and the Color Line: American Race Relations in the Global Arena* (Cambridge, MA: Harvard University Press, 2003); Carol Anderson, *Eyes Off the Prize: The United Nations and the African American Struggle for Human Rights, 1944–1955* (New York: Cambridge University Press, 2003); Alvin B. Tillery Jr., *Between Homeland and Motherland: Africa, US Foreign Policy, and Black Leadership in America* (Ithaca, NY: Cornell University Press, 2011); Carol Anderson, *Bourgeois Radicals: The NAACP and the Struggle for Colonial Liberation, 1941–1960* (New York: Cambridge University Press, 2015); and Gerald Horne, *Black and Red: W. E. B. DuBois and the Afro-American Response to the Cold War, 1944–1963* (Albany: State University of New York Press, 1986).

10. Anne-Maria Makhulu, *Making Freedom: Apartheid, Squatter Politics, and the Struggle for Home* (Chicago: University of Chicago Press, 2015), 154–55.

11. Alex de Waal has discussed the famine narrative and its consequences in detail. Much of the analysis here benefits from de Waal's insight. See de Waal, *Famine Crimes: Politics and the Disaster Relief Industry in Africa* (Bloomington: Indiana University Press, 1997). See also Andrew Jones, "Band Aid Revisited: Humanitarianism, Consumption and Philanthropy in the 1980s," *Contemporary British History* 31, no. 2 (2017): 189–209.

12. Leland's notion of a U.S. debt to the Global South was not widely shared among African American political leaders. In fascinating ways, this position put him in concert with the young activists of the New Left, principally the Students for a Democratic Society. Their 1962 manifesto—*The Port Huron Statement*—explicitly called upon the United States to

address global hunger, along with nuclear proliferation, racism, homelessness, and poverty. See William L. O'Neill, *The New Left: A History* (Wheeling, IL: Harlan Davidson, 2001), 10–12.

13. "Two Missing Bodies of Air Crash Victims Recovered," *Ethiopian Herald*, August 18, 1989.

14. Quoted in D. Michael Cheers, "Leland's Legacy," *Jet*, September 4, 1989.

15. Nene Foxhall, "Mickey Died to Feed the Hungry, Jackson Says," *Houston Chronicle*, August 19, 1989.

16. Jim Simmon, "Leland Eulogized in US—As Life Goes on in Refugee Camps/ Hundreds Attend Leland Mass/The Rev. Jackson Moves Mourners with Stirring Eulogy," *Houston Chronicle*, August 20, 1989.

17. Ibid.

18. Lorenzo Morris, "African American Representatives in the United Nations: From Ralph Bunche to Susan Rice," in *African Americans in US Foreign Policy*, ed. Heywood et al., 191.

Chapter 1

Note to epigraph: ". . . she'll never know!" "Mickey's Message," Series 13, Box 2, File 10436001, Mickey Leland Archives, Texas Southern University.

1. William Middleton, *Double Vision: The Unerring Eye of Art World Avatars Dominique and John de Menil* (New York: Knopf, 2018), 442.

2. Mickey Leland, University of Houston-Downtown commencement speech, May 13, 1989, Series 11, Box 211, Folder 10313002, Mickey Leland Archives, Texas Southern University.

3. Ibid.

4. At the time, Robert Blauner described Black Power as a collection of movements united in the goal of black economic and political liberation and control of African American communities. See Blauner, "Internal Colonialism and Ghetto Revolt," *Social Problems* 16, no. 4 (April 1969): 402. More recently, scholars have generally defined Black Power as an array of positions and organizations that revolved around the notion of cultural self-determination and economic independence from white capitalism. See, for example, Amy Abugo Ongiri, *Spectacular Blackness: The Cultural Politics of the Black Power Movement and the Search for a Black Aesthetic* (Charlottesville: University of Virginia Press, 2009); and Plummer, *In Search of Power*, 13–16. Joshua Bloom and Waldo E. Martin show that Black Power meant different things to different people by settling on the general definition of "actual economic and political power." See Bloom and Martin, *Black Against Empire*. Cedric Johnson states that the shift from civil rights to Black Power involved moving from the task of attaining equal constitutional rights to seizing state power and asserting self-determination. See Johnson, *Revolutionaries to Race Leaders*, particularly chaps. 3 and 5, conclusion.

5. See, for example, Robeson Taj Frazier's study of black internationalists' solidarity with communist China in *The East Is Black*, particularly 6–7.

6. Williams, "From Anticolonialism to Anti-Apartheid," 80.

7. Countryman, " 'From Protest to Politics,' " 816.

8. Bayard Rustin, "From Protest to Politics: The Future of the Civil Rights Movement," *Commentary* 39, no. 2 (February 1965): 25, http://digital.library.pitt.edu/u/ulsmanuscripts/ pdf/31735066227830.pdf.

9. Ibid., 26.

10. In 1972, Jordan was also the first African American woman to deliver the keynote address at a national political convention of a dominant political party.

11. For details on Jordan's tenure in the Texas state senate, see Mary Ellen Curtin, "Reaching for Power: Barbara C. Jordan and Liberals in the Texas Legislature, 1966–1972," *Southwestern Historical Quarterly* 108, no. 2 (2004): 211–31.

12. Rickford, *We Are an African People*, 6. See also Matthew J. Countryman, " 'From Protest to Politics': Community Control and Black Independent Politics in Philadelphia, 1965–1984," *Journal of Urban History* 32, no. 6 (2006): 813–61. Cedric Johnson argues that the end of ethnic politics came with the rise of moderate black political empowerment. He does not discuss the 1980s and the power of the Congressional Black Caucus under the leadership of Ronald Dellums and Mickey Leland. Johnson argues that the popular pressure to support extensive political change dissolved during the 1970s, but he fails to account for the popular pressure for U.S. divestment from South Africa during the 1980s. See Johnson, *Revolutionaries to Race Leaders*, 217–19.

13. Quoted in Bruce Webb, "Counterculture U: Discontent and Liberation at the University of Houston," *Cite* 82 (Summer 2010): 11–16.

14. William Henry Kellar suggests that a mitigating factor in black protest in Houston was the conservative character of the black leadership and the economic ties many of those leaders had with whites. See Kellar, *Make Haste Slowly: Moderates, Conservatives, and School Desegregation in Houston* (College Station: Texas A&M University Press, 1999), 117–20.

15. Middleton, *Double Vision*, 437.

16. Gene Locke, phone interview by the author, July 12, 2009.

17. Jacqueline Trescott, "Leland and the War on Hunger: For the Congressman, an Activist Path," *Washington Post*, September 27, 1985.

18. Omowali Luthuli-Allen, phone interview by the author, October 26, 2009.

19. Plummer, *In Search of Power*; Timothy B. Tyson, *Radio Free Dixie: Robert F. Williams and the Roots of Black Power* (Chapel Hill: University of North Carolina Press, 1999). Attacks from European and U.S. financial and political institutions and internal disunity were detrimental to vestiges of Third World solidarity. The scholarship on the Third World and the Non-Aligned movement has enjoyed something of a renaissance. On the Bandung Conference, see Prashad, *The Darker Nations*, 31–50.

20. Fanon Ché Wilkins, "The Making of Black Internationalists: SNCC and Africa Before the Launching of Black Power, 1960–1965," *Journal of African American History* 92, no. 4, New Black Power Studies (Autumn 2007): 469.

21. Quoted in ibid., 468.

22. I address the issue of African American community development more explicitly in the following chapter. Recent scholarship has offered a rich, textured reconstruction of the history of grassroots community development projects that extended explicitly from, or at least embodied, Black Power aspirations. See, for example, Rickford, *We Are an African People*; and Ongiri, *Spectacular Blackness*. See also Komozi Woodard, *A Nation Within a Nation: Amiri Baraka (LeRoi Jones) and Black Power Politics* (Chapel Hill: University of North Carolina Press, 1999).

23. Charles Pinderhughes, "How *Black Awakening in Capitalist America* Laid the Foundation for a New Internal Colonialism Theory," *Black Scholar* 40, no. 2 (Summer 2010): 71, 75.

24. Harold W. Cruse provides the earliest and most compelling discussion of internal colonialism; see Cruse, "Revolutionary Nationalism and the Afro-American," *Studies on the Left* 2, no. 3 (1962): 12–25, http://my.ilstu.edu/~jkshapi/Cruse_Revolutionary%20 Nationalism.pdf. Its most influential proponents among U.S. academics were Robert L. Allen and Robert Blauner. In *Black Awakening in Capitalist America: An Analytic History* (Trenton, NJ: Africa World Press, 1990), Allen went as far as describing a transition from direct to indirect rule within black America. Blauner conceded the limits of the colonial analogy for understanding African American material conditions in the 1960s but found the concept of colonialism as practice useful. One significant difference between internal colonialism in the United States and what Blauner labels "traditional colonialism" is the absence of fully developed indigenous institutions outside the church among African Americans. See Blauner, "Internal Colonialism and Ghetto Revolt." Scholars have applied the internal colonialism framework to study the economic and political conditions of other nonwhite communities in the United States. See, for example, Ramón A. Gutiérrez, "Chicano Struggles for Racial Justice: The Movement's Contribution to Social Theory," in *Mexicans in California: Transformations and Challenges*, ed. Ramón A. Gutiérrez and Patricia Zavella (Urbana: University of Illinois Press, 2009), 94–110. See also Harold W. Cruse, *Rebellion or Revolution* (New York: William Morrow, 1968). Barry Sautman's description of internal colonialism is helpful and fitting. See Sautman, "Is Xinjiang an Internal Colony?" *Inner Asia* 2, no. 2 (2000): 243.

25. Cruse, "Revolutionary Nationalism and the Afro-American." Activists applied a wide variety of meanings and goals to "revolution." I contend that most regarded revolution in ways similar to Bayard Rustin's definition from 1964. He insisted that his use of the term did not connote violence but instead referred to the "qualitative transformation of fundamental institutions, more or less rapidly, to the point where the social and economic structure which they comprised can no longer be said to be the same." See Rustin, "From Protest to Politics," 65.

26. HARYOU, *Youth in the Ghetto: A Study of the Consequences of Powerlessness and a Blueprint for Change* (New York: Harlem Youth Opportunities Unlimited, 1964). In the 1970s and early 1980s, scholars applied the internal colonialism framework to Puerto Rican, Chicano, and Native American communities as well as African Americans. On the role of social science in school desegregation, see Kenneth B. Clark, *Prejudice and Your Child*, 2nd ed. (Middletown, CT: Wesleyan University Press, 1988); and Clark, *Dark Ghetto: Dilemmas of Social Power*, 2nd ed. (Middletown, CT: Wesleyan University Press, 1989), chap. 6.

27. Thomas C. Holt, *Children of Fire: A History of African Americans* (New York: Macmillan, 2011), 347.

28. Luthuli-Allen interview.

29. Amilcar Cabral, "The Weapon of Theory" (address delivered to the First Tricontinental Conference of the Peoples of Asia, Africa, and Latin America, Havana, January 1966), https://www.marxists.org/subject/africa/cabral/1966/weapon-theory.htm. Cedric Johnson describes Cabral's notion of "class suicide" as one of the guiding axioms of radical intellectuals' self-conceptions and social theories, along with Frantz Fanon's theory of native intellectuals' need to embrace the peasantry as the foundation of national culture. See Johnson, *Revolutionaries to Race Leaders*, 170; see also Fanon, *The Wretched of the Earth*, trans. Richard Philcox (New York: Grove Press, 2005).

30. Rickford, *We Are an African People*, 3.

31. Cynthia A. Young, "Havana up in Harlem: LeRoi Jones, Harold Cruse and the Making of a Cultural Revolution," *Science and Society* 65, no. 1 (Spring 2001): 28.

32. C. L. R. James, *You Don't Play with Revolution: The Montreal Lectures of C. L. R. James*, ed. David Austin (Oakland, CA: AK Press, 2009).

33. On the spectrum of Black Power, see Countryman, "From Protest to Politics." See also Ongiri, *Spectacular Blackness*, 2–3. Pan-Africanism, which intersected with Black Power, had its own spectrum. One end was represented by Kwame Ture (Stokely Carmichael) and the position that Africa was the center of nationalism and nation building. The Republic of New Africa held a competing vision, which located the heart of African American nationalist aspirations in the Deep South and an independent African America through the appropriation of five states: Alabama, South Carolina, Louisiana, Mississippi, and Georgia. On the Republic of New Africa and pan-Africanism, see Rickford, *We Are an African People*, 43, 159; and Muhammad Ahmed, "The Roots of the Pan-African Revolution," *Black Scholar* 3, no. 9 (May 1972): 51–52. On distinctions between the civil rights movement and Black Power, see Sundiata Keita Cha-Jua and Clarence Lang, "The 'Long Movement' as Vampire: Temporal and Spatial Fallacies in Recent Black Freedom Studies," *Journal of African American History* 92, no. 2 (Spring 2007): 265–88, 274.

34. Stokely Carmichael, "Toward Black Liberation," *Massachusetts Review* 7, no. 4 (1966): 639–51, http://nationalhumanitiescenter.org/pds/maai3/segregation/text8/carmichael.pdf. For a discussion of Carmichael's definition of Black Power, see Clayborne Carson, *In Struggle: SNCC and the Black Awakening of the 1960s* (Cambridge, MA: Harvard University Press, 1995), 215–16.

35. John Dittmer, *The Good Doctors: The Medical Committee for Human Rights and the Struggle for Social Justice in Health Care* (New York: Bloomsbury, 2009).

36. Luthuli-Allen interview.

37. Leland found McGovern's political message and his run for president in 1972 inspiring and refreshing. He volunteered for McGovern's campaign in Houston and afterward was profoundly troubled by what his loss signaled for the direction of national politics in the United States. Omowali Luthuli-Allen, phone interview by the author, October 29, 2009.

38. Barbara J. Keys, *Reclaiming American Virtue: The Human Rights Revolution of the 1970s* (Cambridge, MA: Harvard University Press, 2014), 4.

39. Middleton, *Double Vision*, 436–38, 439–40.

40. Cruse, *Rebellion or Revolution*, 70.

41. White liberal patronage of talented black artists, politicians, and others has a legacy tinged by paternalism, creative control, and implicit racism. White patrons and philanthropists supported African American students and musicians throughout the twentieth century. The white patronage of Harlem Renaissance artists and writers has been well documented. See, for example, David Levering Lewis, *When Harlem Was in Vogue* (New York: Penguin Books, 1997). Tiffany Ruby Patterson has richly detailed the benefits and pitfalls of Zora Neale Hurston's experiences with her white benefactors in "Patronage: Anatomy of a Predicament," in *Zora Neale Hurston: And a History of Southern Life* (Philadelphia: Temple University Press, 2005).

42. Quoted in Dominique Browning, "What I Admire I Must Possess," *Texas Monthly*, April 1983.

43. Quoted in Middleton, *Double Vision*, 442–43.

44. Wilkins, "The Making of Black Internationalists," 479.

45. Ibid., 483–85.

46. Luthuli-Allen interview, October 26, 2009.

47. There are numerous published accounts of African American experiences in Ghana during the Nkrumah years. Maya Angelou's memoir is arguably the definitive text. See Angelou, *All God's Children Need Traveling Shoes* (New York: Vintage, 1991). For an engaging analysis of the African American expatriate community in Ghana, see Walters, *Pan Africanism in the African Diaspora*. See also Gaines, *African Americans in Ghana*. For a fascinating study of the diaspora's political and spiritual cultures' intersection with Tanzanian politics, see Monique A. Bedasse, *Jah Kingdom: Rastafarians, Tanzania, and Pan-Africanism in the Age of Decolonization* (Chapel Hill: University of North Carolina Press, 2017). Bedasse describes Tanzania's politics as resonating with Black Power advocates, expatriates, and political tourists between 1965 and 1976, including Malcolm X, Amiri Baraka, Angela Davis, and Eldridge Cleaver. See Bedasse, *Jah Kingdom*, 66–68.

48. Bedasse, *Jah Kingdom*, 67.

49. Ibid.

50. Ibid., 53–54.

51. Plummer, *In Search of Power*, 205.

52. Bedasse, *Jah Kingdom*, 67. Bedasse argues that Tanzania was attractive to "diasporic Africans" because it rose in the wake of Ghana's fall as a beacon of pan-Africanism but also because its political project matched diasporic nationalist ideals of self-determination and self-reliance, particularly as expressed through the Black Power and Rastafari movements. See Bedasse, *Jah Kingdom*, chap. 2, particularly 49–68.

53. "The Search for Mickey Leland," *Houston Chronicle*, August 10, 1989.

54. William Edgett Smith, *We Must Run While They Walk: A Portrait of Africa's Julius Nyerere* (New York: Random House, 1972).

55. Gene Locke, phone interview by the author, July 12, 2009.

56. Crawford, "Mickey Leland, Fighting Hunger from Capitol Hill."

57. Luthuli-Allen interview, October 26, 2009.

58. Leo Zeilig is one of the few scholars to examine student movements throughout Africa and link their organizations and aspirations to movements elsewhere in the world from the 1960s to the 1990s. See Zeilig, *Revolt and Protest: Student Politics and Activism in Sub-Saharan Africa* (New York: Tauris, 2013).

59. Zewde, *The Quest for Socialist Utopia*, 45. See also Andargachew Tiruneh, *The Emergence and Proliferation of Political Organizations in Ethiopia* (Los Angeles: Tsehai, 2015), 43.

60. For a detailed account of life in and around Addis Ababa University during the early 1970s, see Ahmed, "Addis Ababa University," 293–94.

61. On U.S. interests in the Middle East and Ethiopia during the 1970s, see Donna R. Jackson, *Jimmy Carter and the Horn of Africa: Cold War Policy in Ethiopia and Somalia* (Jefferson, NC: McFarland, 2007), 6.

62. Jack Shepherd, "Ethiopia: The Use of Food as an Instrument of US Foreign Policy," *African Issues* 14 (1985): 5.

63. Tiruneh, *Emergence and Proliferation of Political Organizations in Ethiopia*, 44–45.

64. Zewde, *Documenting the Ethiopian Student Movement*, 14.

65. Zewde, *Quest for Socialist Utopia*, 101.

66. Tiruneh, *Emergence and Proliferation of Political Organizations in Ethiopia*, 45.

67. Quoted in Zewde, *Documenting the Ethiopian Student Movement*, 34.

68. "The Dilemma of Famine in Ethiopia," *Combat*, January 1975.

69. De Waal, *Famine Crimes*, 106.

70. Peter Gill, *Famine and Foreigners: Ethiopia Since Live Aid* (Oxford: Oxford University Press, 2010), 33.

71. Zewde, *Quest for Socialist Utopia*, 184.

72. Tiruneh, *Emergence and Proliferation of Political Organizations in Ethiopia*, 59.

73. Zewde, *History of Modern Ethiopia*, 231.

74. Tiruneh, *Emergence and Proliferation of Political Organizations in Ethiopia*, 46.

75. For a more detailed description of the Derg's response and its accusations against the imperial government's handling of famine, see Shepherd, *The Politics of Starvation*, ix–x.

76. Patman, *The Soviet Union in the Horn of Africa*, 154.

77. Gill, *Famine and Foreigners*, 29.

78. Tareke, *The Ethiopian Revolution*, 41–42.

79. Teshale Tibebu, personal correspondence with the author, September 29, 2017. See also, Teshale Tibebu, *The Making of Modern Ethiopia, 1896–1974* (Lawrenceville, NJ: Red Sea Press, 1995), 168–69.

80. Quoted in James Finn, ed., *Ethiopia: The Politics of Famine* (Lanham, MD: University Press of America, 1990), 12.

81. Ibid., 14.

82. Quoted in ibid., 15.

83. From 1975 to 1978, the government established Peasant Associations (PAs) composed of household heads in each community. The PAs had the authority to redistribute land, maintain common assets, resolve conflicts, and enable development activities to take place in their areas. They were intended to be a form of popular self-administration. By 1978 they were co-opted by the government to serve as local extensions of Mengistu's authority. See Dessalegn Rahmato, "Agrarian Change and Agrarian Crisis: State and Peasantry in Post-Revolution Ethiopia," *Africa* 63, no. 1 (January 1993): 38.

84. Quoted in Helen Winternitz, "Ethiopia's Poor See Gain from Revolution but Memory of 'Red Terror' Still Lingers," *Sun (London)*, August 31, 1981.

85. Shepherd, *The Politics of Starvation*, 3.

86. Tiruneh, *Emergence and Proliferation of Political Organizations in Ethiopia*, 105.

87. Tibebu, *Making of Modern Ethiopia*, 168–69.

88. Westad, *Cold War*, 488.

89. Ibid., 489.

90. Tareke, *The Ethiopian Revolution*, 41–42.

91. Christopher Clapham describes in detail the evolving structure of communism in Ethiopia and the structure of the Communist Workers' Party of Ethiopia in "The State and Revolution in Ethiopia," *Review of African Political Economy* 16, no. 44 (1989): 5–17.

92. Sell, *From Washington to Moscow*, 84.

93. Patman, *The Soviet Union in the Horn of Africa*, 176–77.

94. Steven L. Varnis, *Reluctant Aid or Aiding the Reluctant? US Food Aid Policy and Ethiopian Famine Relief* (New Brunswick, NJ: Transaction Publishers, 1990), 41.

95. Jesse Ferris, *Nasser's Gamble: How Intervention in Yemen Caused the Six-Day War and the Decline of Egyptian Power* (Princeton, NJ: Princeton University Press, 2013), 102.

96. Jacqueline McGlade, "More a Plowshare than a Sword: The Legacy of US Cold War Agricultural Diplomacy," *Agricultural History* 83, no. 1 (Winter 2009): 81.

97. "How Meles Zenawi Went from Medical School Dropout to Prime Minister," *Guardian*, August 21, 2012, http://www.theguardian.com/global-development/2012/aug/21/meles-zenawi-dropout-prime-minister.

98. Theodore Vestal, "Meles Zenawi (1955–2012)," *International Journal of Ethiopian Studies* 6, nos. 1–2 (2012): 195.

99. Varnis, *Reluctant Aid or Aiding the Reluctant?* 65.

100. Ethiopia's conflicts absorbed more than half of its national budget. The official explanations were the escalating civil wars, the worst drought in living memory, decreased foreign exchange earnings, scant national savings, and lack of investment. See Tareke, *The Ethiopian Revolution*, 157.

101. Alex de Waal, *Evil Days: Thirty Years of War and Famine in Ethiopia* (New York: Human Rights Watch, 1991), 169.

102. Graham Hovey, "US Moving Toward Military Ties with Somalia, Recognizing Risks," *New York Times*, February 10, 1980.

103. Ibid.

104. Mitchell, *Jimmy Carter in Africa*, 185.

105. Don Oberdorfer, "The Superpowers and the Ogaden War," *Washington Post*, March 5, 1978. See also Nancy Mitchell, *Jimmy Carter in Africa: Race and the Cold War* (Stanford, CA: Stanford University Press, 2016), 201.

106. Piero Gleijeses, *Conflicting Missions: Havana, Washington, and Africa, 1959–1976* (Chapel Hill: University of North Carolina Press, 2002), chap. 12.

107. Piero Gleijeses, *Visions of Freedom: Havana, Washington, Pretoria, and the Struggle for Southern Africa, 1976–1991* (Chapel Hill: University of North Carolina Press, 2013), 324. See also Colin Legum, "The African Crisis," *African Affairs* 57, no. 3 (1978): 634.

108. Legum, "The African Crisis," 635.

109. "Text of PMAC Announcement Regarding Closure of Certain US Installations," April 23, 1978, National Security Affairs, Brzezinski Material Country File, Ethiopia, Box 21, Presidential Papers of Jimmy Carter..

110. Lester R. Brown and Edward C. Wolf, "Origins of the African Food Crisis," *Challenge* 27, no. 6 (1985): 50.

Chapter 2

Note to epigraph: "'Say Brother' Mickey Leland: The Man and the Mission," WGBH, Boston Public Radio, Series 14, 14AVT63_589943, Mickey Leland Archives, Texas Southern University.

1. Quoted in Browning, "What I Admire I Must Possess."

2. Andrew Yemma, "Mickey Leland III—Activist Turned Politician," *Baltimore Afro-American*, May 17, 1975. Leland was not unique in defining revolution as social transformation by not necessarily violent means. Bayard Rustin regarded the fundamental transformation of institutions as revolutionary. See Rustin, "From Protest to Politics."

3. "Black Texas Legislator Learns from 'Ordeal,'" *Atlanta Daily World*, May 31, 1973.

4. Yemma, "Mickey Leland III—Activist Turned Politician."

5. William K. Stevens, "Nominee to Succeed Rep. Jordan Plans to Use Influence for Blacks," *New York Times*, June 5, 1978.

6. "Leland Seeks 3rd Texas Term," *Baltimore Afro-American*, February 21, 1976.

7. "Drug Pricing Proposal Withdrawn in the House," *Houston Post*, April 11, 1972, Series 1, Box 1, Folder 3001, Mickey Leland Archives, Texas Southern University.

8. See, for example, "Freeway Plan Abandoned," *Houston Post*, May 18, 1973, Series 1, Box 1, Folder 5002; "TMA Lobby Killed His Bill, Leland Says," *Houston Chronicle*, May 20, 1973, Series 1, Box 1, Folder 10003, both in Mickey Leland Archives, Texas Southern University.

9. Quoted in Yemma, "Mickey Leland III—Activist Turned Politician."

10. Ibid.

11. Quoted in "We May Know Leland Better in Death than in Life," *Houston Post*, August 19, 1989, Series 15, Box 4, Folder 10712009, Mickey Leland Archives, Texas Southern University.

12. Mary Ellen Curtin, "Reaching for Power: Barbara C. Jordan and Liberals in the Texas Legislature, 1966–1972," *Southwestern Historical Quarterly* 108, no. 2 (2004): 219.

13. Jordan's career was not without controversial episodes. In 1968, as a member of the Texas delegation to the 1968 Democratic National Convention, she voted against seating Julian Bond's contingent from Georgia and the peace plank for the Democratic platform. She was also roundly criticized by student activists for not defending protests at Prairie View A&M in 1971. She was not without her detractors, many of whom saw her as overly supportive of President Lyndon Johnson and too timid and conservative on issues the mainstream Democratic Party regarded as radical. Potentially more damaging to Jordan's standing and prospect for locking in African American support for a prospective congressional campaign in 1972 was the news that her state senate district was to be eliminated and the new district would include the wealthy, white River Oaks section of Houston. She won election in the new district with 80 percent of the vote, despite the strong push against her by more politically radical African Americans within the Democratic Party. See Curtin, "Reaching for Power," 227–29.

14. Chandler Davidson, interview by Billie Carr, *Houston Breakthrough* (April 1978): 4, Special Collections, University of Houston Digital Library, http://digital.lib.uh.edu/collection/feminist/item/257/show/227.

15. Quoted in Jane Ely, "Leland a Lot Like His Favorite Folk," *Houston Post*, May 28, 1978.

16. "Leland Will Be Heard in House," *Baltimore Afro-American*, June 24, 1978.

17. Joel Glenn Richardson to Ronald Dellums, August 21, 1989, Box 37, Folder 44, Ronald Dellums Papers, African American Museum and Library at Oakland.

18. Leland Legacy Memorial Service hosted by Steve Smith, August 22, 1989, CBS KHOU, Houston, Series 14, 14AVT62_589944, Mickey Leland Archives, Texas Southern University.

19. Countryman, "From Protest to Politics," 840.

20. There was a small number of African Americans and people of African descent in the foreign service during the nineteenth century. William Alexander Leidesdorff, born in St. Croix, served as vice-consul in Yerba Buena, Mexico, what is today San Francisco, beginning in 1845. In 1889, President Benjamin Harrison appointed Frederick Douglass consul general to the Republic of Haiti. Twenty additional African Americans were appointed to foreign service posts in Africa and Latin America between 1897 and 1909. For more details, see Ronald W. Walters, "Racial Justice in Foreign Affairs," in *African Americans in Global Affairs:*

Contemporary Perspectives, ed. Michael L. Clemons (Boston: Northeastern University Press, 2010), 7–9.

21. Richard J. Payne. "Black Americans and the Demise of Constructive Engagement," *Africa Today* 33, no. 2/3, South Africa, Namibia and Human Rights: The Case for Strengthened Sanctions (2nd qtr.–3rd qtr., 1986): 86.

22. For a detailed discussion of African American ambassadors, see Morris, "African American Representatives in the United Nations."

23. Borstelmann, *The Cold War and the Color Line*, 258. Jimmy Carter was more damning of South Africa's domestic policies than previous U.S. presidents had been. Carter administration officials privileged human rights and development over anticommunism in Africa, particularly during Carter's first two years in office. Carter altered his approach away from human rights during the Iran hostage crisis of 1979–81 and toward stances that aligned more closely with the Cold War focus of his predecessors. See Jackson, *Jimmy Carter and the Horn of Africa*, 137. Carter sent a signal to Pretoria and, mostly likely, to African American political leaders that his administration did not extend blind support to white-minority rule. He sent his strongest signal in this regard in response to the murder of black anti-apartheid leader Steven Biko in 1977 by South African police while he was in their custody. In an unprecedented gesture from the United States in support of black dissent in South Africa, the president sent a senior State Department official to attend Biko's funeral. See Borstelmann, *The Cold War and the Color Line*, 245.

24. Ronald W. Walters, "African-American Influence on US Foreign Policy Toward South Africa," in *Ethnic Groups and US Foreign Policy*, ed. Mohammed E. Ahrari (New York: Greenwood Press, 1987), 73.

25. As quoted in Mitchell, *Jimmy Carter in Africa*, 141. See also Morris, "African American Representatives in the United Nations," 187.

26. Mitchell, *Jimmy Carter in Africa*, 142.

27. Crawford Young, "Ralph Bunche and Patrice Lumumba: The Fatal Encounter," in *Trustee for the Human Community: Ralph J. Bunche, the United Nations, and the Decolonization of Africa*, ed. Robert A. Hill and Edmond J. Keller (Athens: Ohio University Press, 2010), 128–47.

28. Tillery, *Between Homeland and Motherland*, 131.

29. Cedric Johnson, *Revolutionaries to Race Leaders: Black Power and the Making of African American Politics* (Minneapolis: University of Minnesota Press, 2007), 57.

30. Tillery, *Between Homeland and Motherland*, 132.

31. Congressman Diggs linked U.S. support for South Africa and Portugal. He blamed the problems in U.S. foreign policy for undermining the United States' standing in the Global South. His direct involvement in meetings in Africa and with African heads of state reflected a sense of common cause with Africans. See, for example, his statement to Congress's Committee on Foreign Affairs, February 3, 1972, Moorland Spingarn Research Center, Howard University, http://www.avoiceonline.org/document.html?idq = urn%3Autlol%3Aavoice.txu -diggs-224-f27-01&exhq = anti-apartheid&themeq = &wpq = 1&pageq = 6. See also "Text of Congressman Diggs's Press Statement," September 16, 1972, Moorland Spingarn Research Center, Howard University, http://www.avoiceonline.org/document.html?idq = urn%3Autlol %3Aavoice.txu-diggs-201-f10-01&exhq = anti-apartheid&themeq = &pageq = 5.

32. "Diggs Urges Better US Attitude Toward Africa," *Chicago Defender*, January 3, 1959, 12.

33. Michael L. Krenn, *Black Diplomacy: African Americans and the State Department, 1945–1969* (New York: M. E. Sharpe, 1999), 122.

34. Gleijeses, *Visions of Freedom*, 177.

35. Malcolm X University was a sister organization to the Center for Black Education, which had recently opened in Washington, D.C. Kwame Ture (Stokely Carmichael) was a member of the advisory board for Malcolm X University. Stokely Carmichael and Kwame Ture, "'We Are All Africans': A Speech by Stokely Carmichael to Malcolm X Liberation University," *Black Scholar* 27, nos. 3–4 (1997): 65–68.

36. Plummer, *In Search of Power*, 271.

37. Robin D. G. Kelley, *Freedom Dreams: The Black Radical Imagination* (Boston: Beacon Press, 2002), 104.

38. Ibid. See also Richard Price, "12,000 March to Support Africa," *Washington Post*, May 28, 1972. Some reports put the number of participants closer to thirty thousand. See also Donald R. Culverson, "The Politics of the Anti-Apartheid Movement in the United States, 1969–1986," *Political Science Quarterly* 111, no. 1 (Spring 1996): 137.

39. Cedric Johnson describes the founding of the Africa Liberation Support Committee and the African Liberation Day events in *Revolutionaries to Race Leaders*, 137–47.

40. Michael D. Petit, "Liberation Day to Usher in a New Era of Awakening: Cong. Diggs," *Milwaukee Star*, May 5, 1972.

41. Quoted in Price, "12,000 March to Support Africa."

42. Quoted in Petit, "Liberation Day to Usher in a New Era of Awakening."

43. On Amiri Baraka as a bridge between black radical politics and elected office, see Johnson, *Revolutionaries to Race Leaders*; Woodard, *A Nation Within a Nation*; Tillery, *Between Homeland and Motherland*; and Chappell, *Waking from the Dream*.

44. Johnson, *Revolutionaries to Race Leaders*, 57.

45. Ibid., 62.

46. See, for example, Johnson, *Revolutionaries to Race Leaders*.

47. Robin D. G. Kelley, *Into the Fire: African Americans Since 1970* (New York: Oxford University Press, 1996), 32.

48. Robert C. Smith makes a similar argument about the centrality of Black Power for black solidarity and black political interest groups. Smith, "Power and the Transformation from Protest to Policies," *Political Science Quarterly* 96, no. 3 (Autumn 1981): 434–35.

49. On the evolution of Amiri Baraka's political ideas and community engagement, see Daniel Matlin, "'Lift up Yr Self!': Reinterpreting Amiri Baraka (LeRoi Jones), Black Power, and the Uplift Tradition," *Journal of American History* 93, no. 1 (June 2006): 91–116.

50. Countryman, "From Protest to Politics," 816.

51. Ibid., 817.

52. Nicholas Grant, *Winning Our Freedoms Together: African Americans & Apartheid, 1945–1960* (Chapel Hill: University of North Carolina Press, 2017), 13.

53. Ibid.

54. "Demand US Sanctions on South Africa," *New York Amsterdam News*, October 20, 1962, 44. On the American Council on African Affairs, see David L. Hostetter, *Movement Matters: American Antiapartheid Activism and the Rise of Multicultural Politics* (New York: Taylor and Francis, 2006), chap. 1.

55. Kelley, *Into the Fire*, 32.

56. Plummer, *In Search of Power*, 254.

57. Tillery, *Between Homeland and Motherland*, 135.

58. Until 1970, U.S. support for the apartheid regime in South Africa was consistent with its general approach to African affairs. U.S. presidents supported NATO allies, most of which, at the time, were former colonial powers in Africa. These presidents also favored ruling European settler minorities in places like Rhodesia and Namibia. President Dwight Eisenhower supported France's claim to Algeria. John F. Kennedy and Richard Nixon provided Portugal with military assistance during its war to defeat liberation in Mozambique, Angola, Guinea, and Cape Verde (though Kennedy expressed sympathy for liberation movements in Africa) but failed to ensure Portuguese victory.

59. Daniel Sargent, "Oasis in the Desert? America's Human Rediscovery," in *The Breakthrough: Human Rights in the 1970s*, ed. Jan Eckel and Samuel Moyn (Philadelphia: University of Pennsylvania Press, 2014), 130.

60. Lasse Heerten, "The Dystopia of Postcolonial Catastrophe: Self-Determination, the Biafran War of Secession, and the 1970s Human Rights Movement," in *The Breakthrough: Human Rights in the 1970s*, ed. Jack Eckel and Samuel Moyn (Philadelphia: University of Pennsylvania Press, 2014), 19.

61. Ibid., 29–30.

62. "Biafra Picture Colored Diggs," *Afro-American (Los Angeles)*, March 8, 1969, 1, ProQuest Historical Newspapers.

63. "Rep. Diggs, Others in Biafra, Nigeria," *New York Amsterdam News*, February 15, 1969, 2, ProQuest Historical Newspapers.

64. Kelley, *Into the Fire*, 91.

65. Carolyn P. DuBose, *The Untold Story of Charles Diggs: The Public Figure, the Private Man* (Arlington, VA: Barton Publishing, 1998), 63.

66. As quoted in Krenn, *Black Diplomacy*, 131.

67. Hostetter, *Movement Matters*, 74.

68. John W. Templeton, "Cuban Soldiers in Angola Not US Business: Diggs," *Baltimore Afro-American*, April 17, 1976, 1, ProQuest Historical Newspapers.

69. "Black Caucus Member Rips Lifting of Rhodesia Ban," *Milwaukee Star*, May 5, 1972.

70. Alvin B. Tillery Jr., "Foreign Policy Activism and Power in the House of Representatives: Black Members of Congress and South Africa, 1968–1986," *Studies in American Political Development* 20, no. 1 (2006): 89.

71. Hostetter, *Movement Matters*, 67–68.

72. Charles C. Diggs Jr., "Relations with Africa Sought; Article Type," *Milwaukee Star*, May 15, 1976.

73. Ronald W. Walters, "US-South African Relations: A Legislative Review," Southern African Development Coordination Conference, Sponsored by the Congressional Black Caucus Foundation, February 1985, Box 17, Ronald Dellums Papers, African American Museum and Library at Oakland. The only opposition to apartheid in South Africa before 1977 came from within the African American community. W. E. B. DuBois, Paul Robeson, and Martin Luther King Jr. were important vocal critics of the repressive white-minority regime. The Council on African Affairs was among the first organizations to consistently raise the issue of political repression in South Africa. After the police massacre of peaceful protesters in Sharpeville on March 21, 1960, African American condemnation gained wider reception within the

United States. The U.S. government's position remained ambiguous, as it neither discouraged nor encouraged investment. See Von Eschen, *Race Against Empire*, for a detailed analysis of the Council on African Affairs and the challenges of engaging African issues amid growing U.S. domestic and international anticommunism.

74. Tillery, *Between Homeland and Motherland*, 139.

75. Congressional Black Caucus, "The African-American Manifesto on Southern Africa," *Black Scholar* 8, no. 4 Black Politics 1977 (January-February 1977): 27.

76. Ibid., 30.

77. Ibid., 32.

78. Ibid., 30.

79. Randall Robinson, "Testimony Before the Subcommittees on Africa and International Economic Policy and Trade," *Issue: A Journal of Opinion* 9, no. 1/2 (Spring-Summer 1979): 17.

80. Rob Skinner describes the anti-apartheid movement as comprising myriad social and political organizations. There was no single transnational network of activists and, therefore, it must be understood as a "movement of movements." See Skinner, *Foundations of Anti-Apartheid*, 200.

81. Hostetter describes this distinctive synthesis as critical to TransAfrica's success at key moments. Hostetter, *Movement Matters*, 77–78.

82. Ronald V. Dellums, *Lying Down with the Lions: A Public Life from the Streets of Oakland to the Halls of Power* (Boston: Beacon Press, 2000), 106.

83. "President Reagan's Foreign Economic Aid Budget," Food Policy Notes, Interreligious Taskforce on US Food Policy, Note 81–8, March 6, 1981, Box 54, William Gray Papers, Schomburg Center for Research in Black Culture, New York Public Library.

84. Statement of U.S. Representative William H. Gray III, on Behalf of the Congressional Black Caucus, March 26, 1981, Congressional Records, Office Files, Box 54, William Gray Papers, Schomburg Center for Research in Black Culture, New York Public Library.

85. Howell Raines, "Reagan and Blacks," *New York Times*, September 17, 1982.

86. Shepherd, *The Politics of Starvation*, 29–30.

87. "Black America Has Overlooked the Racist Policies of Ronald Reagan," *Journal of Blacks in Higher Education*, no. 64 (Summer 2009): 13.

88. Renouard, *Human Rights in American Foreign Policy*, 182.

89. Barbara J. Keys, *Reclaiming American Virtue: The Human Rights Revolution of the 1970s* (Cambridge, MA: Harvard University Press, 2014), 4–5.

90. Ibid., 273.

91. Sergio Ramirez, *Adiós Muchachos: A Memoir of the Sandinista Revolution* (Durham, NC: Duke University Press, 2012), 77.

92. Ibid., 78.

93. There are persuasive arguments against a discernible Kirkpatrick Doctrine in Latin America. See, in particular, Mark Falcoff, "Latin America: Was There a 'Kirkpatrick Doctrine'?" in *President Reagan and the World*, ed. Eric J. Schmertz, Natalie Datlof, and Alexej Ugrinsky (Westport, CT: Greenwood Press, 1997). See also Christopher Bright, "Neither Dictatorships nor Double Standards: The Reagan Administration's Approach to Human Rights," *World Affairs* 153, no. 2 (1990): 66.

94. For a succinct and compelling discussion of the evolution of human rights as policy during the Reagan presidency, see Aryeh Neier, "Human Rights in the Reagan Era: Acceptance

in Principle," *Annals of the American Academy of Political and Social Science* 506, no. 1 (November 1989): 30–41.

95. Ramirez, *Adiós Muchachos*, 94.

96. Westad, *Cold War*, 499.

97. Ramirez, *Adiós Muchachos*, 96.

98. Mickey Leland, "The United States and Central America,," Statement of the Congressional Black Caucus Delivered by Congressman Mickey Leland on April 10, 1981, Series 11, Box 49, Folder 8067001, Mickey Leland Archives, Texas Southern University.

99. Ronald Dellums to President Daniel Ortega Saavedra, July 19, 1985, Box 37, Folder 38, Ronald Dellums Papers, African American Museum and Library at Oakland.

100. James M. Scott, *Deciding to Intervene: The Reagan Doctrine and American Foreign Policy* (Durham, NC: Duke University Press, 1996), 165.

101. William Gray III, "Memorandum: Notes on Meeting with Secretary of State Haig and Members of the Congressional Black Caucus on Foreign Affairs Braintrust on April 30, 1981," May 12, 1981, Box 54, William Gray III Papers, Schomburg Center for Research in Black Culture, New York Public Library.

102. On the Boland amendments and Congress's use of legislation to restrict President Reagan's use of covert foreign policy initiatives, see Louis Fisher, "How Tightly Can Congress Draw the Purse Strings?" *American Journal of International Law* 83, no. 4 (1989): 758–66.

103. Lynda V. E. Crawford, "Mickey Leland, Fighting Hunger from Capitol Hill," *Seed, Ending US and World Hunger*, July/August 1989, Series 11, Box 215, Folder 10381001, Mickey Leland Archives, Texas Southern University.

104. "Leland to Testify on Hunger Among Blacks," *Baltimore Afro-American*, October 29, 1983.

105. CARE Special Report, December 7, 1984, CARE Documents, Ethiopia 1984–1985, Box 199, Rare Books and Manuscripts Division, New York Public Library.

106. As quoted in Peter Gill, *A Year in the Death of Africa: Politics, Bureaucracy and the Famine* (London: Paladin Grafton Books, 1986), 42.

107. CARE Special Report, December 7, 1984, CARE Documents, Ethiopia 1984–1985, Box 199, Rare Books and Manuscripts Division, New York Public Library.

108. Foreign Relations Committee Hearing, January 17, 1985, 5.

109. Shepherd, "Ethiopia," 5.

110. Ibid., 4.

111. Kathryn Sikkink, *Mixed Signals: US Human Rights Policy and Latin America* (Ithaca, NY: Cornell University Press, 2014), 155.

112. Joe Renouard argues that Reagan was never as doctrinaire as his critics and supporters believed. See Renouard, *Human Rights in American Foreign Policy*, 198.

113. Congress created USAID in 1961 through the Foreign Assistance Act of the same year to oversee bilateral development aid. For a brief outline of USAID's history, see Allison Stanger, "The Slow Death of USAID," in *One Nation Under Contract: The Outsourcing of American Power and the Future of Foreign Policy* (New Haven, CT: Yale University Press, 2009).

114. Kathleen Teltsch, "US Presses for Increased Relief Aid for Famine-Stricken Ethiopia," *New York Times*, August 19, 1983.

115. "Hunger in America," C-Span, December 16, 1985, http://www.c-spanvideo.org/program/PoliticalInterview46.

116. Rodney Ellis, interview by the author, June 16, 2012, New York.

117. Honorable Mickey Leland of Texas, "A Need for a Select Committee on Hunger," *Congressional Record*, April 27, 1982, Series 4, Box 24, Folder 1853001, Mickey Leland Archives, Texas Southern University.

118. Associated Press, "House Creating Special Unit to Study Worldwide Hunger," *New York Times*, February 26, 1984.

119. Crawford, "Mickey Leland, Fighting Hunger from Capitol Hill."

120. Associated Press, "House Creating Special Unit to Study Worldwide Hunger,"

121. Ibid.

122. Plummer, *In Search of Power*, 310–11.

123. Gregory Mann, *From Empires to NGOs in the West African Sahel: The Road to Non-governmentality* (New York: Cambridge University Press, 2015), 205.

124. Erhagbe, "Congressional Black Caucus and United States Policy Toward Africa," 91; see also Charles C. Diggs, Jr., "The Drought in the Sahel," *Black Scholar* 5, no. 10, The Sixth Pan-African Congress (July-August 1974): 42.

125. Amanda K. McVety, *Enlightened Aid: US Development as Foreign Policy in Ethiopia* (New York: Oxford University Press, 2012), 164.

126. Ibid., 165.

127. Michael Barnett and Thomas G. Weiss divide modern humanitarianism into three periods: the early nineteenth century through World War II; 1945 until the end of the Cold War; and 1990 to the present. See Barnett and Weiss, "Humanitarianism: A Brief History of the Present," in *Humanitarianism in Question: Politics, Power, Ethics*, ed. Barnett and Weiss (Ithaca, NY: Cornell University Press, 2008), 21.

128. David Chandler, *From Kosovo to Kabul and Beyond: Human Rights and International Intervention* (London: Pluto Press, 2006), 32.

129. Barnett and Weiss, "Humanitarianism," 34.

130. Patman, *The Soviet Union in the Horn of Africa*, 278.

Chapter 3

1. Fekade Azeze, *Unheard Voices: Drought, Famine and God in Ethiopian Oral Poetry* (Addis Ababa: Addis Ababa University Press, 1998).

2. Agurt and Agurtachäw are local names given to the 1984–85 famine in northern Shewa. This poem declares the arrival and the early effects of the 1984–85 famine, but it has yet to take its toll on the peasants' households. See ibid., 48–49.

3. Ibid., 41–43.

4. Ibid., 175.

5. Michael Barnett and Thomas G. Weiss, "Humanitarianism: A Brief History of the Present," *Humanitarianism in Question: Politics, Power, Ethics*, ed. Michael Barnett and Thomas G. Weiss (Ithaca, NY: Cornell University Press, 2008), 26.

6. "Hunger in America," C-Span, December 16, 1985, http://www.c-spanvideo.org/program/PoliticalInterview46.

7. Graham Hancock, *Ethiopia: The Challenge of Hunger* (London: Gollancz, 1985), 12.

8. De Waal, *Famine Crimes*, 82.

9. D. J. Clark, "The Production of a Contemporary Famine Image: The Image Economy, Indigenous Photographers and the Case of Mekanic Philipos," *Journal of International Development* 16, no. 5 (July 2004): 693–704, http://www.imaging-famine.org/papers/djclark_famine1.pdf.

10. Alula Pankhurst, *Resettlement and Famine in Ethiopia: The Villagers' Experience* (Manchester: Manchester University Press, 1992), 23.

11. Jones, "Band Aid Revisited."

12. James H. Meriwether details the events that defined the "Year of Africa" in *Proudly We Can Be Africans.*

13. James C. McCann, *People of the Plow: An Agricultural History of Ethiopia, 1800–1990* (Madison: University of Wisconsin Press, 1995), 145.

14. Clifford D. May, "Hunger's Toll: A Generation of Ethiopians," *New York Times,* November 29, 1984.

15. David F. Gordon and Howard Wolpe, "The Other Africa: An End to Afro-Pessimism," *World Policy Journal* 15, no. 1 (Spring 1998): 49–59. See also Peter J. Schraeder, "Speaking with Many Voices: Continuity and Change in U.S. Africa Policies," *Journal of Modern African Studies* 29, no. 3 (September 1991): 391.

16. *Politics of Hunger in the Sudan, Joint Hearing Before the Select Committee on Hunger and the Subcommittee on Africa of the Committee on Foreign Affairs, House of Representatives,* 100th Cong. 4 (March 2, 1989).

17. On Mengistu's agricultural policies, see Rahmato, "Agrarian Change and Agrarian Crisis."

18. Gill, *A Year in the Death of Africa,* 17.

19. D. J. Clark examined the factors that contributed to photographers' and journalists' choices of subjects during Bob Geldof's trip to Ethiopia in 2003. Clark argued that they selected locations and individuals that represented the extreme stereotype of the Ethiopian famine victim rather than those that were more representative of the famine experience. See Clark, "Production of a Contemporary Famine Image," 699–702.

20. "Greatest News Reports on TV Ever No. 1—Ethiopia, 1984," https://www.youtube .com/watch?v = uDZ4_NH4y7w.

21. As quoted in Hancock, *Ethiopia,* 8.

22. Michael Buerk, *The Road Taken: An Autobiography* (London: Hutchinson, 2004), 290.

23. Claire Bertschinger, *Moving Mountains* (London: Doubleday, 2005), 126–27.

24. Quoted in Buerk, *Road Taken,* 294.

25. Robert D. Kaplan, *Surrender or Starve: The Wars Behind the Famine* (Boulder, CO: Westview Press, 1988), 38.

26. Carl Wilkinson, "Live Aid in Their Words," *Guardian,* October 17, 2004.

27. The ICRC was organized in the mid-1860s during the wars in Europe. Over the course of 120 years, before it was one of the leading NGOs operating in Ethiopia during its food crisis, the ICRC splintered into numerous organizations, loosely configured under the ICRC as a decentralized administrative umbrella. See David P. Forsythe, "Human Rights and the International Committee of the Red Cross," *Human Rights Quarterly* 12, no. 2 (May 1990): 265–89. On the ICRC in Ethiopia, see p. 268.

28. Alexander Poster, "The Gentle War: Famine Relief, Politics, and Privatization in Ethiopia, 1983–1986," *Diplomatic History* 36, no. 2 (April 2012): 400.

29. Jones, "Band Aid Revisited," 189.

30. Ibid., 192.

31. Tareke, *The Ethiopian Revolution,* 149.

32. Between 1984 and 1986, Mengistu hastily, forcibly, and pitilessly uprooted 594,190 people from the cool, dry highlands of Shewa, Tigray, and Wollo and moved them to the hot,

wet lowlands of Gojjam, Illubabor, Kefa, and Wellega at an estimated cost of $374 million. See Tareke, *The Ethiopian Revolution*, 157.

33. "Public Law 480 Programs," *Issue* 8, nos. 2–3 (Summer–Autumn 1978): 75–84.

34. Dawit Wolde Giorgis discusses Mengistu's famine relief plans in detail; see Giorgis, *Red Tears: War, Famine and Revolution in Ethiopia* (Trenton, NJ: Red Sea Press, 1989). For additional narratives of the Mengistu and Western famine relief initiatives, see Varnis, *Reluctant Aid or Aiding the Reluctant?*

35. Civil war in Ethiopia during the period in question and more recently has been the subject of numerous detailed, well-researched studies. Gebru Tareke's *Ethiopian Revolution* offers the most comprehensive and useful descriptions and analysis of the Ethiopian revolution and its political aftermath. Tareke has also discussed the weakening of the Ethiopian army and the beginning of the end of the Mengistu regime. See Tareke, "From Af Abet to Shire: The Defeat and Demise of Ethiopia's 'Red' Army, 1988–89," *Journal of Modern African Studies* 42, no. 2 (June 2004): 239–81. Although written at the high point of the second major famine of the decade and a turning point in the civil wars, Kaplan's *Surrender or Starve* provides a strong analysis of the links between war and famine in the Horn. On the guerrilla tactics and general history of the TPLF, see John Young, *Peasant Revolution in Ethiopia: The Tigray People's Liberation Front, 1975–1991* (Cambridge: Cambridge University Press, 2006); Aregawi Berhe, *A Political History of the Tigray People's Liberation Front (1975–1991): Revolt, Ideology and Mobilisation in Ethiopia* (Los Angeles: Tsehai Publishers, 2009); and Donald L. Donham, "Revolution and Modernity in Maale: Ethiopia, 1974 to 1987," *Comparative Studies in Society and History* 34, no. 1 (January 1992): 28–57. On the EPLF, see David Pool, *From Guerrillas to Government: The Eritrean People's Liberation Front* (Athens: Ohio University Press, 2001).

36. Alex de Waal puts the figure at six hundred thousand. See de Waal, *Evil Days*, 124–25.

37. Ibid.

38. Statement by Representative Mickey Leland, November 1, 1984, Series 4, Box 29, Folder 2012001, Mickey Leland Archives, Texas Southern University.

39. Ibid.

40. Associated Press, "Congress Members Depart for Ethiopia," November 23, 1984, Friday, AM Cycle.

41. Throughout the 1980s, considerable popular culture production influenced public conceptions of the social, cultural, and political issues in Ethiopia and South Africa, particularly through music. The charity supergroup Band Aid's "Do They Know It's Christmas" in 1984 was among the earliest, most popular, and most controversial recordings. The recording's commercial success was followed by Live Aid, a global megaconcert. Discussions of Band Aid and Live Aid have largely been limited to journalist authors. Bob Geldof describes the activities surrounding these events and his humanitarian initiatives in Africa in a memoir, *Is That It? An Autobiography* (New York: Grove Press, 1987). See also David Bailey, *Imagine: A Book for Band Aid* (London: Thames and Hudson, 1985). Singer and activist Harry Belafonte sought to emulate the success of Bob Geldof's Band Aid; he encouraged musicians Michael Jackson and Lionel Richie to work with producer and musician Quincy Jones to create *We Are the World*. It raised $50 million for famine relief and supplies in Africa (see Hostetter, *Movement Matters*, 106). Hostetter details numerous cultural and artistic projects in the United States during the 1980s that centered on apartheid or life in South Africa. See Hostetter, "Lost in the Stars: Apartheid and American Popular Culture," in *Movement Matters*. For

a broader analysis of humanitarian aid and controversies surrounding it, see Linda Polman, *The Crisis Caravan: What's Wrong with Humanitarian Aid?* trans. Liz Waters (New York: Metropolitan Books, 2010); and, for a scathing critique of the famine relief industry, see de Waal, *Famine Crimes*.

42. Shepherd, "Ethiopia," 6.

43. Kathleen Teltsch, "US Presses for Increased Relief Aid for Famine-Stricken Ethiopia," *New York Times*, August 19, 1983.

44. Edward Kissi, "Beneath International Famine Relief in Ethiopia: The United States, Ethiopia, and the Debate over Relief Aid, Development Assistance, and Human Rights," *African Studies Review* 48, no. 2 (September 2005): 123.

45. Mickey Leland, "What African Americans Can Do About Starvation in Africa," *Ebony*, October 1989.

46. Ibid.

47. Meriwether, *Proudly We Can Be Africans*, 209, 229, 239–40; Plummer, *In Search of Power*, 6.

48. Quoted in Chris Elfring, "Africa Tomorrow: If We Act Today," *BioScience* 35, no. 7 (July–August 1985): 401.

49. Tommie St. Hill, "Gray to Look Over Crisis in Ethiopia," *Philadelphia Tribune*, November 20, 1984.

50. Lynda V. E. Crawford, "Mickey Leland, Fighting Hunger from Capitol Hill," *Seed, Ending US and World Hunger*, July/August 1989, Series 11, Box 215, Folder 10381001, Mickey Leland Archives, Texas Southern University.

51. Ibid.

52. Christopher Matthews, "The Road to Korem," *New Republic*, January 21, 1985. In 2009, Matthews devoted a segment of his MSNBC news program to a Leland tribute in which he describes his trip to Korem and his relationship with Leland. See https://www.youtube.com/watch?v=A-aBIC9GyFo.

53. Ibid.

54. Clifford D. May, "Hunger's Toll: A Generation of Ethiopians," *New York Times*, November 29, 1984.

55. "Congressmen Return After Viewing African Famine," *Baltimore Afro-American*, December 8, 1984.

56. Statement by Rep. Mickey Leland, American School Food Service Association, Capital Hilton Hotel, Washington, DC, February 27, 1985, Series 4, Box 50, File 4697001, Mickey Leland Archives, Texas Southern University.

57. Kaplan, *Surrender or Starve*, 28.

58. Alison Leland, phone interview by the author, November 24, 2009.

59. Quoted in "Congressmen Return After Viewing African Famine."

60. Associated Press, "Legislators Tell of Anguish at Seeing Victims of Hunger," November 30, 1984.

61. Alison Leland, interview by the author, July 22, 2010, Houston, Texas.

62. Remarks by Mickey Leland, January 3, 1985, Box 50, Folder 4697, Mickey Leland Archives, Texas Southern University.

63. Jacqueline Prescott, "Leland and the War on Hunger: For the Texas Congressman, an Activist's Path," *Washington Post*, September 27, 1985.

64. Ibid.

65. Robert Houdek, phone interview by the author, February 12, 2014.

66. "Leland Delegation to Go to Ethiopia," *Houston Chronicle*, November 2, 1984.

67. For an elaboration of this argument, see James Peck, *Ideal Illusions: How the US Government Co-Opted Human Rights* (New York: Metropolitan Books, 2010), 18–35.

68. Ibid., 19.

69. Ward Sinclair, "US Aid to Ethiopia Stirs Controversy: Reagan's Response to Drought at Issue," *Washington Post*, October 31, 1984.

70. Ibid.

71. *The Famine Effects on African Refugees: Hearing Before the Subcommittee on Immigration and Refugee Policy of the Committee on the Judiciary*, 99th Cong., 1st Sess., on Oversight on the Issue of Emergency Food Aid and Famine Relief to Refugees in Sub-Saharan Africa, February 7, 1985 (statement by Peter McPherson, United States Senate, Committee on the Judiciary).

72. Ibid.

73. David K. Willis, "US Steps up Pressure on Ethiopia," *Christian Science Monitor*, February 26, 1985, https://www.csmonitor.com/1985/0226/opete.html.

74. *The Famine Effects on African Refugees: Hearing Before the Subcommittee on Immigration and Refugee Policy of the Committee on the Judiciary*, 99th Cong., 1st Sess., on Oversight on the Issue of Emergency Food Aid and Famine Relief to Refugees in Sub-Saharan Africa, February 7, 1985 (statement by Senator Edward Kennedy).

75. *Famine and Recovery in Africa: The US Response: Joint Hearing Before the Select Committee on Hunger and the Subcommittee on Africa of the Committee on Foreign Affairs, House of Representatives*, 99th Cong., 1st Sess. 2 (December 5, 1985) (statement of Congressman Howard Wolpe).

76. *Hearing Before the Select Committee on Hunger, Africa: Famine Relief and Rehabilitation, United States Congress on Hunger, House of Representatives*, 99th Cong. 3 (July 25, 1985) (statement by Congressman Mickey Leland).

77. Keys, *Reclaiming American Virtue*, 3.

78. *Africa: Famine Relief and Rehabilitation: Hearing Before the Select Committee on Hunger, House of Representatives*, 99th Cong., 1st sess. 37 (July 25, 1985).

79. *Human Rights and Food Aid in Ethiopia: Hearing Before the Subcommittee on Human Rights and International Organizations and the Subcommittee on Africa of the Committee on Foreign Affairs, House of Representatives*, 99th Cong., 2nd [i.e., 1st] Sess. (October 16, 1985) (statement of Congressman Howard Wolpe).

80. Ibid. (statement of Congressman Gerald Solomon).

81. Richard J. Payne, "Black Americans and the Demise of Constructive Engagement," *Africa Today* 33, no. 2/3, South Africa, Namibia and Human Rights: The Case for Strengthened Sanctions (2nd qtr.-3rd qtr., 1986): 86.

82. Ibid. (statement of Assistant Secretary of State Chester Crocker).

83. Giorgis, *Red Tears*, 197.

84. "Interview with Mengistu Haile Mariam," *Ethiopian Herald*, March 1, 1985.

85. Ibid.

86. Ibid.

87. Sinclair, "US Aid to Ethiopia Stirs Controversy."

88. Shepherd, "Ethiopia," 6.

89. Ibid.; "Senate Approves an Extra $60 Million in Food Aid for Africa," *New York Times*, March 31, 1985.

90. "Leland Meets with Ethiopian Relief Commissioner," press release, Select Committee on Hunger, May 22, 1985, Series 1, Box 14, Folder 1985, Mickey Leland Archives, Texas Southern University.

91. The United States was part of a coalition, which included Zaire, the Frente Nacionale de Libertação de Angola (FNLA), União Nacional para a Independêcia Total de Angola (UNITA), and South Africa, to oust the ruling Movimento Popular de Libertação de Angola (MPLA) government. For a detailed history of U.S. involvement in Angola, see Gleijeses, *Visions of Freedom*. See also William Minter, "The US and the War in Angola," *Review of African Political Economy* 18, no. 50 (March 1991): 135–44.

92. Mickey Leland to Congressional Colleagues, "Update: African Famine Situation," May 8, 1986, http://www.avoiceonline.org/document.html?idq = urn%3Autlol%3Aavoice .txu-gwc-56-f5-07-01&exhq = anti-apartheid&themeq = &pageq = 40.

93. Ibid.

94. Barnett and Weiss describe the early 1990s as a turning point in the internationalizing of the humanitarian aspects of armed conflict. See Barnett and Weiss, "Humanitarianism," 26–27.

95. Ibid., 30.

96. Chandler, *From Kosovo to Kabul and Beyond*, 48.

97. Ibid., 48–49.

98. Other scholars have similarly argued that the fight against apartheid led by the Black Caucus during the 1980s marked the period of greatest strength for African Americans in Congress. For an earlier articulation of this assertion, see Tuck, "African American Protest During the Reagan Years." I take the argument a step further. As an ethnic bloc, African Americans experienced their greatest influence on foreign policy in and outside of government during this period.

Chapter 4

Note to epigraph: Mickey Leland Speech, Houston Alumni Task Force of the University of Texas, Outstanding Black Alumnus Awards, Saturday, April 22, 1989, Series 11, Box 210, Folder 10289001, Mickey Leland Archives, Texas Southern University.

1. Nicholas Grant, *Winning Our Freedoms Together: African Americans & Apartheid, 1945–1960* (Chapel Hill: University of North Carolina Press, 2017), 1.

2. African American journalists questioned South African social and economic policies as early as the 1940s. See Von Eschen, *Race Against Empire*, 86–87.

3. For a detailed argument along these lines, see Håkan Thörn, "The Meaning(s) of Solidarity: Narratives of Anti-Apartheid Activism," *Journal of Southern African Studies* 35, no. 2 (June 2009): 417–36.

4. Hilary Spaire, "Liberation Movements, Exile, and International Solidarity: An Introduction," *Journal of Southern African Studies* 35, no. 2, Liberation Struggles, Exile and International Solidarity (June 2009): 273. See also Håkan Thörn, "Solidarity Across Borders: The Transnational Anti-Apartheid Movement," *Voluntas: International Journal of Nonprofit Organizations* 17, no. 4 (December 2006): 286.

5. Hilary Spaire, "Liberation Movements, Exile, and International Solidarity: An Introduction," *Journal of Southern African Studies* 35, no. 2, Liberation Struggles, Exile and International Solidarity (June 2009): 273.

6. Christabel Gurney, "The 1970s: The Anti-Apartheid Movement's Difficult Decade," *Journal of Southern African Studies* 35, no. 2 (June 2009): 471; Hostetter, *Movement Matters*, 2.

7. Thörn, "Solidarity Across Borders," 285–86.

8. Cooper, *Africa Since 1940*, 57–58.

9. Gleijeses, *Visions of Freedom*, 197.

10. Herbst, "Prospects for Revolution in South Africa," 665.

11. Quoted in Glenn Frankel, "South Africa's Costly Crackdown: Emergency Fails to Quell Unrest, Narrow Political Chasm," *Washington Post*, October 15, 1985.

12. Ibid.

13. Ibid.

14. Dr. Martin Luther King Jr., speech on South Africa in London, December 1964, http://www.rfksafilm.org/html/speeches/pdfspeeches/13.pdf.

15. Ibrahim Sundiata, "Obama, African Americans, and Africans: The Double Vision," in *African Americans in US Foreign Policy: From the Era of Frederick Douglass to the Age of Obama*, ed. Linda Heywood et al. (Urbana: University of Illinois Press, 2015), 203.

16. Ibrahim Sundiata, "Obama, African Americans, and Africans: The Double Vision," in *African Americans in US Foreign Policy: From the Era of Frederick Douglass to the Age of Obama*, ed. Linda Heywood et al. (Urbana: University of Illinois Press, 2015), 203.

17. Michael L. Clemons, "Conceptualizing the Foreign Affairs Participation of African Americans: Strategies and Effects of the Congressional Black Caucus and TransAfrica," in *African Americans in Global Affairs: Contemporary Perspectives*, ed. Michael L. Clemons (Boston: Northeastern University Press, 2010), 57.

18. Ibid., 50–51.

19. Renouard, *Human Rights in American Foreign Policy*, 227.

20. Mary Frances Berry, *History Teaches Us to Resist: How Progressive Movements Have Succeeded in Challenging Times* (Boston: Beacon Press, 2018), 89.

21. For a narrative of the embassy meeting and the subsequent launching of the FSAM, see Hostetter, *Movement Matters*, 65–67.

22. Jesse Jackson, address before the Democratic National Convention, July 18, 1984, *Frontline*, WGBH Educational Foundation, https://www.pbs.org/wgbh/pages/frontline/jesse/speeches/jesse84speech.html.

23. Hostetter, *Movement Matters*, 134; Jesse Jackson, 1988 DNC speech, https://www.youtube.com/watch?v=h8bwh61xTGA.

24. As quoted in Hostetter, *Movement Matters*, 80.

25. Quoted in Nesbitt, *Race for Sanctions*, 103.

26. Quoted in Gleijeses, *Visions of Freedom*, 179; see also Richard Deutsch, "Reagan's Unruly Review," *Africa Report* 26, no. 3 (May–June 1981): 23.

27. Joe Renouard describes a trend of greater American intolerance for undemocratic practices in noncommunist nations aligned with the United States extending back to the 1970s. Reagan also had to respond to a Congress reclaiming its role in foreign affairs that had diminished during the Cold War, and both Democrat and Republican members of Congress found human rights a convenient tool for doing so. See Renouard, *Human Rights in American Foreign Policy*, 11.

28. Ronald Reagan, "Address to the Nation About Christmas and the Situation in Poland," December 23, 1981, http://www.presidency.ucsb.edu/ws/?pid = 43384.

29. George Crockett, Julian Dixon, Mickey Leland, and William Clay to President Reagan, July 1, 1983, Moorland-Spingarn Research Center, Howard University, http://www .avoiceonline.org/document.html?idq = urn%3Autlol%3Aavoice.txu-gwc-55-f3-15&exhq = anti-apartheid&themeq = &pageq = 14.

30. Randall Robinson, "Putting Our Country on the Right Side of History," *Washington Post*, February 3, 1985.

31. Randall Robinson and Clarence Lusane, "An Interview with Randall Robinson: State of the US Anti-Apartheid Movement," *Black Scholar* 16, no. 6 (November–December 1985): 41.

32. Ibid., 42.

33. Culverson, "Politics of the Anti-Apartheid Movement in the United States," 143.

34. On constructive engagement in the context of the Reagan administration's approach to southern Africa, see Scott, *Deciding to Intervene*, 116–26.

35. Erhagbe, "The Congressional Black Caucus and United States Policy Toward Africa," 89.

36. "One Minute: Prohibit the Use of So. African Vessels for the Transport of Food Aid," May 13, 1985, Series 2, Box, 39, Folder 744003, Mickey Leland Archives, Texas Southern University. See also H.R. 2746, A Bill to Prohibit the Transportation of South African Vessels of Agricultural Commodities Provided Under the Agricultural Trade Development and Assistance Act of 1954, 99th Cong., Series 2, Box 39, Folder 744003, Mickey Leland Archives, Texas Southern University.

37. Mickey Leland to the Honorable Peter M. McPherson, April 4, 1985; Peter M. McPherson to Mickey Leland, Chairman of the Select Committee on Hunger, May 13, 1985, both in Series 2, Box 39, Folder 744003, Mickey Leland Archives, Texas Southern University.

38. "One Minute: Prohibit the Use of So. African Vessels for the Transport of Food Aid," May 13, 1985, Series 2, Box, 39, Folder 744003, Mickey Leland Archives, Texas Southern University.

39. Mickey Leland and Walter Fauntroy to Robert Mugabe, August 8, 1986, http:// www.avoiceonline.org/document.html?idq = urn%3Autlol%3Aavoice.txu-gwc-58-f7-04& exhq = Anti-apartheid&themeq = &pageq = 45.

40. Maurice Dawkins, "Savimbi: Africa's Cornerstone for Democracy," *Baltimore Afro-American*, July 5, 1986.

41. Ibid.

42. Ibid.; Minter, "The US and the War in Angola," 136.

43. Ibid., 137.

44. Press release, 1982, Series 7, Box 5, Folder 4827, Mickey Leland Archives, Texas Southern University.

45. Hostetter, *Movement Matters*, 34.

46. Erhagbe, "The Congressional Black Caucus and United States Policy Toward Africa," 89.

47. Hostetter, *Movement Matters*, 34.

48. Press release, 1982, Series 7, Box 5, Folder 4827, Mickey Leland Archives, Texas Southern University.

49. "Report on Companies Doing Business in South Africa, Memorandum to CBC Members from Ronald Dellums," January 29, 1986, http://www.avoiceonline.org/document

.html?idq = urn%3Autlol%3Aavoice.txu-gwc-57-f1-18&exhq = anti-apartheid&themeq = & wpq = 1&pageq = 37.

50. *Prepared Statement of David P. Hauck Before the Subcommittee on Foreign Affairs, House of Representatives*, January 31, 1985, Box 47, Ronald Dellums Papers, Southern Africa Development Coordination Conference, the African American Museum and Library at Oakland.

51. Renouard, *Human Rights in American Foreign Policy*, 230.

52. Don Phillips, "House Votes to Ban Nearly All S. African Trade," *Washington Post*, August 12, 1988.

53. Scott, *Deciding to Intervene*, 19.

54. Mickey Leland, *Official Statement from the House Floor*, Series 11, Box 133, Folder 8938, Mickey Leland Archives, Texas Southern University.

55. Ronald Dellums to the Congressional Black Caucus, May 29, 1985, Moorland-Spingarn Research Center, Howard University, http://www.avoiceonline.org/document .html?idq = urn%3Autlol%3Aavoice.txu-gwc-57-f1-22&exhq = anti-apartheid&themeq = & wpq = 2&pageq = 20.

56. Chester A. Crocker fleshed out in detail the pillars of constructive engagement in a seminal article. See Crocker, "South Africa: Strategy for Change," *Foreign Affairs* 59, no. 2 (Winter 1980): 323–51.

57. Gleijeses, *Visions of Freedom*, 281–82.

58. As secretary of state, Shultz had a higher rank and therefore would have had more influence on the president than Buchanan. On South Africa, however, Reagan believed his core values were at stake. It seemed illogical to him to undermine an ally and Africa's most economically advanced nation. On the conflict within the Reagan administration over South Africa, see Gleijeses, *Visions of Freedom*, 289–93.

59. Beth A. Fischer challenges conventional conceptions of Reagan's role in ending the Cold War. She argues that Reagan took up a nuanced conception of the superpowers' relationship well before Mikhail Gorbachev took office. Rather than a shift in Washington in response to changes emanating from Moscow, Reagan and Gorbachev approached each other with a desire for lasting peace and mutual understanding. Reagan's position changed through an awareness of the realities of the Soviet position on arms control. He was also evidently moved after he viewed the film *The Day After*, which portrayed the brutal, agonizing experiences of life in the aftermath of a nuclear exchange. See Fischer, *The Reagan Reversal: Foreign Policy and the End of the Cold War* (Columbia: University of Missouri Press, 1997). In his review of Beth Fischer's book, Philip J. Briggs points to events that made Reagan comfortable with pursuing a change in U.S.-Soviet relations, including the successful U.S. invasion of Grenada in the fall of 1983. See Briggs, "Review of *The Reagan Reversal: Foreign Policy and the End of the Cold War*, by Beth A. Fischer," *American Political Science Review* 93, no. 3 (September 1999): 712–13. See also Westad, *Cold War*, 537.

60. Fischer argues that a common enemy and the possibility of an inadvertent nuclear holocaust brought a radical change to the relationship between Reagan and Gorbachev. She suggests that Reagan initiated the ideological and political turn that ultimately brought them together. Fischer, *Reagan Reversal*, particularly 141–43. On Reagan's second-term shift, see also Renouard, *Human Rights in American Foreign Policy*, 200–201, 205–7.

61. Fischer, *Reagan Reversal*, 141.

62. Renouard, *Human Rights in American Foreign Policy*, 168.

63. Ronald Reagan, "Address to the Nation and Other Countries on United States-Soviet Relations," January 16, 1984, https://reaganlibrary.archives.gov/archives/speeches/1984/116 84a.htm.

64. Westad refers to Reagan's suggestion that the two governments work toward building common ground as being delivered "somewhat whimsically." Westad, *Cold War*, 537. Reagan's speeches at the end of 1983 and early 1984 reflected his evolving thinking on U.S.-Soviet relations and the efficacy of nuclear proliferation.

65. Ibid.

66. See, for example, Jeffrey Herbst, "Analyzing Apartheid: How Accurate Were US Intelligence Estimates of South Africa, 1948–94?" *African Affairs* 102, no. 406 (January 2003): 81–107.

67. *The Current Crisis in South Africa: Hearing Before the Subcommittee on Africa of the Committee on Foreign Affairs, House of Representatives*, 98th Cong., 2nd Sess. (December 4, 1984).

68. "Tutu Presses Sanctions Campaign," *New Pittsburgh Courier*, May 28, 1988.

69. Ibid.

70. *The Current Crisis in South Africa* (statement by Bishop Desmond Tutu).

71. Gleijeses, *Visions of Freedom*, 284–85.

72. For a detailed discussion of the events that surrounded the introduction of the Comprehensive Anti-Apartheid Act of 1986, see Nesbitt, *Race for Sanctions*, chaps. 7, 8.

73. Vicki Haddock, "House Action on South Africa Career 'High Point' for Dellums," *Oakland (CA) Tribune*, June 19, 1986. See also Hostetter, *Movement Matters*, 132.

74. As quoted in Gleijeses, *Visions of Freedom*, 290–91.

75. Ibid., 291.

76. As quoted in Michael Clough, "Southern Africa: Challenges and Choices," *Foreign Affairs* 66, no. 5 (Summer 1988): 1068.

77. As quoted in Gleijeses, *Visions of Freedom*, 292.

78. Thomas J. Redden Jr., "The US Comprehensive Anti-Apartheid Act of 1986: Anti-Apartheid or Anti-African National Congress?" *African Affairs* 87, no. 349 (October 1988): 597. Conservatives in the United States emphasized the likelihood of increased Soviet influence in South Africa with the fall of its repressive regime, as had happened in Nicaragua, Ethiopia, and Angola. In Congress, Senators Jesse Helms and Jeremiah Denton led the fight against the spread of communism in South Africa. These two politicians were to Reagan's political right, and Helms went so far as to attempt to stall Chester Crocker's confirmation as Reagan's assistant secretary of state for African affairs. See Redden, "US Comprehensive Anti-Apartheid Act of 1986," 599.

79. The Anti-Apartheid Act of 1986 blocked U.S. investment in South Africa, but the act did not prevent South Africans from investing in U.S. companies. Leland tried to gain support for his resolution that would prevent "apartheid-generated profits" in U.S. business enterprises. See Memo from Mickey Leland, "South African Investment in the United States," February 3, 1989, Series 2, Box 45, Folder 840002, Mickey Leland Archives, Texas Southern University.

80. Quoted in Lena Williams, "Congressional Black Caucus Rejoices in Growing Strength," *New York Times*, October 6, 1986.

81. Gleijeses, *Visions of Freedom*, 293–94.

82. Peter J. Schraeder, "Speaking with Many Voices: Continuity and Change in U.S. Africa Policies," *Journal of Modern African Studies* 29, no. 3 (September 1991): 402.

83. "Message to the House of Representatives Returning Without Approval a Bill Concerning Apartheid in South Africa," September 26, 1986, Ronald Reagan Presidential Library and Museum, https://www.reaganlibrary.gov/research/speeches/092686h.

84. The first congressional override of a presidential veto was a World War II immigration measure; the second was President Nixon's 1973 War Powers Act. See "Laying Down the Law, Reagan Loses and Sanctions Take Effect," *Time*, October 13, 1986.

85. Letter to the Speaker of the House and the Senate Majority Leader on the Economic Sanctions Against South Africa, September 29, 1986, Ronald Reagan Presidential Library and Museum, https://www.reaganlibrary.gov/research/speeches/092986a.

86. Nesbitt, *Race for Sanctions*, 103.

87. Ronald Reagan, "State of the Comprehensive Anti-Apartheid Act of 1986," October 2, 1986. Ronald Reagan Presidential Library and Museum, https://www.reaganlibrary.gov/research/speeches/100286d.

88. Michael Isikoff, "Threat to Profits Spurs U.S. Exodus from South Africa," *Washington Post*, November 17, 1986.

89. Ibid.

90. Ibid.

91. Michael Isikoff, "U.S. Firms Keeping Ties Despite Exit," *Washington Post*, October 22, 1987.

92. "Reluctant Leland Says He'll Vote for Sanctions Against South Africa," *Houston Post*, August 3, 1986; Energy and Commerce, H.R. 1580, Series 4, Box 42, Folder 2665, Mickey Leland Archives, Texas Southern University.

93. Floor statement concerning Anti-Apartheid Act amendments, August 11, 1989, Energy and Commerce, H.R. 1580, Foreign Affairs, South Africa, Series 4, Box 42, Folder 2665, Mickey Leland Archives, Texas Southern University.

94. Michael Isikoff, "US Firms Keeping Ties Despite Exit," *Washington Post*, October 22, 1987.

95. Michael Isikoff, "Threat to Profits Spurs U.S. Exodus from South Africa," *Washington Post*, November 17, 1986.

96. Honorable Mickey Leland of Texas, Apartheid Profits Disincentive Act, *Congressional Record*, September 22, 1987, Series 2, Box 54, Folder 1042001, Mickey Leland Archives, Texas Southern University.

97. *Statement of Newmont Mining Corporation on Section 905 of H.R. 3 National Security and Essential Commerce, by Richard B. Leather, Executive Vice-President, Before the Subcommittee on Commerce, Consumer Protection and Competitiveness of the Committee on Energy and Commerce*, October 20, 1987, Series 2, Box 54, Folder 1042017, Mickey Leland Archives, Texas Southern University.

98. *Testimony of Mr. T. Boone Pickens Jr. Before the House Energy and Commerce Committee, Subcommittee on Commerce, Consumer Protection and Competitiveness*, Tuesday, October 20, 1987, Series 2, Box 54, Folder 1042017, Mickey Leland Archives, Texas Southern University.

99. Mickey Leland, keynote address, Congressional Black Caucus Dinner, October 1984, Series 11, Box 133, Folder 8922, Mickey Leland Archives, Texas Southern University.

100. Ibid.

101. "Hunger in America," C-Span, December 16, 1985, http://www.c-span.org/video/ ?125868-1/hunger-america.

102. Statement by Congressman Toby Roth, Developments in South Africa: United States Policy Responses: Hearing Before the Subcommittee on Africa of the Committee on Foreign Affairs, House of Representatives, 99th Cong., 2nd Sess. (March 12, 1986).

103. Statement by Congressman Howard Wolpe, Human Rights and Food Aid in Ethiopia: Hearing Before the Subcommittee on Human Rights and International Organizations and the Subcommittee on Africa of the Committee on Foreign Affairs, House of Representatives, 99th Cong., 2nd [i.e., 1st] Sess. (October 16, 1985).

104. Ibid.

105. Renouard cites the 85 percent figure for "black Africans" in Human Rights in American Foreign Policy, 234.

106. Ibid., 234–35.

107. Statement of the Assistant Secretary of State for International Organization Affairs Alan L. Keyes Before the US Senate Committee on Foreign Affairs' Subcommittee on African Affairs, March 6, 1986, United Nations Archives, New York, s-1043–0024–03.

108. Ibid.

109. Congressman Mickey Leland, "On Congressional Duties—At Home and Abroad," Houston Informer, October 17, 1987.

110. Ibid.

111. Opening Statement Before the Africa Subcommittee and International Economic Policy and Trade Subcommittee, March 22, 1988, Series 11, Box 184, Folder 9709, Mickey Leland Archives, Texas Southern University.

112. Ibid.

113. Gerald Horne, From the Barrel of a Gun: The United States and the War Against Zimbabwe, 1965–1980 (Chapel Hill: University of North Carolina Press, 2001), 282.

Chapter 5

1. Letter to the President from 94 Members of Congress, "Regarding Current Food Situation in Africa," February 29, 1984, ID #197364, FO003–02, WHORM: Subject File, Ronald Reagan Library.

2. Mickey Leland, letter to the editor, Baltimore Afro-American, December 1, 1984.

3. Frank Newport, Jeffrey M. Jones, and Lydia Saad, "Ronald Reagan from the People's Perspective: A Gallup Poll Review," Gallup, June 7, 2004, http://www.gallup.com/poll/11887/ ronald-reagan-from-peoples-perspective-gallup-poll-review.aspx.

4. Letter to the President from 94 Members of Congress, "Regarding Current Food Situation in Africa," February 29, 1984, ID #197364, FO003–02, WHORM: Subject File, Ronald Reagan Library.

5. Jasper Womach, "Report for Congress: Agriculture: A Glossary of Terms, Programs, and Laws," 2005 ed., https://web.archive.org/web/20110810044532/http://ncseonline.org/nle/ crsreports/05jun/97-905.pdf. See also "US Wheat Reserve Tapped for Food Aid," Baltimore Afro-American, December 8, 1984.

6. Mickey Leland to President Ronald Reagan, November 19, 1984, ID #260875, ND 402FO003-02, WHORM: Subject File, Ronald Reagan Presidential Library.

7. Ronald Hanna, "Black Congressmen Head Fact-Finding Ethiopia Tour," *Baltimore Afro-American*, December 1, 1984.

8. "US Wheat Reserve Tapped for Food Aid."

9. "Wheat Reserve Signing Ceremony," December 3, 1984, ID #247103, FO003–02 WHORM: Subject File, Ronald Reagan Library.

10. "Ronald Reagan's Remarks at the Signing Ceremony for the Release of Wheat Reserves," December 5, 1984, ID #47103, FO003–02 WHORM: Subject File, Ronald Reagan Library.

11. Ibid.

12. "$1 Billion Sought to Feed Africans," *New York Times*, December 9, 1984.

13. Quoted in Larry Minear, "The Forgotten Human Agenda," *Foreign Policy* 73 (Winter 1988–89): 90.

14. See, for example, Ronald Reagan, "Address to the Nation on the Economy," February 5, 1981, https://reaganlibrary.archives.gov/archives/speeches/1981/20581c.htm; "Address to the Nation on the Economy," October 13, 1982, https://reaganlibrary.archives.gov/archives/speeches/1982/101382d.htm; "Ronald Reagan: Radio Address to the Nation on the Federal Budget Deficit," December 17, 1988, http://www.presidency.ucsb.edu/ws/?pid = 35274.

15. Congress granted President Reagan $18.2 billion for foreign aid toward the 1985 fiscal year budget, $4.7 more than 1984 but $11 billion less than what the president requested. "Reagan Gets Most of '85 Foreign Aid Wish List," *CQ Almanac 1984*, 40th ed. (Washington, DC: Congressional Quarterly, 1985), 390–98, http://library.cqpress.com/cqalmanac/cqal84 -1151564. Although Reagan increased the aid level, he targeted fewer recipients. Two countries, Egypt and Israel, received more than one-third of U.S. foreign aid at the time. George D. Moffett III, "Reagan's Imprint on Foreign Aid: Under Reagan, US Aid Is Tied More Tightly to National Security," *Christian Science Monitor*, May 23, 1985, http://www.csmonitor.com/ 1985/0523/zaid1-f1.html.

16. *Statement by Congressman Mickey Leland, Senate Committee on Labor and Human Resources*, September 25, 1985, Series 11, Box 33, Folder 8921, Mickey Leland Archives, Texas Southern University.

17. Mickey Leland to President Ronald Reagan, October 15, 1985, ID #342202, HE003, WHORM: Subject File, Ronald Reagan Library.

18. *Statement by Congressman Mickey Leland, Senate Committee on Labor and Human Resources*, September 25, 1985.

19. "Hunger in America," C-Span, December 16, 1985, http://www.c-spanvideo.org/ program/PoliticalInterview46.

20. Statement by Rep. Mickey Leland, American School Food Service Association, Capital Hilton Hotel, Washington, DC, February 27, 1985, Series 4, Box 50, File 4697001, Mickey Leland Archives, Texas Southern University.

21. Ibid.

22. *Opening Statement by Congressman Mickey Leland, United States Congress, House Select Committee on Hunger: Famine and Recovery in Africa: The US Response: Joint Hearing Before the Select Committee on Hunger and the Subcommittee on Africa of the Committee on Foreign Affairs*, 99th Cong., 1st Sess. (December 5, 1985).

23. Rep. Mickey Leland, House Select Committee on Hunger, address at University of Houston, November 24, 1987, Series 11, Box 178, File 9551001, Mickey Leland Archives, Texas Southern University.

24. Ibid.

25. "Hunger in America."

26. Statement, Congressman Mickey Leland, 17th African-American Conference, Gaborone, Botswana, January 12, 1987, Series 11, Box 164, File 9366001, Mickey Leland Archives, Texas Southern University.

27. Quoted in George D. Moffett III, "Donor Nations Seek Long-Term Solutions to Famine in Africa," *Christian Science Monitor*, March 5, 1985, https://www.csmonitor.com/1985/0305/along.html.

28. Mickey Leland, interview by Lester Wolf, "ASK Congress" discussion on Congress, Hunger, Houston, Economy, International Aid, Iran Contra, Congressional Affairs, August 16, 1987, Series 14, 14AVT114_589915, Mickey Leland Archives, Texas Southern University.

29. *House Committee on Foreign Affairs, Subcommittee on Human Rights International Organizations, Human Rights and Food Aid in Ethiopia: Hearing Before the Subcommittee on Human Rights and International Organizations and the Subcommittee on Africa of the Committee on Foreign Affairs*, 99th Cong., 2nd [i.e., 1st] Sess. (October 16, 1985).

30. Ibid.

31. "We Have Tightened Our Belt to Withstand Drought Problem: Comrade Mengistu," *Ethiopian Herald*, November 18, 1984.

32. Giorgis, *Red Tears*, 128.

33. Press release, "Leland Refutes Allegations That US Food Aid Was Misused in Ethiopia," September 24, 1986, Series 11, Box 154, Folder 9246, Mickey Leland Center Archives, Texas Southern University.

34. Toby Roth to Congressional Colleagues, "Support Human Rights in Ethiopia," January 1987, Series 2, Box 1, Folder 11001, Mickey Leland Archives, Texas Southern University.

35. Ibid.

36. Robert Houdek, phone interview by the author, February 12, 2014.

37. Quoted in Clifford D. May, "Ethiopia Says US Aid Won't Heal Rift," *New York Times*, November 16, 1984.

38. Press release, "News from Congressman Mickey Leland," February 11, 1987, Series 11, Box 164, File 9354001, Mickey Leland Archives, Texas Southern University.

39. Quoted in Blaine Harden, "US Law Bars Aid That Could Develop Ethiopian Agriculture," *Washington Post*, December 1, 1984.

40. John Lewis Gaddis, "The Reagan Administration and Soviet-American Relations," in *Reagan and the World*, ed. David E. Kyvig (New York: Greenwood Press, 1990), 18.

41. Ibid., 23.

42. Ibid., 24.

43. Jan S. Adams, *A Foreign Policy in Transition: Moscow's Retreat from Central America and the Caribbean, 1985–1992* (Durham, NC: Duke University Press, 1992), 47–48.

44. Quoted in Tareke, "From Af Abet to Shire," 242.

45. Michael Barnett, *Empire of Humanity: A History of Humanitarianism* (Ithaca, NY: Cornell University Press, 2011), 162.

46. E. A. Wayne, "Ethiopian Regime Looks West for Helping Hand," *Christian Science Monitor*, May 8, 1989, https://www.csmonitor.com/1989/0508/ahorn.html.

47. Robert Service, *The End of the Cold War, 1985–1991* (New York: Public Affairs, 2015), 393–94.

48. Ibid., 394.

49. Congressman Mickey Leland to Speaker of the House James Wright, April 9, 1987, Series 11, Box 168, File 9385002, Mickey Leland Archives, Texas Southern University.

50. Ibid.

51. Seth Kantor, "US Considering Plan with Soviets to Feed Angolans," *American Statesman*, October 22, 1987.

52. Kathy Kiely, "Leland Says US Won't Help Starving in Mozambique," *Houston Post*, n.d., Series 11, Box 179, File 9575002, Mickey Leland Archives, Texas Southern University.

53. On Cuban medical internationalism, see, for example, John M. Kirk, *Healthcare Without Borders: Understanding Cuban Medical Internationalism* (Gainesville: University of Florida Press, 2015); Robert Huish and John M. Kirk, "Cuban Medical Internationalism and the Development of the Latin American School of Medicine," *Latin American Perspectives* 34, no. 6 (2007): 77–92; and Isaac Saney, "Homeland of Humanity: Internationalism Within the Cuban Revolution," *Latin American Perspectives* 36, no. 1 (2009): 111–23.

54. Congressman Mickey Leland to Speaker of the House Jim Wright, March 31, 1987, Series 4, Box 68, Folder 2181001, Mickey Leland Archives, Texas Southern University.

55. Congressman Mickey Leland to Speaker of the House James Wright, April 9, 1987.

56. "Briefing Memo: Joint US/Soviet Initiatives, Prepared by Mickey Leland, Chairman, Select Committee on Hunger," April 1987, Series 11, Box 168, File 9385002, Mickey Leland Archives, Texas Southern University.

57. Seth Kanto, "Soviet, US Plan Joint Relief Bid for Starving Africans," *Atlanta Journal and Constitution*, April 20, 1987. On the goals, accomplishments, and impressions of the delegation's meetings with Soviet leaders, see Bill Keller, "House Group in Soviet Union Hopeful on Arms," *New York Times*, April 19, 1987; David S. Broder, "Soviets Charm Hill Delegation: Although Skeptical, Visitors See Golden Opportunity," *Washington Post*, April 26, 1987.

58. Mark Nelson, "Soviets Impress Lawmakers," *Dallas Morning News*, April 24, 1987.

59. "US-Soviet Food Program Set for Africa," *Globe and Mail*, April 21, 1987.

60. Ibid.

61. David B. Ottaway, "US Shuns Joint Effort on Mozambican Food Relief," *Washington Post*, June 2, 1987.

62. Kiely, "Leland Says US Won't Help Starving in Mozambique."

63. Seth Kantor, "Teaming Up to Feed the Needy," Cox News Service, n.d., Series 11, Box 179, Folder 9575001, Mickey Leland Archives, Texas Southern University.

64. Gleijeses, *Visions of Freedom*, 310.

65. Robert S. Greenberger, "Angolan Rebel Leader Beseeches Washington to Broaden Support," *Wall Street Journal*, January 31, 1985.

66. Gleijeses, *Visions of Freedom*, 310.

67. Kiely, "Leland Says US Won't Help Starving in Mozambique."

68. Quoted in "Defeat Effort to Deny Aid to Front Line States," *New York Amsterdam News*, December 26, 1987.

69. Ibid.

70. Randall Robinson at the Cleveland City Club, "US/South Africa Policy," November 12, 1982, https://www.youtube.com/watch?v=EBa7RYWLXTM.

71. Leland interview by Kathy Kiley, Mickey Leland Audio, Series 14, Tape 1, 14AVC01_489804, Mickey Leland Archives, Texas Southern University.

72. Ibid.

73. Simon Anekwe, "Fear Ethiopia Faces Famine," *New York Amsterdam News*, October 3, 1987.

74. Ibid.

75. Mickey Leland, "No Excuse for Attack," *Philadelphia Tribune*, November 3, 1987, 10A.

76. Ibid.

77. "Ethiopian Rebels Claim to Hold 2 Soviet Officers," *Washington Post*, March 20, 1988.

78. Mary Battista, "Ethiopia Orders a Halt to Food Relief in North," *Washington Post*, April 7, 1988.

79. Ibid.

80. Bogdan Szajkowski, "Ethiopia: A Weakening Soviet Connection?" *World Today* 45, nos. 8–9 (August–September 1989): 155. By comparison, the Soviet Union spent 15 percent of its regular budget on defense. See ibid., 155.

81. "Excerpts from Gorbachev's Speech: 'Universal Human Values,'" *Washington Post*, December 8, 1988.

82. Gerald J. Bender, James S. Coleman, and Richard L. Sklar, eds., *African Crisis Areas and US Foreign Policy* (Berkeley: University of California Press, 1985), 13.

83. Ibid. On the fallacy of exported revolution, see Piero Gleijeses, *Conflicting Missions: Havana, Washington, and Africa, 1959–1976* (Chapel Hill: University of North Carolina Press, 2002).

84. Campbell Craig and Fredrik Logevall, *America's Cold War: The Politics of Insecurity* (Cambridge, MA: Harvard University Press, 2009), 322–23.

85. Nene Foxhall, "Leland Taking Foe Seriously, Challenger Spates Shows Congressman No Mercy," *Houston Chronicler*, February 12, 1988, Series 8, Box 4, Folder 5182002, Mickey Leland Archives, Texas Southern University.

86. Mickey Leland, Houston Alumni Task Force of the University of Texas, Outstanding Black Alumnus Awards, Saturday, April 22, 1989, Series 11, Box 210, Folder 10289001, Mickey Leland Archives, Texas Southern University.

87. Kathy Kiely, "Leland Called 'Incredible' on Hunger Mission to Sudan," *Houston Post*, April 13, 1989.

Chapter 6

Note to epigraph: "'Say Brother' Mickey Leland: The Man and the Mission," WGBH, Boston Public Radio, Series 14, 14AVT63_589943, Mickey Leland Archives, Texas Southern University.

1. Alison Leland, interview by the author, July 22, 2010, Houston, TX.

2. Simon Anekwe, "Leland Urges Sudan Relief," *New York Amsterdam News*, January 7, 1989.

3. Jane Perlez, "Ethiopia Leader Tells of Execution of Coup Figure," *New York Times*, May 19, 1989.

4. Jane Perlez, "Ethiopia Asking US for Full Diplomatic Ties," *New York Times*, April 20, 1989.

5. Mickey Leland, "We Need Better Relations with Africa," *New York Times*, July 21, 1989.

6. Leland, quoted in ibid.; "Ethiopian Regime Looks West for Helping Hand," *Christian Science Monitor*, May 8, 1989.

7. "President Underscores Ethiopia's Preparedness for Strengthening Bilateral Relations with USA," *Ethiopian Herald*, Saturday, April 1, 1989.

8. Jane Perlez, "Sudanese Rebel Seeks Credibility in US Visit," *New York Times*, June 4, 1989.

9. Quoted in E. A. Wayne, "Ethiopian Regime Looks West for Helping Hand," *Christian Science Monitor*, May 8, 1989.

10. Perlez, "Sudanese Rebel Seeks Credibility in US Visit."

11. Ibid.

12. Alex de Waal, *The Real Politics of the Horn of Africa: Money, War and the Business of Power* (Malden, MA: Polity Press, 2015), 45.

13. Jane Perlez, "House Panel Questions UN Effort in Sudan," *New York Times*, April 9, 1989; Secretary General to Mengistu, April 14, 1989, United Nations Archives, New York, s-1024–0150–0021.

14. Secretary General to Mengistu, April 14, 1989.

15. Barbara Al Tayeb, "Ambitious Relief Plan Starts in Famine-Stricken Sudan," United Press International, April 1, 1989.

16. Select Committee Trips and History, n.d., p. 24, Series 4, Box 167, Folder 2830003, Mickey Leland Archives, Texas Southern University.

17. *Report on Congressional Delegation to the Horn, Foreign Affairs, Ethiopia, Select Committee on Hunger* (1989), Series 5, Box 21, Folder 1989, Mickey Leland Archives, Texas Southern University.

18. Select Committee Trips and History, n.d., p. 11.

19. *Report on Congressional Delegation to the Horn, Foreign Affairs, Ethiopia, Select Committee on Hunger* (1989), Series 5, Box 21, Folder 1989, Mickey Leland Archives, Texas Southern University.

20. Select Committee Trips and History, n.d., p. 11.

21. Jane Perlez, "In Ethiopia, Yet Another Burden: The Castoffs of Neighbors' Wars," *New York Times*, August 7, 1989.

22. Mickey Leland, Houston Alumni Task Force of the University of Texas, Outstanding Black Alumnus Awards, April 22, 1989, Series 11, Box 210, Folder 10289001, Mickey Leland Archives, Texas Southern University.

23. Select Committee Trips and History, n.d., p. 13.

24. Tareke, "From Af Abet to Shire," 240.

25. Select Committee Trips and History, n.d., p. 17.

26. Sonya Ross, "Rebel Leader Says Peace Possible in War-Torn Sudan," Associated Press, June 6, 1989, Series 4, Box 15, Folder 2768001, Mickey Leland Archives, Texas Southern University.

27. Select Committee Trips and History, n.d., p. 19.

28. Mickey Leland, "What Afro-Americans Can Do About Starvation in Africa," *Ebony*, April 1989.

29. Ibid.

30. Quoted in Perlez, "House Panel Questions UN Relief Effort in Sudan."

31. Mickey Leland, Houston Alumni Task Force of the University of Texas, Outstanding Black Alumnus Awards, April 22, 1989.

32. George McElroy, "Quite a Role for a 'Fifth Ward Firebrand,'" *Houston Informer*, August 14, 1989, Series 13, Box 16, Folder 10622007, Mickey Leland Archives, Texas Southern University.

33. Mickey Leland, Select Committee on Hunger, to Donald Payne, June 1989, Series 11, Box 178, Folder 9548, Mickey Leland Archives, Texas Southern University.

34. Mickey Leland, Houston Alumni Task Force of the University of Texas, Outstanding Black Alumnus Awards, April 22, 1989.

35. Kathy Kiely, "Leland Called 'Incredible' on Hunger Mission to Sudan," *Houston Post*, April 13, 1989.

36. *Nightline*, April 10, 1989.

37. Polman, *The Crisis Caravan*, 127–28.

38. Adrian Martin, "Environmental Conflict Between Refugee and Host Communities," *Journal of Peace Research* 42, no. 3 (2005): 337–38.

39. Sheila Rule, "Refugees from Sudan Strain Ethiopia Camps," *New York Times*, May 1, 1988.

40. Holly Philpot, "Operation Lifeline Sudan: Challenges During Conflict and Lessons Learned" (Case-Specific Briefing Paper, Humanitarian Assistance in Complex Emergencies, University of Denver, 2011), 4.

41. Jennifer Dixon, "Congressmen Say Allies Not Helping Relief Effort for Starving," Associated Press, Washington, DC, April 13, 1989.

42. Philpot, "Operation Lifeline Sudan," 10.

43. David B. Ottaway, "Ethiopia Allows Non-UN Sudan Aid Convoy," *Washington Post*, April 28, 1989.

44. Mickey Leland, Houston Alumni Task Force of the University of Texas, Outstanding Black Alumnus Awards, April 22, 1989.

45. Neil Henry, "Rep. Leland Still Missing in Ethiopia—Day-Long Search Provides No Clues to Fate of Plane," *Washington Post*, August 9, 1989.

46. Sheila Rue, "Refugees from Sudan Strain Ethiopia Camps," *New York Times*, May 1, 1988.

47. Donna Britt, "Alison Leland, Carrying on—One Year After the Plane Crash That Claimed the Life of Rep. Mickey Leland, His Widow Looks to the Future with Hope and Remembers the Past with Love," *Washington Post*, August 5, 1990.

48. Alison Leland, interview by the author, July 22, 2010, Houston, Texas.

49. Brooke A. Masters, "Crash Victims in Ethiopia Bound by Love for Humanity—8 Strove to Make Society Better for All," *Washington Post*, August 15, 1989.

50. Glenn Fowler, "Ivan Tillem, 32; Lost in Ethiopia," *New York Times*, August 14, 1989.

51. *Accident Investigation Report on RRC DHC-6 Aircraft Near Gambella, Civil Aviation Ethiopia*, June 30, 1990, Series 15, Box 4, Folder 10711001, pp. 13–14, Mickey Leland Archives, Texas Southern University.

52. Neil Henry, "Red Flag Marks Fatal Spot—Fellow Pilot Ducks Under Clouds for Look," *Washington Post*, August 15, 1989.

53. Ibid.

54. *Accident Investigation Report on RRC DHC-6 Aircraft Near Gambella, Civil Aviation Ethiopia*, 15.

55. Ibid., 13–14.

56. Kathy Lewis and Andrew Kirtzman, "Friends, Colleagues Recall Their Last Contacts with Mickey Leland," *Houston Post*, August 20, 1989, Series 15, Box 4, Folder 107120121, Mickey Leland Archives, Texas Southern University.

57. Robert Houdek, phone interview by the author, February 12, 2014.

58. Associated Press, "Leland Crash Probe Finds Pilot Error—Ethiopia Faults Crew for Decision to Fly," *Washington Post*, August 25, 1990.

59. *Accident Investigation Report on RRC DHC-6 Aircraft Near Gambella, Civil Aviation Ethiopia*, 14.

60. Evan Ramstad, "Pilot Error, Weather Cited in Crash That Killed Texas Congressman," Associated Press, August 24, 1990.

61. "President Mengistu Receives Message from George Bush," *Ethiopian Herald*, August 12, 1989.

62. "Mengistu Sends Message to the US President," *Ethiopian Herald*, August 11, 1989.

63. Jane Perlez, "US Helicopters Join Search for Leland," *New York Times*, August 13, 1989.

64. "Intensive Search for Missing RRC Aircraft Continues," *Ethiopian Herald*, August 13, 1989; Associated Press, "Leland Crash Probe Finds Pilot Error."

65. "Intensive Search for Missing RRC Aircraft Continues."

66. Ibid.; Neil Henry, "Leland Plane Found Crashed into Mountain—No Survivors," *Washington Post*, August 14, 1989.

67. Henry, "Leland Plane Found Crashed into Mountain—No Survivors,"

68. "12 Bodies Recovered, Search for Other Crash Victims Goes on," *Ethiopian Herald*, Tuesday, August 13, 1989.

69. Elizabeth Hudson, "'We Have Lost One of Our Most Important Leaders'—Houston Constituents, Colleagues Gather to Remember Their Longtime Congressman," *Washington Post*, August 14, 1989.

70. President George H. W. Bush, "Statement on the Death of Representative Mickey Leland," August 18, 1989, Public Papers-1989, George Bush Presidential Library and Museum, http:/bushlibrary.tamu.edu.

71. United Press International, "Bush Expresses Condolences," *Atlanta Daily World*, August 15, 1989.

72. Kim Cobb, William E. Clayton Jr., and Sonja Garza, "Ethiopia Bids Goodbye to 9 Victims," *Houston Chronicle*, August 23, 1989.

73. Emergency Committee for African Refugees, "US Policy and the Current Refugee Crisis in Africa," *Issue* 12, nos. 1–2 (Spring–Summer 1982): 11.

74. "President Pays Tribute to Mickey Leland," *Ethiopian Herald*, August 13, 1989.

75. "President Receives Condolence Message from George Bush," *Ethiopian Herald*, August 16, 1989.

76. "Herman Cohen Concludes Visit," *Ethiopian Herald*, August 8, 1989.

77. Don Oberdorfer and Adela Gooch, "US Sees Hope for Better Ties with Ethiopia—Aid in Leland Search Viewed as Promising," *Washington Post*, August 15, 1989.

78. David Keen, *The Benefits of Famine: A Political Economy of Famine and Relief in Southwestern Sudan, 1983–1989* (Athens: Ohio University Press, 2008), 205.

79. Stephen Spector, *Operation Solomon: The Daring Rescue of the Ethiopian Jews* (New York: Oxford University Press, 2005), 14.

80. "Joint Statement on Ethiopia," June 2, 1990, CARE Papers, Box 1202, Rare Books and Manuscripts Division, New York Public Library.

81. Tony Hall to Rudy von Bernuth, June 6, 1990, CARE Papers, Box 1202, Rare Books and Manuscript Division, New York Public Library.

82. As quoted in Gill, *Famine and Foreigners*, 75.

83. Theodore Vestal describes Meles's definition of democracy as mirroring Lenin's democratic centralism rather than the widely accepted definitions of traditional democracy. Members of the ruling party decided matters of policy by majority vote. See Vestal, "Meles Zenawi," 196.

84. Terrence Lyons, "Post–Cold War US Policy Toward Africa: Hints from the Horn," *Brookings Review* 10, no. 1 (Winter 1992): 33.

85. Ibid., 32.

86. Nene Foxhall, "Mickey Died to Feed the Hungry, Jackson Says," *Houston Chronicle*, August 19, 1989.

87. Harry Wall, "Texas Maverick Who Built Lasting Bonds Between Minorities," *Jerusalem Post*, August 17, 1989.

88. Robert P. Hey, "Mickey Leland: Champion of the Hungry," *Christian Science Monitor*, August 15, 1989, https://www.csmonitor.com/1989/0815/amick.html.

89. Alison Leland, interview by the author, July 22, 2010, Houston, TX.

Conclusion

1. Remarks by President Obama and Prime Minister Hailemariam Desalegn of Ethiopia in joint press conference, July 27, 2015, https://www.whitehouse.gov/the-press-office/2015/07/27/remarks-president-obama-and-prime-minister-hailemariam-desalegn-ethiopia.

2. See, for example, Andrew Nachemson, "Obama's Ethiopia Visit Legitimizes Authoritarian Government, Critical Expats Say," *Washington Times*, July 21, 2015.

3. For a general biography of Meles Zenawi and his government, see Vestal, "Meles Zenawi." Peter Gill is effusive in his praise of Meles's genius, leadership, and personality, but in chapter 9 of his book he details many of the ways Meles had clamped down on speech freedoms in Ethiopia. See Gill, *Famine and Foreigners*.

4. On Meles and civil liberties, see "The Unhappy Legacy of Meles Zenawi," Freedom House, August 22, 2012, https://freedomhouse.org/blog/unhappy-legacy-meles-zenawi.

5. Walters, "Racial Justice in Foreign Affairs," 18.

6. David F. Gordon, "Congress and the Future of U.S. Foreign Policy Toward Africa," *Issue: A Journal of Opinion* 24, no. 1, Issues in African Higher Education (Winter–Spring 1996): 5.

7. On the fragility of the inner city as an "internal colony," see Plummer, *In Search of Power*, 8.

8. Tom Kentworthy, "Congressional Black Caucus Facing New Circumstances After 20 Years," *Washington Post*, September 17, 1989.

9. Shelly Leanne, "The Clinton Administration and Africa: Perspective of the Congressional Black Caucus and TransAfrica," *African Issues* 26, no. 2 (1998): 17–22.

10. Mika Aaltola, "Emergency Food Aid as a Means of Political Persuasion in the North Korean Famine," *Third World Quarterly* 20, no. 2 (1999): 373.

11. Charles P. Henry also points to the lack of a "consensus to act." He notes the demise of pan-African solidarity and African American commitment to human rights as significant

factors that foreclosed on African American responses to events in Africa. He also points to a prevailing sense of racial justice rather than pan-Africanism that motivated responses to Haiti and South Africa. See Henry, "The Rise and Fall of Black Influence on US Foreign Policy," in *African Americans in Global Affairs: Contemporary Perspectives*, ed. Michael L. Clemons (Boston: Northeastern University Press, 2010), 214–16.

12. Adekeye Adebajo, "Africa, African Americans, and the Avuncular Sam," *Africa Today* 50, no. 3 (Spring 2004): 103.

13. William Gray to George Crockett, March 2, 1990, Box 18, MG 469, Apartheid/South Africa and Foreign Affairs Files, William Gray III Papers, Schomburg Center for Research in Black Culture, New York Public Library.

14. Karen De Witt, "Hunger Strike on Haiti: Partial Victory at Least," *New York Times*, May 9, 1994; Howard Kurtz, "A Striking Success," *Washington Post*, June 23, 1994.

15. Steven Holmes, "With Persuasion and Muscle, Black Caucus Reshapes Haiti Policy," *New York Times*, July 14, 1994.

16. Holmes, "With Persuasion and Muscle, Black Caucus Reshapes Haiti Policy."

17. Henry, "The Rise and Fall of Black Influence on US Foreign Policy," 212–13.

18. House Foreign Affairs Committee, UN Intervention in Somalia, C-Span, December 17, 1992, https://www.c-span.org/video/?36232-1/un-intervention-somalia.

19. Congressional Black Caucus Issue, C-Span, June 16, 1993, https://www.c-span.org/video/?43148-1/congressional-black-caucus-issues&showFullAbstract=1.

20. Matthew A. Baum, "How Public Opinion Constrains the Use of Force: The Case of Operation Restore Hope," *Presidential Studies Quarterly* 34, no. 2 (June 2004): 213.

21. Ibid., 218.

22. Shelly Leanne, "The Clinton Administration and Africa: Perspective of the Congressional Black Caucus and TransAfrica," *Issue: A Journal of Opinion* 26, no. 2, The Clinton Administration and Africa (1993–1999) (1998): 19.

23. See Adebajo, "Africa, African Americans, and the Avuncular Sam," 98.

24. Gwendolyn Mikell, "Women Mobilizing for Peace: African-American Responses to African Crises," *International Journal on World Peace* 17, no. 1 (March 2000): 73.

25. "USA: Call for US to Embargo Imports of Nigerian Oil," Associated Press, n.d., https://www.youtube.com/watch?v=82iw3NXZZdk.

26. For a good outline of the African Growth and Opportunity Act's main features and its relation to the long-term trade relationship between African countries and the United States, see Carol B. Thompson, "US Trade with Africa: African Growth and Opportunity?" *Review of African Political Economy* 31, no. 101 (2004): 457–74.

27. Leanne. "The Clinton Administration and Africa: Perspective of the Congressional Black Caucus and TransAfrica," 18.

28. Steven Greenhouse, "Administration Is Faulted over Conference on Africa," *New York Times*, June 27, 1994.

29. Barbara Lee, "The Black Community and the Non-Aligned Movement," *Black Scholar* 18, no. 2, Eighth Non-Aligned Summit Harare—1986 (March–April 1987): 2–8.

30. Menna Demassie, "Congress from the Inside: U.S.-African Foreign Policy and Black Ethnic Politics," *PS: Political Science and Politics* 44, no. 3 (July 2011): 686.

31. Leanne, "The Clinton Administration and Africa: Perspective of the Congressional Black Caucus and TransAfrica," 18.

32. "US President on Historic Visit to the AU," press release, July 28, 2015, http://cpauc .au.int/en/content/us-president-historic-visit-african-union.

33. "Remarks by President Obama to the People of Africa," White House, Office of the Press Secretary, July 28, 2015, https://www.whitehouse.gov/the-press-office/2015/07/28/ remarks-president-obama-people-africa.

34. For a compelling analysis of Barack Obama's Africa policies through 2015, see Nicolas van de Walle, "Obama and Africa: Lots of Hope, Not Much Change," *Foreign Affairs* 94, no. 5 (September–October 2015): 54–61.

35. Nicole Degli Innocenti, "Powell Condemns Mugabe over Zimbabwe Crisis," *Financial Times*, May 26, 2001, 1.

36. Adebajo, "Africa, African Americans, and the Avuncular Sam," 104.

37. Walters, "Racial Justice in Foreign Affairs," 24.

Bibliography

Aaltola, Mika. "Emergency Food Aid as a Means of Political Persuasion in the North Korean Famine." *Third World Quarterly* 20, no. 2 (1999): 371–86.

Adams, Jan S. *A Foreign Policy in Transition: Moscow's Retreat from Central America and the Caribbean, 1985–1992*. Durham, NC: Duke University Press, 1992.

Adas, Michael. "From Settler Colony to Global Hegemon: Integrating the Exceptionalist Narrative of the American Experience into World History." *American Historical Review* 106, no. 5 (December 2001): 1692–1720.

Adebajo, Adekeye. "Africa, African Americans, and the Avuncular Sam." *Africa Today* 50, no. 3 (Spring 2004): 93–110.

Ahmed, Hussein. "Addis Ababa University: Fifty-Three Years on an Insider's View." *Cahiers d'Études Africaines* 46, no. 182 (2006): 291–312.

Ahmed, Muhammad. "The Roots of the Pan-African Revolution." *Black Scholar* 3, no. 9 (May 1972): 48–55.

Alexis, Marcus. "Assessing 50 Years of African-American Economic Status, 1940–1990." *American Economic Review* 88, no. 2 (1998): 368–75.

Allen, Robert L. *Black Awakening in Capitalist America: An Analytic History*. Trenton, NJ: Africa World Press, 1990.

Anderson, Carol. *Bourgeois Radicals: The NAACP and the Struggle for Colonial Liberation, 1941–1960*. New York: Cambridge University Press, 2015.

———. *Eyes Off the Prize: The United Nations and the African American Struggle for Human Rights, 1944–1955*. New York: Cambridge University Press, 2003.

Angelou, Maya. *All God's Children Need Traveling Shoes*. New York: Vintage, 1991.

Arulanantham, Ahilan T. "'A Hungry Child Knows No Politics': A Proposal for Reform of the Laws Governing Humanitarian Relief and 'Material Support' of Terrorism." An Issue Brief for the American Constitution Society for Law and Policy, Washington, DC, June 2008. https://www.acslaw.org/wp-content/uploads/2018/07/Arulanantham_Issue_Brief.pdf.

Asserate, Asfa-Wossen. *King of Kings: The Triumph and Tragedy of Emperor Haile Selassie I of Ethiopia*. London: Haus, 2015.

Azeze, Fekade. *Unheard Voices: Drought, Famine and God in Ethiopian Oral Poetry*. Addis Ababa: Addis Ababa University Press, 1998.

Bailey, David. *Imagine: A Book for Band Aid*. London: Thames and Hudson, 1985.

Baines, Gary. "The Master Narrative of South Africa's Liberation Struggle: Remembering and Forgetting June 16, 1976." *International Journal of African Historical Studies* 40, no. 2 (2007): 283–302.

Barnett, Michael. *Empire of Humanity: A History of Humanitarianism.* Ithaca, NY: Cornell University Press, 2011.

———. "Humanitarianism Transformed." *Perspectives on Politics* 3, no. 4 (December 2005): 723–40.

Barnett, Michael, and Thomas G. Weiss. "Humanitarianism: A Brief History of the Present." *Humanitarianism in Question: Politics, Power, Ethics*, edited by Michael Barnett and Thomas G. Weiss. Ithaca, NY: Cornell University Press, 2008.

Baum, Matthew A. "How Public Opinion Constrains the Use of Force: The Case of Operation Restore Hope." *Presidential Studies Quarterly* 34, no. 2 (June 2004): 187–226.

Bedasse, Monique A. *Jah Kingdom: Rastafarians, Tanzania, and Pan-Africanism in the Age of Decolonization.* Chapel Hill: University of North Carolina Press, 2017.

Beltramini, Enrico. "SCLC Operation Breadbasket: From Economic Civil Rights to Black Power." *Fire!!!* 2, no. 2 (2013): 5–47.

Bender, Gerald J., James S. Coleman, and Richard L. Sklar, eds. *African Crisis Areas and US Foreign Policy.* Berkeley: University of California Press, 1985.

Benti, Getahun. *Addis Ababa: Migration and the Making of a Multiethnic Metropolis, 1941–1974.* Trenton, NJ: Red Sea Press, 2007.

Berhe, Aregawi. *A Political History of the Tigray People's Liberation Front (1975–1991): Revolt, Ideology and Mobilisation in Ethiopia.* Los Angeles: Tsehai Publishers, 2009.

Berry, Mary Frances. *History Teaches Us to Resist: How Progressive Movements Have Succeeded in Challenging Times.* Boston: Beacon Press, 2018.

Bertschinger, Claire. *Moving Mountains.* London: Doubleday, 2005.

Biko, Steve. *I Write What I Like: Selected Writings.* Edited by Aelred Stubbs. Chicago: University of Chicago Press, 2002.

Biondi, Martha. *The Black Revolution on Campus.* Berkeley: University of California Press, 2012.

"Black America Has Overlooked the Racist Policies of Ronald Reagan." *Journal of Blacks in Higher Education*, no. 64 (Summer 2009): 13–14.

Blauner, Robert. "Internal Colonialism and Ghetto Revolt." *Social Problems* 16, no. 4 (April 1969): 393–408.

Blix, Gunnar, Yngve Hofvander, and Bo Vahlquist, eds. *Famine: A Symposium Dealing with Nutrition and Relief Operations in Times of Disaster.* Uppsala: Almqvist and Wiksell, 1971.

Bloom, Joshua, and Waldo E. Martin Jr. *Black Against Empire: The History and Politics of the Black Panther Party.* Berkeley: University of California Press, 2016.

Bon Tempo, Carl J. *Americans at the Gate: The United States and Refugees During the Cold War.* Princeton, NJ: Princeton University Press, 2008.

Borstelmann, Thomas. *The Cold War and the Color Line: American Race Relations in the Global Arena.* Cambridge, MA: Harvard University Press, 2003.

Briggs, Philip J. Review of *The Reagan Reversal: Foreign Policy and the End of the Cold War*, by Beth A. Fischer. *American Political Science Review* 93, no. 3 (September 1999): 712–13.

Bright, Christopher. "Neither Dictatorships nor Double Standards: The Reagan Administration's Approach to Human Rights." *World Affairs* 153, no. 2 (1990): 51–80.

Brown, Lester R., and Edward C. Wolf. "Origins of the African Food Crisis." *Challenge* 27, no. 6 (1985): 50–52.

Buerk, Michael. *The Road Taken: An Autobiography.* London: Hutchinson, 2004.

Cabral, Amilcar. "The Weapon of Theory." Address delivered to the First Tricontinental Conference of the Peoples of Asia, Africa, and Latin America, Havana, January 1966. https://www.marxists.org/subject/africa/cabral/1966/weapon-theory.htm.

Campbell, James T. *Middle Passages: African American Journeys to Africa, 1787–2005*. New York: Penguin, 2007.

Carmichael, Stokely (Kwame Ture). "Toward Black Liberation." *Massachusetts Review* 7, no. 4 (1966): 639–51. http://nationalhumanitiescenter.org/pds/maai3/segregation/text8/carmichael.pdf.

———. " 'We Are All Africans': A Speech by Stokely Carmichael to Malcolm X Liberation University." *Black Scholar* 27, nos. 3–4 (1997): 65–68.

Carnochan, W. B. *Golden Legends: Images of Abyssinia, Samuel Johnson to Bob Marley*. Stanford, CA: Stanford University Press, 2008.

Carson, Clayborne. *In Struggle: SNCC and the Black Awakening of the 1960s*. Cambridge, MA: Harvard University Press, 1995.

Cha-Jua, Sundiata Keita, and Clarence Lang. "The 'Long Movement' as Vampire: Temporal and Spatial Fallacies in Recent Black Freedom Studies." *Journal of African American History* 92, no. 2 (Spring 2007): 265–88.

Chandler, David. *From Kosovo to Kabul and Beyond: Human Rights and International Intervention*. London: Pluto Press, 2006.

Chappell, David L. *Waking from the Dream: The Struggle for Civil Rights in the Shadow of Martin Luther King, Jr.* Durham, NC: Duke University Press, 2014.

Chávez, John R. "Aliens in Their Native Lands: The Persistence of Internal Colonial Theory." *Journal of World History* 22, no. 4 (December 2011): 785–809.

Clapham, Christopher. "The State and Revolution in Ethiopia." *Review of African Political Economy* 16, no. 44 (1989): 5–17.

Clark, D. J. "The Production of a Contemporary Famine Image: The Image Economy, Indigenous Photographers and the Case of Mekanic Philipos." *Journal of International Development* 16, no. 5 (July 2004): 693–704.

Clark, Kenneth B. *Dark Ghetto: Dilemmas of Social Power*. 2nd ed. Middletown, CT: Wesleyan University Press, 1989.

———. *Prejudice and Your Child*. 2nd ed. Middletown, CT: Wesleyan University Press, 1988.

Clemons, Michael L., ed. *African Americans in Global Affairs: Contemporary Perspectives*. Boston: Northeastern University Press, 2010.

———. "Conceptualizing the Foreign Affairs Participation of African Americans: Strategies and Effects of the Congressional Black Caucus and TransAfrica." In *African Americans in Global Affairs*, edited by Clemons, 33–64.

Clough, Michael. "Southern Africa: Challenges and Choices." *Foreign Affairs* 66, no. 5 (Summer 1988): 1067–90.

Colburn, Forrest D. "The Tragedy of Ethiopia's Intellectuals." *Antioch Review* 47, no. 2 (Spring 1989): 133–45.

Congressional Black Caucus. "The African-American Manifesto on Southern Africa." *Black Scholar* 8, no. 4 Black Politics 1977 (January–February 1977): 27–32.

Cooper, Frederick. *Africa Since 1940: The Past of the Present*. Cambridge: Cambridge University Press, 2009.

Copson, Raymond W. *The Congressional Black Caucus and Foreign Policy (1971–2002)*. New York: Novinka Books, 2003.

Countryman, Matthew J. " 'From Protest to Politics': Community Control and Black Independent Politics in Philadelphia, 1965–1984." *Journal of Urban History* 32, no. 6 (2006): 813–61.

Craig, Campbell, and Fredrik Logevall. *America's Cold War: The Politics of Insecurity.* Cambridge, MA: Harvard University Press, 2009.

Crocker, Chester A. *High Noon in Southern Africa: Making Peace in a Rough Neighborhood.* New York: W. W. Norton & Co., 1993.

———. "South Africa: Strategy for Change." *Foreign Affairs* 59, no. 2 (Winter 1980): 323–51.

Crummey, Donald E. *Farming and Famine: Landscape Vulnerability in Northeast Ethiopia, 1889–1991.* Edited by James C. McCann. Madison: University of Wisconsin Press, 2018.

Cruse, Harold W. *Rebellion or Revolution.* New York: William Morrow, 1968.

———. "Revolutionary Nationalism and the Afro-American." *Studies on the Left* 2, no. 3 (1962): 12–25. http://my.ilstu.edu/~jkshapi/Cruse_Revolutionary%20Nationalism.pdf.

Culverson, Donald R. "The Politics of the Anti-Apartheid Movement in the United States, 1969–1986." *Political Science Quarterly* 111, no. 1 (Spring 1996): 127–49.

Curtin, Mary Ellen. "Reaching for Power: Barbara C. Jordan and Liberals in the Texas Legislature, 1966–1972." *Southwestern Historical Quarterly* 108, no. 2 (2004): 210–31.

Darch, Colin. "The Ethiopian Student Movement in the Struggle Against Imperialism, 1960–1974." Paper presented at the Annual Social Science Conference of the East African Universities, Dar es Salaam, December 20–22, 1976. http://www.colindarch.info/docs/1976 1222_Ethiopian_student_movement.pdf.

Davis, Louise H. "Feeding the World a Line? Celebrity Activism and Ethical Consumer Practices from Live Aid to Product Red." *Nordic Journal of English Studies* 9, no. 3 (2010): 89–118.

Day, Dorothy. *Loaves and Fishes: The Inspiring Story of the Catholic Worker Movement.* New York: Orbis Books, 1997.

De la Cova, Antonio R. "US-Cuba Relations During the Reagan Administration." In *President Reagan and the World,* edited by Schmertz, Datlof, and Ugrinsky, 381–92.

Dellums, Ronald V. 2000. *Lying Down with the Lions: A Public Life from the Streets of Oakland to the Halls of Power.* Boston: Beacon Press, 2000.

Demassie, Menna. "Congress from the Inside: U.S.-African Foreign Policy and Black Ethnic Politics." *PS: Political Science and Politics* 44, no. 3 (July 2011): 685–87.

Deutsch, Richard. "Reagan's Unruly Review." *Africa Report* 26, no. 3 (May–June 1981): 23.

De Waal, Alex. "Ethiopia: Transition to What?" *World Policy Journal* 9, no. 4 (Fall–Winter 1992): 719–37.

———. *Evil Days: Thirty Years of War and Famine in Ethiopia.* New York: Human Rights Watch, 1991.

———. *Famine Crimes: Politics and the Disaster Relief Industry in Africa.* Bloomington: Indiana University Press, 1997.

———. *Famine That Kills: Darfur, Sudan.* New York: Oxford University Press, 2005.

———. *The Real Politics of the Horn of Africa: Money, War and the Business of Power.* Malden, MA: Polity Press, 2015.

Dickson, David A. "American Society and the African American Foreign Policy Lobby: Constraints and Opportunities." *Journal of Black Studies* 27, no. 2 (1996): 139–51.

Diggs, Charles C., Jr. "Action Manifesto." *Issue: A Journal of Opinion* 2, no. 1 (Spring 1972): 52–60.

————. "The Drought in the Sahel." *Black Scholar* 5, no. 10 (1974): 37–42.

Dikötter, Frank. *Mao's Great Famine: The History of China's Most Devastating Catastrophe, 1958–1962*. New York: Bloomsbury, 2010.

Dittmer, John. *The Good Doctors: The Medical Committee for Human Rights and the Struggle for Social Justice in Health Care*. New York: Bloomsbury, 2009.

Donham, Donald L. "Revolution and Modernity in Maale: Ethiopia, 1974 to 1987." *Comparative Studies in Society and History* 34, no. 1 (January 1992): 28–57.

DuBose, Carolyn P. *The Untold Story of Charles Diggs: The Public Figure, the Private Man*. Arlington, VA: Barton Publishing, 1998.

Dudziak, Mary L. *Cold War Civil Rights: Race and the Image of American Democracy*. Princeton, NJ: Princeton University Press, 2010.

Eckert, Andreas. "African Nationalists and Human Rights, 1940–1970s." In *Human Rights in the Twentieth Century*, edited by Hoffman, 283–300.

Elfring, Chris. "Africa Tomorrow: If We Act Today." *BioScience* 35, no. 7 (July–August 1985): 400–402.

Emergency Committee for African Refugees. "US Policy and the Current Refugee Crisis in Africa." *Issue* 12, nos. 1–2 (Spring–Summer 1982): 10–12.

Erhagbe, Edward O. "The Congressional Black Caucus and United States Policy Toward Africa: 1971–1990." *Transafrican Journal of History* 24 (1995): 84–96.

Falcoff, Mark. "Latin America: Was There a 'Kirkpatrick Doctrine'?" In *President Reagan and the World*, edited by Schmertz, Datlof, and Ugrinsky.

Fanon, Frantz. *The Wretched of the Earth*. Translated by Richard Philcox. New York: Grove Press, 2005.

Fassin, Didier. *Humanitarian Reason: A Moral History of the Present*. Translated by Rachel Gomme. Berkeley: University of California Press, 2012.

Ferris, Jesse. *Nasser's Gamble: How Intervention in Yemen Caused the Six-Day War and the Decline of Egyptian Power*. Princeton, NJ: Princeton University Press, 2013.

Finn, James, ed. *Ethiopia: The Politics of Famine*. Lanham, MD: University Press of America, 1990.

Firebrace, James, and Stuart Holland. *Never Kneel Down: Drought, Development and Liberation in Eritrea*. Trenton, NJ: Red Sea Press, 1985.

Fischer, Beth A. *The Reagan Reversal: Foreign Policy and the End of the Cold War*. Columbia: University of Missouri Press, 1997.

Fisher, Louis. "How Tightly Can Congress Draw the Purse Strings?" *American Journal of International Law* 83, no. 4 (1989): 758–66.

Forsythe, David P. "Human Rights and the International Committee of the Red Cross." *Human Rights Quarterly* 12, no. 2 (May 1990): 265–89.

Fraser, Cary. "A Requiem for the Cold War: Reviewing the History of International Relations Since 1945." In *Rethinking the Cold War*, edited by Allen Hunter, 93–115. Philadelphia: Temple University Press, 1998.

Frazier, Robeson Taj. *The East Is Black: Cold War China in the Black Radical Imagination*. Durham, NC: Duke University Press, 2014.

Freeman, Joshua B. *American Empire, 1945–2000: The Rise of a Global Power, the Democratic Revolution at Home*. New York: Penguin, 2012.

Gaddis, John Lewis. *The Cold War: A New History*. New York: Penguin, 2005.

———. "The Reagan Administration and Soviet-American Relations." In *Reagan and the World*, edited by Kyvig, 17–38.

———. *The United States and the End of the Cold War: Implications, Reconsiderations, Provocations.* Oxford: Oxford University Press, 1992.

Gaines, Kevin K. *American Africans in Ghana: Black Expatriates and the Civil Rights Era.* Chapel Hill: University of North Carolina Press, 2006.

Geldof, Bob. *Is That It? An Autobiography.* New York: Grove Press, 1987.

Gill, Peter. *Famine and Foreigners: Ethiopia Since Live Aid.* Oxford: Oxford University Press, 2010.

———. *A Year in the Death of Africa: Politics, Bureaucracy and the Famine.* London: Paladin Grafton Books, 1986.

Giorgis, Dawit Wolde. *Red Tears: War, Famine and Revolution in Ethiopia.* Trenton, NJ: Red Sea Press, 1989.

Gleijeses, Piero. *Conflicting Missions: Havana, Washington, and Africa, 1959–1976.* Chapel Hill: University of North Carolina Press, 2002.

———. *Visions of Freedom: Havana, Washington, Pretoria, and the Struggle for Southern Africa, 1976–1991.* Chapel Hill: University of North Carolina Press, 2013.

Gordon, David F., and Howard Wolpe. "The Other Africa: An End to Afro-Pessimism." *World Policy Journal* 15, no. 1 (Spring 1998): 49–59.

Grandin, Greg. *Kissinger's Shadow: The Long Reach of America's Most Controversial Statesman.* New York: Metropolitan Books, 2015.

Grant, Nicholas. *Winning Our Freedoms Together: African Americans & Apartheid, 1945–1960.* Chapel Hill: University of North Carolina Press, 2017.

Gurnery, Christabel. "The 1970s: The Anti-Apartheid Movement's Difficult Decade." *Journal of Southern African Studies* 35, no. 2 (June 2009): 471–87.

Gutiérrez, Ramón A. "Chicano Struggles for Racial Justice: The Movement's Contribution to Social Theory." In *Mexicans in California: Transformations and Challenges*, edited by Ramón A. Gutiérrez and Patricia Zavella, 94–110. Urbana: University of Illinois Press, 2009.

Haile, Rebecca G. *Held at a Distance: My Rediscovery of Ethiopia.* Chicago: Academy Chicago Publishers, 2007.

Hall, Tony. *Changing the Face of Hunger.* Nashville, TN: W. Publishing, 2006.

Hancock, Graham. *Ethiopia: The Challenge of Hunger.* London: Gollancz, 1985.

Harlem Youth Opportunities Unlimited (HARYOU). *Youth in the Ghetto: A Study of the Consequences of Powerlessness and a Blueprint for Change.* New York: Harlem Youth Opportunities Unlimited, 1964.

Heerten, Lasse. "The Dystopia of Postcolonial Catastrophe: Self-Determination, the Biafran War of Secession, and the 1970s Human Rights Movement." In *The Breakthrough: Human Rights in the 1970s*, edited by Jack Eckel and Samuel Moyn. Philadelphia: University of Pennsylvania Press, 2014.

Helfenstein, Josef, and Laureen Schipsi, eds. *Art and Activism: Projects of John and Dominique de Menil.* New Haven, CT: Yale University Press, 2010.

Henry, Charles P. "The Rise and Fall of Black Influence on US Foreign Policy." In *African Americans in Global Affairs*, edited by Clemons, 192–221.

Herbst, Jeffrey. "Analyzing Apartheid: How Accurate Were US Intelligence Estimates of South Africa, 1948–94?" *African Affairs* 102, no. 406 (January 2003): 81–107.

——. "Prospects for Revolution in South Africa." *Political Science Quarterly* 103, no. 4 (Winter 1988–89): 665–85.

Heywood, Linda, Allison Blakely, Charles R. Stith, and Joshua C. Yesnowitz, eds. *African Americans in US Foreign Policy: From the Era of Frederick Douglass to the Age of Obama.* Urbana: University of Illinois Press, 2015.

Hill, Robert A., and Edmond J. Keller, eds. *Trustee for the Human Community: Ralph J. Bunche, the United Nations, and the Decolonization of Africa.* Athens: Ohio University Press, 2010.

Hlongwane, Ali Khangela. "The Mapping of the June 16, 1976, Soweto Student Uprisings Routes: Past Recollections and Present Reconstruction(s)." *Journal of African Cultural Studies* 19, no. 1 (June 2007): 7–36.

Hoffman, Stefan-Ludwig, ed. *Human Rights in the Twentieth Century.* Cambridge: Cambridge University Press, 2011.

——. "Introduction: Genealogies of Human Rights." In *Human Rights in the Twentieth Century*, edited by Hoffman, 1–26.

Holloway, Jonathan S. *Confronting the Veil: Abram Harris Jr., E. Franklin Frazier, and Ralph Bunche, 1919–1941.* Chapel Hill: University of North Carolina Press, 2002.

Holt, Thomas C. *Children of Fire: A History of African Americans.* New York: Macmillan, 2011.

Horne, Gerald. *Black and Red: W. E. B. DuBois and the Afro-American Response to the Cold War, 1944–1963.* Albany: State University of New York Press, 1986.

——. *From the Barrel of a Gun: The United States and the War Against Zimbabwe, 1965–1980.* Chapel Hill: University of North Carolina Press, 2001.

Hostetter, David L. *Movement Matters: American Antiapartheid Activism and the Rise of Multicultural Politics.* New York: Taylor and Francis, 2006.

Hush, Robert, and John M. Kirk. "Cuban Medical Internationalism and the Development of the Latin American School of Medicine." *Latin American Perspectives* 34, no. 6 (2007): 77–92.

Intondi, Vincent J. *African Americans Against the Bomb: Nuclear Weapons, Colonialism, and the Black Freedom Movement.* Stanford, CA: Stanford University Press, 2015.

Iriye, Akira, Petra Goedde, and William I. Hitchcock, eds. *The Human Rights Revolution: An International History.* Oxford: Oxford University Press, 2012.

Irwin, Ryan M. *Gordian Knot: Apartheid and the Unmaking of the Liberal World Order.* New York: Oxford University Press, 2012.

Jackson, Donna R. *Jimmy Carter and the Horn of Africa: Cold War Policy in Ethiopia and Somalia.* Jefferson, NC: McFarland, 2007.

James, C. L. R. *You Don't Play with Revolution: The Montreal Lectures of C. L. R. James.* Edited by David Austin. Oakland, CA: AK Press, 2009.

Johnson, Cedric. *Revolutionaries to Race Leaders: Black Power and the Making of African American Politics.* Minneapolis: University of Minnesota Press, 2007.

Johnson, Douglas H. *The Root Causes of Sudan's Civil Wars: Old Wars and New Wars.* New York: James Currey, 2016.

——. *The Root Causes of Sudan's Civil Wars: Peace or Truce.* New York: James Currey, 2012.

Jones, Andrew. "Band Aid Revisited: Humanitarianism, Consumption and Philanthropy in the 1980s." *Contemporary British History* 31, no. 2 (2017): 189–209.

Kaplan, Robert D. *Surrender or Starve: The Wars Behind the Famine.* Boulder, CO: Westview Press, 1988.

Kapuściński, Ryszard. *The Emperor: Downfall of an Autocrat.* Translated by William R. Brand and Katarzyna Mroczkowska-Brand. New York: Vintage Books, 1989.

Kataria, Kanta. "M. N. Roy's Conception of New Humanism." *Indian Journal of Political Science* 66, no. 3 (July–September 2005): 619–32.

Keen, David. *The Benefits of Famine: A Political Economy of Famine and Relief in Southwestern Sudan, 1983–1989.* Athens: Ohio University Press, 2008.

Kellar, William Henry. *Make Haste Slowly: Moderates, Conservatives, and School Desegregation in Houston.* College Station: Texas A&M University Press, 1999.

Kelley, Robin D. G. *Freedom Dreams: The Black Radical Imagination.* Boston: Beacon Press, 2002.

———. *Into the Fire: African Americans Since 1970.* New York: Oxford University Press, 1996.

Kempton, Daniel R. "Africa in the Age of Perestroika." *Africa Today* 38, no. 3 (1991): 7–29.

Keys, Barbara J. *Reclaiming American Virtue: The Human Rights Revolution of the 1970s.* Cambridge, MA: Harvard University Press, 2014.

Kirk, John M. *Healthcare Without Borders: Understanding Cuban Medical Internationalism.* Gainesville: University of Florida Press, 2015.

Kissi, Edward. "Beneath International Famine Relief in Ethiopia: The United States, Ethiopia, and the Debate over Relief Aid, Development Assistance, and Human Rights." *African Studies Review* 48, no. 2 (September 2005): 111–32.

Krenn, Michael L. *Black Diplomacy: African Americans and the State Department, 1945–1969.* New York: M. E. Sharpe, 1999.

Kyvig, David E., ed. *Reagan and the World.* New York: Greenwood Press, 1990.

Leanne, Shelly. "The Clinton Administration and Africa: Perspective of the Congressional Black Caucus and TransAfrica." *African Issues* 26, no. 2 (1998): 17–22.

Lee, Barbara. "The Black Community and the Non-Aligned Movement." *Black Scholar* 18, no. 2, Eighth Non-Aligned Summit Harare—1986 (March–April 1987): 2–8.

Legum, Colin. "The African Crisis." *African Affairs* 57, no. 3 (1978): 633–51.

Leland, Mickey. "The Politics of Hunger Among Blacks." *Black Scholar* 21, no. 1, Hunger in Black America (January–March 1990): 2–5.

Lemi, Adugna. "Anatomy of Foreign Aid to Ethiopia: 1960–2003." Economics Faculty Publication Series, Paper 13, 2008. http://scholarworks.umb.edu/econ_faculty_pubs/13.

Leogrande, William M., and Philip Brenner. "The House Divided: Ideological Polarization over Aid to the Nicaraguan 'Contras.'" *Legislative Studies Quarterly* 18, no. 1 (February 1993): 105–36.

Levering Lewis, David. *When Harlem Was in Vogue.* New York: Penguin Books, 1997.

Lie, Jon Harald Sande, and Axel Borchgrevink. "Layer upon Layer: Understanding the Gambella Conflict Formation." *International Journal of Ethiopian Studies* 6, nos. 1–2 (2012): 135–59.

Loescher, Gil. *The UNHCR and World Politics: A Perilous Path.* Oxford: Oxford University Press, 2001.

Lubin, Alex. *Neoliberalism, Security, and the Afro-Arab International.* Chapel Hill: University of North Carolina Press, 2014.

Lyons, Terrence. "Post–Cold War US Policy Toward Africa: Hints from the Horn." *Brookings Review* 10, no. 1 (Winter 1992): 32–33.

Magaziner, Daniel. "'Black Man, You Are on Your Own!': Making Race Consciousness in South African Thought, 1968–1972." *International Journal of African Historical Studies* 42, no. 2 (2009): 221–40.

Makhulu, Anne-Maria. *Making Freedom: Apartheid, Squatter Politics, and the Struggle for Home*. Chicago: University of Chicago Press, 2015.

Malan, Rian. *My Traitor's Heart: A South African Exile Returns to Face His Country, His Tribe, and His Conscience*. New York: Grove Press, 1990.

Mamdani, Mahmood. *Saviors and Survivors: Darfur, Politics, and the War on Terror*. New York: Doubleday, 2009.

Mann, Gregory. *From Empires to NGOs in the West African Sahel: The Road to Nongovernmentality*. New York: Cambridge University Press, 2015.

Martin, Adrian. "Environmental Conflict Between Refugee and Host Communities." *Journal of Peace Research* 42, no. 3 (2005): 329–46.

Matlin, Daniel. " 'Life Up Yr Self!': Reinterpreting Amiri Baraka (LeRoi Jones), Black Power, and the Uplift Tradition." *Journal of American History* 93, no. 1 (June 2006): 91–116.

Maxwell, Simon. "Does European Aid Work? An Ethiopian Case Study." Institute of Development Studies, Working Paper 46, University of Sussex, 1996.

McCann, James C. *People of the Plow: An Agricultural History of Ethiopia, 1800–1990*. Madison: University of Wisconsin Press, 1995.

McGlade, Jacqueline. "More a Plowshare than a Sword: The Legacy of US Cold War Agricultural Diplomacy." *Agricultural History* 83, no. 1 (Winter 2009): 79–102.

McVety, Amanda K. *Enlightened Aid: US Development as Foreign Policy in Ethiopia*. New York: Oxford University Press, 2012.

Meillassoux, Claude. "Development or Exploitation: Is the Sahel Famine Good Business?" *Review of African Political Economy* 1, no. 1 (1974): 27–33.

Mengiste, Maaza. *Beneath the Lion's Gaze: A Novel*. New York: Norton, 2010.

Meriwether, James H. *Proudly We Can Be Africans: Black Americans and Africa, 1935–1961*. Chapel Hill: University of North Carolina Press, 2002.

Middleton, William. *Double Vision: The Unerring Eye of Art World Avatars Dominique and John de Menil*. New York: Knopf, 2018.

Mikell, Gwendolyn. "Women Mobilizing for Peace: African-American Responses to African Crises." *International Journal on World Peace* 17, no. 1 (March 2000): 61–84.

Mills, Kurt. *International Responses to Mass Atrocities in Africa: Responsibility to Protect, Prosecute, and Palliate*. Philadelphia: University of Pennsylvania Press, 2015.

Minear, Larry. "The Forgotten Human Agenda." *Foreign Policy* 73 (Winter 1988–89): 76–93.

Minter, William. "The US and the War in Angola." *Review of African Political Economy* 18, no. 50 (March 1991): 135–44.

Mitchell, Nancy. *Jimmy Carter in Africa: Race and the Cold War*. Stanford, CA: Stanford University Press, 2016.

Molvaer, Reidulf Knut. *Tradition and Change in Ethiopia: Social and Cultural Life as Reflected in Amharic Fictional Literature ca. 1930–1974*. Addis Ababa: Tsehai Publishers, 2008.

Morris, Lorenzo. "African American Representatives in the United Nations: From Ralph Bunche to Susan Rice." In *African Americans in US Foreign Policy*, edited by Heywood et al., 177–99.

Moses, Wilson Jeremiah. *Alexander Crummell: A Study of Civilization and Discontent*. Amherst: University of Massachusetts Press, 1989.

———. *The Golden Age of Black Nationalism, 1850–1925*. Oxford: Oxford University Press, 1978.

Mottern, Nicholas. *Suffering Strong: The Journal of a Westerner in Ethiopia, the Sudan, Eritrea and Chad.* Trenton, NJ: Red Sea Press, 1987.

Moyn, Samuel. *Human Rights and the Uses of History.* New York: Verso, 2014.

Mufson, Steven. *Fighting Years: Black Resistance and the Struggle for a New South Africa.* Boston: Beacon Press, 1990.

Naidoo, Jay. *Fighting for Justice: A Lifetime of Political and Social Activism.* Johannesburg: Picador Africa, 2010.

Nair, Parvati. *A Different Light: The Photography of Sebastião Salgado.* Durham, NC: Duke University Press, 2011.

Neier, Aryeh. "Human Rights in the Reagan Era: Acceptance in Principle." *Annals of the American Academy of Political and Social Science* 506, no. 1 (November 1989): 30–41.

Nesbitt, Francis Njubi. *Race for Sanctions: African Americans Against Apartheid, 1946–1994.* Bloomington: Indiana University Press, 2004.

Nmoma, Veronica. "The Shift in United States–Sudan Relations: A Troubled Relationship and the Need for Mutual Cooperation." *Journal of Conflict Studies* 26, no. 2 (2006): 44–70.

Noguera, Pedro A. "Charismatic Leadership and Popular Support: A Comparison of the Leadership Styles of Eric Gairy and Maurice Bishop." *Social and Economic Studies* 44, no. 1 (1995): 1–29.

Northrup, David. *Africa's Discovery of Europe: 1450–1850.* Oxford: Oxford University Press, 2002.

Olson, William C. "The US Congress: An Independent Force in World Politics?" *International Affairs* 67, no. 3 (July 1991): 547–63.

O'Neill, William L. *The New Left: A History.* Wheeling, IL: Harlan Davidson, 2001.

Ongiri, Amy Abugo. *Spectacular Blackness: The Cultural Politics of the Black Power Movement and the Search for a Black Aesthetic.* Charlottesville: University of Virginia Press, 2009.

O'Sullivan, Kevin. "The Search for Justice: NGOs in Britain and Ireland and the New International Economic Order, 1968–82." *Humanity* 6, no. 1 (2015): 173–87.

Pankhurst, Alula. *Resettlement and Famine in Ethiopia: The Villagers' Experience.* Manchester: Manchester University Press, 1992.

Pankhurst, Richard. *The History of Famine and Epidemics in Ethiopia Prior to the Twentieth Century.* Addis Ababa: Relief and Rehabilitation Commission, 1985.

Parker, Deloyd. "In Good Faith: Remembering John de Menil." In *Art and Activism*, edited by Helfenstein and Schipsi, 114–15.

Patman, Robert G. *The Soviet Union in the Horn of Africa: The Diplomacy of Intervention and Disengagement.* New York: Cambridge University Press, 1990.

Patterson, Tiffany Ruby. *Zora Neale Hurston: And a History of Southern Life.* Philadelphia: Temple University Press, 2005.

Peck, James. *Ideal Illusions: How the US Government Co-Opted Human Rights.* New York: Metropolitan Books, 2010.

Philpot, Holly. "Operation Lifeline Sudan: Challenges During Conflict and Lessons Learned." Case-Specific Briefing Paper, Humanitarian Assistance in Complex Emergencies, University of Denver, 2011.

Pinderhughes, Charles. "How *Black Awakening in Capitalist America* Laid the Foundation for a New Internal Colonialism Theory." *Black Scholar* 40, no. 2 (Summer 2010): 71–78.

Plummer, Brenda Gayle. "The Changing Face of Diplomatic History: A Literature Review." *History Teacher* 38, no. 3 (May 2005): 385–400.

———. *In Search of Power: African Americans in the Era of Decolonization, 1956–1974.* Cambridge: Cambridge University Press, 2013.

———. *Rising Wind: Black Americans and US Foreign Affairs, 1935–1960.* Chapel Hill: University of North Carolina Press, 1996.

Polman, Linda. *The Crisis Caravan: What's Wrong with Humanitarian Aid?* Translated by Liz Waters. New York: Metropolitan Books, 2010.

Pool, David. *From Guerrillas to Government: The Eritrean People's Liberation Front.* Athens: Ohio University Press, 2001.

Poster, Alexander. "The Gentle War: Famine Relief, Politics, and Privatization in Ethiopia, 1983–1986." *Diplomatic History* 36, no. 2 (April 2012): 399–425.

Prashad, Vijay. *The Darker Nations: A People's History of the Third World.* New York: New Press, 2008.

———. *The Poorer Nations: A Possible History of the Global South.* New York: Verso Books, 2014.

Prendergast, John. "The Political Economy of Famine in Sudan and the Horn of Africa." *African Issues* 19, no. 2 (Summer 1991): 49–55.

"Public Law 480 Programs." *Issue* 8, nos. 2–3 (Summer–Autumn 1978): 75–84.

Rahmato, Dessalegn. "Agrarian Change and Agrarian Crisis: State and Peasantry in Post-Revolution Ethiopia." *Africa* 63, no. 1 (January 1993): 36–55.

Ramirez, Sergio. *Adiós Muchachos: A Memoir of the Sandinista Revolution.* Durham, NC: Duke University Press, 2012.

Redda, Araya. "The Famine in Northern Ethiopia." *Review of African Political Economy* 10, nos. 27–28 (1983): 157–64.

Redden, Thomas J., Jr. "The US Comprehensive Anti-Apartheid Act of 1986: Anti-Apartheid or Anti–African National Congress?" *African Affairs* 87, no. 349 (October 1988): 595–605.

Reitan, Ruth. *The Rise and Decline of an Alliance: Cuba and African American Leaders in the 1960s.* East Lansing: Michigan State University Press, 1999.

Renouard, Joe. *Human Rights in American Foreign Policy: From the 1960s to the Soviet Collapse.* Philadelphia: University of Pennsylvania Press, 2015.

Rickford, Russell. *We Are an African People: Independent Education, Black Power, and the Radical Imagination.* New York: Oxford University Press, 2016.

Robinson, Randall. "Testimony Before the Subcommittees on Africa and International Economic Policy and Trade." *Issue: A Journal of Opinion* 9, no. 1–2 (Spring–Summer 1979): 17–20.

Robinson, Randall, and Clarence Lusane. "An Interview with Randall Robinson: State of the US Anti-Apartheid Movement." *Black Scholar* 16, no. 6 (November–December 1985): 40–42.

Rotberg, Robert I. "The Reagan Era in Africa." In *Reagan and the World*, edited by Kyvig, 119–37.

Roy, Manabendra Nath. *M. N. Roy, Radical Humanist: Selected Writings.* New York: Prometheus Books, 2004.

Rustin, Bayard. "From Protest to Politics: The Future of the Civil Rights Movement." *Commentary* 39, no. 2 (February 1965): 25–31. http://digital.library.pitt.edu/u/ulsmanuscripts/pdf/3173506 6227830.pdf.

Salgado, Sebastião. *Sahel: The End of the Road*. Berkeley: University of California Press, 2004.

Saney, Isaac. "Homeland of Humanity: Internationalism Within the Cuban Revolution." *Latin American Perspectives* 36, no. 1 (2009): 111–23.

Sargent, Daniel. "Oasis in the Desert? America's Human Rediscovery." In *The Breakthrough: Human Rights in the 1970s*, edited by Jan Eckel and Samuel Moyn. Philadelphia: University of Pennsylvania Press, 2014.

Sautman, Barry. "Is Xinjiang an Internal Colony?" *Inner Asia* 2, no. 2 (2000): 239–71.

Schmertz, Eric J., Natalie Datlof, and Alexej Ugrinsky, eds. *President Reagan and the World*. Westport, CT: Greenwood Press, 1997.

Schmidt, Elizabeth. *Foreign Intervention in Africa: From the Cold War to the War on Terror*. Cambridge: Cambridge University Press, 2013.

Scott, David. *Refashioning Futures: Criticism After Postcoloniality*. Princeton, NJ: Princeton University Press, 1999.

Scott, James M. *Deciding to Intervene: The Reagan Doctrine and American Foreign Policy*. Durham, NC: Duke University Press, 1996.

Scott, Michael, and Mutombo Mpanya. *We Are the World: An Evaluation of Pop Aid for Africa*. Washington, DC: InterAction, 1994.

Selassie, B. Kifle. "The Class Struggle or the Struggle for Positions? A Review of Ethiopian Student Movements Between 1900 and 1975." Working paper presented at the UNESCO symposium "The Role of African Student Movements in the Political and Social Evolution of Africa from 1900 to 1975," Dakar, Senegal, April 5–9, 1988.

Selassie, Bereket H. "The American Dilemma on the Horn." In *African Crisis Areas and US Foreign Policy*, edited by Bender, Coleman, and Sklar, 163–77.

Sell, Louis. *From Washington to Moscow: US-Soviet Relations and the Collapse of the USSR*. Chapel Hill: University of North Carolina Press, 2016.

Sen, Amartya. *Development as Freedom*. New York: Anchor Books, 1999.

Service, Robert. *The End of the Cold War, 1985–1991*. New York: Public Affairs, 2015.

Shepherd, Jack. "Ethiopia: The Use of Food as an Instrument of US Foreign Policy." *African Issues* 14 (1985): 4–9.

———. *The Politics of Starvation*. Washington, DC: Carnegie Endowment for International Peace, 1975.

Sikkink, Kathryn. *Mixed Signals: US Human Rights Policy and Latin America*. Ithaca, NY: Cornell University Press, 2014.

Singh, Nikhil Pal. *Black Is a Country: Race and the Unfinished Struggle for Democracy*. Cambridge, MA: Harvard University Press, 2005.

Skinner, Rob. *The Foundations of Anti-Apartheid: Liberal Humanitarians and Transnational Activists in Britain and the United States, c. 1919–64*. New York: Palgrave Macmillan, 2010.

Smart, Pamela G. "Aesthetics as a Vocation." In *Art and Activism*, edited by Helfenstein and Schipsi, 21–39.

Smith, Robert C. "Black Power and the Transformation from Protest to Policies." *Political Science Quarterly* 96, no. 3 (Autumn 1981): 431–43.

Smith, William Edgett. *We Must Run While They Walk: A Portrait of Africa's Julius Nyerere*. New York: Random House, 1972.

Sorenson, John. *Imagining Ethiopia: Struggles for History and Identity in the Horn of Africa*. New Brunswick, NJ: Rutgers University Press, 1993.

Spaire, Hilary. "Liberation Movements, Exile, and International Solidarity: An Introduction." *Journal of Southern African Studies* 35, no. 2, Liberation Struggles, Exile and International Solidarity (June 2009): 271–86.

Spector, Stephen. *Operation Solomon: The Daring Rescue of the Ethiopian Jews.* New York: Oxford University Press, 2005.

Stanger, Allison. *One Nation Under Contract: The Outsourcing of American Power and the Future of Foreign Policy.* New Haven, CT: Yale University Press, 2009.

Stewart, Jeffrey C. "A New Negro Foreign Policy: The Critical Vision of Alain Locke and Ralph Bunche." In *African Americans in US Foreign Policy*, edited by Heywood et al., 30–57.

Stith, Charles R. "Epilogue: The Impact of African Americans on US Foreign Policy." In *African Americans in US Foreign Policy*, edited by Heywood et al., 213–24.

Sundiata, Ibrahim. "Obama, African Americans, and Africans: The Double Vision." In *African Americans in US Foreign Policy*, edited by Heywood et al., 200–212.

Suri, Jeremi. *Power and Protest: Global Revolution and the Rise of Détente.* Cambridge, MA: Harvard University Press, 2003.

Szajkowski, Bogdan. "Ethiopia: A Weakening Soviet Connection?" *World Today* 45, nos. 8–9 (August–September 1989): 153–56.

Tareke, Gebru. *The Ethiopian Revolution: War in the Horn of Africa.* New Haven, CT: Yale University Press, 2009.

———. "From Af Abet to Shire: The Defeat and Demise of Ethiopia's 'Red' Army, 1988–89." *Journal of Modern African Studies* 42, no. 2 (June 2004): 239–81.

"Who Supports UNITA and RENAMO?" *Black Scholar* 18, no. 6, Southern Africa: The Frontline War (November–December 1987): 47–48.

Thompson, Carol B. "US Trade with Africa: African Growth and Opportunity?" *Review of African Political Economy* 31, no. 101 (2004): 457–74.

Thomson, Alex. "Incomplete Engagement: Reagan's South Africa Policy Revisited." *Journal of Modern African Studies* 33, no. 1 (1995): 83–101.

———. *US Foreign Policy Towards Apartheid South Africa, 1948–1994.* New York: Palgrave Macmillan, 2008.

Thörn, Håkan. "The Meaning(s) of Solidarity: Narratives of Anti-Apartheid Activism." *Journal of Southern African Studies* 35, no. 2 (June 2009): 417–36.

———. "Solidarity Across Borders: The Transnational Anti-Apartheid Movement." *Voluntas: International Journal of Nonprofit Organizations* 17, no. 4 (December 2006): 285–301.

Tibebu, Teshale. *The Making of Modern Ethiopia, 1896–1974.* Lawrenceville, NJ: Red Sea Press, 1995.

Tillery, Alvin B., Jr. *Between Homeland and Motherland: Africa, US Foreign Policy, and Black Leadership in America.* Ithaca, NY: Cornell University Press, 2011.

———. "Foreign Policy Activism and Power in the House of Representatives: Black Members of Congress and South Africa, 1968–1986." *Studies in American Political Development* 20, no. 1 (2006): 88–103.

Tiruneh, Andargachew. *The Emergence and Proliferation of Political Organizations in Ethiopia.* Los Angeles: Tsehai, 2015.

Toscano, Alberto. "The Tactics and Ethics of Humanitarianism." *Humanity* 5, no. 1 (Spring 2014): 123–47.

Tuck, Stephen. "African American Protest During the Reagan Years: Forging New Agendas, Defending Old Victories." In *Ronald Reagan and the 1980s: Perceptions, Policies, Legacies*, edited by Cheryl Hudson and Gareth Davies, 119–34. New York: Palgrave Macmillan, 2008.

Tyson, Timothy B. *Radio Free Dixie: Robert F. Williams and the Roots of Black Power*. Chapel Hill: University of North Carolina Press, 1999.

Van de Walle, Nicolas. "Obama and Africa: Lots of Hope, Not Much Change." *Foreign Affairs* 94, no. 5 (September–October 2015): 54–61.

Van Dyke, Kristina. "The Menil Collection: Houston, Texas." *African Arts* 40, no. 3 (Autumn 2007): 36–49.

Varnis, Steven L. *Reluctant Aid or Aiding the Reluctant? US Food Aid Policy and Ethiopian Famine Relief*. New Brunswick, NJ: Transaction Publishers, 1990.

Vaughan, Sarah. "Ethnicity and Power in Ethiopia." PhD diss., University of Edinburgh, 2003.

Vaux, Tony. *The Selfish Altruist: Relief Work in Famine and War*. Sterling, VA: Earthscan, 2001.

Vestal, Theodore. "Meles Zenawi (1955–2012)." *International Journal of Ethiopian Studies* 6, nos. 1–2 (2012): 195–99.

Von Eschen, Penny M. *Race Against Empire: Black Americans and Anticolonialism, 1937–1957*. Ithaca, NY: Cornell University Press, 1997.

Waller, James. *FAU: Portrait of an Ethiopian Famine*. Jefferson, NC: McFarland, 1990.

Walters, Ronald W. "African-American Influence on US Foreign Policy Toward South Africa." In *Ethnic Groups and US Foreign Policy*, edited by Mohammed E. Ahrari, 65–82. New York: Greenwood Press.

———. *Pan Africanism in the African Diaspora: An Analysis of Modern Afrocentric Political Movements*. Detroit: Wayne State University Press, 1993.

———. "Racial Justice in Foreign Affairs." In *African Americans in Global Affairs*, edited by Clemons, 1–31.

Wardlaw, Alvia J. "John and Dominique de Menil and the Houston Civil Rights Movement." In *Art and Activism*, edited by Helfenstein and Schipsi, 103–13.

Watenpaugh, Keith David. "The League of Nations' Rescue of Armenian Genocide Survivors and the Making of Modern Humanitarianism, 1920–1927." *American Historical Review* 115, no. 5 (December 2010): 1315–39.

Webb, Bruce. "Counterculture U: Discontent and Liberation at the University of Houston." *Cite* 82 (Summer 2010): 11–16.

Westad, Odd Arne. *The Cold War: A World History*. New York: Basic Books, 2017.

———. *The Global Cold War: Third World Interventions and the Making of Our Times*. Cambridge: Cambridge University Press, 2007.

Whitehead, R. G. "The Causes, Effects, and Reversibility of Protein-Calorie Malnutrition." In *Famine*, edited by Blix, Hofvander, and Vahlquist, 41–53.

Wilentz, Sean. *The Age of Reagan: A History, 1974–2008*. New York: Harper Perennial, 2008.

Wilkins, Fanon Ché. "The Making of Black Internationalists: SNCC and Africa Before the Launching of Black Power, 1960–1965." *Journal of African American History* 92, no. 4, New Black Power Studies (Autumn 2007): 467–90.

Williams, Gary. "Prelude to an Intervention: Grenada 1983." *Journal of Latin American Studies* 29, no. 1 (1997): 131–69.

Williams, Ronald, II. "From Anticolonialism to Anti-Apartheid: African American Political Organizations and African Liberation, 1957–93." In *African Americans in Global Affairs*, edited by Clemons, 65–90.

Winter, Roger P. "Refugees, War and Famine in the Sudan." *African Issues* 19, no. 2 (Summer 1991): 56–61.

Wolde-Mariam, Mesfin. *Rural Vulnerability to Famine in Ethiopia, 1958–1977.* New York: Advent Books, 1977.

Wolpe, Howard, J. Stephen Morrison, and Stephen Weissman. "Seizing Southern African Opportunities." *Foreign Policy*, no. 73 (Winter 1988–89): 60–75.

Woodard, Komozi. *A Nation Within a Nation: Amiri Baraka (LeRoi Jones) and Black Power Politics.* Chapel Hill: University of North Carolina Press, 1999.

Young, Crawford. "Ralph Bunche and Patrice Lumumba: The Fatal Encounter." In *Trustee for the Human Community,* edited by Hill and Keller, 128–47.

Young, Cynthia A. "Havana up in Harlem: LeRoi Jones, Harold Cruse and the Making of a Cultural Revolution." *Science and Society* 65, no. 1 (Spring 2001): 12–38.

———. *Soul Power: Culture, Radicalism, and the Making of a US Third World Left.* Durham, NC: Duke University Press, 2006.

Young, John. *Peasant Revolution in Ethiopia: The Tigray People's Liberation Front, 1975–1991.* Cambridge: Cambridge University Press, 2006.

———. "Regionalism and Democracy in Ethiopia." *Third World Quarterly* 19, no. 2 (1998): 191–204.

Zeilig, Leo. *Revolt and Protest: Student Politics and Activism in Sub-Saharan Africa.* New York: Tauris, 2013.

Zewde, Bahru, ed. *Documenting the Ethiopian Student Movement: An Exercise in Oral History.* Addis Ababa: Forum for Social Studies, 2010.

———. *A History of Modern Ethiopia, 1855–1991.* 2nd ed. Athens: Ohio University Press, 2001.

———. *The Quest for Socialist Utopia: The Ethiopian Student Movement, c. 1960–1974.* Rochester, NY: James Currey, 2014.

Index

Page numbers in italics refer to figures and tables.

Acknowledgments

I learned of Congressman Mickey Leland on the evening of August 8, 1989, while watching the *NBC Evening News* in my family's apartment in New York City. I was rapt as news anchor Tom Brokaw announced the disappearance and ongoing search for Mickey's plane. He presented a touching and illuminating summary of Leland's political career, highlighting his humanitarian initiatives in the United States and Africa, punctuated with footage of Mickey in Ethiopian villages and feeding centers. I was fifteen and consumed with a desire to help bring about justice in the United States and Africa. Decades later, I was determined to write about Mickey and the politics and political moment he embodied, for it was a time that indelibly shaped my sense and that of many others of my generation of what Africa and blackness mean and who we are in relation to both.

Many people helped bring this book to life. Alison Leland, Mickey's widow, was extremely gracious and generous with her time. Jew Don Boney was an essential part of my early research. Patriccus Fortiori, with his unmatched patience and dedication to the Leland Center, helped me fill significant research gaps during follow-up trips to Houston. I managed to speak with only a small number of people from Mickey's wide circle of friends and colleagues, but I benefited immensely from these conversations. Special thanks to Matchash Maddox, Cleo Johnson, Omowali Luthuli-Allen, Gene Locke, Alan Wheat, Harry Hurt, Marty LaVor, Miranda Katsoyanis, Rodney Ellis, Anthony Hall, and the late congressman William Gray.

In addition to collections at the Mickey Leland Center Archives, I consulted documents from a host of other institutions, including the Rare Books and Manuscripts Division of the New York Public Library, the Schomburg Center for Research in Black Culture, the Jimmy Carter Presidential Library, the African American Museum and Library at Oakland, the Moorland-Spingarn Research Center at Howard University, the Ronald Reagan Presidential Library, the National Archives in Washington, D.C., the United Nations Archives in New York, the Menil Collection, and the Institute of Ethiopian Studies at the University of Addis Ababa. Many expert archivists assisted me along the way, but Raymond Wilson of the Reagan Library is, beyond a doubt, the most thorough, patient, and dedicated archivist in the business. I am grateful to Rachael Hill, James de Haan, and Candice Washington, who kindly chased down documents at different libraries. I owe a large debt of gratitude to the Institute for African Studies at Columbia University, where Mamadou Diouf and Jinny Prais provided me with space and a vibrant intellectual community in which to write and share my ideas.

In Addis Ababa, my friends Emebet Worku and Aida Muluneh (HU!) connected me with invaluable contacts in the city, at the University of Addis Ababa, and in Mekele. In Mekele, Atsbaha Abraha Gebrehiwot and Mitiku Gabrehiwot kindly educated me on the local sites and experiences of the 1980s famines.

A wide circle of friends and colleagues helped me think through the early stages of writing this book. My writing group partners Abosede George, Natasha Lightfoot, Natasha Gordan-Chimpembere, Toja Okoh, Hlonipha Mokoena, and Vanessa Perez provided feedback on the initial idea for this book. Clarence Haynes, Guthrie Ramsey, Daniel Magaziner, Jonathan Gray, Minkah Makalani, Gregory Mann, Christian Crouch, and Jennifer Johnson gave me feedback on early drafts of the manuscript and the book proposal. It never ceased to amaze me when friends and colleagues agreed to read the full, unedited manuscript. Erika Asikoye, Brian McNamara, Jesse Shipley, Derek Musgrove, and Michael Gomez all helped me tighten my argument, analysis, and prose. My Department of History colleagues Teshale Tibebu and Harvey Neptune both read full drafts of the manuscript and provided thoughtful insights and corrections. A special note of thanks to Quincy Mills. If this brother had not been a phone call away, I would be a very different scholar and this would be a different book. I am truly grateful for his honesty, support, and friendship through the years.

The University of Pennsylvania Press has been the ideal home for this project, and I have immensely enjoyed working with the editors, particularly Peter Agree, Bob Lockhart, and Erica Ginsburg. Bob, my primary editor, remained responsive, supportive, and instructive from our initial email exchanges (and lunches) to publication. I learned a great deal about writing and editing from him. Thanks also to Carl Bon Tempo and the anonymous reviewers who made note of errors and pointed toward ways to improve the manuscript's structure and argument. There is no better editor, critic, supporter, friend, and coconspirator through this life than my wife, Janai Nelson.

CPSIA information can be obtained
at www.ICGtesting.com
Printed in the USA
LVHW010303101122
732752LV00003B/359